Beirut on the Bayou

Beirut on the Bayou

Alfred Nicola, Louisiana, and the Making of Modern Lebanon

RAIF SHWAYRI

SUNY PRESS

Published by State University of New York Press, Albany

Printed in the United States of America

For information, contact State University of New York Press, Albany, NY
www.sunypress.edu

Production, Dana Foote
Marketing, Fran Keneston

Library of Congress Cataloging-in-Publication Data

Shwayri, Raif
Beirut on the Bayou: Alfred Nicola, Louisiana, and the making of Modern Lebanon / Raif Shwayri
ISBN 978-1-4384-6095-6 (hardcover: alk paper)
ISBN 978-1-4384-6096-3 (ebook)

Library of Congress Control Number: 2015944372

10 9 8 7 6 5 4 3 2 1

To Nadim Habib Shwayri

What's past is prologue . . .

—Shakespeare

Contents

Part II
Alfred in Louisiana

Part III
Alfred's legacy

Appendices

Plates follow pages 78 and 232

Maps

The map entitled "Lebanon's confessional mosaic as it stands today: Cultural diversity or powder keg?" appears as the first plate in the second gallery.

Maps drawn and designed by François Eid

Acknowledgments

The idea of writing this book was not entirely mine. It is true that the story of my grandfather's experiences in Louisiana has always fascinated me, as well as that of the Moujaes family, with its long heritage in stonemasonry and silk trading, but after the publication of my first book in 2008, writing was not on my agenda, as my work at Al-Kafaàt consumed most of my writing (and reading) time. Then, in June 2012, two years into the affiliation that was in progress and that brought the State University of New York to partner with AL KAFAAT UNIVERSITY (AKU), Sally Crimmins Villela, assistant vice chancellor for global affairs, threw me back into academia. By nominating me for the John W. Ryan Fellowship for International Education, which SUNY bestowed on me later that year, Sally brought me in front of students, researchers, and faculty across SUNY colleges, lecturing on education for development and on "unifying people and societies through shared knowledge." The book matured on the trail that took me across the state of New York, from campus to campus, occasions for me to meet with people and dig into the histories of the Lebanese who immigrated to America. The book developed naturally out of that experience. Two visits—to Ellis Island and to Lockport, Louisiana—helped me to shape the narrative. At these places, I met Alfred Nicola. He was there at the Ellis Island Great Hall, where he waited his turn before one of the inspectors in high chairs when he was just seventeen years of age. I met him on the towpaths that he walked for eighteen years down in the bayous of Louisiana, with a heavy valise on his back. I found his story so poignant that I knew I wanted him to be the focal subject of the book. But to understand him, I had to understand where he came from, which meant digging into his lineage to understand the choices he made in life. Family history is not enough if we want to understand the choices anyone makes; we must also look at the environment that forges personalities and sets lives on different paths. The history of Alfred and his family could therefore only be understood when juxtaposed with the history of Lebanon in the making.

My discussions with Adib Aoun Moujaes put me on track when researching the origins of the Moujaes family. A lawyer of repute and a historian, son of a justice of the peace under the mutasarifiya, his suggestions and tips helped me structure my research work. I was privileged to have had the opportunity to sit with him a short time before he passed away, and am only sorry he will not get to read the finished work. I am equally grateful to Adib's son, Khalil Moujaes, a fine lawyer in his own right, a friend and cousin, for reading my history of the Moujaes family. In researching the ancestry of the family and tracing it back to Arabia Felix (now modern-day Yemen) and later to the Arabian Desert and the confines of Syria and Turkey, I spent many long and pleasurable hours decrypting manuscripts, interpreting maps, and reading travelers' logbooks. I have many resource centers to thank for that: the Jafet Memorial Library at the American University of Beirut, the Library of Oriental Studies at St. Joseph University in Beirut, the British Library (particularly the Maps and Manuscripts Reference Team), and the Palestine Exploration Fund in London, where I found good help in reviewing maps of Syria and Palestine of the late nineteenth century.

Researching Lebanese American history was equally thrilling, especially at the Smithsonian Archive Center at the National Museum of American History in Washington, DC, where I was able to dig into the many cartons of photographs and documents donated by Alixa Naff, an extraordinary woman who spent her life building a unique collection on the Lebanese American experience. My gratitude goes to the staff of the Archive Center for their highly professional support, and for adapting to my travel constraints and bending a few rules when it came to opening hours. On the same topic, I am grateful to Eugene Nassar, the founder of the Ethnic Heritage Studies Center at Utica College, for his input and the information he shared (and for the great Lebanese meal he treated me to at the Phoenician Restaurant in Utica!).

In Louisiana, the compass had a name: Fred Joseph Jr., son of another Fred, nephew of Alfred and his cousin too, who bore witness to Alfred's style and endeavors and who ended naming his two sons very tellingly: Al and Fred. I can never thank Fred enough for the time he made for me on my two research visits to Louisiana and the long discussions we had while driving across Bayou Lafourche and eating po' boys with the fishermen in Gulfport. I also thank him for introducing me to the local tastes and customs, with his son Brent and friend Amanda, and for reviewing the section on Alfred Nicola in Louisiana. A day with Glen Pitre, the well-known Cajun cinema producer and director, is all you need if you are looking at delving into the deep Louisianan culture. I am grateful to him for passing on to me his passion for New Orleans and sharing with me his intimate knowledge of the Cajun country (and entrusting me with many of his movies). The New Orleans Archives and Library was one of my favorite destinations as I was able there to consult the individual registrations logbooks and view the newspapers of the epoch from when Alfred was in Louisiana. Viewing was made so simple with the search engines that the library has made available in a very distinctive and friendly environment.

Back in Lebanon, my aunt Lodi was of immense help with providing an accurate account of the events in the life of her father, Alfred Nicola, after his return to Beirut. Our discussions frequently found us trading information on Alfred in Lebanon for that of Alfred in Louisiana, the product of my detective work in the United States. I am also grateful to her for sharing pictures of Alfred and his family, some of which are included in the photo galleries in this book. I was privileged to hear firsthand anecdotes on Lebanon in the period of Bashir the Great from Amir Hareth Chehab, who did not stint in giving me personal materials, and for that I am ever so grateful. I also must pay a tribute to Riad Khneisser of the Shwayr Community Center Library and Municipality, who helped provide rare documents and share much of the peoples' histories, which have traveled across generations in oral traditions. Much gratitude I owe to the talented architect, historian, and cartographer François Eid for drawing the maps for this book. His composition depicting the distribution of religious communities across Lebanon is more the design of a master clockmaker than that of a cartographer.

At Al-Kafaàt, I must credit Rose Khneisser, my personal assistant, and Enham Khneisser, both from Shwayr, for their personal input in the collection of information.

This book would not have been were it not for two remarkable people who supported the work wholeheartedly: the co-directors of SUNY Press, Donna Dixon and James Peltz. Working with them for three years was a unique and delightful experience, one I have come to treasure profoundly. If Donna was the conductor, James was my alter ego, to whom I owe the book's title as well as the final editing. I am equally thankful to the production editor, Dana Foote, and Silvia Benvenuto, who produced the index, as well as Fran Keneston for the marketing and outreach. Three fine ladies who have added a touch of class to this book. I will always be indebted to my dear friend Jim Ketterer, Senior Fellow at Bard College, an expert in regional history and politics, for having spent long years in the Middle East, for reading the manuscript, and entrusting me with valuable comments.

Finally, it is to Rosemary Ortlieb-Padgett that I devote the last words of gratitude. Dean of international relations at Nassau Community College, Global Fellow for Lebanon through the Office of Global Affairs at SUNY System Administration, and today a trustee of AKU, her input was immeasurable across all stages of the making of the book. She was my research and travel companion, a detective and reporter when not photocopying manuscripts and digging out archival material, first reader, and a proofreader as well. I treasure our long brainstorming discussions, which most of the time ended in arguments, and commend her for the time and dedication she has put into this endeavor to make it a success.

Note: Throughout the book, I have chosen to use US transliterations for names of historical people and places, but for contemporary people I have tried to keep the spelling they personally use.

Introduction

February 2012. We arrived at JFK in plenty of time for our flight to New Orleans, but we had an unusual hiccup: At check-in, my e-reservation simply wouldn't go through. Rosemary Ortlieb, my partner in researching this book, had reserved our tickets online, and she spelled my name the way I usually spell it: Shwayri, an Anglicized spelling of Choueiri (the French transliteration of the original Arabic). I have been using the Anglicized spelling ever since I entered the American University of Beirut, just like my numerous predecessors from the Shwayri/Choueiri family. Unfortunately, on my passport, my name is spelled Choueiri, not Shwayri.

Needless to say, the attending Delta ground crew wouldn't have it. I could not be admitted. Even if they let me through, they said, the security check would deny me boarding. Rosemary pleaded the case at length, to the airline clerks as well as to Expedia, the ticket issuer, but nobody would listen. After 9/11, the security regulations have been understandably strict. "This man will not be admitted because Shwayri on the ticket is not Choueiri on the passport, and unless you have a corresponding ticket (or passport), you can't board the flight." I eventually had to buy a new ticket and toss the other one. And a last-minute ticket is priced full rack. Ironically enough, a rack rate is a business class ticket that moves you to the front of the line in security. I had gone from persona non grata to VIP. The agent at security fiddled with my passport and fed it through a laser "truth-teller" that confirmed my honest intentions, and in no time I was through the scanners and into the waiting lounge.

The rest of the journey was sheer pleasure: large seats with large armrests and generous legroom, along with coffee and snacks—in other words, maximum comfort. As New Orleans came into view outside the windows of the plane, I couldn't help making a mental comparison: Here I was, arriving at my destination in the most comfortable conditions, with a ticket that bore the exact date of my return, a cell phone in my pocket and a few credit cards to cover whatever expense, looking forward to a luxurious room at the Hilton on Canal Street and a program on arrival that accounted for all logistics. My grandfather, however, came to the United

States with barely enough money to pay for his journey, on ships undetermined, from harbors unknown, to a future uncertain. He left Beirut when it was still ruled by the Ottoman Empire and the country of Lebanon did not exist yet, for a country that had recently been wracked by a terrible civil war—but where, it was said, there was money to be made. He was only seventeen years old, had never had a shave, could not read or write, had no friends awaiting him on destination, no friends with him on board, no money in his pockets to quench a thirst or feed a hungry stomach. I was able to call home the moment I landed to make sure Reina had tucked our children into bed and that the plumber had showed up to fix the leak in our kitchen, but my grandfather stood speechless in the midst of the overwhelming crowd that massed in front of the high desks at Ellis Island, waiting to be assigned a name, to be checked for tropical diseases, and, if found to be disease free, to be set loose to navigate the wide country of America and contribute to the wealth of a nation still very much in the making. Between our trips, one hundred and ten years had passed.

Although I never met my grandfather, he has fascinated me. The resolve and resilience revealed in his story have a lesson to teach, one that my father passed on to my sisters, my brother, and me. He was righteous, honest, and well intentioned. He was a hard worker, an introspective, self-educated, serious man. He didn't engage in small talk and innuendos, just incisive words when it mattered to say them, simple and hardly complicated. "People are all *ḳhayr* and *Baraḳa*," he would say, "goodness and blessing," when he heard people criticizing others for their differences. *Goodness* and *blessing*—his two words, almost his mission in life—these he earned from his life in Louisiana.

He peddled for eighteen years in the harshest conditions, traveling barefoot to the bayous and Grand Isle and along the Gulf of Mexico. I retraced his steps by car, with Fred Joseph, my cousin from Lockport, Louisiana, and we had the assurance of good winds and a sense of security that weather forecasts give you today, so important if you want to avoid hurricanes. But in my grandfather's time, the only forecasts were in reading the clouds and interpreting the flight of seagulls. He defied every possible danger, from natural disasters to thieves who came after the valise filled with the money he made as a peddler, a walking store. He sent money home and kept his household in Beirut alive. He paid off the mortgage his father had contracted and freed the family home. And when his father died while he was peddling for a living down in Lafourche Parish, he sent money home so that his mother and brothers and sisters could live decently.

By the time he returned home, eighteen years later, he had earned a considerable amount of money. He bought property in the now-French-colonized, newly created country of Lebanon, and over the years, his holdings grew. Part of his estate fell to his youngest child, Nadim, my father, who used this seed capital to start Al-Kafaàt, a unique charity organization that serves Lebanon and Lebanese youth.

Habib Shwayri arrived at Ellis Island in 1902 and was admitted under the name Alfred Nicola (the name by which I shall refer to him in this book). This book tells his story and that of his family, as well as the legacy he has left, which blossomed into the institution that serves so many in Lebanon today. It tells the story of people who toiled hard to make ends meet while, all around, a society was in gestation, a country was in the making, born from the collision of colonial powers and an elite establishment that sought to use the power of government for personal rather than social enrichment.

Wherever I have been to look for him—in Shwayr, in Hadath, at archives and libraries, and in Louisiana—he has been there waiting. His fisted hands and lean body, his constant frowns and austerity, have come across in every interview I have conducted and every record I have read, as have his integrity, his love of people, and his generosity. He has been a true companion over the past few years, and as this book goes to publication, I know I shall miss our secret talks and evening stories.

Part I

Alfred remembers

1

Fares Bozeid Moujaes

At the time of the emara

Alfred woke up in the early hours of the day, as was customary for him. He wore his dark gray striped suit and white shirt that bore his initials, and he sat on the porch on his caned wooden seat. He faced the garden and the Mamluk-style fountain, his back to the household through the entrance door, open as always. He sat there, as did the farm owners in his dear Louisiana on their rocking chairs on a hot day, passing the time and talking to the passersby. His wife, Najibeh, prepared coffee for him, a whole pot, which she placed in front of him with the small, cone-shaped cup that held small measures, enough for just one sip, or *shaffeh* as it is called. Of shaffehs he will have many, whether freshly brewed or cold, as he will sit there all day only moving to the dining table, the *sufra*, when called for lunch, which Najibeh dexterously prepares for her large family. Alfred never set foot in Najibeh's kitchen, not that he couldn't brew his own coffee, but she wouldn't allow it. "Men should be served," she would say and motion him off to his throne whenever he came close to suggesting he help himself. In the house, she laid down the law, to the extent that Alfred more than once suggested, "She should wear the pants." Strong she was, yet she never deviated from the age-old social intricacies that reflected the conservative and patriarchal tendencies so prevalent in the Middle East.

When Alfred stood to shave his beard at the hat stand, the highest piece of furniture in the large sitting room, one of his daughters, Lodi usually, would hold the towel as he chipped off small flakes of soap and lathered them in a bronze cup. And this he did twice every day while humming the tunes of the Byzantine repertoire he had learned at the church next door. Out on the porch, he sipped coffee and smoked the locally manufactured *bafras* or *tatlis*, consuming no fewer than three packs of these cigarettes a day. He sat there every day and contemplated his success, a landowner now, a holder of large estates across the region. Saint Elias, the patron saint of the church next door, had looked over him well. The church had been standing for a long time, long enough to see the first of his Shwayri ancestors settle in the village in 1807.

Alfred knew little of his great grandfather, only that Fares Bozeid Moujaes had been a stonemason and had come from Shwayr and was named for his village of origin when he settled here in Hadath. The name *Moujaes* was dropped for the *Shwayri* of convenience. Alfred didn't know that Fares represented a long line of stonemasons that traced its origins to the southern tip of the Arabian Peninsula. Stone cutting and building were crafts his ancestors had mastered, having engaged in large construction projects back in Yemen, the land of riches and abundance. The Dam of Ma'arib in Yemen, described in history books as a jewel of construction since the early sixth century BCE, was but one example of the ingeniousness of these engineers and builders. Then many tribes fled Yemen after the economy plummeted as a result of internecine wars and the meddling of mighty Rome in the trading of commodities, activities that had once made the fortunes of the original inhabitants. Of these commodities, frankincense was most important, but wealth also came from spices and other rare products of Africa and India, and even the distant Far East.

The migrating tribes trekked across the Arabian Peninsula, many settling in the Hauran area, southwest of Damascus, where they developed commercial ties with the Byzantines, then lords of the land. In this new region, the gifted builders developed their skills further and put them to use under the Byzantine emperors, who required many stonemasons and paid them lavishly, as did Justinian, who built fortress after fortress on his eastern flank, which faced the threat of the ruthless Persian Sassanid Empire. But not only fortresses did the ancestors of Fares Bozeid Moujaes build. They also lent their skills to grand realizations ordered by Emperor Justinian who built numerous churches across his empire, the cathedral of Hagia Sophia in Constantinople being unequivocally the most impressive. But empires decline and give way to newer ones, and the Byzantine Empire was no exception. When the Ottomans swept over Hauran in the early years of the sixteenth century, the Moujaes became refugees again and, after a difficult journey to Akkar in the northern mountains, took refuge in the heights of Shwayr.

Alfred knew the village of Shwayr very well. He was a regular visitor and had family and friends there. He even bought property there. Najibeh knew it equally well, as she had lived most of her life in its vicinity, the daughter of Abdallah Meshrek, a learned man who held high positions under the Ottoman governorship.

Founded on a small cliff (its name means "small cliff"), Shwayr faces inward to the east. It sits in a fabulous gorge, formed by the succession of foothills that run from Mount Sannine and drop sharply from five thousand feet to the blue Mediterranean Sea less than fifteen miles away. The sight of the Sannine from Shwayr, with its satin-white snow in spring, is awe inspiring. These are the everlasting snows that were praised in the Bible and by early travelers, but with global warming, changes in demography, and the intensive use of modern technology, the snows of Sannine have become rather seasonal. Despite that, Sannine is lovingly said by locals to "wear winter on its head, spring on its shoulders, autumn in its bosom, and to have summer sleep at its feet." The peak is the sturdy guardian of time and the rearguard of Metn, the large region comprised of the valleys that climb eastward from the sea, cutting into the continuous chain of mountains that run along the longitudinal axis of Lebanon, with Kesrwan to the north and Shouf to the south.

At the time of their migration in the sixteenth century, the Moujaes must have looked at Shwayr as an impregnable fortress, rising three thousand feet above sea level, with a shallow gorge at its feet and facing the mighty Mount Sannine. Facing east, it had its back covered from the sea, invisible to the passing armies and those who sailed along the shores of Lebanon. In a nod to Cairo, it was called Shwayr Al-Qahira ("Cairo" in Arabic), "the Impregnable," an acknowledgment that the town had never been invaded nor occupied by an army, a striking fact in a land that had been crisscrossed constantly by different civilizations since the dawn of time.

For the Moujaes, Shwayr was the perfect asylum. Coming from Hauran, they saw in the hospitable gorge a hideaway from the sacrilegious invaders who dared to profane Hagia Sofia. The righteous Islam of the early caliphs was done with, they thought, and recent events hinted that a new Islam was being ushered in, one that was ruthless and brutal. Shwayr offered a refuge where the Moujaes could practice their Greek Orthodox faith unafraid. They arrived in successive groups between 1517 and 1532, built a church next to a millenary oak, and settled down. (A detailed history of the Moujaes family is given in appendix 2.)

Of silk and stone

The great-grandfather of Alfred Nicola was born in Shwayr in 1788, a period of upheaval across the world. Europe was in turmoil and revolution was looming on the horizon. Royalty in France was on the brink of collapse: the Bourbons were soon to walk to the guillotine, leaving the Jacobins to plunge the country into the Reign of Terror. Had television existed in those days, the parents of Fares would have seen a triumphant Napoleon campaigning in Italy against the Austrians and the United States of America coming to life from the womb of a war for liberty and independence. They would have seen a live broadcast from Philadelphia the day the Declaration of Independence was ratified, and they might even have seen the grand drawings of Charles L'Enfant, whose plans for the new nation's capital were just starting to be put into place when Fares turned five. Great moments in history, certainly, but who in Shwayr was to know? Life at the Moujaes household revolved around simple things, and when Fares turned five, his hands were put to use. He would spend most of his days picking mulberry leaves to feed the tiny worms that sat in container boxes and squeaked all night long in the sitting room where he also made his bed.

Silk growing and trading were common practices among village people in Mount Lebanon, the region in which Shwayr is located. The Moujaes, like many others in Shwayr, depended on this business. It was not their main occupation, as the seasonal sale of cocoons to silk spinners could not possibly feed a family, but it was a source of supplemental income they could rely upon when, come winter, Fares's father returned from the faraway lands where he worked as a stonemason. A master stonemason, Fares's father had built his own house in Shwayr, a simple two-room dwelling walled in stones that he cut himself along with others from the village who shared their labor to build each other's homes. The inside walls were plastered with thick clay, which kept in the warmth in winter when five feet of snow covered the picturesque landscape. The roof was made of earth, piled on a thick mat of straw that rested on large beams and cross poles. It was thick, to keep out the rains, and was compacted with a heavy stone roller during the winter.

Winter months were probably the happiest times for Fares, who had the snow to thank for his father being at home, the only family time they had together. Life in those days was harsh, and nothing came easy. While Fares's father was away most of summer and autumn, his mother spent her time replenishing food stocks for the winter, the *mouneh*, which she kept in the second room, next to the tools, firewood, and other necessities. She stored a large variety of cottage foods in this room: meats, which she diced and fried and kept in clay pots sealed with animal grease; tomato paste in jars; olives and olive oil; all sorts of marmalades; syrups made from blueberries and mulberries; dried fruits such as figs, apricots, and raisins; nuts and pine nuts; oats and wheat. She made her own flour from the wheat, grinding it with a pestle and then baking it in the *mawqadeh*, the fireplace that had so many functions in this same sitting room. The smoke-blackened ceiling contrasted with the chalky white-plastered walls and the floor of packed-down, iron-colored sand.

The whiteness of the walls was striking, repainted completely each summer after a season of silkworm nurturing. This season started in spring when the tiny worms were eager to start their metamorphosis, about the time when Fares's father, like every other stonemason of Shwayr, left his family for work in "foreign lands," or *ard al-gherbeh*. The life of the Bozeid Moujaes was orchestrated by the cycle of the seasons. A turning point in Shwayr came at Easter, when Orthodox Lent and its fifty-day fasting period came to an end and the Eid was proclaimed in great pomp. Families celebrated together the resurrection of Christ before the men packed their tools and headed out to a new season of construction work.

While his father was away, Fares's mother filled the walls of her sitting room with a framework of poles made of mulberry tree branches, tying them into a grid in which the mulberry leaves were positioned. In this, the worms were placed, and they ate the leaves with an ogre-like appetite. Fares helped pick the large, thick, crunchy leaves and bring them to the framework every day, and the worms grew bigger by the hour. From tiny, squeaking bugs, the silkworms grew massive and then stopped eating to begin the pupal transformation into chrysalides. After forty days, the tiny insects yielded a forest of large silk cocoons that Fares's mother sold by the bundle to spinners who crisscrossed the countryside on buying trips.

The silk industry was very prosperous then and would develop further in the coming century to become the main source of wealth in Mount Lebanon. Sericulture had existed there since the seventeenth century, thanks to the forward thinking of Amir Fakhreddine (1572–1635), the ruler of a large territory that extended in its heyday from Gaza in the south, to Latakia in the north, and deep into the Syrian hinterland as far as Palmyra in the east. He governed under the tutelage of the Ottomans, who confirmed him in his role of governor of the *sanjak* of Saida, a province that fell at that time under the auspices of the *wali* (the provincial governor) of Damascus and included all the mountains extending from Kesrwan to the Shouf. Saida, the biblical Sidon, was a harbor city that served these highlands, as did Tripoli, in the north, serve the Syrian hinterland.

Being so powerful, Fakhreddine managed to sign the tax-farming contract, the *muamala*, with the wali, which gave him the right to manage the territories to his benefit and, from the standpoint of the Ottomans, to enrich the imperial treasury in Istanbul from levies on the local populations. For the Ottomans, the rationale was clear: who other than a local and powerful dignitary could levy taxes across a rugged and inaccessible terrain and hold the populations in check? Fakhreddine was the obvious choice. The amir, however, had other plans, and taking advantage of the war that was raging between the Ottomans and the newly established Safavid dynasty in Persia, he turned his emara into a socioeconomic model that gave birth to a new system of governance. He collected less tax, improved the conditions of the working class, developed irrigation systems with the help of the Venetians (with whom he openly maintained relations), organized a standing army, and built fortresses across his ever-enlarging territories.

The Ottomans soon grew disenchanted with this exuberant and indomitable amir, and for a time Fakhreddine had to lay low, and so sailed for Tuscany. He remained in Florence for four years, where he learned from his friends, the Medici, the intricacies of governing a transforming society where art and architecture coexisted with modern economics and riches poured in from newly discovered continents. By extending their hospitality, the Medici befriended a potential ally who could be useful if, come the day, they mounted a new crusade to liberate the Holy

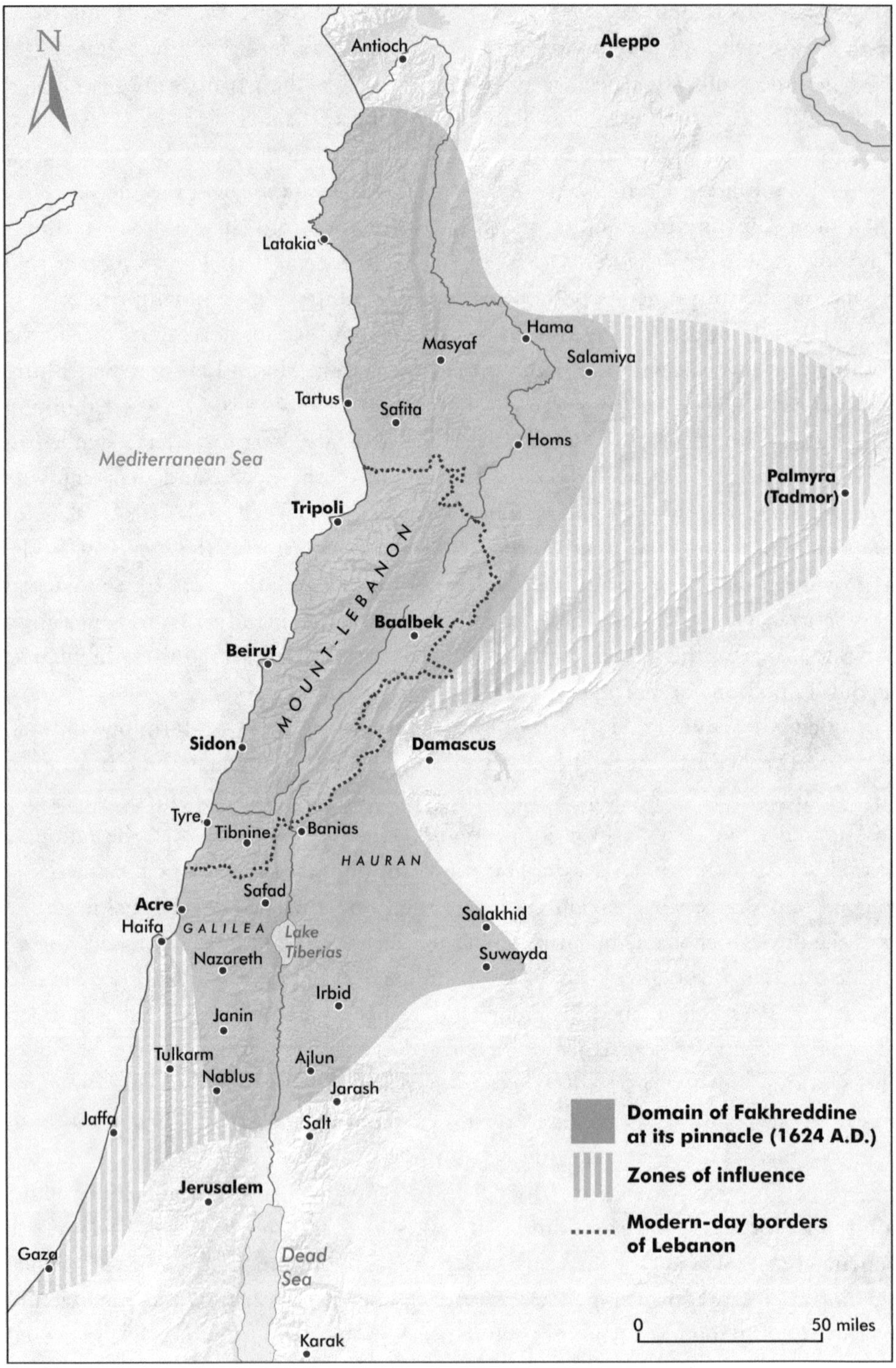

Map 1. The territorial expansion of Fakhreddine the Great

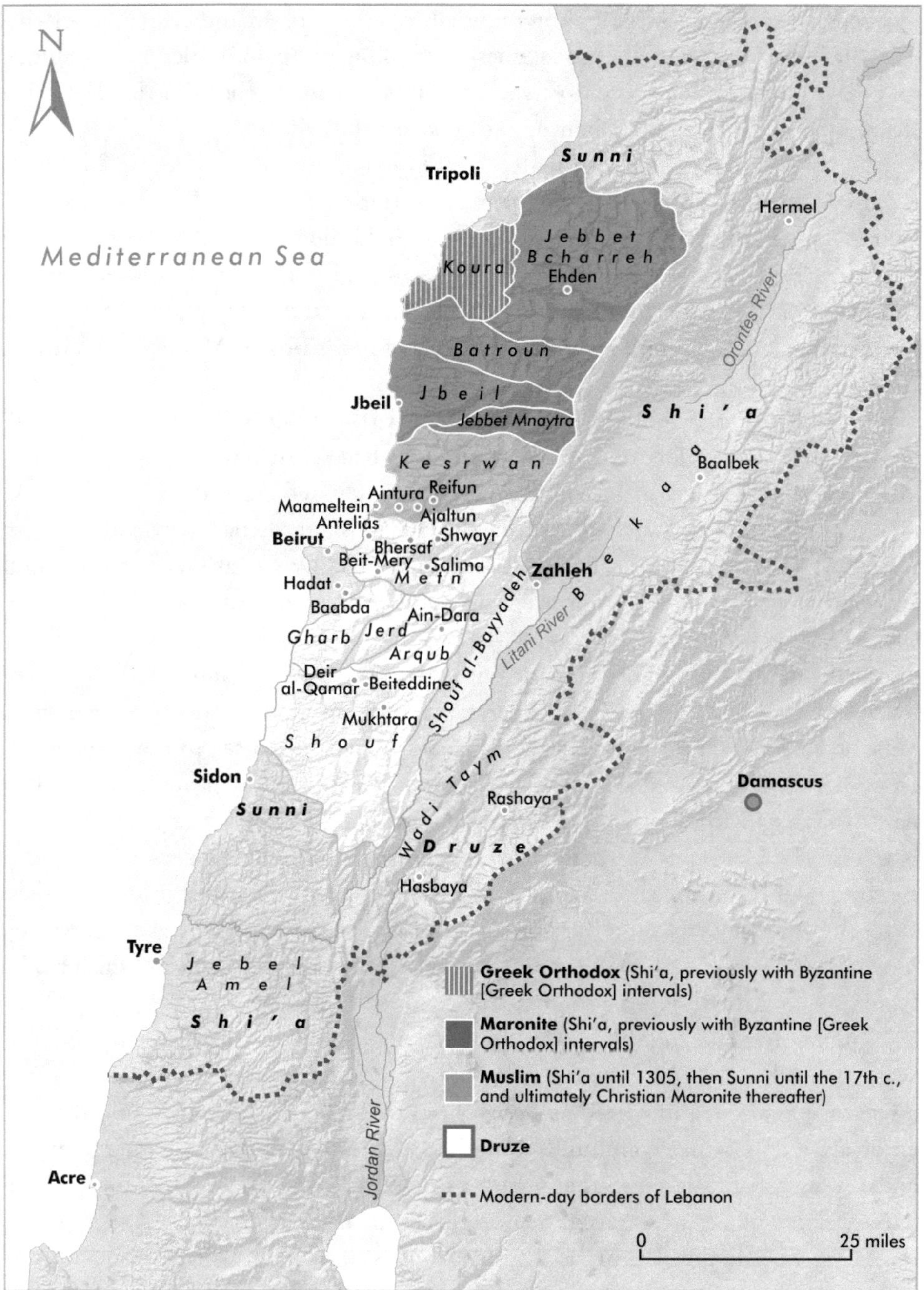

Map 2. The seven fiefdoms (emara) in the times of Amir Fakhreddine

Shrines of Jerusalem. Amir Fakhreddine also spent time in the Kingdom of the Two Sicilies in Napoli as a personal guest of the king of Spain. Exiled Fakhreddine may have been, but the four to five years he spent in the bustling lands of the Renaissance gave the amir alliances and food for thought.

After brokering a deal with the Ottomans to return home, in 1618, Fakhreddine spent time organizing his administration and rebuilding his village of Deir al-Qamar, turning it into the power center of his dominions. And when it came to construction, Fakhreddine knew where to get good stonemasons. If his architects and engineers were mostly Florentines, the stone workers were from Hauran and Shwayr, many of the Moujaes family, ancestors of Fares Bozeid Moujaes and Alfred Nicola.

At the time of Fakhreddine, the southern part of modern-day Mount Lebanon was inhabited by the Druze, a dissident sect that had splintered from Muslim Shi'a in the eleventh century in Fatimid Egypt and sought refuge in the hills that took their name. Until the nineteenth century, the part of Mount Lebanon extending from Kesrwan to the Shouf was called the Mountain of the Druze; at that time, "Mount Lebanon" only referred to the northern part that had come to be inhabited by Maronite Christians about the same time (see "Mount Lebanon in history," appendix 1, for a discussion of the origins of the different communities of Lebanon). Communities lived separately and had very little interaction until Amir Fakhreddine, enlightened most probably by his years in exile, endeavored to build an agrarian economy based on crop and silk production. For this, labor was needed, and Fakhreddine saw the hard-working Christian Maronite community living in the north as a good source of workers. The Maronites had come to the region after having been persecuted by the Byzantines and were pushed into Mount Lebanon from their lands on the Orontes River, in western Syria near the northern frontier of modern-day Lebanon. In the mountains, where rains were plentiful, they mastered terrace agriculture, which made them experts at subduing the inhospitable, cold, and hilly terrain.

Manpower was not all Fakhreddine wanted, however; he also had political reasons to usher the Maronites into the lands of the Druze. The amir was himself a Druze, and although he lived and governed among his coreligionists, they did not enjoy unity. The Druze community was divided by power struggles among families, and also by tribal differences that separated those who identified with their Yemeni ancestry from others who traced their origins to the north of the Arabian Peninsula, the Qaysi. Simply put, Fakhreddine needed allies to balance his lack of popularity among a large portion of the Druze. He could not turn to the Sunni community, as it was too close to the Ottomans, who shared their religion. He could not turn to the Shi'a either, because they were close to the Persian Safavid dynasty; such a move would be interpreted as a *casus belli* by the Ottomans, who were at war with their neighbors. He also could not turn to the Greek Orthodox, who answered to the Patriarch in Phanar, in Istanbul itself, and were therefore equally close to the Sublime Porte, the seat of Ottoman power. So Fakhreddine chose the Maronites, who formed an indigenous church in the highlands up north and who were less likely to respond to Ottoman overtures. To improve relations with them, he gave their clergy swathes of land in the Druze Mountains to build churches. It is at this moment in the history of Lebanon that religion started to interfere with politics, a state of affairs that is intrinsic to the power balance of Lebanon today. Modern politics in Lebanon is in many ways the continuation of the sociopolitical system that came into play in these early times. Away from their homes and living among a fierce and combative population (one valley in the Metn Mountains is called the valley of skulls, *wadi jamajem*, after the high number of fighters who fell during a battle between Druze families), the Maronite workers needed protection, and their rallying point, the church, amassed power and never lost it.

Palace builders

The Ottomans did not approve of Fakhreddine and his methods, but their hands were tied after losing so much territory to the Europeans at the Battle of Lepanto in 1571. Their hands were also tied by the Persian enemy marauding on their eastern flank, and more by the economic losses they had suffered as a consequence of the inflation in Europe that accompanied the flow of riches from the Americas. The Ottomans needed to maximize tax collections to offset these losses and left the Druze amir alone as long as he paid his dues to the Porte on time.

This state of affairs changed when Europe was drawn into a war of its own, the Thirty Years' War, which started in 1618 and diverted the European chancelleries' attention away from their Ottoman neighbors. Another stroke of good fortune for Istanbul was the death in 1629 of Shah Abbas, the strong leader of the Safavids in Persia, and the subsequent decay of his empire. Thus, two threats to the Ottoman Empire, the Europeans and the Safavids, were lifted without any effort on the part of Istanbul. This sudden change of fortune gave the Ottomans the time they needed to reorganize internally, and soon the clock started to tick for the impetuous amir who had dared to mock the sovereignty of the House of Othman for nearly half a century.

Fakhreddine was arrested in 1634 and sent to Istanbul, where his fate was sealed a year later along with three of his sons. His legacy, however, remained, although his direct successors, approved by the Porte, did not rise to the standard of his greatness. Not until the end of the seventeenth century, when Fakhreddine's family, the Maans, had no male heirs, was an alternative line of succession sought. Was it the Druze dignitaries who proposed it, or the Ottomans who imposed their will? Either way, the succession was given to the Shihab family, cousins by marriage to the Maans.

Rustum Moujaes, a master stonemason from Shwayr, arrived one April morning in 1804 to pay the parents of Fares Bozeid Moujaes a visit. He had work to offer and Fares's father was all ears. The two men had worked together before on a number of construction projects across the country, and Fares's father was eager to begin another one. Lent was approaching, and no job offers had yet come his way, not surprising given the difficult economic times. The ruthless wali of Saida, Al-Jazzar, had forced the new master of the mountains, Amir Bashir, to flee on more than one occasion, leaving the country in the hands of incompetent power-mongers from his own family, and the people of Mount Lebanon suffered the consequences. What Rustum had to offer was a grand project, the grandest possible perhaps: nothing less than a palace for the great Amir Bashir himself in Beiteddine.

Bashir II Shihab, also called Bashir the Great, was the strongman of the family, and one who was by many accounts the only notable successor to Fakhreddine. He was seventh in line to govern after the Shihab came to replace the Maan in the emara, and he proved to be both an enlightened leader and a ruthless despot, governing by force and intimidation. The amir had asked Rustum to gather his workers at Beiteddine immediately after the Eid. Fares Bozeid Moujaes turned sixteen that year, and his father decided he was old enough to make the trip as one of the workers.

The Shihab knew the Moujaes, having been neighbors in Hauran in the early times. Originally, the Shihab came from Najaf, valiant fighters whose elder was a Companion of the Prophet and fought many wars under his banner, not least that of Yarmouk against the Byzantines in what is today Syria. For compensation, the Caliph Omar, friend and successor of the Prophet, endowed them with wide swathes of land across Hauran and the lowlands southwest of Damascus. They lived there for nearly five centuries and relied on the Moujaes to build their homes. Then, when pressured in the eleventh century by both Nureddin Zengi and Saladin, the rulers of Syria and Egypt, to take sides in their internecine wars, the Shihab chose instead to leave Hauran and crossed the Anti-Lebanon Mountains to settle in the valley called Wadi Taym. As Sunnis, the Shihab were related to the Prophet, a fact that could legitimize either Zengi or Saladin, for supremacy in the Near East, were the Shihab to take sides. They also had a standing army of fifteen thousand warriors, no less a reason for the two contenders to make overtures to them and try to gain their support. On arriving in Wadi Taym, the Shihab picked a long fight with a crusader's army and took hold of its fortress, which they refashioned as a palace, again with the help of the Moujaes from Hauran. This palace of the Shihab, recently refurbished, still stands in the town of Hasbaya.

The Ottomans were content to see the Shihab family assume the succession in the mountains. First, they were Sunni, which meant the Shihab would be less inclined to deny them their allegiance. They also came from Wadi Taym, far from the Druze Mountains, and so did not take part in the internecine fights among the Druze families. From the standpoint of the Ottomans, the Shihab would have no reason to take sides with either the Yemeni or Qaysi groups; they would only levy taxes for the Porte and gain ascendancy for themselves in the process. The first Shihab to govern, however, were rather weak, many acting treacherously toward one another. Some went as far as poisoning their next of kin in order to be able to sign the *muamala* with the Ottomans themselves and so become *multazim*, or tax farmers.

One of the Shihab, Amir Haidar, did quell the ancient contention between the two Druze clans. At the Battle of Ain Dara, in 1711, he affirmed the dominance of the Qaysite clan over the Yemeni. The defeated were either massacred or exiled to Hauran, while the triumphant families divided the spoils that the Shihab were happy to bestow. The Abillamah, a princely family that was given the whole sanjak of Metn for tax-farming by the Maan in the early seventeenth century, was promoted to the title of amir from that of *muqaddam* (the titles are all from the military and were introduced by the Ottomans: *sheikh* is the lowest rank, followed by *muqaddam*, *caimaqam*, and *amir*, which has come to signify "prince" in the vernacular). They lived in Mtein, in the vicinity of Shwayr, the village of the Moujaes, and when tax time came, the parents of Fares Bozeid Moujaes settled their dues and paid the *miri* to the collectors of the Abillamah. Their palaces are still there to see, built around a square used for horseback riding and where the population attended the amirs' celebrations.

The year 1711 was an important one in the history of modern Lebanon. The outcome of the Battle of Ain Dara and the triumph of the Qaysites consolidated the emara, the socioeconomic system that Fakhreddine had scrupulously built and that Amir Bashir, with his political maneuverings, would anchor permanently in the Lebanese political ethos for the next two hundred years. This ethos has survived, practically unchanged, to the present day.

No sooner had the Qaysi-Yemeni conflict been more or less resolved than another political division arose that would poison Druze relations for years to come. One fast-rising family after Ain Dara was the Jumblatt family, who had fought on the side of the Shihab family and helped consolidate power after inheriting the substantial wealth of the Qadi family, which had died out without a direct heir. All the estates and wealth of the Qadi went to a son-in-law, Ali Jumblatt, a turn of affairs that a large group of Druze families resented. New alliances were formed over this controversy, each striving to control the mountains by seeking to appoint its own candidate to the succession of the emara. Divided as they were, members of the Shihab family ended up aligning against each other, siding with the antagonistic families, the Jumblatti and Yazbaki.

Bashir II Shihab entered the scene at a crucial time in the history of Lebanon. For a long time he had lived in Deir al-Qamar, the seat of Amir Youssef Shihab, his uncle. Young Bashir came to his uncle at an early age, after being orphaned and raised in the Christian family of Chidiac in the Kesrwan Mountains. His father had converted to Christianity as was the trend among non-Christian muqataaji, who were surrounded by growing numbers of Maronite serfs in the second half of the eighteenth century. If *cujus regio, ejus religio* was the standard in the Germanic principalities of sixteenth-century Europe, the muqataaji of the Druze Mountains had every reason to go the other way and follow the religion of their subjects.

The landowners operated their estates by employing peasants, a form of serfdom but one regulated by social norms that were appropriate to the mountains. Unlike serfs in Europe or Romanov Russia, peasants were free to move and settle anywhere, which meant the landowners needed to indulge their subjects to a certain degree to keep them in their employ. Conversion to Christianity made for good employee relations. This did not mean that social interactions were not held to a strict and formal protocol. To the contrary, when Fares Bozeid Moujaes and his father decided to leave Shwayr for Beiteddine and take the job offered by Rustum Moujaes, they certainly had to visit the Abillamah amir and ask for his permission to do so. Muqataajis made law and gave protection. The Abillamah, by the way, also converted to Christianity when the Metn Mountains came to be densely inhabited by Christians, a second conversion for them, given that they already turned Druze earlier, relinquishing the Sunni religion into which they had been born in the Arabian Peninsula. Plural communities formed as a consequence of this religious blending, affecting the social and political landscape. At this time, Mount Lebanon came to refer to the entire chain of mountains that encompassed the previously all-Christian and Druze parts, while the name Mountain of the Druze fell out of general use and became identified only with the mountain in Hauran.

It was from Hauran that young Bashir II Shihab came to Deir al-Qamar and lived under the protection of his uncle Amir Youssef until he developed ambitions of his own. He soon struck an alliance with his namesake from the Jumblatt family, Sheikh Bashir, who was an important strongman of the mountains at the end of the eighteenth century.

Of strongmen, the period had many, and one to contend with was the ruthless Ahmad Al-Jazzar, the governor of Saida, which had become an independent *pashalik* in 1660. Bosnian by birth, Al-Jazzar, whose nickname ("butcher," in Arabic) testified to his coldblooded personality, had merits in the eyes of the Ottoman sultan. He defended astutely the harbor town of Beirut against the Russians when their ships shelled the Ottoman troops stationed there in 1772. The ramparts he built in record time did not yield despite the severity of the attack. (In the end, the Russians did capture Beirut in 1773 and kept the flag of the tsarina flying for a year.)

Al-Jazzar received the governorship of Saida as a result of his valor and gained the favors of the Ottomans, who turned a blind eye on his rapaciousness: after the Russians left, he confiscated Beirut from Amir Youssef and relocated the seat of his pashalik to Acre. In doing so, he captured two thriving maritime merchant cities that were serving the blossoming sericulture economy of the mountains. By the time Fares Bozeid Moujaes and his father came to Beiteddine, exports of raw silk accounted for nearly half of the economy of Mount Lebanon. Another quarter of the economy was the trade in olives and olive oil. The landscape had changed radically by the turn of the century, with cereal crops giving way to mulberry trees, olive groves, and vineyards. Al-Jazzar understood the importance of the coastal lands to the people of the mountains and apportioned for his benefit the stretches that fell from Acre to Tripoli. That way, he could control access to the Mediterranean and tax the routes used by marine merchants across a number of port cities in the Levant.

Impressed by Al-Jazzar's strong personality, the sultan appointed him governor of Damascus in 1780. The ruthless wali seemed unstoppable. In his new post, he could easily dispose of Amir Youssef since it was he, Al-Jazzar, the governor of Saida now in Acre, who would decide with whom to renew the muamala, the tax-farming contract that Amir Youssef now enjoyed. The contract was renewed every year, and the Ottoman governor could review the terms and play the contenders, usually from the same families, against one another in order to extract larger payments, since the amount for the contract was set in advance. It also granted the wali the advantage of maintaining a grip on local politics by dividing the families and ruling them. Sheikh Bashir Jumblatt knew this too, and when the time for renewing the muamala came, he presented the younger Bashir as a candidate, even though his protégé was a poor and inexperienced young man whose only virtue (or so they thought) was belonging to the Shihab family.

Spotting a golden opportunity, Al-Jazzar pitted the two Shihab against one another, using the young Bashir to force Amir Youssef to offer a larger payment, the muamala being signed off to the highest bidder. Finally, with the promise from young Bashir to pay an incredible figure (which Bashir intended to levy on the peasants over a number of years), Al-Jazzar granted him the muamala for the Druze Mountains. More rounds of offers and counteroffers took place, prompted by the voracious greed of Al-Jazzar, until Amir Youssef was finally summoned to Acre and assassinated on the orders of the wali. As soon as Amir Bashir was confirmed in his new position, he purged the mountains of all potential rivals, and after another round of power struggles, again fomented by Al-Jazzar, he went as far as disfiguring the sons of the deceased Amir Youssef, blinding them and exiling them to Jbeil. (The worst thing that could befall a member of the gentry was disfigurement, usually having the eyes plucked out and the tongue cut off, as this meant falling from grace. "Gentry" in Arabic is synonymous with "face," *wujaha'a*.)

The real test of force for Al-Jazzar, however, came in 1798 in the person of Napoleon Bonaparte. It also turned out to be a real test of government for Amir Bashir. Bonaparte was campaigning in Egypt, and after his swift defeat of the Mamluks at the Battle of the Pyramids, he took his army east, only to come face to face with Al-Jazzar. The French laid siege in front of Acre, attempting to force an opening to the north. That way, Napoleon's army could circumvent the English, who controlled the Mediterranean, and be first to arrive at the gates of Istanbul.

Al-Jazzar, the "soldier-adventurer" as Engin Akarli calls him, resolutely held his position, surprising the French general, whose Italian campaign against the Austrians in 1796 had set him on his legendary course. To turn the situation in his favor, Napoleon needed local help, a diversion in the form of an attack on the flank of the Ottomans. The obvious choice to lead the diversion was Amir Bashir, and Napoleon sent an officer to Deir al-Qamar with a clear message to rally him.

The amir, however, was a master of brinksmanship and used astute political maneuverings to keep both contenders in check. Helping Napoleon meant earning the harsh reprisals of Al-Jazzar in case the Frenchman failed; neglecting the appeal of Napoleon meant Amir Bashir would be marginalized if the general did win the battle and occupied Mount Lebanon. Not wanting to deceive either of them, the amir managed to satisfy both by reassuring each of the contenders of his undivided allegiance.

About this time, news of the Empress Josephine's infidelities arrived, adding to the bitterness of the military stalemate that Napoleon was enduring under the walls of Acre. With his navy broken and his army decimated by disease, Napoleon surrendered his command to General Kléber and left for Paris aboard a frigate. (This ship came within an ace of falling into English hands, and probably would have, if the infatuated Admiral Nelson hadn't been determined to spend time with Emma Hamilton on the island of Sicily.)

With Napoleon gone, the triumphant Al-Jazzar was now in a position to cash in on his victory from his overlord, the sultan of the Ottomans, who confirmed him as a wali for life. Amir Bashir fled for Egypt, anticipating the wrath of Al-Jazzar, but eventually worked his way back to the wali's grace through diplomacy. The price to pay for this leniency of the wali would prove to be full of consequence for Mount Lebanon.

The cat-and-mouse interplay between Amir Bashir and Al-Jazzar continued for a few more years, until the aging Bosnian passed away in 1804. The more moderate Suleiman Pasha replaced Al-Jazzar as wali of Saida, a seat he would keep for fourteen years. These were years of prosperity for Mount Lebanon as

Amir Bashir, without Al-Jazzar breathing down his neck, was free to develop his dominions, starting with the building of his Beiteddine palace.

Fares Bozeid Moujaes and his father came to Beiteddine in the company of Rustum Moujaes and some forty other workers in early May 1804. They joined others from Hauran and many more from across the Syrian lands, a large contingent of construction workers who were placed under the direction of master architects and engineers, many of whom had traveled from Florence. The relations that Mount Lebanon amirs maintained with Italian principalities and duchies since the times of Fakhreddine were very strong. The doge of Venice, for example, was a regular supplier of weapons (the Arabic name for Venice is *boundoukia*, which means "rifle"), and Tuscany supplied illustrious architects and shipped construction materials, such as granite and stained glass, especially for Beiteddine. Amir Bashir started work on the palace in 1788, but progress was intermittent and took eighteen years to complete. On more than one occasion, he had to flee Mount Lebanon, as he did between 1800 and 1804, when no fewer than five amirs were appointed successively in his stead to rule the mountains. The construction really took off after Al-Jazzar passed away in 1804, when the amir was no longer pressured by the powerful wali of Acre.

With its multiple squares, different levels, imposing volumes, and impressive character, the whole organized with a refined and cohesive identity, the palace was intended as a power center where Amir Bashir not only resided but managed his dominions. Here he oversaw secretaries and clerks, devised a modern administration, and entertained a court that lived by the regal protocols observed by distinctive European royalties. Some two thousand people were employed at Beiteddine, and the stables had stalls for fifteen hundred horses.

Shwayr and its people enjoyed a privileged relationship with Amir Bashir, who exempted them from taxes, not a common act and one that suggests the close bonding that united the Shihab and the Shwayr families. A popular ode of the period that still lives in oral memory alludes to the work achieved by Rustum Moujaes in Beiteddine:

> My lord has erected a palace, was not content with bare buildings,
> He brought a Shwayri stonemason, and had him work the edifice.
> (*Sayyidi a'mmar amara, ma kaffa amareta,*
> *Wa jabla maallem Shwayri, yen'eshla hajara.*)

Oral tradition and poetry have more to share on this subject, some of it fictitious but equally interesting in what it tells us about how the people, mostly peasants living on muqataaji estates, viewed their amir. The stonework turned out to be so grand, says one story, and Amir Bashir was so charmed by the result, that he asked to have the hands of all the Shwayri stonemasons chopped off to keep them from replicating the jewel of Beiteddine. This never happened, of course, yet this was the kind of hearsay that added mystery to the enigma that was the amir.

One of those mysteries was religion; the exact religion of the amir was not common knowledge, and he was careful to accept all religions but belong to none: he had serious inclinations toward Christianity, but probably for the political reasons explained earlier. In the Hammam that he built in Beiteddine and where he spent a whole day every week with his close counselors, Amir Bashir had a cross formed in a constellation of stained glass, cleverly concealed in the ceiling of the shower rooms, which glowed radiantly when the sun was at its zenith. (The tourist guides at Beiteddine regularly make a stop there to show the visitors the reflection of the cross on their sunglasses.) In short, Amir Bashir was from Sunni Muslim stock, born a Christian, and lived among the Druze. He built a small chapel in Beiteddine, a mosque, and a *ḳhalweh*, a community space for the Druze *uqqal*; so he could practice all three religions. A common joke in this regard claims, "Amir Bashir was born a Christian, lived a Druze, and died a Muslim." Although, during his time in power, religious differences were increasingly causing problems, he handled them with relative ease, being a resolute and strong character. It is unfortunate that we cannot say the same of his successors. For while Amir Bashir was able to suppress people's excess anxiety from sectarian strife, others only exacerbated it.

A true people's man, Amir Bashir received whomever came to see him, always dressed in his grandiloquent robes, observing etiquette carefully. A layman always bowed on entry as a sign of reverence and never came close to the amir, who remained seated in the *diwan*. The higher a visitor's rank, the more affable the amir would be, the closest encounter being reserved for a muqataaji, who was entitled to kiss the shoulder of Amir Bashir while the amir stood a few steps from his seat. He listened with genuine concern to the complaints of the people who solicited his help, especially the less fortunate, and gave orders to his secretaries to resolve their problems immediately. The meetings with his ministers and counselors took place in the government rooms, spacious diwans with red velvet seats, with walls and ceilings covered with cedar wood and decorated with fine paintings. Most of the meeting rooms had a water curtain built into the walls that flowed continuously. A precursor of air conditioning systems, the water curtain also had the useful effect of camouflaging sound. Weary of spies around him, the amir spoke firmly but kept his voice low when he spoke of confidential matters, always standing next to the water curtains. When receiving ambassadors with important messages to convey, he often used small cubicles that were soundproofed with highly decorated thick cedar planks.

Over time, Amir Bashir erected another four palaces, less grandiose though equally refined, in Deir al-Qamar and Beiteddine, three for his children and a dowager palace intended for his wife. One of them has been converted into a boutique hotel by the Ministry of Tourism of Lebanon and has one of the best views of Beiteddine. It is called (A)Mir Amin, after one of the amir's sons. If you cannot stay overnight, I recommend you sip a shaffeh of cardamom coffee at the hotel terrace and enjoy the marvelous views over this part of Mount Lebanon.

One cannot speak of Beiteddine without referring, if only briefly, to the "idiot of Shanay," a Chaplinesque character intimately associated with the palace. A frequent visitor of the amir who was seen as a kind of court jester, he is said to have found a solution to the amir's water shortage problem. His suggestion: drag the nearby Safa water source to Beiteddine by having all the men of the amir stand side by side across the distance and dig one length of earth each. In this way, a canal was dug and water flowed; so, on the suggestion of the alleged village idiot of Shanay, Beiteddine became self-sufficient in water (which still flows to this day). The epic *Akhwat Shanay* was brought to the stage by an ingenious theater director in the 1970s and dramatizes with wit and simplicity much of the wisdom of a past century. Included in that wisdom is the amir's own observation, "Among the idiots, I have found the wisest of men."

Unlike his father, Fares Bozeid Moujaes did not remain to see the work on Beiteddine palace completed. He left in 1807 to start a new life of his own, having just turned nineteen.

From Beiteddine to Hadath

The sons of Amir Youssef were not the only members of the Shihab family who were blinded at the hands of Amir Bashir's men. Many others received similar treatment, two of whom were Bashir's cousins, Fares and Selman, the sons of Sid Ahmad Melhem Shihab. Sightless and unwelcome, the two brothers followed other members of the family and came to live in Baabda. On the recommendation of his father, Fares Bozeid Moujaes went with them. Now a skilled stonemason, having earned his experience at his father's side at Beiteddine, he could lend a hand, with others that Rustum Moujaes designated, to build the Shihab residences in their new retreat.

A three-day ride from Beiteddine, Baabda would be the seat of the Shihab in winter when the snows fell on Deir al-Qamar. This small coastal mountain overlooked a fertile plain on the southern edge of Beirut called Hadath, where the Shihab raised crops and produced silk. Standing on their balconies on the heights of Baabda, they could see the large swathes of land in Hadath that were theirs.

Beirut at this time was only a small fishing harbor, of little importance compared with the seafaring towns of Saida and Tripoli. Fewer than seven thousand souls lived inside the walls and seven gates of the ancient city, within which were such landmarks as the casern of Fakhreddine (occupied by Ottoman troops at that time), Saint George's Orthodox Church, the Mosque of Omar, and the *Burj*, one of the towers that dotted the city's walls, which had its base in the Mediterranean Sea. Fares Bozeid Moujaes resided at the construction sites in Baabda before moving into a rented house in Hadath. There he dropped his family name and came to be called Shwayri after the village of his origins. He lived next door to Saint Elias Church.

In the meantime, Amir Bashir's power was expanding over all Mount Lebanon. The tax-farming muamala signed with the wali of Acre gave him rights over the southern mountains; another, signed with the wali of Tripoli, put the northern mountains under his control (a river between the northern and southern mountains still retains the name Maameltein, the "two muamalas"). On the strength of these two muamalas, Amir Bashir governed a large dominion, the largest to regroup under a local amir since Fakhreddine. Yet, unlike Fakhreddine, who held the rank of wali, a title bestowed by the Sultan in Istanbul, Bashir was only a signatory of the muamalas and was entirely subject to the whims of the walis in Acre and Tripoli.

Under Suleiman Pasha, Amir Bashir had faced no serious threats; however, the successor to the passive wali at Acre proved to be, if not as ruthless as Al-Jazzar, at least his equal in the thirst for power and money. Abdallah Pasha succeeded the aging Suleiman in 1818 and within two years imposed on Amir Bashir a significant increase in the muamala. To raise these funds, the amir had to levy additional taxes on the muqataajis; they, in turn, imposed the financial burden on the peasants who actually farmed the land. In the southern mountains where the Druze muqataajis still made the law, the tax increase went unnoticed. It was paid by the amir's namesake, Sheikh Bashir Jumblatt himself, the wealthy man of the Druze Mountains, who understood the dangers of imposing higher taxes on the peasants.

In the north, the story was different. There was no Sheikh Bashir to step in and pay the tax, and the muqataajis in the Christian Mountains either did not understand the threat that was posed or did not have the means to cushion the surtax. As a result, the peasants in the north, faced with an impossible debt to settle, fomented a rebellion. The Maronite Church became the cornerstone of this political movement, and its zealous clergy encouraged the aggrieved populace. Led by a bishop, the Maronite peasants in the north went rogue in 1820, and Amir Bashir had to use force to quell the uprising. Riding with Sheikh Bashir and his men, the amir finally defeated the rebels. Although the bishop was killed, the amir did not use punitive measures against the peasants themselves, who ended up paying the surtax.

The peasant resistance of 1820 reignited in 1821 with another round of armed grievances; these Amir Bashir also tamed by force, again with the help of Sheikh Bashir and his private army. The outcome may have seemed satisfactory at the time, as the walis of Tripoli and Acre received the full amount of taxes they imposed and Amir Bashir got to keep his seat as ruler of the mountains, but these events had ushered in a new and unexpected religious divide in Mount Lebanon. By bringing the Christian Maronite peasants to bay under the arms of the Druze in order to extract a surtax to benefit the Ottoman walis, Amir Bashir opened a denominational fracture that still deeply divides the identity of Lebanon today.

The wali of Acre, Abdallah Pasha, faced other troubles in his domain; the large cities in the Syrian hinterland were growing weary of his excesses. By controlling the trading routes across the coast and the ports of Acre and Sidon, the wali could tax all goods that boarded ships or mounted camels across his dominions. At this time, the economy of Mount Lebanon was flourishing. So was that of Damascus and a number of other towns such as Zahleh, the *haut lieu* of the fertile Bekaa plateau, then under the governance of the wali of Damascus. The general prosperity prompted Abdallah Pasha to increase taxes on all products that transited his regions, sometimes even seizing shipments and attacking caravans that transported goods to Damascus.

Irritated by the demands of his insatiable colleague, the wali of Damascus started preparations for war and called for the two Bashirs, the amir and the sheikh, to support him. Having earned the governance of Mount Lebanon from the wali of Acre, Amir Bashir chose to stand by Abdallah Pasha, probably weighing the consequences of siding against him. For his part, Sheikh Bashir, seeing his chance to strike a blow at Amir Bashir, whose dominion surpassed his own, swore allegiance to the wali of Damascus. By standing against him, the sheikh hoped to undo the Amir and replace him with another Shihab, one he could control, and so regain the power that his onetime ally and namesake had taken from him. And for a time, the sheikh's plan did work. Amir Bashir had to leave Beiteddine and sought asylum in Egypt, disembarking at Damietta. (It is interesting to note that Amir Bashir made the journey aboard a frigate made available to him by Admiral Sydney Smith, the British naval officer who controlled the Mediterranean.)

Amir Bashir arrived in an Egypt that was developing at a quick pace to the colorful rhythms of its *nahda*, the cultural renaissance that accompanied a series of reforms. Against all expectations, it was not an Egyptian who was responsible for this renewal, but an Albanian military man. He had been sent to Egypt in 1801 by the Ottoman Sublime Porte, after the army of Napoleon Bonaparte had left, to silence the remaining Mamluks who, still under the sway of the French general, were attempting to regain control. Muhammad Ali was the man's name, and he was to occupy the center stage of Middle Eastern politics for half a century.

In record time, Muhammad Ali reorganized the Egyptian army, built a navy that outshone any other in the Mediterranean, developed his administration, and sent officials for special training in France. He did this with the active participation of French officers who had fought in the army of Bonaparte and stayed behind, some changing their names to sound more Middle Eastern. After the fall of Bonaparte and the restoration of the Bourbons in France, Muhammad Ali welcomed wholeheartedly any officers of Napoleon who were incapable of coping with the *de facto* regime in Paris. Colonel Joseph Sève was probably the most important of these. He had fought valiantly in Russia and came to Egypt after the emperor was exiled to take command of the army. He was known thereafter as Suleiman Pasha, also the *frensawi*, or Frenchman. Before long, Muhammad Ali became too strong for Istanbul to deny him the sovereignty that the people of Egypt had already granted him, and he became the sole ruler of the land while still reporting to the Sultan in Istanbul. In time, the viceroy of Egypt would gain complete independence from the Porte.

Muhammad Ali received Amir Bashir in great pomp. He had every interest in seeing the amir of Mount Lebanon reinstated and strong, for he viewed him as an ally in a struggle looming on the horizon, a struggle that might eventually engulf all of Syria and steal it from the Ottomans. But that time had not yet come, and for now, Muhammad Ali was still pledging allegiance to the Sublime Porte, coming with his army to aid the sultan when needed. Muhammad Ali sent his son, Ibrahim Pasha, for example, on a campaign to restrain the Wahhabi movement that was causing strife in Najaf; this brought Mecca and Medina into Muhammad Ali's fold for a time, defusing a threat to the Ottomans' power that came at the beginning of the nineteenth century.

The ultra-fundamentalist Wahhabi movement was started by an imam, Muhammad ibn Abd al-Wahhab, and, after 1790, started to spread to Aleppo and Damascus before being fought back in 1811 by the Ottomans and none other than Amir Bashir, who had been called in to the rescue. The threat was lifted, but many clerics in Damascus had been converted to the new teachings and started preaching a return to Orthodoxy. As a result, a number of Christians from Damascus and Syria, mostly tradespeople, were forced to seek refuge in Mount Lebanon, settling in commercial hubs such as Zahleh in the Bekaa plateau, where they introduced a cosmopolitan *savoir faire*.

Eventually, Muhammad Ali interceded with the sultan on behalf of Amir Bashir, who duly regained his seat in Mount Lebanon. On his return, he was received by the wali of Acre in triumph, the Sultan in Istanbul having relieved the wali of Damascus of his duties (to the dismay of Sheikh Bashir Jumblatt, who had bet on the wrong outcome). The sheikh tried to regain the favors of the amir, his ally from previous times, but to no avail. In the end, the sheikh was detained and killed by the wali of Acre in 1825. Amir Bashir was once again the strongman of Mount Lebanon, having rid himself of every possible contender and normalized the balance of power with the wali of Acre. Soon, though, he would have to repay

Muhammad Ali for his support, and the price would change the sociopolitical nature of Mount Lebanon and the coastal cities.

As these events were unfolding, the Greeks were in open rebellion against the Ottomans, whom they viewed as an oppressive occupation force. The Greeks wanted independence and made it clear that they would not lay down their arms before they achieved it. Except for Austria, which feared the emancipation virus would contaminate its own subjects, the other European countries sympathized with and endorsed the Greeks' goal. The English poet Lord Byron was one of many who came to fight alongside the Greeks, adding a twist of romance to a bloody backdrop. He died in Missolonghi at the age of thirty-six and is still revered today by the Greeks as a national hero.

The Sultan in Istanbul appealed to Muhammad Ali to take charge and tame the Greek insurrection at any cost. Muhammad Ali sent his son Ibrahim Pasha to fight the rebels, but after a promising start, Ibrahim Pasha could not contain the rebellion, which was erupting violently in many different locations. Muhammad Ali had brokered his intervention in Greece in return for the Peloponnese, which the sultan was happy to cede to Egypt, but the outcome of the Battle of Navarino and later the Treaty of Adrianople in 1829 gave Greece its independence and dealt a blow to the Sublime Porte, which was coming into increasing disarray. When, in the end, Muhammad Ali did not get the Peloponnese, he demanded Syria as a substitute prize. The weak Sultan Mahmud II ceded the Island of Crete for compensation, but when Muhammad Ali started massing his troops to invade Syria, the sultan could only acquiesce to Ali's demand.

Back in Hadath, Fares Bozeid Moujaes was overwhelmed with work; as soon as he finished one construction project, he embarked on another. Hadath had been his home ever since he arrived in 1807, but he went back to Shwayr practically every year, and in 1810, he returned with a wife, a girl from his village and church, as tradition demanded. The couple had a son, Habib, born in 1813. Like his father before him, Habib learned early to share his bedroom with the squeaking bugs and work the silk bundles. Silk production and trading were becoming ever more dominant in the economy of Hadath and the entire region of the Sahel. Sadly, Fares Bozeid lost his wife early and he ended up remarrying in 1824, to another girl from his village and church. She gave him a second son in 1826, whom he named Youssef.

Neither Habib nor Youssef would become stonemasons.

2

Habib Fares Shwayri

At the time of the caimaqamat

Alfred Nicola was on time, dressed in a white-striped dark suit, a Beranger hat in his hand, ready before his household and waiting for the others in the sitting room. With an instinctive regard for punctuality, he protested whenever someone ran behind schedule, and he made it clear that everybody recognized his dissatisfaction. Najibeh joined him and tried to calm his nerves, reminding him that this was a big day and that the girls were making themselves beautiful. But that was no excuse. Then, one after the other, family members came out of their rooms, all dressed for the occasion in their most beautiful garments, which pleased both parents and seemed to appease Alfred.

Emily wore a white satin dress, distinguished with a fluffy brooch; Lodi, a light pink dress with white gloves; Nada, a burgundy dress with a flower on the collar, a daisy she had made herself with the dexterity in handling knitting needles that the Shwayri girls learned from their mother. Nicolas wore a white jacket and golf-style shoes in black and white, while Nadim, last to join the gathering, looked handsome in his plain dark suit, the first he had ever worn and which his mother had given him for the occasion. They were all going to Nadim's graduation ceremony from secondary school, a proud moment for Najibeh, who had taught Nadim the Arabic language herself, often using the psalms of Solomon and David, reading material that Nadim had a particular passion for. The graduation was held on the campus of the American University of Beirut, where the secondary school made its home, part of an American-style education that extended from preschool to postgraduate studies. Alfred Nicola knew the university by its former name, the Syrian Protestant College, an institution of repute that led people to often call Lebanon "the lighthouse of education in the Middle East."

Nicolas, proud owner of a vehicle now that he had become a successful lawyer, drove his sisters, and the others followed in the car of Abu-Aziz, the superintendent of Alfred's domains, whose services were put to use for the occasion. The ceremony was memorable, and Nadim grasped his baccalaureate degree with pride, happy to have reached a major milestone, one that would open the way to business and economics studies, which he would pursue with great distinction at the same American University. Delighted by the day's events, Alfred took out his pocket watch, the one he had been wearing for thirty years and which he had bought in New Orleans, the same brand of watch that he had sold hundreds of on his peddling journeys in Louisiana, and gave it to Nadim. It was his gift to his son, the youngest of the family, and, like so many youngest children in so many families, the most affectionate.

American missionaries had come to Mount Lebanon as early as the 1820s and were received with some cordiality by the Druze families. The Maronites, however, did not want the proselytizing Protestants anywhere near their children, and the Maronite clergy were fierce with any of their followers who considered converting to a Protestant creed. The missionaries had some success with the Greek Orthodox community, and a Scottish clergyman did start a school in Shwayr that bred two generations of literate Shwayris, many of whom converted to Presbyterianism. But it was among the Druze that the missionaries had the most success, not on religious grounds, not because the Druze embraced Christianity, but rather because oriental hospitality flowed with a certain generosity among the Druze.

In earlier times, the Ottomans had denied entry across all of the Levant to European travelers, whether they came for trade, missionary work, or any other purpose. Trade across the whole empire was orchestrated to the rhythms of the Sublime Porte, and trade in many products was monopolized by Istanbul. Tobacco, silk, and food crops, to name but three, were handled by the Ottomans without any competition from outside markets. That was the situation until the Porte started losing control, first in the Balkans and then after the Greek Rebellion; there was also internal dissent, as was the case with the Janissaries, the elite corps of the empire, and the separatist movement led by Muhammad Ali in Egypt.

At each junction, the Ottoman sultan used force to tame rebellion, but with little success. He lost Greece, disbanded the Janissaries after killing a great number of them, and then had to deal with an Egyptian army that was modern enough to stand up to his own. And it did in 1831, when the ever-present Ibrahim Pasha, the son of Muhammad Ali, went on a campaign across Syria, laying siege to the harbor city of Acre. As he had three decades earlier, when he was called upon by Bonaparte to fight on his side, Amir Bashir tried to use his finely honed diplomatic skills to evade the call of Ibrahim Pasha to help break the walls of the city. But the Egyptian Pasha would not accept his prevarications, and the amir soon saw his men on horseback fighting the war of Acre. The city ended up falling, bombed from the sea by a strong naval force and encircled on land by the troops of Ibrahim and Bashir. Then, leaving Amir Bashir and his army to control Syria, Ibrahim Pasha went north, struck at the Ottoman army at Antioch, and camped in Konya in the heartland of the Ottoman Empire, at a strategic distance to pose a threat to Istanbul. His ultimate goal was clear: the sultan had to recognize the sovereignty of Muhammad Ali over Egypt and Syria.

Alarm bells rang everywhere, the loudest in the European nations, which had every interest in keeping the Ottoman Empire standing—for a while at least. The British, who held sway over India and much of South Asia, were horrified at the thought of Muhammad Ali taking control of their trade and maritime routes. Even the French, who had supported Muhammad Ali since the beginning, would not let him deliver the fatal blow to "the sick man of Europe." The Russians feared that the breakup of the Ottoman Empire would let loose the Balkan countries, a threat Tsar Nicholas could not control. For the Austrians and Prussians, the emergence of these countries meant the unleashing of nationalistic aspirations, not a palatable prospect since their own empires subjugated minorities too.

In the end, Ibrahim Pasha backed down and withdrew his army to Syria, but in doing so he pushed the sultan into the hands of the Europeans and Russians, who turned out to be his lesser-of-two-evils. The rapid arrival of Westerners showed the growing influence of Europe. Missionaries with various agendas poured into the Ottoman Empire, as did eccentrics who came to spy, early versions of Mata Hari. One of them, Lady Hester Stanhope, a wealthy Conservative Party militant and niece of William Pitt, was bored with her chatelaine life and moved to the vicinity of Saida, where she was soon to wield so much authority that Amir Bashir sent her precious gifts and Ibrahim Pasha sought to neutralize her.

The Druze populations were shattered by the Egyptian occupation. Their ties with Amir Bashir were cut, and many fled to Hauran, rejoining their kinsmen there, escaping the wrath of the amir, who disarmed all those who stayed behind. The Maronites stayed on, replacing the Druze escapees, earning the titles for their abandoned *muqataas* and making their communities stronger. The Druze did not just clash in internecine wars; they lost numbers dramatically in battles with Amir Bashir, who did not hesitate to use Maronite militias to fight them in their own stronghold in Hauran. The demographics of Mount Lebanon changed, showing a radical sectarian turnabout. In the Shouf and Metn, the original home of the Druze community, over sixty percent of the people were now Maronite Christians; Maronites made up ninety percent of Kesrwan, where the Shi'a Muslims were reduced to an insignificant minority.

The Europeans did not stand idly by and watch as these changes took place. All too often, they awakened religious prejudices that added fuel to the fire. The British armed the Druze, the French pleaded for the Maronites, the Russians spoke for the Greek Orthodox, and the Austrians, not to be outdone, adopted the Greek Catholics. Every European power had a local community to defend and to use in the game. With the Druze undermined, the first two years of Ibrahim Pasha's occupation of Mount Lebanon and the coastal strip were rather blissful for the Maronites, and ironically led to the emergence of a new social order, with Beirut at its epicenter.

Rebirth of Beirut

Alfred Nicola did not know his grandfather Habib Fares, son of Fares Bozeid Moujaes. He had passed away long before Alfred was born. He knew his great-uncle Youssef, though, in his early years, and knew that Youssef had married twice and, when he passed, left a grieving second wife with a daughter and two sons, as well as a child from his first marriage. That child eventually sailed for Brazil, while Youssef's second wife went to America with her two sons and lived in New Orleans, peddlers all three. Alfred knew their story well because he too had crossed the Atlantic, following in their footsteps, and shared many of their pains and joys.

From stories about his grandfather Habib Fares, Alfred knew about the joys and hardships of working in the silk industry in the environs of Beirut. Habib Fares did well for himself and at his death had considerable wealth for that time. Early in his life, Habib Fares had raised silk worms at home, as many families did in those days, and sold bundles of the cocoons to the collectors employed by silk factories who went door to door, town to town, gathering the thin threads that created so much wealth. In time, Habib Fares started supplying the factories himself, earning greater returns; later still, with the advent of international markets in Beirut, he collected silk across the entire Sahel region to sell to French and English merchants at the souks of Beirut.

The journey from Hadath to Beirut took two hours on horseback, longer with a cart, and Habib Fares undertook it twice a week to sell the wagonloads of bundles he had spent the other days collecting. When the silk season ended, Habib Fares made the same journey in reverse, buying cotton textiles from the English at the souks of Beirut and selling them in Hadath and the Sahel region. Eventually, he bartered many of his silk bundles for fabrics, some manufactured by textile factories in Lyon from possibly the same silk cocoons he had sold to French merchants earlier.

Once a simple fishing harbor town halfway between Saida and Tripoli, Beirut rose unexpectedly during the nineteenth century to a lofty position as a key port city. For two millennia it was rarely mentioned in writing, except by Roman historians who cited the posting of a Roman garrison in Beirut, a rough hostel city that had little to offer. Beirut remained very much the same under the successive occupations by Byzantine, Arab, and then Ottoman rulers. The mosque al-Omari in the heart of Beirut, in the old Beirut *intra muros*, is indicative of this history. Once a Byzantine church, built on the remains of a Roman temple, and supposedly a Phoenician temple before that, it was turned into a Catholic church by the Crusaders before it fell to the Ottomans, who adorned it with two minarets and named it after the Caliph Omar.

Despite this incredible span of history, for the traveler in the early days of the nineteenth century, Beirut was certainly an Arab city by all standards. The maze of inchoate passageways, where life in all its variety took place, was typical of the oriental bazaars in every city of the Levant. Souks covered the landscape, and people did not really separate what was public from what was private, what was professional from what was personal. The poor lived in single-room apartments above their shops, which they accessed from an exterior flight of steps, the wealthy in larger houses that opened onto the street via a short alley, often dark and unwelcoming, but leading to a captivating central garden around which the household functions occurred.

At work, the artisans called for hummus or for a shaffeh from the coffee-boy, an indigent child who worked for the *fawwal* or *kahwaji* present on every corner, and had their breakfast or lunch while sitting on the porches of their shops. Whether dressed in large pantaloons, the *charwal*, or for the less well off, a *deshdasheh*, the flowing outfit that reached the floor, and wearing the *tarboosh*, the traditional Moroccan fez that traveled across the fluid boundaries of the empire, all the inhabitants of Beirut had their occupations. There were more souks than one can imagine, all grouped by activities, each group forming a kind of corporation. The souks took the name of their activities: the *najjareen*, or carpenters; the *otur*, or perfumers; the *haddadeen*, or metalworkers; the *seegha*, or jewelers; and so on.

The southern part of the city housed the markets for local people's needs, such as the vegetable market next to Saint George, the Greek Orthodox church. The northern part of the city was home to the noisier markets; those that were repulsive, such as souk *dabbagha*, the tanneries; and also foreign traders, being close to the sea. In the center of the city, along the road that divided the two markets, city officials and moneychangers worked. The city center was also the site of a military casern, erected in the seventeenth century by Fakhreddine, where a corps of janissaries served the governor, a servant of the empire appointed by the wali of Saida.

Each souk had an unofficial representative, a well-respected person viewed as an elder, whether in age, experience, or social status, and who spoke for the group. In short, the artisans built a social order that integrated multiple aspects of everyday life, insuring their livelihoods in the absence of any real form of government.

Later years revealed that these local mechanisms of self-government, woven across centuries, would delay Lebanon's ability to forge a nationwide power structure.

Beirut in those days had seven gates in its high walls, the number seven symbolizing holy attributes in Islamic culture. The main gate faced the military casern and led into a mosque, also attributed to Fakhreddine, and it was called *bab saray*, or gate of the casern. All the city gates were open during the day but closed at night; the unfortunate traveler who arrived at the city after dark had to sleep outside the gates. Every year, the governor of the city bestowed the keys of the gates to seven different *a'yan*, prominent men in the city. Each man was responsible for maintaining a gate, keeping its passages lit at all times. This duty conferred honor to the appointee, and the long and heavy keys were eagerly sought by all the dignitaries of the city.

After 1800, Beirut began to grow in importance, and under Egyptian rule, which began in 1831, a series of unexpected events catapulted the city into the future. While other foreign diplomats were headquartered in Saida, the consul for Britain moved his residency to Beirut, although keeping his title "Consul of Britain at Saida and Acre." The French consul soon followed suit. They viewed Beirut not only as an industrious artisan city but also as a port, with a harbor that was secure, ideal for year-round coastal shipping.

A more noteworthy decision that changed Beirut forever was made by Ibrahim Pasha, the son of Muhammad Ali, who at this time ruled Syria. Anxious to avoid the contagious diseases that traveled aboard merchant ships, Ibrahim Pasha instituted quarantine in Beirut harbor, and all ships inbound to the Levant across the Mediterranean were now forced to anchor in Beirut harbor and undergo a sanitary inspection. Ships from Europe were signed in by one of the officials, who made a cursory inspection. For ships departing from any port across the Ottoman Empire, the checkup was stricter and often meant the detention of passengers and cargoes for long periods of time. Passengers were quarantined at the lazaretto, a complex of four buildings erected at the harbor. (Despite the best efforts of the French engineers who designed the quarantine, conditions of detention were such that many who were in good health contracted diseases at the lazaretto.)

The quarantine had a very healthy effect on the local economy however. Previously, a shipment destined for Damascus would sail into Saida, get offloaded, and then be carried in caravans across Mount Lebanon to the Syrian hinterland. Offloading in Beirut, the shipment took the Damascus road to the east and short-circuited Saida. Trade at Saida and Tripoli, as well as Acre, slackened, to the benefit of Beirut, which became a major hub. Soon the walls of the ancient city could no longer contain the bustling activity.

Other measures instituted by Ibrahim Pasha also empowered Beirut as the new economic engine of Mount Lebanon. Drawing on his father's achievements

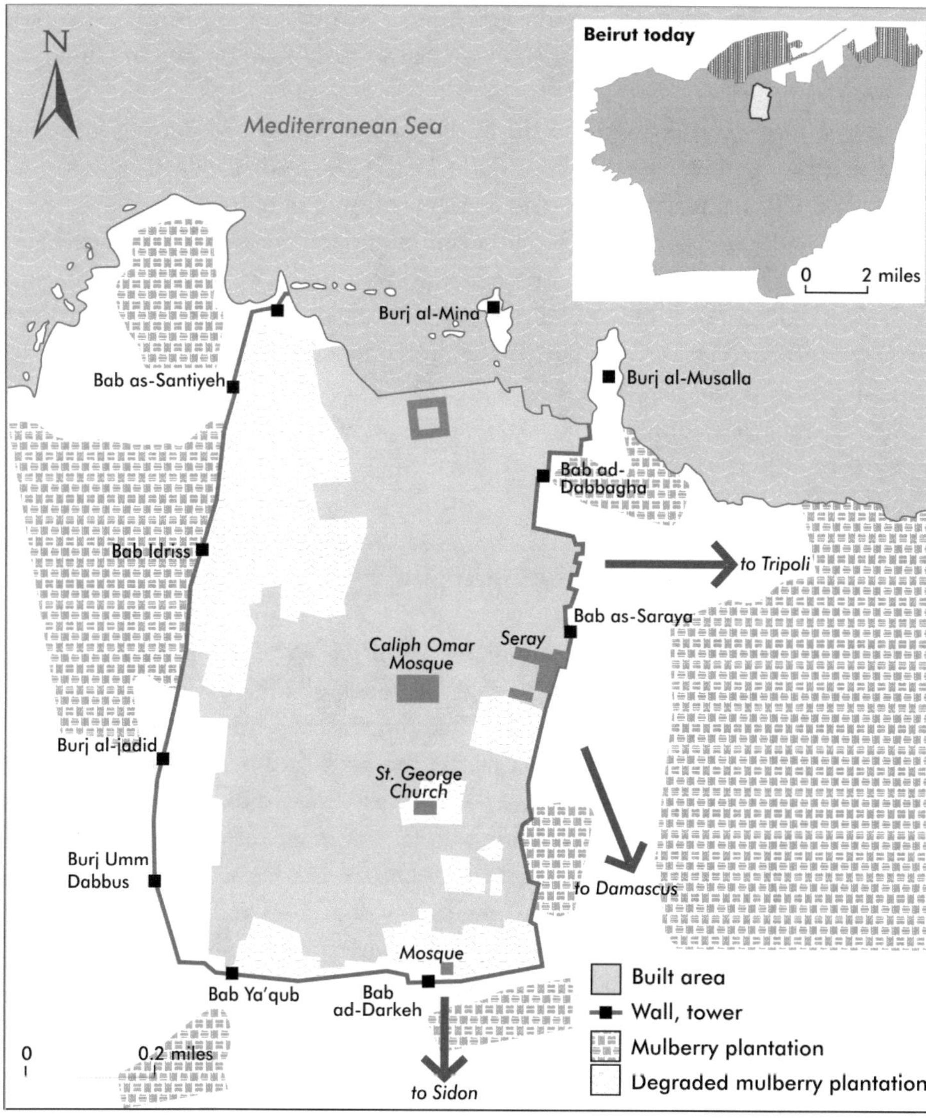

Map 3. Beirut *intra muros* in 1830 (based on the cartography works of Michael Davie)

in modernizing Egypt, Ibrahim Pasha organized the administration, developed the communications, encouraged foreign trade, and above all, masterminded the establishment of consultative councils for every large town and city. Each council had twelve members, half of whom were Christian, quite a novelty in a country where Christians were labeled *dhimmi* (subjected yet legally protected groups), and banned from holding office. Under the new rules, the Christian populations were treated as equals and were allowed, like the Jews, to dress like the Muslim populations, shedding the distinctive attire that they had been forced to wear by the Ottomans for three centuries.

These changes contributed to the birth of a merchant class, starting in Beirut and radiating to other cities between the port and the Syrian hinterland, such as Zahleh in the Bekaa plateau. The road to Damascus began outside the main gate of the city, near the cemeteries of the Sunni community on the east side, where Martyrs' Square lies today. The road for Saida and Acre, and, by extension, Jerusalem, was at the southern gate of the city, *bab dirqah*. Both roads ran along the outskirts of Hadath, the first on the east, the second on the north—an advantageous turn of events for a town that had been little more than a vegetable garden for the Shihab in their Baabda promontory. And Habib Fares Shwayri certainly understood the importance of that.

Toward civil war

Sitting in his Beiteddine palace, Amir Bashir had reason to rejoice in 1833. With his government as strong as ever, he was the ruler of Mount Lebanon and the principal ally of the Egyptian overlord, Ibrahim Pasha; furthermore, he had no rival across his entire dominion, now that the Jumblatts had been exiled to Hauran along with other muqataaji families. The amir relied more than ever for support on the Maronite Patriarch, now a strong counterpart in power politics with a large community that spread across all of Mount Lebanon. The opening of Beirut to international trade brought wealth to the amir's dominion and gave work to his people, the true ingredients for peace and prosperity in his mountains. The year 1833 was probably the best he had ever had. And yet, the worst of his nightmares was about to begin.

Having swept across Syria and defied the Ottoman army, Ibrahim Pasha had a standing army of seventy thousand soldiers positioned in the region, and with the threat of a counterattack always present, he was reluctant to disband it. The cost of keeping this army was a drain on the Egyptian treasury, and Muhammad Ali decided the locals must pay for it instead. From Alexandria, he ordered Ibrahim Pasha to impose taxes and use every means to collect them. To the traditional tax on income and the occasional poll tax, Ibrahim Pasha added imaginative new ones: marriage tax, childbirth tax, civil servant appointment tax, even holiday presents for senior officials were institutionalized. Any occasion seemed good enough to impose levies on the people. Not content with that, he hampered the thriving economy with so-called reforms that made him an intermediary in all economic transactions. For example, he bought the produce of the land and then sold it, setting the prices on both transactions to maximize profits. This double monopoly on major products such as silk, cotton, and tobacco caused an unprecedented burden, which, coupled with the imposed taxes, led to economic disarray among the people.

Although threatened by these developments, Amir Bashir could do nothing. Allies they might be, but Bashir didn't have the rank of a wali as far as Ibrahim Pasha was concerned. When the Pasha visited Beiteddine, Amir Bashir walked all the way down to the central court to greet his guest, the overlord who controlled his fate. Ibrahim didn't need to justify himself to Bashir and was unresponsive to the amir's appeals, leaving him to face his angry people alone. Those people were losing faith in Bashir. He already had broken up the Druze families and sent many away, and was not even able to defend the interests of those who had supported him faithfully all along.

To make matters worse, Ibrahim Pasha ordered conscription, wanting to draft local men into his army, a drastic step in his iron-fist policy toward Mount Lebanon. Also distressing was his decision to collect weapons from the people, peasants and muqataajis alike. For those who did not have a weapon, the order was to buy one and relinquish it to the authorities. Weakened by the battles they had already fought, the Druze suffered further when their sons were taken into the Egyptian army, though an arrangement had been made to keep them in a separate battalion. As for the Maronites, the Patriarch managed to keep his faithful flock from conscription, using his strong ties with the French to good advantage.

These were trying times for Ibrahim Pasha, too. The Sultan in Istanbul was gaining territory and drawing the Europeans closer to his realm. In the sultan's eyes, Ibrahim Pasha had undermined his prestige by the occupations of Anatolia and Syria, actions that also had dire consequences on the sultan's treasury. Not only did the Sublime Porte lose the important income from Mount Lebanon and Syria, the Ottoman sultan lost face in front of his large caucus at a time when the empire was waning. Sultan Mahmud II needed to rethink his policies, weave a new network of allies, and, above all, evict the Egyptian adventurer from his Syrian dominions.

However much he despised Muhammad Ali, the sultan appreciated his achievements: a modern army, a modern administration, and, most importantly, a modern economy attuned to the West. To stay in control, the sultan understood that he had to modernize his empire as well, and that meant opening it to those same nations that seemed intent on usurping his throne and partitioning his dominions. He already had indulged the Russian tsar with a secret convention that, in return for protection from the Egyptian ogre, gave Russia access to the warm waters of the Mediterranean along with a tight control on the Dardanelles strait. But that was not enough to restore his sovereignty.

So, with deep misgivings, the sultan signed trade agreements with the European nations, starting in 1838 with Britain and followed by agreements with the

French, the Austrians, and, again, the Russians. Under these *Capitulations*, as they came to be known, a word that reveals the Sultan's state of mind when signing them, the Ottomans agreed to lift trade restrictions, adopt fair tax regulations on imports, and undo their monopolies on practically all commodities. The modern reforms that Sultan Mahmud, and later his son, Sultan Abdul Majid, decided to implement, partly to match his Egyptian opponent, partly to satisfy the demands of his new allies, came a year later in 1839, in the form of the Edict of Gülhane, which signaled a new style that was to characterize the Ottoman Empire throughout the last chapter of its existence: *Tanzimat*. That was the name given to the reforms that started that year and that brought enormous change to the relationship between the Porte and its administrations and local populations across the empire. The reforms included the suppression of tax-farming contracts, the building of government institutions, equal treatment for all under the law, the imposition of security measures over individual property, and a review of trade relationships with an intent to develop Western-style market-driven economies. With the Capitulations and the Tanzimat, the European nations had cornered the sultan and could now manipulate him at ease, assuming they could overcome their own differences. Between the French and the British, relations were barely cordial, and the Russians, Austrians, and Prussians also nursed grievances among themselves. Each country had special interests, all too often divergent, and these conflicting interests affected the unfolding of events.

In Mount Lebanon, the policies adopted by Ibrahim Pasha to restrict the liberties of the locals drew antagonistic reactions from all communities. In an unprecedented gathering, representatives from all religious communities met in Antelias, on the coastal rim of Mount Lebanon, and pledged, with the patron saint of the village church as witness, to unite to terminate the occupation of Ibrahim Pasha. (The Antelias meeting was often referred to as the precursor to the Pact of National Unity that would come a century later and institute the basis for the modern-day Lebanese Republic.) Talk of rebellion was everywhere, across all of Mount Lebanon, and when it waned, as it did by the summer of 1840, the consuls of the European nations and their countless agents tried to keep it alive in the minds of the peasants, paying them money and giving out weapons wherever they went. Despite these efforts, the rebellion did die out before it began, but not before giving the European nations an excuse to intervene militarily.

A joint campaign to drive Ibrahim Pasha out of Syria and Mount Lebanon was instigated in 1841 in London and involved all the major European powers except France; due to their controversial relationship with Muhammad Ali, the French stayed out, leaving their Egyptian ally to fight the coalition by himself. On the Egyptian side, preparations for war moved ahead, and Suleiman Pasha, the French colonel from the army of Napoleon and now the commander of the Egyptian forces, went to Beirut to take up its defense. Soon, British warships entered the harbor and shelled the city mercilessly. But that was only to divert attention, for the British ships sailed farther north and landed troops in Jounieh.

Amir Bashir now faced a serious dilemma. British agents were distributing weapons to the Druze, inciting them to rebellion; the amir himself was invited to change sides, assured that he could keep his seat if he did. But the amir was cautious, still expecting the French to intervene on behalf of their ally Muhammad Ali, and also because his own sons and grandsons were fighting in the army of Ibrahim Pasha. Then, in a town called Bhersaf in the heart of Metn, the Egyptian and Ottoman armies, the latter supported by a British force, met for a decisive battle that ended with Ibrahim Pasha's very disorderly retreat.

When news of the Battle of Bhersaf reached Amir Bashir, he understood the consequences of his own inaction and left Beiteddine for Saida, where he surrendered to the Ottomans. This move, he hoped, would earn him asylum with the British and buy him enough time to work his way back into the good graces of the sultan. The British, however, did not offer the amir many options, and he was exiled in Malta.

The short reign of Ibrahim Pasha came to an end, and the absence of Amir Bashir created a void in governance. This the British had anticipated, and they were already prepared to fill it with their own candidate: while negotiating with Amir Bashir about his defection from the Egyptian camp, the British were secretly conspiring with another member of the Shihab family, preparing him to become the new amir. Leaving no details to chance, they took every care to get his signature on a document that described the exact limits of his role once he was brought to power. This candidate, another Bashir, nicknamed Bashir-the-Flour (or Abu-t'heen, which means "father-flour") for having traded this commodity at a time when famine struck Mount Lebanon, turned out to be as arrogant a leader as he was uncharismatic and pathetic. He had two virtues though, equally precious in the eyes of the Maronite Patriarch: he was a Shihab, and he belonged to the Maronite side of the family.

Taking office in 1841, Bashir-the-Flour decided to rule from Baabda, the winter town of the Shihab where Fares Bozeid Moujaes had worked half a century earlier, probably on the very same mansion that was now the seat of the new amir, and uptown from Hadath, where his son Habib Fares Shwayri was now earning his living as a merchant. The reign of Bashir-the-Flour was to be short lived; a mere sixteen months would pass before he would be overthrown. During that period, however, for as long as the amir lived in Baabda, the town took on the allure of a princely domain, with a large court revolving around it, a court with regal tastes in clothing—and clothing was what Habib Fares did best.

At this time, ready-to-wear dresses and suits did not exist; people had their clothes tailored, purchasing cloth from the souks in Beirut or, more commonly, from itinerant vendors who traveled with samples. Habib Fares was one of these vendors. A man of taste with an ingenious mind for business, he did not fear hard labor and long hours of work. Trading raw cotton and silk bundles for cloth at the souks, he built strong relationships with local and European merchants and suppliers. The rest was simple. He rented a small space next door to his house where he stored silk bundles and cotton as well as the diverse fabrics he gradually accumulated on his journeys to Beirut. He sold cloth to tailors, and tailors recommended him to their clients, and soon Habib Fares had a long list of customers who depended on him for their wardrobes. When he came of age, his brother Youssef worked with him, and in time each saw himself overwhelmed with responsibilities. Youssef collected silk and cotton while Habib Fares negotiated for fabrics in the souks; they both dealt with customers, and they both did it well, seeing their orders multiply. Of course, the times were not easy, and the British shelling of Beirut the previous year had hurt business, but it soon picked up, and always would do so afterward, through all the upheavals that Mount Lebanon was still to witness.

In that same year, 1841, Habib and Youssef saw the passing of their father, Fares Bozeid Moujaes, the sturdy stonemason from Shwayr who had made his home in Hadath. His funeral took place at Saint Elias in Hadath, the church where he had married, where his two sons had also married, and where all the ceremonies of the descendants of Fares Bozeid would take place for the two centuries to come.

With Amir Bashir in exile and the Egyptian army gone, the Druze populations, who had been displaced during the previous decade due to their loyalty to the Ottomans, came home to find a new social order in place. New tenants were working the land, many of them Maronites, who were now a large community across Mount Lebanon and would eventually outnumber the Druze themselves. The returning Druze were muqataajis and had tenured rights to the land and its produce, and they now saw themselves scorned by the same people whom they once had employed, the peasants and the serfs of the previous decades. Conflicts emerged, but the Druze found no sympathetic ear among the Ottoman administrators or with the new amir in Baabda. The fate of the muqataaji system was sealed in the Tanzimat of Sultan Abdul Majid, son and successor of Mahmud, and there was no possible return to the old ways. Even without legislation, tax farming had fallen into oblivion once the new class of merchants had emerged, Beirut acting as a catalyst. A market economy supplanted the old semi-feudal and semi-tribal social organization, benefiting a thriving community of enterprising individuals who were attracted to the capitalism that held sway on the decks of British and French vessels. The Druze, who had suffered the harsh reprisals of Amir Bashir while in exile, spoke a language that sounded anachronistic to the new generation, a situation that widened the gap between the religious communities of Mount Lebanon.

Another blow to social cohesion in Mount Lebanon came with a pamphlet that the Maronite Patriarch took the initiative to print and distribute in 1841. To formalize the position of his Church, the Patriarch stated that "no other ruler over Mount Lebanon will be accepted but a Maronite from the Shihab family"; he went on to claim, "the Maronites, wherever they are to be found, are under the protection of France as they have been in the past." The Druze saw the declarations of the Patriarch as sheer provocation; they could not possibly accept the return of the exiled amir to rule over them or, for that matter, any other member of the Shihab family.

A third gap in trust came with the creation of a consultative council, called a *diwan*, which Bashir-the-Flour attempted to form at the suggestion of the provincial Ottoman wali of Saida. It intended to bring together individuals from different communities to resolve the conflicts that arose among the different religious groups. The Druze families saw this as an attempt to circumvent their positions as muqataajis by entrusting to a council, over which they had no control, decisions that mattered to their community alone. This gap was too wide to close, and the rattling of sabers began.

The clash came when the amir left Baabda to take up residence in Deir al-Qamar, the old power center of Fakhreddine but now overwhelmingly Maronite, to finalize the establishment of the diwan. Seizing this opportunity, the Druze muqataajis and their peasants encircled Deir al-Qamar and threatened the life of the amir. The Maronite inhabitants of Deir al-Qamar came to the amir's rescue, and the battle began. On hearing the news, the Patriarch sent envoys, many of them clergymen, from village to village, inciting the Maronites to war and even threatening them with a fall from grace if they did not take up arms. The Druze had decided to rid themselves of the Shihab once and for all, but the Maronites, enflamed by events, were determined not to let this happen. All over Mount Lebanon, militias formed, mostly Maronite peasants summoned by their clergy. In major towns, camps were organized, the largest in Baabda, home of the Shihab family, where twelve thousand would-be soldiers gathered.

As the drumbeats of war grew louder, there can be no doubt that Habib Fares and his brother Youssef were made anxious by the troops massing all around. One reason to be afraid was that their coreligionists, the Greek Orthodox, had not sided with the Maronites. Instead, many Greek Orthodox were allied to the Druze, a fact that might lead to reprisals against innocent citizens like themselves if the enflamed Maronites went on a rampage.

From the beginning, however, the Maronite efforts were badly managed, suffering from a lack of leadership and unity. Each camp had its own reasons for fighting and each ended up picking on isolated and unengaged villages. This caused the deaths of fifteen hundred people and the destruction of forty-five hundred homes, but the bloodbath that had threatened to engulf all of Mount Lebanon never occurred.

After more than three weeks of intentional nonaction, the Ottomans finally acted, and the wali of Saida sent a delegation to escort the amir out of Deir al-Qamar to safety. It is said that the amir was nevertheless brutalized by Druze partisans who attacked him as he started his descent from the Shouf. The story doesn't say if this happened with or without the consent of the escorting officials, but it does confirm the intentions of the Sublime Porte to take matters in hand and appoint an Ottoman governor to rule Mount Lebanon.

The time was ripe to impose Omar Pasha, nicknamed "the Austrian" because of his origins, on the governance of Mount Lebanon, a one-year interlude that served only to further escalate sectarian strife and polarize the sociopolitical order. More than ever, the Druze and Maronite populations were in discord, unable to outgrow their historical feuds to engage in the construction of a modern nation. Omar Pasha first tried the diplomatic route; when that proved unsuccessful, he flexed his muscles and imprisoned the influential heads of the major families, also to no avail. He was simply unacceptable to both parties. Unable to agree on anything else, the Druze and Maronites did see eye to eye on this and engineered his departure. In fact, they resorted to their respective protectors among the European quintet to broker this arrangement with the Porte.

In return for the withdrawal of Omar Pasha and the abolition of the direct governance of Mount Lebanon from Istanbul, the French, speaking for the Maronites, agreed to drop their demand for a Shihab ruler. Instead, a new system of government was devised, one that seemed to please both sides: Mount Lebanon would be divided into two districts, one Maronite in the north, the other Druze in the south, administered by two *caimaqams*, or governors, of the respective communities and appointed by the wali of Saida to "stand in his stead." In this way, the seeds for permanent discord were planted and Mount Lebanon was headed for more bloodshed.

The failure of the caimaqamat system

"Easier said than done" describes the partition of Mount Lebanon. The plan, suggested originally by Klemens von Metternich, the diplomatic Machiavelli of the time and the minister of foreign affairs of the Austro-Hungarian Empire (and one of the key architects of the stabilizing Concert of Europe), was as difficult to implement as it was damaging in effect. The interreligious conflict that caused the Druze and Maronite populations to cross swords developed into an intra-community conflict, with family rivalries in each camp, especially among the Maronites. As usual, the conflicts were exacerbated by the ever-present consuls of the European nations, who found ready followers among the gullible, the power hungry, and those eager to regain their former privileges. Names of candidates for governors of both districts were circulated by the consuls; Said, the son of Sheikh Bashir Jumblatt, was backed by the British for the Druze region, and a member of the Abillamah family, the second largest princely family after the Shihabs, was touted by the French as the amir for the Maronite district.

As if the choice of candidates for the *caimaqams* was not enough source of conflict, a long list of unresolved issues promised even more unrest. The exact boundaries of the partition were one stumbling block, especially since the Ottomans hoped to carve out a large chunk of the northern district, namely Jbeil, Batroun, and Bcharreh, the hills that formed Mount Lebanon proper in the early days, and join it to the *wilayat* of Tripoli. This area would be governed by the Ottoman wali of Tripoli, depriving the Maronites of a considerable source of wealth.

For its part, and no doubt pressed by the Russians, the Greek Orthodox community was not ready to submit to a Maronite governor and pleaded for its own district, essentially a third caimaqamat. To boost the chances of their coreligionists, the Russians even proposed the complete incorporation of Mount Lebanon into the Ottoman Empire, a diplomatic feint with no chance of success, but one that might improve the chances of the earlier Greek Orthodox proposal. Other problems also arose, the most difficult being the question of the countless villages with mixed populations of Maronites and Druze. In which district did they belong?

Villages with mixed populations were most common in the south, especially in the Metn and Shouf mountains, where Maronites, encouraged by Fakhreddine and his successors in previous centuries, had been given property to settle. Encouraged by their church leaders, the Maronites of the southern district now refused to submit to a Druze caimaqam, insisting they answer instead to the caimaqam of the northern district, irrespective of geography. In support of their position, the Maronites cited the Patriarch's pamphlet of 1841, which clearly stated, "The Maronites, wherever they were to be found, were under the protection of the French." For those who still ventured to make the new order work, diplomacy proved impossible.

In the end, the wali of Saida spoke and named two caimaqams for the districts: from the Jurd region, a member of the Arslan family as caimaqam for the Druze district; and from the Metn region, a member of the Abillamah family as caimaqam for the Maronite district. The Arslan caimaqam was not the candidate backed by the British consul, but the Abillamah caimaqam was quite to the liking of the French. In the Maronite district, however, a number of families were infuriated by the appointment of a member of the Abillamah family to govern them, and they immediately began plotting against him. The Khazen of Kesrwan, long acknowledged as vice consul for France in Beirut, threatened to bring the matter up before the Pope, were the new Abillamah caimaqam not forced to share power. The Druze, much diminished by the events of the previous years, chose to form their own council of families to second the Arslan caimaqam.

The thorny issue of what to do about the Maronite populations living in the southern district remained. In this debate, the French consul played a leading role. Emboldened by his recent success at persuading the Ottoman wali to drop his ambitions over the territories of the Maronites in the north, the consul now asked for nothing less than the restoration of the Shihab family. This was nothing but a diplomatic ploy, meant to stall the Ottoman administration and provoke the Druze population. The ruse, a classic example of "ask for the moon and settle for less," worked; the consul went on to earn the Maronites in the southern district independence from the Druze. At the same time, the Patriarch fomented agitation among his followers, adding to the tension.

There are conflicting accounts of the events that culminated in the second civil confrontation of 1845. Some cast blame on the Druze, some on the Maronites, depending on their own religious and political convictions, depending on whether they were Druze, Sunni, Maronite, or British or French travelers of the era. A researcher on the history of Beirut, May Davie, has said that "history is written with ideologies," and this is certainly true of the 1845 conflict. Contrast English colonel Charles Churchill's account of the civil war of 1845 with that of the French general Auguste-Alexandre Ducrot, and you will find any number of incompatibilities. Both men were present in Mount Lebanon at the same time, during the days when the preparations for war were at their height, yet their accounts diverge radically on whom to hold responsible for the fighting. Each was defending his caucus, Churchill the Druze and Ducrot the Maronites, interpreting history according to the whims of their foreign offices.

The truth is that both communities bear an equal measure of responsibility. The Druze muqataajis had been sidelined for too long, having dispersed across the Anti-Lebanon, a mountain range in the eastern part of the region, in the previous decade and returning to find a new order in which the Maronites had taken their place. The Maronites, for their part, were still hoping for the reunification of all Mount Lebanon under a Maronite amir, one from the Shihab family, and they were as tenacious as ever about restoring the exiled Amir Bashir. For the Patriarch, war was the ultimate solution now that diplomacy had failed to bring Bashir back. Even Amir Bashir, exiled in Malta, was involved, conniving with the Patriarch through back channels of communication until the Ottomans learned of it and transferred him to Istanbul.

War was clearly imminent, and all communities quickly took sides. The Greek Orthodox sided with the Druze, the Shi'a with the Maronites, if only to oppose their age-old rivals, the Sunni, who stood with the Druze and who followed the marching orders of the Ottoman administration. Once the fighting began, neither side could gain the upper hand. Although outnumbered, the valiant Druze fighters compensated with superior fighting skills. In the villages, losses were appalling, with majorities inflicting carnage on minority communities.

After a month of bloodshed, no victor had emerged, and the time was ripe for diplomatic solutions. After some initial peace talks, which took place between the two sides on the instigation of the wali of Saida, the minister of foreign affairs of the Sublime Porte, Shakib Effendi, came to Beirut to take matters into his own hands. By delegating Shakib Effendi, no ordinary diplomat, the sultan intended to find a permanent solution to the ongoing problems of Mount Lebanon. A plenipotentiary in Greece during the separatist crisis, Shakib Effendi had negotiated the London treaty in 1840 and was a rigorous statesman with a powerful base in Istanbul. He had the authority to implement radical change and do it on the spur of the moment.

Upon arrival in Beirut, Shakib Effendi seized weapons across Mount Lebanon, starting in the most mutinous villages, such as Deir al-Qamar and Zahleh. Next, he imprisoned a number of muqataaji dignitaries suspected of fomenting rebellion, isolated the two caimaqams, and ordered the European consuls to recall their agents from the mountains and confine them to Beirut. Shakib Effendi didn't shy away from the seemingly intractable problems inherent to the caimaqamat order. He delineated the border between the two districts, adopting the Damascus road as the natural frontier. He also constituted councils for both districts to second the governors, each composed of a *wakeel*, or executive overseer, and consultative adjudicators from all religious groups. These adjudicators handled the matters of their own coreligionists, and when a dispute arose between the Druze and Maronite communities, the case was put to the respective judges together. Deir al-Qamar, the largest town with a mixed population, was made subject to the wali of Saida directly, who appointed a director to it, the *mutasallem*, aided by a council of local dignitaries.

These "arrangements" of Shakib Effendi, as they came to be known, initiated a form of government that embraced sectarian representation, an underlying feature that became a constitutional principle still very much alive in Lebanon. As it turned out, the power of the councils was limited, as no single decision could be made without the approval of all the members, a case of *liberum veto*. As for Deir al-Qamar, subjecting it to the governance of the wali of Saida satisfied the Maronites in that it kept the town away from the authority of the Druze. In general, the arrangements were well received and Mount Lebanon was poised to enjoy a period of tranquility that would last some fifteen years, despite the omnipresent tensions that persisted from all sides until the collapse of 1860.

During these years, Habib Fares was enjoying marriage and fatherhood, having taken a wife in 1840, a girl from the Moujaes family in Shwayr, before the first civil war had started. In all, Habib fathered five children, of whom Nicolas was the first, born in 1841. Nicolas became his father's workmate, a position he enjoyed for twenty years before his father passed away in 1868; then he kept working with his uncle, Youssef, until the latter passed away in 1890.Youssef had lost his first wife early, and he had remarried, also to a Moujaes girl, a woman we shall encounter in Louisiana while trailing Alfred Nicola in the second part of this book.

Once the Edict of Gülhane in 1839 ushered in the Tanzimat reforms, the reorganizations imposed by the sultan, changes occurred rapidly in Mount Lebanon. The new legislation opened the Ottoman Empire to European merchants, and Beirut's prime location on commercial routes made it the region's capital city for trade. In the same year that the edict was signed, the French Portalis brothers came to Beirut and started a silk factory in the Jurd region, bringing modern spinning techniques to Mount Lebanon. The demand for Syrian silk had boomed once the Tanzimat reduced custom duties and made the crossing between Beirut and Marseille more secure. Steamers now made this voyage in one-quarter of the time required by older sailing ships, and fierce competition between steamship companies resulted in reduced shipping fees, all factors that promoted Beirut as the gateway for commerce in Mount Lebanon and Syria at large.

And in this economic boom, the Christian populations of Beirut and Mount Lebanon enjoyed the upper hand. One reason was that the Druze viewed European businesses with a jaundiced eye, assuming they were undermining the strength of the muqataaji order and extracting wealth that rightly belonged to the Druze. Similar views were held by the Sunni community, which had always been privileged by the Ottomans and now felt destabilized by the European capitalists. As it turned out, the European factories did tend to employ Christian women and buy goods and services from local businesspeople who were Christian, such as Habib Fares and his brother Youssef. Nevertheless, the inherited social order of the Christian sector also rested on the muqataaji system, and Christian officials and dignitaries did not necessarily want to lose this, however interested and implicated they were in the new capitalist alternative. Many felt they could have their own system, a hybrid between the old and the new, keeping the privileges that allowed them to dominate helpless peasants while enjoying the benefits of booming business.

Not surprisingly a power struggle emerged. As the peasants of a previous time turned increasingly into a business-minded class, they simply would not submit to the old feudal families, who still clung to their muqataaji ranks and benefits. To poison the atmosphere further, a new Maronite Patriarch was elected in 1854, who came from the peasant class and had accounts to settle with former overlords. That same year, the Crimean War began, causing the French and British to side with the Ottomans against the tsar of Russia. Caused by a dispute over the Holy Shrines in Jerusalem, the conflict festered into an open war that gave Napoleon III a chance to reintegrate the club of nations after France's deliberate isolation from the league that had dominated the events of 1840.

The war in Crimea lasted two years, during which time the local politics of Mount Lebanon and the activities of the European consuls were largely put on hold. Nevertheless, it was a war that would change the course of local events and impose even more reforms on the "Sultan of the Muslims," whose title was reduced to "Sultan of the Ottomans." This name change was only one of many reforms, called the *Hatti Hamayun*, issued by the sultan in 1856 as a result of the Crimean War. The edict covered many topics, both social and economic, including the continued emancipation of non-Muslim subjects begun in 1839 and the rights of private banks to settle and do business in the sultan's domains.

None of these reforms was to the liking of Muslim subjects in large cities, such as Beirut and Damascus, who saw them both as demeaning and, for the more pious among them, immoral: European-style banking was contrary to the *sharia*, and no Muslim could undertake to earn interest from moneylending. In response, the Muslim community in Beirut turned its back on the reforms and the economic opportunities they offered, allowing the Christians to make the most of them. Not that all the reforms were to the tastes of all Christians, either, who suspected the emancipation acts might open the door to their conscription into the Ottoman army. What is more, both Muslims and Christians saw the Hatti Hamayun as an act of surrender, one that signaled the weakness, the hollowing out, of the Ottoman Empire, now definitely the "sick man of Europe." That the sultan had to ask the Europeans for cash advances to finance his military operations in 1854, a first in the empire's four-hundred-year history, was a clear symptom of this distress.

In the politics of Mount Lebanon, the 1850s saw a revival of internecine conflicts among the Druze families along the lines of the old Jumblatti-Yazbaki divide. These family feuds were fueled by the European consuls, the French and the British taking opposite sides with the belligerents, to the amusement of the Ottoman administration, who seemed to view a war of attrition in the Druze community as a good thing. (A return to direct rule by an Ottoman was the ultimate objective of the wali, and internal conflicts within the community might help bring about this end.) At one point, relations between the Druze and the Ottomans grew chilly, stemming from Druze annoyance and disappointment at what they viewed as an Ottoman policy to keep them secluded in Mount Lebanon. It didn't take long, however, for the uqqal, the elite group of sages that governs the Druze community, to patch up relations, and as a sign of allegiance, a brigade of Druze soldiers was even sent to fight the Crimean War alongside the Ottomans.

On the Christian side, the situation was more dramatic. Their aging caimaqam passed away in 1854, a crucial time in the history of the region. Conflict arose within the governing family, the Abillamah, who had more than one contender for the succession. Other Maronite families, particularly the Khazen and Hobeiche, questioned the very appointment of an Abillamah for the position of caimaqam. The resulting struggle for power was overwhelming and multifaceted: the muqataaji families against the new caimaqam, who was to be another Abillamah; the Maronite Patriarch against the muqataaji families; muqataaji families against muqataaji families; foreign diplomats with the Church against notable muqataaji families; other diplomats with some muqataaji families against the Church; the people, peasants in the main, against their overlords and the muqataaji establishment altogether. Safe to say, nobody in the Maronite district was on very good terms with anybody else, and if the Europeans and the Ottomans hadn't been too busy in Crimea to stir up strife in Mount Lebanon as they usually did, an all-out war would have erupted even sooner than it did.

The new Maronite Patriarch, Paul Massad, was a commoner and spoke the language of the peasants. He also understood the power his Church exercised over a community that spread across Mount Lebanon, and he decided to use it to undo the rule of the muqataajis and assume control himself. Some say the Patriarch hoped to establish a Maronite emara, an independent entity that would reunite the Maronites under a theocratic government that he would lead. Whatever his thoughts and whatever support he got from the French diplomats always present in his entourage, it remains that Massad sustained the peasants in their dissenting views and was a strong partisan when their revolt came.

Regarding the revolt, the Ottoman position was as duplicitous as ever, the wali of Saida claiming to side with the peasants when they went to solicit his aid but also promising the overlords to crush the revolt when the muqataajis sought his support. In the midst of these typical Mount Lebanon double standards and intricate deceits, the Hatti Hamayun had a clarifying impact. By advocating the equality of men before the law, the sultan had given the masses cover for what they in fact had already achieved. The relationship between the muqataajis and their workers was deteriorating at a fast pace. Greed was a common characteristic of the overlords, many of whom were corrupt, and the taxes they imposed on the peasants had become excessive. In response, the peasants held mass meetings, the one in Ajaltoun in the Kesrwan Mountains in 1858 being first and probably the most notable. It happened under the nose of the Khazen, who were accused by the peasants of bigotry and oppressive behavior. The movement turned into an open revolt, and soon the peasants threw the Khazen out, intimidating some and taking the lives of others, then occupying their domains.

Similar meetings popped up everywhere, and soon every town had its own coordinator, whom peasants called Sheikh Shabab ("Youth"), a play on the muqataaji title of sheikh, a title exclusively bestowed by the Porte but now used derisively by the commoners to refer to the "young" militants. The meetings resulted in the self-appointment of *wakeels*, or peoples' representatives, and the forty-two wakeels had an outstanding figure to lead them, a peasant named Tanios Shaheen. As this peasant movement grew stronger and more organized, the Patriarch became convinced that the time had come for a new era in the history of Mount Lebanon, one that would institute Christian leadership over a system of governance that integrated the emerging forces of human and economic capital.

1860, the year of transformations

The Maronite Church had long understood the importance of maintaining a close rapport with the papal authority, starting its own college in Rome as early as the sixteenth century. The Roman Church, for its part, was eager for the Eastern Church, with its monothelitist origins, to align itself more closely with Roman Catholic doctrine; this plan of action suited the Maronite patriarchs, who had everything to gain from an association with the Pope. By the nineteenth century, the Maronite clergy included highly educated members who had studied in Rome and were well-versed in Roman Catholic practices, both sacred and political. Patriarch Paul Massad was one of them. Educated at the Maronite college in Rome, he was nonetheless a man of the people and understood very well the frustrations of the peasants.

By the time of the peasant revolt in 1859, the Maronite Church had become a very powerful player in the Mount Lebanon economy. Over the three previous centuries, muqataaji families had endowed the Church with large tracts of land, and the monks had nurtured them well. If the families had given land freely at first, it was to enhance their own domains, for the Maronite monks were skilled agriculturists, planting trees, cultivating grains, and excelling in terrace agriculture. Under the monks, harvests were abundant, and the muqataaji families by custom earned a share of this wealth, an underlying reason for their original "philanthropy." The Church's wealth and the shares it paid were regulated by a statute of mortmain (perpetual ownership), prescribed by Ottoman law, that covered the possessions of all religious groups, the *waqf*. In fact, before modern banking, it was not uncommon for muqataaji families to turn over their personal funds to the waqf for safekeeping, providing the Church with a great deal of capital to enhance its domains.

By the middle of the nineteenth century, the wealth and power of the Maronite Church surpassed that of the muqataaji families. The Church bought more and more property, becoming in time the largest landowner in Mount Lebanon. It also became the largest employer, far surpassing the muqataaji themselves at their traditional activity—intensive agriculture. As an employer, the Church offered more to its working peasants. It educated their children, building schools wherever there was a Maronite community, which, by the nineteenth century meant the northern and the southern districts of Mount Lebanon equally. By the time the Hatti Hamayun was decreed in 1856, the Church was strong, wealthy, and active across the whole country, and its members were well educated.

By contrast, the old muqataaji families steadily lost influence. In constant discord, they splintered into countless factions, their estates divided endlessly, generation after generation. Many spent so much money trying to buy positions of social and political control by entertaining Ottoman walis (who played them for fools) that they wound up penniless. Simply put, the muqataaji families were clinging to an obsolete system, refusing to face the new social order that was on the rise and seemingly as unstoppable as a force of nature.

The excessive taxation of the muqataaji and the imposition of frivolous nuisance taxes, such as the wedding-gift levy, prompted Maronite peasants in the northern district to call for revolution. The peasants were doubtlessly inspired by the teachings of missionaries from Europe and America, who had been at work for some time among them, establishing schools and missions. The Roman Catholic missionaries emphasized the rhetorical and dialectical thinking of the age of enlightenment in revolutionary Europe; Protestant pastors delivered the lessons of a reformed and transcendent humanity. Perhaps the most important teachings to take root among the Maronites were those of the Jesuits. Their mission in Mount Lebanon, founded in the seventeenth century, was interrupted by Pope Clement IV's suppression of the order in 1773, but they were back in strength after being reinstated some forty years later.

The religious debates that had shaken Europe for two centuries were echoed in Mount Lebanon and Beirut once the city was opened to outside religions as a result of the Tanzimat. Both Protestants and Catholics proselytized widely, and the Jesuits drove the Greek Catholics to cut their ties with Greek Orthodoxy, helping them escape from Damascus and Aleppo when the tensions there were high and settle in the Bekaa, Beirut, and Mount Lebanon.

During the period when the Jesuits were suppressed, another congregation took charge in its stead, the Congregation of the Mission, also called the Lazarists. Generations of Lebanese studied at the Lazarist school of Aintoura, an institution that has played an important role in the modern history of the country. The Lazarists were imbued with the humanistic values that accompanied the Counter-Reformation and were not indifferent to the cause of the peasants. They supported Tanios Shaheen and opened the doors of their convent in Reifoon for the wakeel to hold revolutionary meetings.

The revolution, as long as it was contained in the Maronite district in the north, was seen as a conflict between the classes, feudalism versus egalitarian principles. The peasants, led by a powerful Maronite Church, had earned the support of European Catholic missions and also a number of European diplomats, who supplied weapons and money. Enjoying legal cover from the sultan's own decree of Hatti Hamayun, the rebels used arms to rid themselves of the oppressive, obsolete, and corrupt muqataaji system and its feudal families. When the revolt entered the southern district, the district under the governance of a Druze caimaqam and where mixed populations lived, the story was totally different.

In the mixed town of Beit Mery in the Metn region, a small conflict among neighbors escalated into widespread religious strife that would prove disastrous for all of Mount Lebanon and, by extension, Damascus. Early attempts to quell the conflict failed, and soon total violence erupted in practically every region, even regions where different religious communities had lived side by side for three hundred years. In some places, the Ottoman garrisons played a passive role, not intervening; in others, such as Rashaya and Hasbaya in Wadi Taym, the stronghold of the Shihab family, the garrisons gathered the Christian populations in the *saray*, the government buildings, where they were slaughtered by Druze fighters.

Among the dead were a number of Shihab amirs. In a way, they had paid with their blood for the practices of their forbears, for Amir Bashir at the height of his power had exiled the Druze and cast out their overlords. The Shihab family was held responsible for the resulting downfall of the Druze community, and it was time for revenge. The Ottoman garrisons were sympathetic to the Druze, led by governors who did not view the sultan's reforms favorably, regarding the Hatti Hamayun as a stark departure from Muslim orthodoxy. So not only did the garrisons turn a blind eye to the atrocities, some actually took part in the killing.

Patriarch Paul Massad expected a favorable turn of events for his flock in the southern district, believing the rebellion would move as swiftly there as it had in Kesrwan. After all, the Maronites had the strength of numbers and, although weakened by struggles over leadership, their militias were seen as superior, able to deal the Druze a decisive blow. After what had happened to the Khazen family in Kesrwan, however, the Patriarch developed deep misgivings about Tanios Shaheen, who now spoke of a "popular republic" and was organizing the public affairs of the villages that fell under his sway. The Patriarch now favored Youssef Karam to lead the rebellion, a more disciplined figure than Shaheen, and one whose hands were not bloodied by the demise of the muqataaji. At best, Tanios Shaheen was a local rebel, Massad thought, but Youssef Karam was a natural leader of men, one to win the favors of the Ottomans and allow the Church to play the supreme role he had in mind. In this plan, the Patriarch hoped to restore the Khazen and keep the muqataaji system, but in his own fashion and under the authority of the Church.

When news of the massacres of Christians in Wadi Taym arrived, Tanios Shaheen was stationed in Antelias, on the coastline of Metn, at the head of an army from Kesrwan. Youssef Karam was a day's march away from Zahleh, at the head of a large army of fighters from his far northern mountain retreat of Ehden. Zahleh, at that time, was a wealthy town, a commercial epicenter for Syrian trade, a short distance from Damascus and on the road leading to the coastal city of Beirut. It was densely populated by Christians who had fled half a century earlier from the reprisals and repression of the Wahhabis and other followers of Arabian fundamentalism. After contact with Roman Catholic missionaries, they acknowledged the authority of the Pope and broke ranks with the Orthodox Church, forming a separate church that came to be known as the Greek Catholic Church (as opposed to Greek Orthodox).

Tensions had been building in Zahleh, and in other large towns, where Christians did not ignore or downplay the new privileges granted them by the Hatti Hamayun; instead, to show off their wealth, they often paraded through the streets in rich attire, denied them until quite recently. Such displays provoked the Ottomans, running counter to their own religious observances. The Druze were also provoked, viewing the Christians as the serfs of yesterday, who, by political conniving, had come to dominate Druze fiefdoms.

For the Druze, therefore, the time had come for revenge, and Zahleh was suddenly overwhelmed by Druze fighters, who quickly dispatched the badly managed and ill-prepared militias that stood in its defense. Despite calls for help and incessant orders from Church officials to head to Zahleh and relieve the city, Youssef Karam would not move from his position. (He was probably keen to please the Ottoman wali in Saida, who had the authority to appoint him as the future caimaqam of the northern district.) At this same time, the Maronites were also committing deadly offenses, their militias devastating the Druze villages of Qornayel, Salima, Ain-Dara, and Btekhnay in a deadly game of tit for tat that saw much innocent blood spilled.

The Druze fighters, reinforced by their coreligionists from Hauran, were still outnumbered by the Maronites, but they nevertheless had mastery of the field. Having dealt a serious blow to the Shihab on their turf in Wadi Taym, a large dispatch of Druze was sent to root out what was left of them in their strongholds of Baabda and Hadath, the hometown of the Shwayri and where Habib Fares and his brother Youssef lived. News of the turmoil came to them after violence erupted in Beit Mery, a town they traveled through on their trips to Shwayr. For a while, Habib and Youssef kept their families in Hadath, hoping the Ottoman army would control the situation, believing the European nations would not let the madness degenerate further. When clashes erupted in Damur and the Jurd, however, the families packed up what they could carry, sealed their houses, hid their stocks of silk bundles and fabrics, and left for Shwayr. Days after they left, the Druze fighters clashed with ineffective Christian militias, and Baabda, Hadath, and many villages nearby were soon in flames.

Tanios Shaheen came to the rescue but was turned away by the Ottoman governor, who reassured the wakeel that he would control the region. That control never came, however, and the results were deplorable. Amir Bashir's successor and namesake, Bashir III, the gloomy Bashir-the-Flour, was beheaded in Baabda, in a residence known well by Habib and Youssef and their father before them. After Zahleh, the next largest town with a mixed community was Deir al-Qamar, the seat of Fakhreddine in the seventeenth century. A prosperous town at the time of the 1860 carnage, the scenario there was much the same as in Hasbaya and Rashaya. Men, women, and children took refuge in the saray and were slaughtered. Some Druze notables were dismayed by their deaths, including Sheikh Said Jumblatt, who did not refuse asylum to the Maronites who sought his protection.

The Sultan in Istanbul shed tears, it is said, when he learned of the massacres. The man who wanted history to remember him as the reformer who introduced the Hatti Hamayun and freed the minorities, extending to Christians and Jews the rights of Ottoman subjects, was stained with the blood of the innocent. Deeply affected though he may have been, his sense of *realpolitik* remained intact, and he took quick steps to show the European consuls in Istanbul that he was still in command. From among his lieutenants, he chose a strong character, Fuad Pasha, to deal with the crisis. Multitalented and very competent, Fuad sailed to Crete en route to Mount Lebanon with orders to stop the war, reprimand the perpetrators, and find a workable system of governance. Fuad Pasha was still in Crete when more dark news, perhaps the darkest of all, arrived.

The violence had spread to Damascus. The Christian area of the city, built around the eastern gate of St. Thomas, or *Bab Tuma*, had been invaded by Muslim fighters, many motivated by the prospect of seizing the belongings of wealthy Christians. The cold-blooded killing dragged on for a week under the nose of an Ottoman governor who did nothing to stop the massacre of five thousand innocent people. The consulates were sacked and burned, except the British and the Prussian, and some consuls had been brutalized. The efforts of Muslim notables to stop the bloodshed did little to end the agony, and only a very few found asylum. Of these, Abdel-Kader was particularly stoic, the Algerian amir who had been incarcerated by the French for standing in the way of their colonial designs on his country and later exiled to Damascus.

The massacres of Damascus took the conflict to a new level. The violence in Lebanon could be viewed as a civil war, the warring parties dealing one another serious damage. The event in Damascus was nothing but gratuitous murder, and the Muslim community would be held accountable. Fuad Pasha landed in Beirut and assumed command, staying only for a short while before leaving for Damascus, where the situation called for his immediate presence. There, he found cadavers still lying on the ground, left to rot at the site of Bab Tuma, where the massacres had taken place.

Fuad ordered the burial of the dead and orchestrated the disarmament of the population. He also took steps to lodge the homeless in requisitioned homes and return whatever stolen belongings could be found to owners who were still alive. After a full investigation of the massacre, with eyewitness testimony, the culprits were tried and sentenced.

In the end, one hundred and fifty perpetrators were sentenced to death and executed; another two hundred were found guilty of contumacy. Among those sentenced to death was the governor of Damascus himself, found guilty and hanged. In this, Fuad Pasha had the upper hand, for he was empowered by the sultan with supreme command, able to do whatever he deemed necessary (while conferring with the ever-present consuls of the five interested nations). The list of names of the accused was often lengthened or shortened to accommodate the whims of the consuls, now that the massacres of Damascus had opened the door for them to interfere.

The massacres also gave Napoleon III a strategy to redeem himself in the eyes of the Roman Catholic Church. He had fallen from grace by giving his undivided support to the nationalistic movement in Italy, thus undermining the authority of the Pope (while, however, expanding France's dominions over Savoy and Nice in the process). By supporting the Maronites, subjects of the Catholic Church, he hoped to find favor with church officials in France, and he prepared to mount a military action. To do so, however, he needed the approval of the other European nations, and a summit was called in Paris, bringing together the representatives of Britain, Russia, Austria, Prussia, and France.

Landing troops in Beirut was important for Napoleon III for reasons other than the religious altruism by which he claimed to be motivated. Ferdinand de Lesseps was building the Suez Canal, a project feared by the British prime minister, Lord Palmerston, because it threatened British control of their colonies in India and Asia. For Napoleon III, the Suez Canal would mean circumventing English trade, but mostly he wanted France to enjoy open access to the Chinese market, where quality raw silk was produced in abundance. After an outbreak of *pébrine*, a disease affecting silkworms, and pressed by a powerful industrial lobby versed in the revolutionary ideas of Saint-Simonianism, Napoleon III was after raw silk from Asia for the textile industry that was booming in cities like Lyon.

If these arguments were not enough, the French emperor also saw his campaign to support the despondent Maronites of Mount Lebanon as his hour of glory. He could finally reintegrate the European quintet of nations and take part in oriental politics, having been shunted aside in 1840 after his ill-fated support of Egypt's Muhammad Ali. The summit granted Napoleon III his wish, much to the dismay of the British, who managed only to impose limits on his military incursion. The French could land only twelve thousand troops and had only six months to complete the intervention. The commanding general, Beaufort d'Hautpoul, headed to Beirut where the port was crowded with vessels, French for the most part, but also English, Russian, and even Greek. After a period of intentional stalling, Fuad Pasha met with the French commander to address the issues surrounding Mount Lebanon. Druze notables were imprisoned and a court was opened in Beirut, soon to be relocated to Mukhtara in the Shouf, at the house of Sheikh Said Jumblatt himself, who at that moment was detained with the notables.

The suggestion of the French to take the court to the house of the Jumblatt, the leading family among the Druze notables since 1711, was a diplomatic coup intended to assuage both sides. Eyewitnesses were called for testimony, but none would step forward, the Druze out of solidarity and the Christians for fear of reprisals. Unlike in Damascus, where courts got to the bottom of things in most cases, the trials in Mount Lebanon were a charade and not very convincing. Nevertheless, the lists of accused were assembled, again tweaked at will by the consuls, and finally just under fifty individuals were sentenced to death. The Druze notables were eventually released from prison, except for Sheikh Said Jumblatt, who died of tuberculosis while behind bars. Some historians claim the Druze sheikh died of poisoning, pointing the finger at the Ottoman authorities, who chose to silence the man whom they had stripped of his title of sheikh after arresting him, giving him the title of *bey* instead, a lower title that the Jumblatt have kept since. The Ottoman wali of Beirut met the same fate as his counterpart in Damascus, proof of the impartiality of the sultan, a message that was well understood by the European consuls.

Once the courts had finished their work, the question of governance for Mount Lebanon remained, a return to the dual-district caimaqam system seeming impossible. The six months allotted to Napoleon III at the summit of Paris had expired, and peace across Mount Lebanon was still fragile. With much difficulty, French diplomats succeeded in gaining an extension from Lord Russell, the head of the Foreign Office in London. In the meantime, Fuad Pasha was not idle. He appointed Youssef Karam to the seat of interim caimaqam of the northern district, a position Karam had long coveted, and sent him to fight Tanios Shaheen in his Kesrwan retreat. The latter chose not to fight, ordered his men to lay down their arms, and sought refuge in the convent of the Lazarists in Reifoon. Thus the "popular republic" of the peasants was nipped in the bud, and Tanios Shaheen stepped down from public life and lived among his people until he was an old and much respected man.

Under Youssef bey Karam (the title of *bey* was bestowed on him after taking the seat of caimaqam), the muqataaji families in the northern district were reinstated to their old territories. The Khazen pieced together their original dominions,

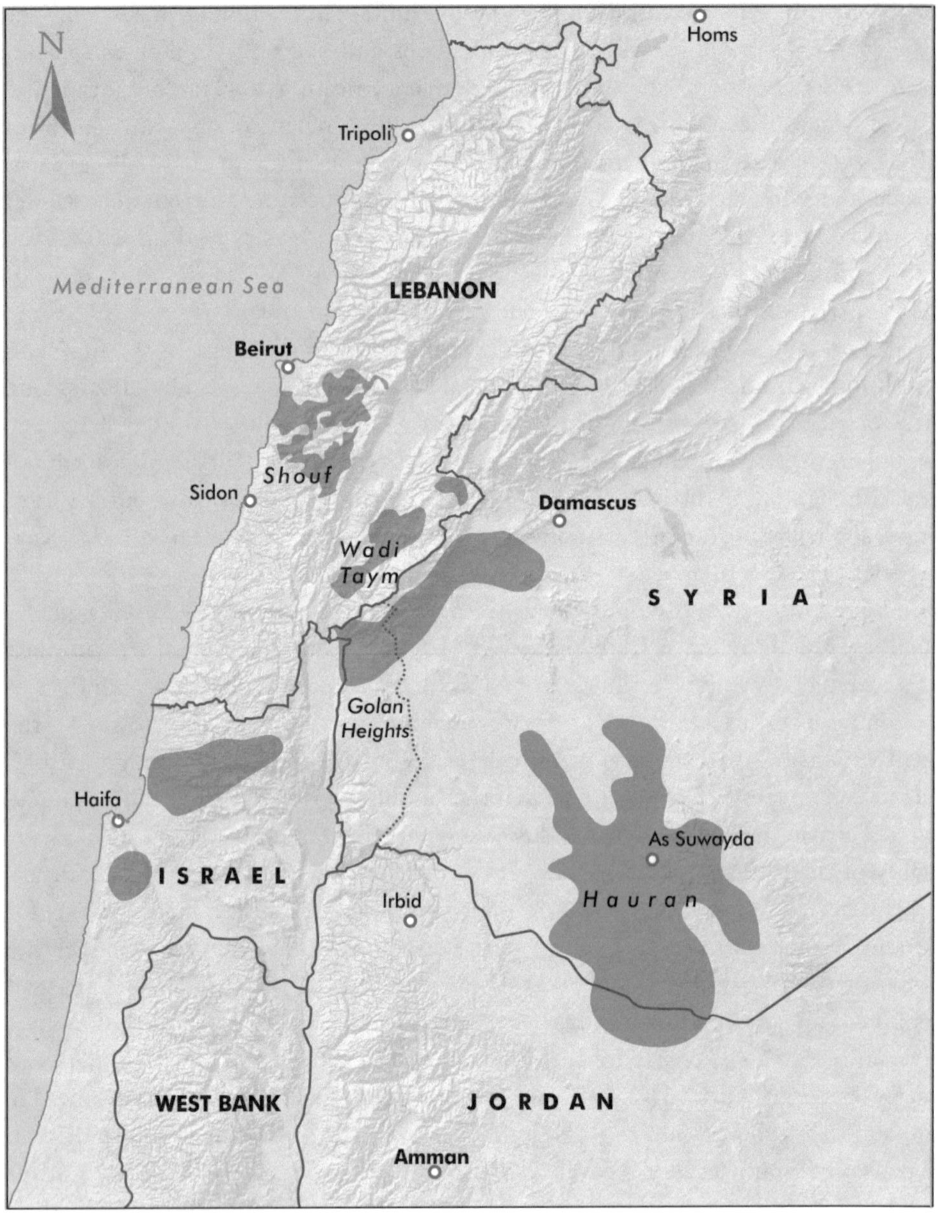

Map 4. The Druze community today: Spread across borders

reestablishing the age-old practices that had ignited the revolt in the first place, as if nothing had happened. The families were counting on General d'Hautpoul to enforce their domain, proud of having been the standard-bearers of French interests in Mount Lebanon for three centuries.

In the southern district, Fuad Pasha attempted to restructure the territory into smaller districts, appointing governors backed by councils of local advisors elected from the different religious groups. The tricky calculus of sectarian representation was taking the lead, a state of affairs that was to become the backbone of the republic-to-be. But Fuad's measures were not enough to bridge the differences in the south, and the reunification of Mount Lebanon under the governance of one wali came under discussion again.

The restoration of the Shihab, advocated by the French consul, was soon dropped in favor of an Ottoman governor who would be Christian and speak the language of the people. (The previous Ottoman walis spoke nothing but Turkish.) Most important, the would-be governor would not be from Mount Lebanon. As advocated by the European consuls, this condition was expected to satisfy the Maronites who would demand a Christian at the head of a reunited Mount Lebanon, and the Druze who would view the muqataaji families, and the Shihab in particular, as out of the question.

As new humanitarian missions and European hospices in Beirut struggled to heal the sick and wounded and rescue the destitute, Habib Fares and Youssef decamped from the heights of Shwayr and returned to their homes in Hadath. Beirut had become a safe haven for refugees, who had fled by the hundreds from Mount Lebanon, the Bekaa, and Damascus. Broken families, traumatized infants, orphaned children, injured and disabled men and women from all walks of life were hosted in schools and government buildings hastily converted into hospices. Beirut in 1860 was wearing black.

In Hadath, the scene was no brighter. An air of desolation and destruction hung over the ruins of homes that had been looted and burned. The news about casualties was grim. Countless friends and neighbors had been killed, including many young boys who had joined makeshift militias and their sheikh shababs, to resist the incursion, and who now were survived by their heartbroken mothers. Habib Fares, Youssef, and their wives and nine children walked home. Although vandalized, their modest home still stood, but their stores of fabrics and silk were destroyed. Nevertheless, all thirteen of them were still alive and together, and for that they were grateful. So they rolled up their sleeves and went back to work.

3

Nicolas Habib Shwayri

At the time of the mutasarifiya

Najibeh called her family for lunch and seated them at the table in the formal dining room, one of the rooms off the large sitting area. In well-to-do family homes, there was always a formal sitting room and an equally formal dining room, not for daily use but for special occasions when guests were invited. Najibeh's children were all home, not a common occurrence, now that Nicolas had a law practice to keep him busy, Nadim was still in college, and Emily had recently married and lived in the far northern city of Tripoli. Today, however, they were all home, and Najibeh prepared *molukia*—finely chopped molukia leaves, which she served on rice, adding rabbit and beef, diced raw onions and grilled breadcrumbs—making it very thick, just as they liked it.

The house of Alfred Nicola was a typical Lebanese construction of the nineteenth century, a spacious building that integrated the styles of the various cultures that had controlled and influenced Lebanon over the centuries. High arc-shaped windows, a pyramidal red-bricked roof, white granite flooring, wrought-iron grillwork, a fountain at the center of the large garden—the house was a melding of Ottoman style, Mamluk refinement, and Italianate flair. This distinctive home, typical of a prosperous family in Beirut, was built by Alfred's father, Nicolas, son of Habib Fares, in 1871.

According to one story, Nicolas built the house at the far end of his estate, away from the main road of Hadath that passed along the northern side of his property. Then someone whispered in his ear that he had committed a serious mistake. The location of his house meant he would be isolated from the people, hidden away in the back when all the excitement was in front, by the road. This argument was persuasive enough for Nicolas to order the walls to be dismantled and reconstructed at a different location. In fact, he moved the house three times before he was finally satisfied, a sign of the financial capabilities of the man and his exacting tastes.

Nicolas was nineteen at the time of the 1860 civil war, when his father and uncle took their families into hiding in Shwayr. After the Hatti Hamayun of 1856 and the beginning of Christian conscription into the Ottoman army, many young Christian men were drafted to serve long terms in different parts of the empire. A deferment from this duty was legally available, but it entailed paying a substantial fee; nevertheless, Habib Fares disbursed it readily on behalf of his four sons, unwilling to see them struggle for five or six years under the banner of the Sultan of Istanbul in some distant war. Habib Fares also made sure his sons avoided the entreaties of the rebels, always in need of recruits. Indeed this was another reason why the retreat to Shwayr in the dark hours of the civil war was an absolute necessity.

Of Habib Fares's four sons, Nicolas, the oldest, was the one who took up his father's business. While in his early teens, he traveled with Habib Fares to the souks in Beirut, now overflowing with European goods. Nicolas went with his father on visits to clients, learning the skills of commerce. Business was booming and Nicolas soon accumulated considerable capital. After a near-total collapse in 1860, the economic situation in Mount Lebanon had bounced back rapidly, helped along by the establishment of a new regime that was solidly anchored by the summer of 1861: the mutasarifiya.

As the mandate for French military intervention neared its expiration, representatives of the five Europeans nations and the envoy of the Ottoman sultan, Fuad Pasha, met and drafted a solution to the problem of Mount Lebanon's governance. Turkish and European historians (and, within that latter group, French, Austrian, and English writers) differ over who proposed the new regime and who presided over the summit. The original proposal probably came from the Prussian representative, augmented by the Austrian, who insisted on the Catholic faith of the governor-to-be; the session itself was headed by Fuad Pasha in person. The proposal was seconded by the English and Russian envoys reluctantly, and the French delegate finally agreed to it despite the fact that his bid to place another Shihab at the head of Mount Lebanon was sidelined.

In the end, and pressured by the imminent departure of General Beaufort d'Hautpoul and his army, the mutasarifiya was a practical solution. Fuad Pasha was relieved as it gave him the opportunity to restore the governance of Mount Lebanon to the direct control of the Sublime Porte, much longed for since the breakup of Mount Lebanon into two districts in 1841. The solution commanded the Ottomans to appoint a Christian governor to a three-year term.

While this new arrangement on its face seemed similar to the system in effect during the early years of the nineteenth century, the differences were actually enor-

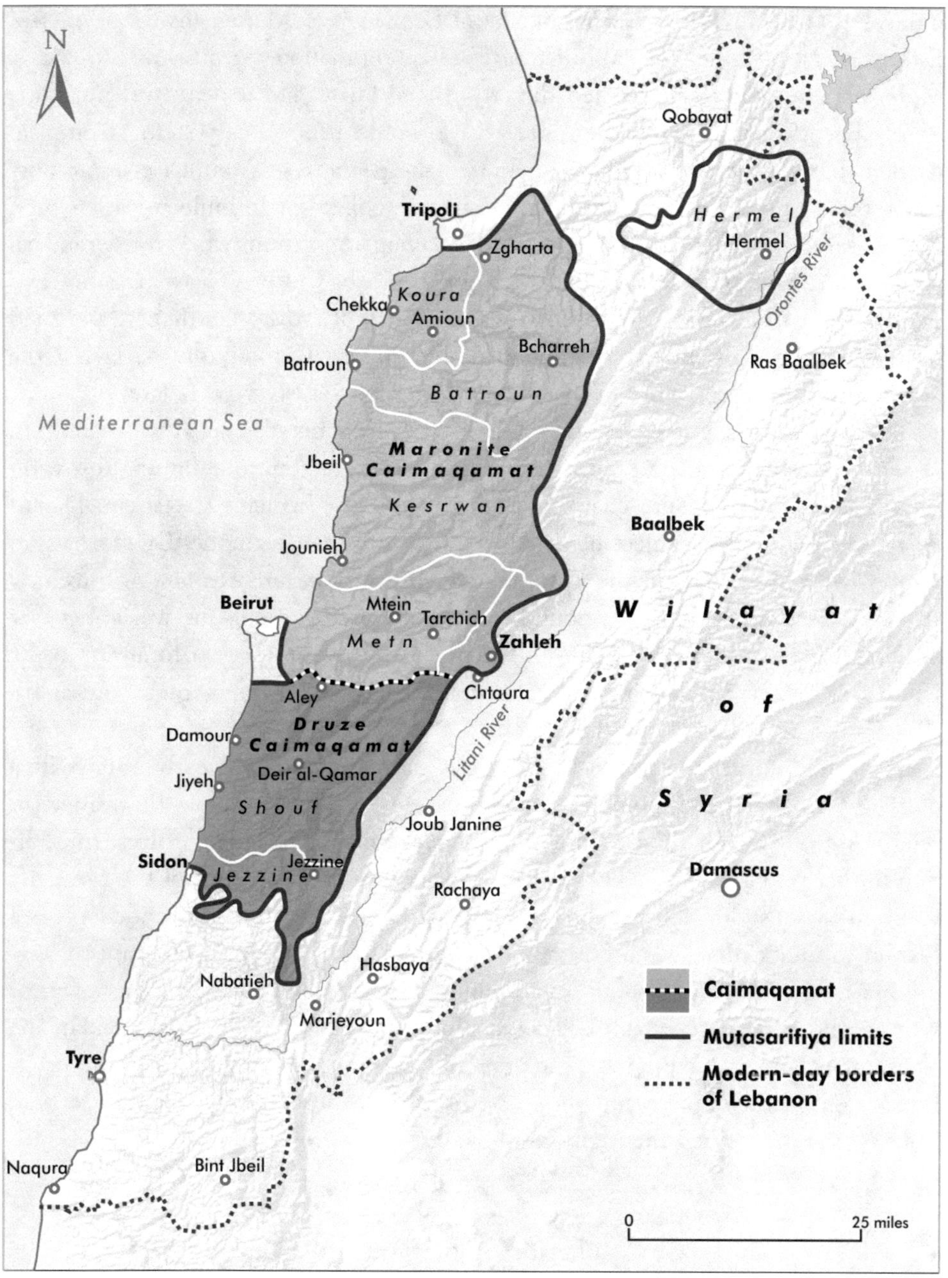

Map 5. Mount Lebanon under the caimaqamat dual regime (1841–1861) and the mutasarifiya (1861–1914)

mous. For one thing, the governor of Mount Lebanon would now answer to the five European nations since they all took part in his nomination, not just the Ottomans. Moreover, the governor reported directly to the Porte, not a petty wali in Saida or Tripoli. Most important, the mutasarifiya would usher in a system of political participation where the once silent majority, the peasants of Mount Lebanon, now had a role to play. The new administration also took pains to build infrastructure, deliver services, and regulate the economy, laying the groundwork for a modern nation-state. The mutasarifiya had both good and bad effects, perhaps more bad than good at times, but at least there was a system at work, one that transcended the petty politics of individual muqataaji families and moody amirs, laying the groundwork for a constitution that finally came to exist sixty years later.

The first three years after the mutasarifiya was adopted, until it was revised in 1864, were challenging, and the system would have ended in total failure, throwing Mount Lebanon back into chaos, were it not for one brilliant statesman: Daoud Pasha. An Armenian subject of the Porte and a Roman Catholic, Daoud had an impressive track record in the Ottoman administration and was able to carefully shape the new mutasarifiya. Among his many accomplishments, he was a member of the Science Academy in Berlin, the recipient of an honorary doctorate from the University of Jena in Thuringia, a Francophile who spoke some Arabic, and above all a humanist and a clever administrator.

Drafted immediately after the religious clashes of 1860, the early mutasarifiya of 1861 formalized the religious differences in government, giving the leaders of religious groups priority in nominating their candidates to public offices. In addition to that problem, Daoud Pasha had to deal with the volte-face of the Maronite Church, which suddenly resented his prerogatives and used the hardheaded Youssef Karam to undermine his authority. The Church still cherished the dream of having her own candidate at the head of Mount Lebanon, not some foreign governor who might rock the boat and ignore her political expectations. In particular, the Maronites wanted to reestablish the emara of previous times, and given the privileged position the Church now enjoyed, bring it under its sway. And to do that, Youssef Karam seemed the likely candidate.

The Organic Statutes

Weary of rumors that claimed the interference of European powers was proof of his decline, the Sultan in Istanbul used every means possible to impress upon his subjects the power and greatness of his Empire. The European quintet, more interested in outcomes than in appearances and formalities, acquiesced to the Sultan's pretenses, allowing the Ottomans to appear to be in total control and take any credit there was to be had. The new mutasarifiya regime, for example, was announced to the people in a series of pomp-filled ceremonies at which declamations were read publicly, dramatically stating the concerns of the Sultan for his subjects and his desire to see to their happiness—although, in reality, the new regime secured the interests of the European nations. Appearances were important, however, especially at a time when the Empire was on the brink of serious disruptions.

The Organic Statutes, as they came to be known, the *Règlement* for the reorganization of Mount Lebanon, were reviewed almost every time a new governor was nominated. The most important review took place in 1864, when the mandate of Daoud Pasha was extended for five years. Geographically, the mutasarifiya covered Mount Lebanon only, not the coastal towns or the important Bekaa plateau. (The seafaring towns along the coast were left out and kept under direct Ottoman control, while the Bekaa was attached to the wilayat of Damascus. In 1887, Beirut was organized into a large wilayat that extended from Jaffa to Latakia.) These boundaries deprived Mount Lebanon of the arable lands of the interior, the Bekaa being the only fertile ground in the vicinity. Also lost were the international gateways of trade that Beirut, Saida, and Tripoli had become.

Politically and administratively, the Statutes of 1864 gave rise to a system that clearly defined the responsibilities of government officials. The statutes provided a framework on which a coherent government system took form, and despite ongoing inconsistencies, opposition, and petty corruption, it gave good results.

At the grassroots level, every town had its representative, voted for by the people directly. These so-called village sheikhs had overall responsibility for their villages, the once-noble title of "sheikh" having been democratized with the coming of the mutasarifiya. They collected taxes, resolved conflicts, and, in their roles as justices of the peace (the so-called sheikh *solh*), were the first rung of a complex judicial hierarchy.

Most important, the village sheikhs elected the members of the district councils, giving real power to the people. Villagers now had a say in the constitution of the councils that governed their districts, a truly novel turn of events. In a way, what Tanios Shaheen had failed to achieve with weapons, the mutasarifiya handed to the people with the stroke of a pen. One can speculate on whether the first led to the second, the armed revolt to the Organic Statutes, but it remains that the political situation had evolved to the satisfaction of the people.

In all, there were seven districts for Mount Lebanon, each governed by a caimaqam who chaired the elected councils. Within each district, groups of villages formed sectors, each controlled by a director appointed by the mutasarif. Sectors were usually formed of coreligionists, or as close to a homogeneous population as possible. Najibeh's father, Alfred Nicola's father-in-law, a highly respected judge, was a *mudeer na'hia*, the director for the sector of Shwayr and its surroundings. In this position, he would be known for his righteousness and for enabling reforms that impacted the lives of the people.

At the pinnacle of the pyramid, the mutasarif governed with an Administrative Council, an advisory panel composed of twelve members appointed by the mutasarif from among the six religious groups: four Maronites, three Druze, two Greek Orthodox, one Greek Catholic, one Shi'a, and one Sunni. The demography of Mount Lebanon being what it was, the Maronite Church challenged the Administrative Council's decision to name only four Maronites among its twelve members, pleading with the mutasarif for more representation. Since the Maronites did account for most of the population in what was known as the northern district under the now-defunct dual caimaqam regime, and no less than one-third of the population in the southern district, the Church argued they should have proportional weight in the council. Daoud Pasha conceded and gave the position of second-in-command to a Maronite, though this ignored the spirit of the Organic Statutes. The seat of vice president of the Administrative Council was to be occupied by a Maronite thereafter, appointed by the mutasarif and not elected, to the satisfaction of the Maronite Patriarch.

In the early years, the Maronite Church fared better than other religious groups under the mutasarif, for in the absence of a genuine political culture among the village sheikhs, uneducated in the main and mostly Maronites, it managed to control the votes to its advantage. In addition, Daoud Pasha, as well as the mutasarif who succeeded him in 1868, was favorably disposed toward the Church and entrusted the Administrative Council with decisions that, strictly speaking, were beyond its consultative role.

Subsequent mutasarifs, however, sought to limit the influence of the Maronite Church, returning the council to its preordained boundaries. All this led to a unique, if ironic, model of power-sharing where the lip-service complicity among different religious groups became essential: the labeling of seats in the council on religious grounds, juxtaposed with a guided electoral college of village sheikhs that was Maronite in the main, resulted in unusual and complex sets of power relations. In a mixed area, where Maronites outnumbered the Druze, a Druze candidate might be elected with Maronite votes, thus making him beholden to them. The same applied in other areas where Druze, Sunni, or Shi'a had a majority and might therefore be able to elect "their" candidates from other religious groups.

The system worked relatively well as long as a mutasarif was there to impose his will, maintaining the chain of command tightly and dictating the marching orders. But in the short interludes that saw the seat of the mutasarif vacant, the system gave away under the personal and political greed of the public servants, whether elected or appointed. When the second mutasarif, Franco Pasha, passed away in 1873, the Porte authorized the vice president of the Administrative Council to act in the interim period, two long months that saw more than one crisis erupt. It was only with the appointment of Rustum Pasha to the seat of mutasarif that the system began to function smoothly again.

The Administrative Council: Prefiguration of the House of Representatives

From the early days of Daoud Pasha's tenure, the Administrative Council gradually amassed power. Formed as a simple advisory committee, it gradually assumed executive powers and in time became the main organ of government. As originally constituted, it could only review budgets, suggest sources of income, control taxation, and advise the mutasarif on matters that he proposed for discussion. That worked fine as long as the central government in Istanbul closed the yearly budget deficits of the mutasarifiya, as was implied in the Organic Statutes, or at least as the council members interpreted them. But the Porte had a different view and charged the operational deficits back to the mutasarifiya, to be paid by additional taxes on the populations or by a surplus in the trade balance.

Chronic budget deficits plagued the mutasarifiya throughout its existence and were responsible for the accrual of power by the Administrative Council, for the council had a strong card to play. The Organic Statutes stipulated that any tax increase proposed by the mutasarif had to be approved by the Administrative Council to be valid. Thus, the council had veto power over any mutasarif's decision to impose a new tax to close a budget deficit. When Rustum Pasha came to power in 1873, he was faced with this dilemma. Expenditures on infrastructure and socioeconomic projects had been extensive under his two predecessors, and the budget was in deficit, so the central government in Istanbul would not approve it. All new taxes were denied by the Administrative Council, and the Porte still refused to cover the deficit.

With no other options available, Rustum Pasha resorted to slashing expenditures, implementing unpopular measures such as reducing administrative personnel. The cuts he imposed, however, did little to close the budget gap; the deficit was still monumental, partially because he wisely continued to invest in much-needed and beneficial infrastructure projects. A way around this financial conundrum—how to spend on necessary development projects when the budget was in the red—was eventually worked out: separate accounting. Certain financial accounts, provincial in nature, were not scrutinized by the central government in Istanbul and, in a way, escaped the screening of the finance diwan. As early as Daoud Pasha, the mutasarif made use of these accounts to funnel funds from taxation to finance investment programs. Called *muhmalat*, these accounts grew in significance, not only for financing projects but also leveraging the birth of an autochthonous political identity.

That the Administrative Council had direct control over these muhmalat accounts is central to this development. By the end of the nineteenth century, most public works across the mutasarifiya were funded through these accounts, turning the Administrative Council into the epicenter of government power. The extent of the council's power prompted strong reactions from the Porte, and after Rustum Pasha's long tenure came to a close in 1883, a new mutasarif was charged by the Porte to trim the excessive authority of the council.

During his tenure, Rustum Pasha had tried to control the council by maintaining a firm grip on the Maronite Church, which he blamed for most of the problems around him. In the growing power of the council, Rustum saw the meddling of the Church, whose four council members and council vice president were all anxious to do the Patriarch's bidding. His successor, Wasa Pasha, continued to focus on the Church, lining up his own Maronite candidates to challenge the election of the members backed by the Patriarch when their three-year terms ended in 1885. However successful Wasa Pasha was at weakening the Administrative Council by forcing its return to a simple advisory role, he could not stop the new awakening that had taken place. The structure and the culture of Mount Lebanon's government were in gestation, a first step in the making of a modern state. Although held in the clamps of religious affinities and often forced to march in lockstep by sectarian labels, the council members were nevertheless the natural and elected representatives of the people of Mount Lebanon.

As the Administrative Council gained power and took on the prerogatives of a real government, local notables increasingly took part in the electoral process. If at the start the mutasarif appointed members from one-time muqataaji families to buy their support for the new system, the 1860 tragedy put an end to muqataaji privileges, and the council opened up to new elites, who came from trade and industry. Having the title of a dignitary was in vogue at this time, and such titles were up for sale, often bought under the counter with *bakhsheesh*, as were government positions themselves that needed to be filled. The people who had lived so long under the repression of the muqataaji families were now liberated, the equals of their previous lords as stipulated by the Hatti Hamayun, and many were earning substantial incomes from trade and also developing their political instincts.

When in session, the council had all the appearance of a modern government assembly. Members dressed fashionably in European-style attire, discarding the traditional pantaloons in favor of suits and ties (though retaining the Moroccan fez, the red tarboosh that became a symbol of this successful era). As infrastructure projects modernized the landscape of Beirut and Mount Lebanon and the bustling harbor produced ever-greater wealth, the more successful the council appeared and the more opulent the seat of government became.

The Organic Statutes of 1861 named the town of Deir al-Qamar as the seat of government, no doubt because it was the scene of the most ruthless bloodshed in

1860; it was also chosen because it was home to two religious groups, Christians and Druze, and had been the emblematic city of the great Amir Fakhreddine. The first mutasarif, Daoud Pasha, found the town too remote for keeping in touch with the people across his expansive territories; Deir al-Qamar was also very cold in winter, with snows covering the region. So Daoud decided to relocate his seat of government in winter to a coastal town, warmer and closer to Beirut, eventually choosing Baabda, where the Shihab family had their residences. He rented the house of a good friend, Fendi Shihab, whom he appointed later as vice president of the council.

The second mutasarif, Franco Pasha, had more grandiose living arrangements, renting the saray of Haidar Shihab in Baabda, a complex finished in 1775 that counted no fewer than fifty-five rooms. By the time of the arrival of the third governor, Rustum Pasha, discord had divided the local community, and the new mutasarif decided to leave Baabda for a neighboring town, opening his offices in Hadath of all places, within walking distance of Habib Fares's and Youssef Shwayri's homes.

When the fourth mutasarif, Wasa Pasha, was named, the people of Baabda were anxious to regain the honor of hosting the government. So they bought the saray that Franco Pasha had once rented and put it at the disposal of the government. The building came at a heavy price—one-thousand Napoleons in gold—but this was financed over twenty years, and all the inhabitants of Baabda contributed, in proportion to their incomes, paying a monthly charge managed by a benevolent committee. The seat of the mutasarifiya would remain at the saray thereafter, sitting in prominence on a hill overlooking Beirut. Still there today, it's the oldest government building in operation.

The return of government to Baabda brought a large number of public servants to the town, and providing them with food, lodging, and other services created profitable opportunities. The council drew people from across the seven districts every day, and especially from Beirut, the commercial seafaring town just a short distance away. In addition, public servants in Beirut often fled the summer heat, taking up residence in the numerous villages of Mount Lebanon.

All this meant good business for Nicolas, Alfred Nicola's father, who saw his fabric business expand rapidly, with a well-dressed, well-to-do clientele just outside his door. Nicolas had taken over from his father, Habib Fares, who passed away in 1868 at the young age of fifty-five. Alfred was born seventeen years later, in 1885, the third child of Nicolas, after Alexander and Julia and before Zahia and George. These were good times in Mount Lebanon, for the mutasarifiya had lived up to people's expectations, maintaining the peace and enabling a modern society to emerge and mature.

Sadly, however, the winds of fate would soon blow in from a different direction, bringing dismay to many in Mount Lebanon, the Shwayri among them, and imposing on Nicolas and his family ordeals they would never have expected.

To finish with Youssef bey Karam

Neither the Maronite Patriarch nor Youssef Karam viewed the mutasarifiya as a worthy or workable system that would last very long, certainly not under the governance of a foreign administrator who knew nothing about the particularities of their mountains. They assumed any mutasarif would soon be overwhelmed by the political intrigues of Mount Lebanon and fail in his mission, a turn of events that would bring the Porte and the consuls back to reality and surrender control to a local Christian. It was just a matter of time, they believed, before Youssef Karam would be called in to rule, a fait accompli.

As time went by, however, more and more people viewed the new regime positively; it had brought security to their families, boosted the local economy, and downplayed the issues of religion and class that had caused such havoc in the past. So when Daoud Pasha was reappointed for a second term in 1864, having done well in his first mandate, the discontent was palpable in Youssef Karam's camp. Karam, the interim caimaqam of a previous era and the courageous fighter of 1860, had become the figurehead of Ehden, the stronghold of the Maronites since very early times, and considered himself the natural leader of Mount Lebanon. Now his seat was being usurped by some foreign dignitary.

A revolt broke out, and Maronite families soon took up arms, divided between those who supported Karam and those who were content with the new regime. As this fighting played out in the northern district, the rest of the mutasarifiya and the coastal towns were unmoved, even uninterested, in the crisis, preferring to live according to the Organic Statutes and looking favorably on the new prospects it brought their way. Ultimately, the Patriarch saw wisdom in sustaining the efforts of the mutasarif, especially when the revision of the statutes in 1864 gave the Maronites a larger role in the decision-making.

Giving the Maronites a de facto vice president in addition to their four seats on the Administrative Council may have been Daoud Pasha's way of defusing the Youssef Karam threat, pleasing the Patriarch enough to persuade him to give up on Karam. Whatever the rationale, clearly the times had changed, and the Patriarch had reasons to support the government and even talked Youssef Karam into collaborating with Daoud Pasha. As a sign of goodwill, the mutasarif appointed Karam as caimaqam over the district of Jezzine in the south, a position that Karam turned down, not willing to give up his northern fiefdom, which was now to be governed, not to make things any easier, by a Shihab caimaqam.

When Daoud Pasha came in person to meet Youssef Karam in Batroun, the latter showed up with no fewer than a thousand men, a move that tipped the balance against the impetuous warlord and gave the mutasarif enough grounds to eliminate him. More clashes ensued, and the regular army tracked Karam to

Ehden, where the rebel went into hiding only to surface at a meeting called by the Patriarch and attended by the French consuls of Beirut and Damascus and the envoy of Daoud Pasha. There it was agreed that Youssef Karam would be exiled to Algeria, a French dominion at the time.

The story does not end there though. At every historical junction, at the end of every mutasarif's term, Youssef Karam would surface once again, perhaps in Istanbul or Rome, or even in Tripoli or Ehden, pressing for his appointment to office or at least for his reinstatement as an acknowledged political figure. By 1867, he was out for good, his power to mobilize forces reduced to insignificance, his only support within the Maronite clergy itself. Some clergy continued to agitate, and Rustum Pasha went so far as to send eighteen clerics to prison in 1877. After exiling a bishop to Jerusalem the following year, he declared, "Lebanon has two enemies, and they both wear black: the sheep and the monks."

Youssef bey Karam passed away in 1889, near Naples. He had always believed that a foreign mutasarif would fail, unable to bond with the local people, and in this, he was proven wrong. Not only did many mutasarifs succeed in their endeavors, they all strove wholeheartedly to give Mount Lebanon a chance to exist as a political entity and play a role in the regional economy. Some of them developed close ties with the people and became emotionally attracted to the mountainous land, even choosing to be buried in Mount Lebanon. Franco Pasha, the Aleppo-born mutasarif who succeeded Daoud Pasha, died in office and was laid to rest, according to his wishes, in Hazmieh, a town near Baabda and Hadath. Not far from there, Rustum Pasha created spectacular gardens where he often wandered; next to the gardens he built a cemetery, where the remains of his predecessor were interred, soon to be joined by others (Wasa Pasha was one of them; his remains were transferred to his native country of Albania in 1978).

A lover of nature and art, the Italian-born Rustum commissioned a stonemason from Shwayr, Tanios Khoury, to build a bridge in his gardens, over the river of Beirut. The bridge was still in use a hundred years later. Bypassed in the twentieth century when Beirut outgrew its traditional boundaries, the fine gardens of the Pasha gave way to modern-day asphalt and concrete. The remains of the bridge, fallen into neglect, are still there to see when one drives through the area now known as Jisr al-Basha, the bridge of the Pasha.

A bustling but constrained economy

The economy of Mount Lebanon in the second half of the nineteenth century centered on the export of silk. Although sericulture had been established early in the seventeenth century under Fakhreddine, it greatly expanded during the ten-year rule of Ibrahim Pasha. In large part, he charted the course that transformed Beirut from an obscure fishing town into a central hub of the major economic routes in the eastern Mediterranean. Endowed with a lazaretto that made her the unrivaled entryway for international trade, and a modern administration that Ibrahim Pasha had borrowed from the French, Beirut outshone the other coastal harbor towns of Tripoli, Saida, and Acre.

Allied, for better or worse, with the Egyptian Ibrahim Pasha, Beirut, and by extension Mount Lebanon, built strong economic ties with Alexandria, a city that imported large amounts of raw silk. Mulberry trees were planted in lieu of traditional crops that were less profitable, and Beirut's first spinning mill opened in 1836, followed by a second in the neighboring Jurd region in 1838, the same year the Edict of Gülhane was signed and while Ibrahim Pasha still made the laws in the region. That both mills were owned by French companies is not surprising, considering the close relations between France and Egypt. International relations were motivated by colonial interests as well as the race to pick up the pieces of the fast-collapsing Ottoman Empire. These interests were not only largely dictated by the colonial offices of the European nations but also by influential industrial groups that had a growing say in power politics.

This period was marked by great prosperity in the silk-based textile industry in Lyon, which led to a growing demand for the raw commodity; however, the cost of local production was prohibitive. With the advent of Louis Philippe in 1830, France entered a period of labor unrest that resulted in successive salary increases in local industries, making it less profitable to produce silk in France. Entrepreneurs in Lyon therefore sought to relocate their production, a decision eased by technical innovation that industrialized spinning mills. Steam had made its debut in the industry, replacing the traditional wood-fired basins that produced the silk, and mills could now deliver larger quantities while maintaining regularity in quality without necessarily having to rely on highly qualified staff. This meant relocation to faraway destinations was simplified.

As the silk industry became internationalized, mill owners viewed Mount Lebanon as the perfect place for their new facilities, on par with Valencia in Spain and certain parts of Italy. Labor in Mount Lebanon was much cheaper, nearly three times less expensive than in Lyon; moreover, the climate was mild, and land was relatively inexpensive. Mills opened at lightning speed, and by 1885 mulberry trees occupied forty percent of the arable land in Mount Lebanon; tellingly, Lyon became the sole purchaser of silk produced on this land. While Alexandria imported half of Mount Lebanon's silk bundles in 1845, by the end of the century Lyon had a near monopoly on the silk industry there.

In 1867, there were 67 mills in Mount Lebanon and Beirut, 10 of which were owned by French spinners that produced half the country's total silk output. By

1885, there were 105 mills, and in 1913 the number went as high as 200. Throughout these decades, the French dominated the industry, wrote the rules, and kept one step ahead of the demands of local workers and service providers. The mill owners integrated their industry totally, engaging in spinning, shipping, insurance, and banking, often all at the same time. In the eyes of the Lyon entrepreneurs, their interests in Mount Lebanon were too big to be left to chance, and they became a formidable lobbying group, capable of influencing the political decisions of the French government itself. This was evident as early as the aftermath of the civil war of 1860, when a humanitarian committee was established by the silk entrepreneurs eager to fund the restoration of homes and get the spinners back to work. And while pleasing the silk entrepreneurs may not have been the prime motive of Napoleon III, it certainly was another good argument for sending troops in 1860.

While Mount Lebanon was important to some French interests, France was hardly dependent on it. Silk from Mount Lebanon represented only ten percent of the total quantity the French imported, Europe and Asia being far larger suppliers. In this one-sided relationship, Mount Lebanon and Beirut relied totally on the French market and its movements. In all, France accounted for two-thirds of the gross revenue produced from the overall exports that were channeled through Beirut. For in addition to silk bundles, French interests were equally represented in the major public works projects built by French contractors, or, when Ottoman legislation did not allow direct concessions, by local entrepreneurs who acted on behalf of their French correspondents.

This situation placed tremendous power in the hands of French spinners and bankers, who dictated their retail prices to the mills in Mount Lebanon according to what suited them, competition being insignificant. There were a few British spinners, of course, one as early as 1844, but the French controlled the business. Even those mills that were owned by locals had their operating budgets funded through local banks that were overseen by the Lyon entrepreneurs. Toward the end of the century, Lyon was sustaining, in one way or another, nearly half the operating budget of the entire silk market across Mount Lebanon and Beirut.

Finding themselves in this relationship of total dependency, the mutasarifiya and all Beirut were attuned to any revolutions and wars in France or those waged by the French around the world. In other words, when France sneezed, the mutasarifiya caught cold. And so the economy of Mount Lebanon suffered with every major crisis that France faced: in 1848, when Europe was swept by revolutions, the monarchy fell and Louis Napoleon was elected president of the republic; in 1852, when France, under the same Napoleon, changed regimes, dropping the republic in favor of the Second Empire; from 1854 to 1856, during the Crimean War; and in the Franco-Prussian War of 1871, when Napoleon was defeated in Sedan and Wilhelm of Prussia was crowned king of Germany. In between these major crises, smaller events—labor strikes, customs adjustments, new laws and regulations—also brought disruptions.

Looking at the trade balance for the period extending from 1840 to 1900, we see in black and white the sudden and grave interruptions that France's crises had on Mount Lebanon's economic well-being. More important, we note the complete deregulation of the trade balance after 1860, with a major deficit growing by the year; before 1860, the balance was nearly in equilibrium. The deficit reached unrivaled peaks in the last two decades of the century, due to the large number of public works projects that were in progress and a surge in housing construction that raised demand for imports of construction materials and consumables.

But the deficit was also the result of a drop in the demand for silk from Beirut. The finished fabrics from the Lyon weaving factories had become too expensive for the European and American markets, even though, paradoxically, the demand for silk was increasing at a fast pace. Simply put, the cost of French production was no longer viable in the face of fierce competition from China and the introduction of synthetic silk. As a result of that, the French entrepreneurs, who had formally organized into the Union of Silk Traders of Lyon, advocated for a state subsidy and were granted substantial support over a period of twenty years.

At the same time, the cost of silk production, from cocoon to bundle, was rising in the mutasarifiya and Beirut. This increase was due to a shortage of manpower, many having opted for emigration, and also the overvaluation of land, as most returning emigrants invested the wealth they had earned abroad in property. So, by the end of the century, mulberry trees began to give way to citrus trees in Beirut and along the coast; to tobacco fields, olive trees, and vineyards at the lower altitudes in Mount Lebanon; to apple trees and other fruits farther up in the mountains; and to potatoes in the Bekaa.

In the midst of this transformation, Nicolas Shwayri, the father of Alfred Nicola, was struggling to make ends meet. Until 1885, his business had held its own; after that, his economic prospects, like those of the entire region, dimmed. A series of political setbacks led to widespread economic decline, starting with the Cretan revolt, which escalated into an all-out war between the Greeks and the Ottomans; next came a new constitution decreed by the sultan for his empire, most likely forced by circumstances and by a young Ottoman elite forming in Istanbul; this was followed by the deposing of the sultan when he suspended the Constitution, and the advent of a new sultan who pledged to put it into practice.

The instability of the Ottoman administration was obvious, and nervousness was reflected in the streets of Beirut. Prices of goods soared, and work became scarce. Many workers left for Egypt, many more for America, and the drainage of manpower was obvious. Over one hundred thousand people from Mount Lebanon alone had emigrated, a fourth of the total population at the time. One spinning mill had to begin employing orphans to compensate for its loss of laborers, entering into an agreement with a French congregation that sponsored it. Yet Nicolas went on, earning less but still enough to support his family. Then, in 1890, his uncle Youssef passed away, leaving behind a wife and four children. It was a particularly hard time, when the economy across the country was at its lowest, yet Nicolas took in Youssef's family and helped as much as he could.

The eldest of Youssef's children, a son from his first marriage, named Fares, immigrated to Brazil, where he had relatives on his mother's side. The others stayed for a while until Youssef's wife, Ann, took her two sons, Habib and Alexander, to seek out her brother who was in business in Louisiana. They left in 1892.

Alfred Nicola dropped out of school early in his childhood and by age twelve was working full time with his hands. Of his siblings, only his elder brother had some education from the time when his father, Nicolas, was still able to pay school fees. For apart from the decline in his sales and the hardship of losing a lucrative business, Nicolas was developing health problems. No doubt the strains of a failing enterprise coupled with unsold stocks of fabric and unpaid invoices got the better of him, for he fell into depression and also developed a heart condition.

Alfred did what he could to alleviate the situation and help his father and his mother, Helena, to maintain a decent standard of living by doing small jobs here and there. He was willing to do anything, but his earnings were not enough. Moreover, his elder brother had no occupation, and his younger brothers were still too small to work. Meanwhile, Nicolas, hounded by business creditors, was forced to borrow money to pay his debts and could not escape mortgaging his property.

Alfred was heartbroken by the change in his father. Nicolas's health continued to deteriorate. Daydreaming nostalgically of better times, he would sit all day in his pajamas, speechless and with empty eyes, forcing a hollow smile on his expressionless face whenever anyone tried to snatch him out of his reveries. How Helena suffered for her husband as she served him attentively, with the same devotion she had for all her family, sitting next to him all day, entertaining him with any story that came her way, stories that Nicolas had no taste for and no ears any longer.

Alfred redoubled his efforts, going out early in the morning to search for work, coming home only late in the evening; yet the money was too little, much too little to cover even the interest on his father's debt. Unless money was forthcoming, consistent sums and fairly quickly, his father's property would be foreclosed, and the family would have nowhere to live. By seventeen, Alfred had work-hardened hands, strong arms and legs, and a sturdy physique that prepared him for the harshest conditions.

News from Alfred's cousins in Louisiana came regularly to Hadath. His cousin Alexander had married Alfred's older sister, Julia, in 1895, three years after leaving for Louisiana with his mother and brother. Alexander had returned to Lebanon for the occasion, and after that, he visited Julia every other year as she stayed in Hadath to look after their children, who were born to the beat of his intermittent travels. Alexander had become a peddler in New Orleans, as had his mother and brother, and one option for Alfred was to follow in their footsteps. He thought it over at length and finally decided he was ready to do it. On Alexander's visit to Beirut in the winter of 1902, he learned that Alfred was preparing to cross the Atlantic.

The mutasarifiya regime provided Mount Lebanon with much of its socioeconomic, legal, educational, and sanitary infrastructure. It conducted a real cadastral survey that resulted in a series of maps still in use today and was responsible for the first serious population census (although many of the population counts were erroneous, due to people's fears that the information was being collected for conscription and tax purposes). During the tenure of the first mutasarif, Daoud Pasha, over one thousand kilometers of roads were cut across the hillsides of Mount Lebanon, linking distant villages and connecting them with the main towns. Later, Franco Pasha formed a commission for public works and employed two European engineers and six building specialists: Youssef Ghosn, Tannus Khneisser, Elias Khoury, Antoun Saadeh, Metry Rustum Shwayri, and Elias Zgheib. Apart from Elias Zgheib, all were from Shwayr, and four (Ghosn, Khoury, Shwayri, and Saadeh) were descendants of the Moujaes family. The commission built bridges across countless rivers and tributaries and installed water conduits to villages.

In the race to modernize, European investors competed to earn concessions, or contracts, from the mutasarif or the wali of Beirut to build the major public works that were planned. Increasingly, the Ottomans, hoping to reduce their dependence on France, tried to avoid French contractors. Yet these sprouted up everywhere, hiding behind shell corporations that sounded local or signing up with local dignitaries who were in business. So in the end, all major public works were either governed by French companies or at least had a major shareholder that was French. The Beirut–Damascus road was entrusted to a French group that counted among its shareholders the shipping company Messageries Impériales, which operated a regular line into Beirut from Marseille, as well as the train companies Paris-Orléans and Paris-Lyon-Méditerranée, which were owned by the Credit Lyonnais bank.

The concession for the Beirut–Damascus road was signed in 1859 and the road opened in 1863, having lent its first section in 1860 to six thousand French troops, who retired to the newly forested park of Beirut to make their camp. Next, the contract for a railway connecting Beirut with Damascus was signed, given to a company with a long Ottoman-sounding name (La Société ottomane de la Voie ferrée économique de Beyrouth à Damas) but whose equities were French. This railway began operations in 1895, and it took only nine hours to cross the eighty-seven miles to Damascus. That same year, the port of Beirut resumed operations, with deeper berths capable of hosting bigger boats. The dredging had been executed by another company with a long name (La Companie impériale ottomane du Port, des Quais, des Entrepôts de Beyrouth) whose headquarters happened to be in Paris.

All these projects cost Beirut and the mutasarifiya incredible amounts of money, the mutasarifiya occasionally helping itself to the coffers of the wali of Beirut, when the interests of the two independent entities collided. The balance of trade was constantly in deficit, and efforts to close the gap through taxation proved fruitless, since so many workers had immigrated to faraway destinations. Not to leave the pressure at that, the fast-rising bourgeois class, sitting on new wealth gained from trade and industry, mainly silk, was developing into a consumer society with a taste for expensive and often imported products. This added financial speculation to an economy that was already stretched to the breaking point.

As a modern city, Beirut needed access to modern banking services. Until the middle of the nineteenth century, this was resolved by private lenders, whom we would call rentiers today, who lent money on preset return rates guaranteed by the Ottoman administration. Then, in 1856, the Ottoman Bank opened as a commercial bank, before it transformed itself in 1863 into a national bank. The bank's new name included references to "Sultan" and "Ottoman," but of the 135,000 shares, 80,000 were British, 50,000 were French, and only 5,000 were really Ottoman.

The influence of European bankers did not stop at the gate of the Ottoman Bank but was omnipresent behind the counters of all the private banks that started to emerge after the Hatti Hamayun and that were initially established to fund the budgets of spinning mills. The actual investment in equipment for a mill was relatively low in comparison with the annual operating budget it required, and cash was only disbursed upon the delivery of the final product. This meant that a spinner would incur enormous costs by June, the usual start of the spinning year, which was hard except for those who had a foot in the banking business as well (the French, in particular). Most spinners therefore either worked intimately with a Lyon-based fabric buyer who advanced the cash in return for them selling at a substantially reduced fee, or they took a bank loan against guarantees. And the Lyon entrepreneurs were not very far from the local banks either. When a hard year came by and the product did not sell well, a local mill, a family business usually, often found itself in financial difficulty and had to sell the business to a competitor or a new entrant.

The Beirut of long ago, with its Arabic souks and chaotic ambiance, was still there at the end of the nineteenth century, with additions that added new prospects to a city in constant flux. One new landmark was the *qishlah*, a casern that housed an

Ottoman garrison; it was built in 1853 on a small hill outside the gates, overlooking the old city. This large building has played an important role in the history of Lebanon, becoming the seat of the French high commissioner under the mandate and serving today as the offices of the prime minister. A second floor was added during the restoration of Beirut in the 1990s, and the roof was covered in red tiling. North of the qishlah and situated on the site of an old wharf, a commercial center was built about the same time as the qishlah and called khan Antoun Bey. (The word *khan*, from Persian, signifies a roadside inn for caravanserais and was appropriated in the common language of the time to mean retail center.) The khan Antoun Bey hosted a number of shops as well as the Ottoman Bank for a while, before it moved to the square facing the high Burj. This square with an ever-changing name was then called Burj Square for the tower that sat on the northeastern corner of the city walls, then Cannon Square during the short interlude when the armada of Catherine the Great of Russia occupied the city in 1773 and unloaded its cannons in a show of force. In 1881, after it was transformed into the grand city entrance, it was renamed Hamidiyyeh Square, in tribute to Sultan Abdul Hamid. Adorned with a central garden that featured the sultan's emblem, the *thugra*, the square lay between the roads leading out of Beirut toward Saida and Tripoli.

Etymologically, the name *beyr'ut* comes from the Aramaic word for "wells," and until late in the nineteenth century the city's only water source was its many wells. As the town grew in population, from seven thousand in 1830 to nearly thirty thousand in 1885, the water from the wells, some of which had become polluted, was no longer sufficient. A concession to build a water line was signed with a French firm, which after incessant negotiations sold its rights to a British company, the Beirut Waterworks Company, which brought water to Beirut in 1884, sourcing it at the Dog River some thirteen miles north of the town. Gas became available in 1879 for street lighting, giving Beirut a thousand lampposts by 1885. Electricity came later, with another concession to a French company, La Société des Tramways et de l'Eclairage, signed in 1894. The city's first tram began carrying passengers in 1908, and electricity finally replaced gas for street lights in 1910.

Mount Lebanon and Beirut attracted other people, too, not just business tycoons and political schemers who came looking to advance their careers, or orientalists in search of the "Levantine wisdom" to enhance their esoteric beliefs. Men and women of good intentions, genuinely moved by the ordeals of the people in Greece, the Balkans, and Syria, and by the massacres of the Armenian population, stepped ashore as early as the eighteenth century and devoted themselves to turning Beirut into "the lighthouse of the East." Educators, scholars, medical doctors, humanists, priests, and pastors, they came, as one of them said, quoting St. John, "that they may have life, and have it more abundantly."

A rivalry developed as a result of their arrival, once the American evangelical missionaries found themselves disputing the turf coveted by the Catholic Jesuits. Yet, as is often true, competition brings out the best, and it certainly did in this case. The Syrian Protestant College (SPC), with its medical school, was established in 1866 and was spearheaded in large part by a great investor in people, Cornelius Van Dyck, a New York medical doctor and humanitarian. Since his arrival in 1840, Van Dyck had started a number of schools across Mount Lebanon; he also helped translate the Bible into Arabic, published in science journals, did not shy away from learning ophthalmology late in life in order to teach it at the medical school, and built the first observatory in the region, one so accurate that its data was collected every day and sent to Vienna via Istanbul. Because the medical school at SPC lacked a hospital, Van Dyck turned to the Knights of St. John, who owned a hospital in Beirut that they entrusted to the care of the German deaconesses of the Kaiserwerth. Students of the SPC fulfilled their training at the German hospital to the satisfaction of the college and the hospital alike.

Ambroise Monod, a Jesuit priest, was another highly motivated and competent person driven by humanistic values. He took upon himself the purchase of the large estate destined to become the Catholic Institute and strove to solicit funding for its construction, which he did after a prolonged stay in New York and London. The institute and a medical center opened in 1883, a very short while after the SPC. In time, these two institutions developed into the American University of Beirut and Saint Joseph University, respectively, and to this day are iconic schools in Lebanon and across the Middle East.

New schools continued to proliferate with the arrival of new congregations and denominations. Every congregation that was already present in the Holy Land opened a chapter in Beirut and built schools across the city and Mount Lebanon: the Society of Jesus (Jesuits), the Order of the Mission (Lazarists), the Institute of the Brothers of the Christian Schools, the Marist Brothers, the Sisters of the Holy Family, the Sisters of Nazareth, the Sisters of Charity, the Israelite Alliance, the Presbyterian Church, the Evangelical Church, and many others. Other schools were founded by the indigenous congregations: the Greek Orthodox (who also founded the Saint George Hospital in 1878), the Maronites, and Greek Catholics.

Public schools began to appear about the same time with the arrival of a charismatic wali in Damascus in 1878, Midhat Pasha. He finally implemented an education decree that had sat on the shelf for years, ignored by his predecessors, and government schools finally were built in every large town. Because the decree was titled *maaref* (knowledge), the public schools were known by that term, an appellation widely in use to this day. Charity being the cornerstone of Islam, Midhat Pasha encouraged the foundation of a charity organization that offered education and assistance to the less fortunate, and the Makassed Institution, which began its work in 1880, is still active today.

The brief Egyptian rule of Syria and Lebanon was decisive in more than one way. As already discussed, by placing the small fishing town of Beirut at the center of international commerce, Ibrahim Pasha planted the seeds of a modern city that only the mutasarifiya, the regime that succeeded in governing Mount Lebanon, could nurture. The mutasarifiya built a system of governance and endowed it with the necessary legal, administrative, financial, and political tools, which were easily transferred into a standing government when the time came. The differences between Beirut and Mount Lebanon resulted from the goals that were set for each independently, by Ibrahim Pasha for the former and by the mutasarifiya for the latter. Each place had an independent system of government from 1860 until World War I, and each was nurtured along a different path that suited its geography, economic realities, and society. A liberal and velvet-smooth regime for Beirut, a resilient and traditional one for Mount Lebanon. They were different yet complementary, each needing the other to exist. The combination became explosive, however, when, under the French mandate, Beirut and Mount Lebanon reunited under a *Grand Liban*.

The other legacy that Beirut, and Mount Lebanon by extension, had gained from Ibrahim Pasha was a safe conduct to a new and thriving cultural identity, one that Muhammad Ali had already instituted in Egypt and that came to be known as the *Nahda*, or Renaissance. A benevolent dictator in his own right, a man of will and no less of vision, Ibrahim Pasha opened the door wide for the Egyptian winds to blow across Beirut and Mount Lebanon, bringing what Egypt had earned during three decades of reforms. Stimulated by the early works of the Institute of Egypt, which Bonaparte had founded during his campaign in Egypt in 1798, and with such distinguished figures as Berthollet and Saint-Hilaire marking this period of enlightenment, the Nahda was marked by the complete transformation of Egypt.

The seeds of knowledge, information, culture, and liberty of expression that were carried by the horsemen of Ibrahim Pasha into Beirut in 1830 found a fertile terrain for germination, and print shops, newspapers, and theaters blossomed. The American foreign mission relocated its printing presses from Malta to Beirut as early as 1836, the Greek Orthodox Church installed theirs in 1842, and the French Jesuits started their Imprimerie Catholique in 1847. Under the guidance of learned men such as Boutros Bustani and Nassif Yazigi, as well as missionaries such as Cornelius Van Dyck, who befriended Bustani during their time together at the SPC, the Arabic language found its way to publication, first with religious literature and later with cultural and political writing. *Hadiqat al-Akhbar* (Garden of Information) was the first daily paper to print in Beirut in 1858 and was followed by others in a prolific tradition of information that continues to our day.

Drama had its own advocate in the person of Maroun Naccache, who presented classic plays beginning in 1848 in his home until he was approved by the Ottoman authorities to start a theater in Beirut five years later. The theater survived many wars and continued hosting experimental works until recent years, when it fell into the grasp of a property promoter who dressed it up for commercial use. Masters of the art of dissimulation under coercive administrations, and in the eloquent suggestion of certain truths with half-words, the sons of the Nahda were reproved on many occasions and sometimes lost their heads; in 1916, that was the fate of fourteen of them who sealed with their blood the closure of four hundred years of Ottoman rule.

On the eve of World War I, Beirut was a radiant city, Arabic and Mediterranean in character, conservative and liberal at the same time, paradoxical yet harmonious, much as China today fosters a socialist order amid a vibrant and liberal economy. Lebanon was the land where everything seemed possible, where companies could complete a million tasks, where laws were accommodating and impartiality a notion that did not lack elasticity. That was the legacy of four centuries of Ottoman rule, a lesson of survival, of sleeping with the devil, of forgetfulness, and of starting all over again. This lesson would prove to be invaluable in the years to come, as more chapters in the making of Lebanon unfolded, first pleasing, then bitter.

The new imperialisms

After 1860, the British showed less favor to the Druze, their former protégés. The death toll across Mount Lebanon had been too high and the recent crimes perpetrated by the Druze seemed unforgivable, and the fact that the Maronites retaliated against the Druze did not make the situation less condemnable. As their new protégés, the British settled on the Jews, if only because all the other religious groups were already in association with one of the European nations. The Jewish community was much smaller than the Druze, but it had been in Mount Lebanon long enough, an industrious people, known for their skill in craftwork, trade, and finance.

Jews had always lived in Deir al-Qamar and maintained good relations with the amirs, Bashir using their services on more than one occasion. During the 1860 war, they did not take sides and were therefore less affected by the skirmishes that took place. What is more, they were systematically left out of the carnage that was perpetrated in Damascus against the Christians, although they had as much wealth as the Christians to arouse the envy of the Muslim perpetrators. They went unharmed because they were less ostentatious than the Christians, who defied the social code of four centuries as soon as the Hatti Hamayun gave them a semblance of equal rights. They consumed alcohol openly, for example, and displayed the wealth they were earning from trading with the Europeans, a trend the Muslims held as unlawful and that, they felt, perhaps more spitefully, denied them access to the same wealth.

The Jews did no less than the Christians to earn good returns and sold to the French, British, and whomever bought from them. But they did not show their wealth, lived in the same houses they always had, wore the same clothes, and refrained from indulging in anything associated with the new bourgeois class. They had the good instinct to downplay their wealth and not provoke the Muslims. Although they themselves escaped the 1860 carnage of Damascus, records show that many Jewish people lent a helping hand to their Christian neighbors during the massacres.

After the mutasarifiya came into existence, the British developed their relationship with the Jewish community in Mount Lebanon and in Palestine. Intimations of the Eretz Israel were already in the air, the Jewish homeland in Palestine, and neither the British nor, for that matter, the Ottomans saw this as a bad thing. The former needed stability across the Suez Canal and the Red Sea, now that the passage provided a link to their Indian and Asian dominions in barely half the time. The Ottomans for their part still remembered the show of force that Ibrahim Pasha brought to their doorsteps in Istanbul in 1839 and thought a new buffer nation might keep the Egyptians away in the future.

The bonding between the British and the Jewish people of Mount Lebanon forged in 1860 developed consistently over the next decades. Theodor Herzl, an Austro-Hungarian writer and political thinker, spearheaded a congress in 1897 in Basel, Switzerland, which drew particularly important conclusions. A Zionist organization was founded whose objectives were to establish a homeland for the Jewish people and to create a federation of Jews across all nations, promoting a permanent settlement in Palestine. At this time, the population of Palestine was mainly Arab, the Jewish community accounting for only seven percent of the total.

In later years, the unfolding of the resolution taken by this first Zionist congress was to prove lethal to the indigenous people of Palestine, whose plight would be to live in camps, as many as half a million in camps in modern-day Lebanon alone, and never be allowed back to their homes. The radicalization of the Palestinian movement in the twentieth century and the use of force spread from the camps and engulfed Lebanon in a long and particularly devastating war.

In the second half of the nineteenth century, the map of Europe was redrawn, almost beyond recognition. The Prussians entered into a large federation with a mosaic of principalities and duchies, which it governed with "blood and iron," to quote Chancellor Otto von Bismarck, who played an important role in the birth of Germany. France was defeated and humiliated, the Prussian victor choosing to crown himself kaiser of Germany at the Hall of Mirrors in Versailles, the chateau of Louis XIV, whose majesty and greatness had never been so despoiled. And of spoliation, the Prussians had done much, not least the annexation of Alsace and Lorraine on the eastern flank of France and the arrest of Napoleon III and his detention in Westphalia, at a chateau where his uncle, the brother of Bonaparte, once sat as king.

Thus the seeds for a coming war were planted, and it was only a question of time before the French came back for revenge. In the meantime, thanks to the industrial revolution, the factories of Krupp, Mauser, and Schneider were mass-producing the weapons that would soon be used in a war of a different magnitude. Kaiser Wilhelm II developed his navy as quickly as possible, hoping to match the British at sea, and setting off an arms race that saw all European states stocking their armories. Italy had her Risorgimento and the new federation was brought to life by a mastermind worthy of his position as prime minister, the Count of Cavour, who also made it possible for Victor Emmanuel of Piedmont to sit as king of Italy. The Papal States were reduced to the size of the Vatican City, and the authority of the Pope was curtailed to the spiritual alone. The Austro-Hungarian Empire was waging its own wars, annexing the kingdoms of Bosnia and Herzegovina in 1878, which had been part of the Ottoman Empire. The tsar of Russia took a very dim view of this affront, perpetrated in his own backyard by Emperor Franz Joseph, and stepped up the tone of his own warmongering. At the turn of the twentieth century, war seemed imminent, and the European leaders seemed almost eager for it to begin.

Such was the mood on the street in June 1902, when Alfred Nicola prepared to leave Hadath. He was barely seventeen years of age. The sight of his father, sitting inert and expressionless, a recluse in his sadness, was hard to accept. Alfred pledged to turn the situation around and win his father back, the jovial and indefatigable entrepreneur who walked for hours through the souks of Beirut and who was impatiently awaited by his faithful customers across Hadath, Baabda, and the entire Jurd.

Like so many others, each with a story to tell, Alfred Nicola became another immigrant from Mount Lebanon. Leaving a land where successive civilizations had risen and fallen since the dawn of time, leaving the crossroads of the three early continents, the immigrants sailed to a faraway continent where a new nation was in need of their industrious hands and their tenacious talents, a land where the future mattered more than the past, and where history was too young to count. There, to America, they marched.

1. The land where the Moujaes families settled for many centuries after migrating northbound from Yemen, at the intersection of modern-day Syria, Jordan, and Israel. In this picture taken from Umm al Qays in Jordan the Sea of Galilee is visible to the west. Further north are the highlands of Jebel Amel and Mount Hermon, and to the east, the Golan.

2. The steep Mount Lebanon chain of mountains with its rough terrain. Crisscrossed since the dawn of time, it became home to Arab tribes and dissenting communities from Egypt and Syria. View from Dimane, the summer residence of the Maronite Patriarch.

3. Across from the cedars reserve of Tannourine is a rugged mountain landscape.

4. The early settlers practiced terrace agriculture and tamed the harsh landscape. View over Douma, another village that was built by stonemasons from Shwayr.

5. The power center of Fakhreddine, who reigned from 1598 to 1635, Deir al-Qamar is an architectural gem. Among the builders were Moujaes stonemasons. Deir al-Qamar has been at the epicenter of all religious conflicts in Lebanon, and hence most of its civil wars.

6. Late afternoon sunlight over the picturesque red-roofed Deir al-Qamar. *Center*, the grand mountain of the Barouk and its large reserve of cedars wear the January snows. Facing Deir al-Qamar, the Palace of Beiteddine stands as a relic and depicts the greatness of Amir Bashir, who reigned from 1792 to 1840.

7. At one of the spacious courts inside the Palace of Beiteddine, which Amir Bashir Shihab the Great built in pomp and magnificence and where Fares Bozeid Moujaes came to work in 1804.

8. Playing in Shwayr, in view of the convent of Saint Elias, is a tradition that has passed down through the generations.

9. The large residence of Haidar Shihab in Baabda was turned into the power center of the mutasarifiya in 1869. It is today the seat of the governorate of Mount Lebanon.

10. An Ottoman banknote of one lira from the late period of the empire. I found it among the possessions of Alfred Nicola that were kept by my father.

11. No less than a third of Syrian emigrants that went to America were women, 1892. (Courtesy of the Smithsonian Archives, Alixa Naff Collection.)

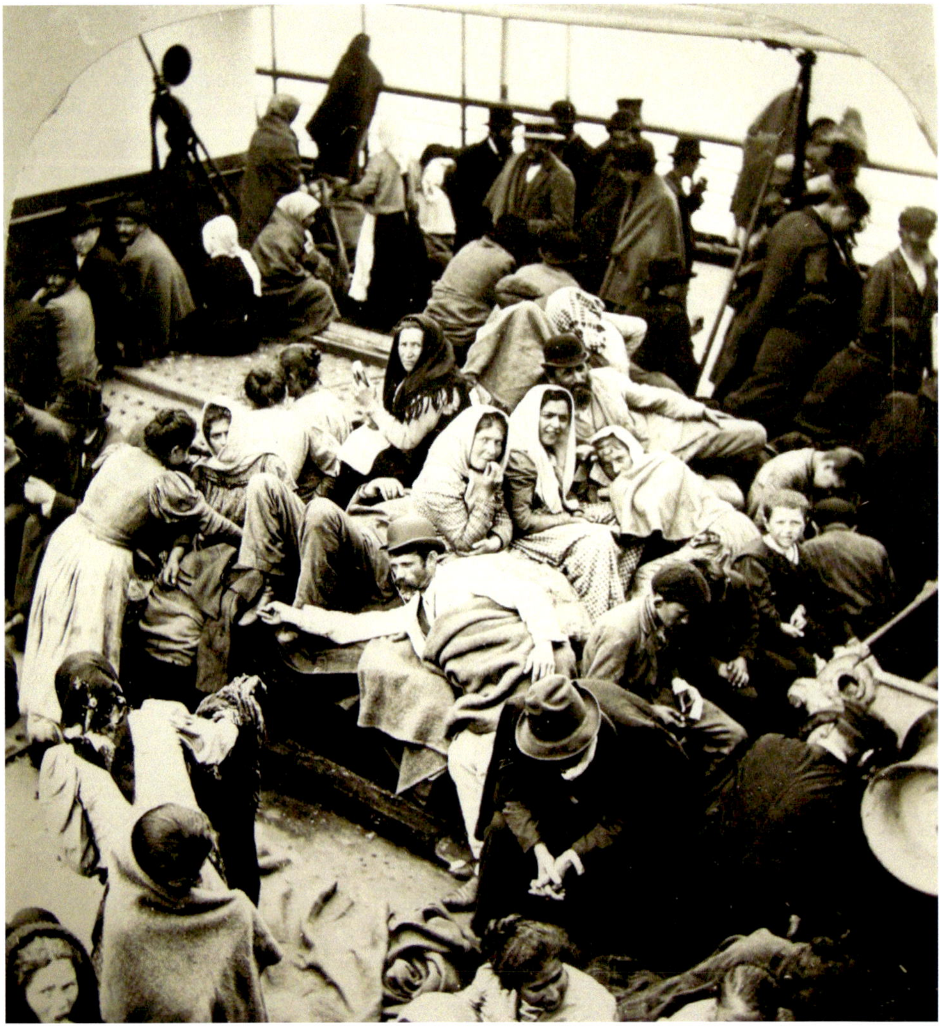

12. Steerage on a vessel bound for Ellis Island in 1902, the year that Alfred Nicola immigrated to the United States. (Courtesy of the Smithsonian Archives, Alixa Naff Collection.)

13. The Great Hall at Ellis Island in the early twentieth century. (Courtesy of the Smithsonian Archives, Alixa Naff Collection.)

14. The Bourbon Street house where Alfred Nicola first resided and where he began peddling in New Orleans. Alfred's aunt Ann Murray and her two sons, Habib and Alexander Joseph, also made this their home, in a simple room in the rear. The apartment is still there, now home to the in-laws of the well-to-do Creole owner.

15. A typical Syrian peddler. (Courtesy of the Smithsonian Archives, Alixa Naff Collection.)

16. The shotgun house where the Nicola and Joseph families lived in Lockport.

17. A typical peddler on his wagon. As his business grew, Alfred Nicola, like his cousins before him, bought a horse (which he named Mac, short for macaque) and a wagon, which he rode for peddling. (Courtesy of the Smithsonian Archives, Alixa Naff Collection.)

18. Helena, Alfred Nicola's mother.

19. Alfred Nicola in Louisiana, a successful young man proudly wearing a solid gold watch on a gold chain in his jacket pocket.

20. Alfred Nicola (*middle*) and his brothers in Louisiana in 1921, a short time before he returned to Hadath. Alexander, on his *right*, sailed back home with him, while George stayed behind and continued working Alfred's peddling routes until 1955.

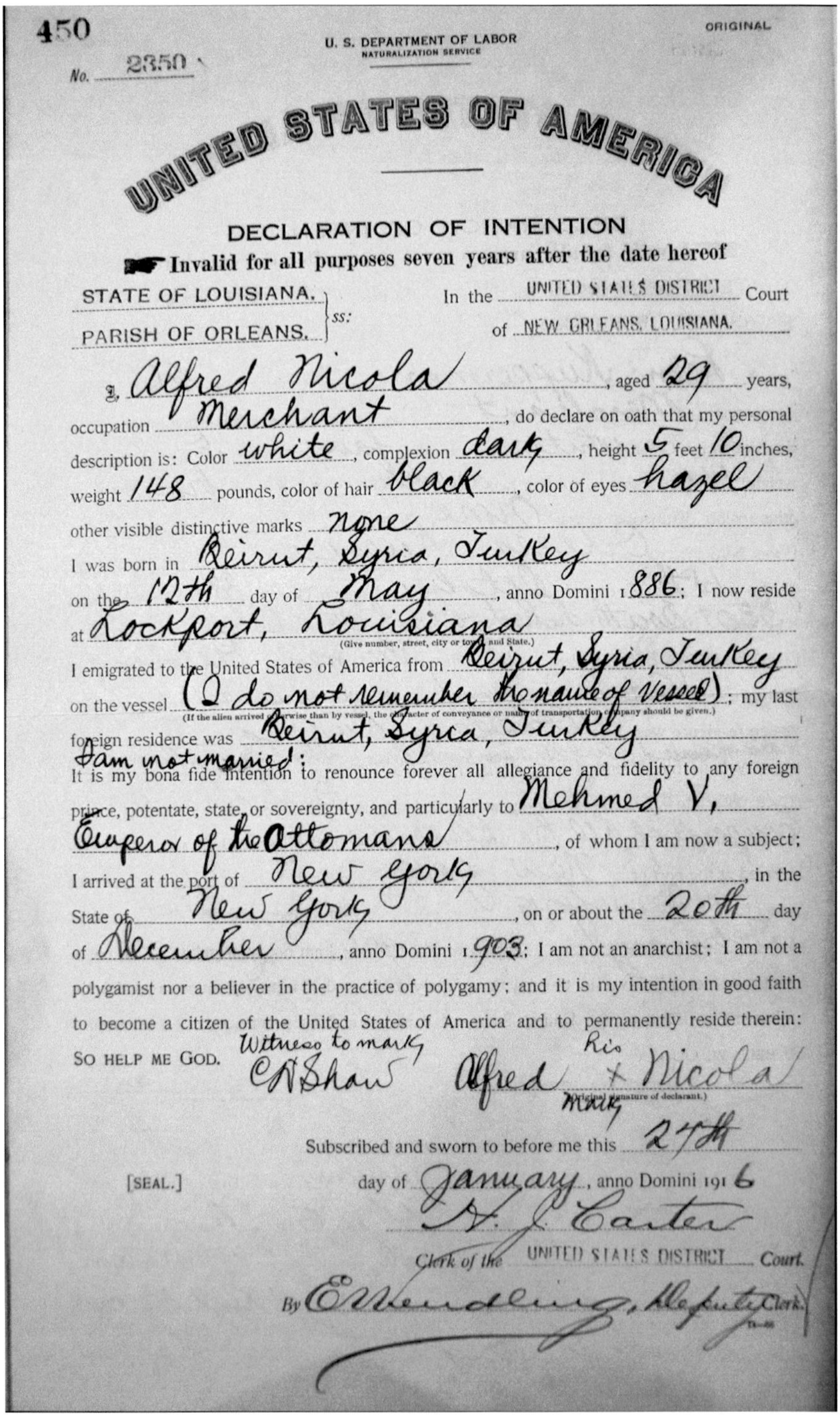

450 ORIGINAL

No. 2350

U. S. DEPARTMENT OF LABOR
NATURALIZATION SERVICE

UNITED STATES OF AMERICA

DECLARATION OF INTENTION

Invalid for all purposes seven years after the date hereof

STATE OF LOUISIANA, } ss: In the UNITED STATES DISTRICT Court
PARISH OF ORLEANS. } of NEW ORLEANS, LOUISIANA.

I, Alfred Nicola, aged 29 years, occupation Merchant, do declare on oath that my personal description is: Color white, complexion dark, height 5 feet 10 inches, weight 148 pounds, color of hair black, color of eyes hazel other visible distinctive marks none
I was born in Beirut, Syria, Turkey on the 12th day of May, anno Domini 1886; I now reside at Lockport, Louisiana (Give number, street, city or town, and State.)
I emigrated to the United States of America from Beirut, Syria, Turkey on the vessel (I do not remember the name of vessel); my last (If the alien arrived otherwise than by vessel, the character of conveyance or name of transportation company should be given.) foreign residence was Beirut, Syria, Turkey
I am not married;
It is my bona fide intention to renounce forever all allegiance and fidelity to any foreign prince, potentate, state, or sovereignty, and particularly to Mehmed V, Emperor of the Ottomans, of whom I am now a subject; I arrived at the port of New York, in the State of New York, on or about the 20th day of December, anno Domini 1903; I am not an anarchist; I am not a polygamist nor a believer in the practice of polygamy; and it is my intention in good faith to become a citizen of the United States of America and to permanently reside therein: So help me God.

Witness to mark
C A Shaw

Alfred his x mark Nicola
(Original signature of declarant.)

Subscribed and sworn to before me this 27th day of January, anno Domini 1916

[SEAL.]

H. J. Carter
Clerk of the UNITED STATES DISTRICT Court.
By E Wendling, Deputy Clerk.

21. The declaration of intention toward naturalization in January 1916. Alfred signed it with an X, witnessed by the clerk H. J. Carter, who noted "his mark" and added his full name. Alfred gave his approximate date of arrival as a year and a half later than the actual date and could not remember the name of the vessel that transported him.

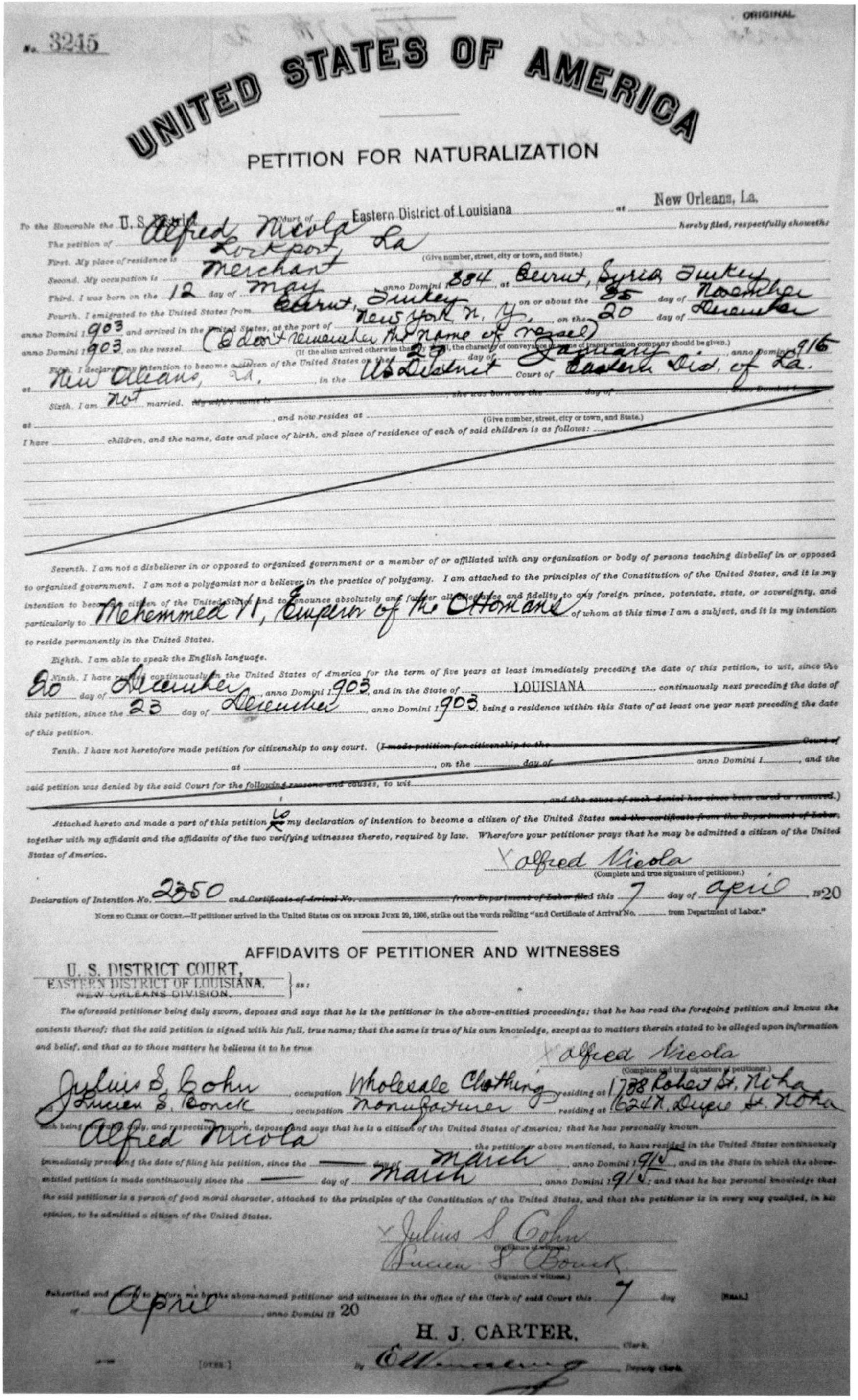

22. For his petition for naturalization four years later, Alfred, by then a literate and well-to-do young man, signed his name in full in front of the same clerk. The witnesses were his business friends Lucien Bonck and Julius Cohn.

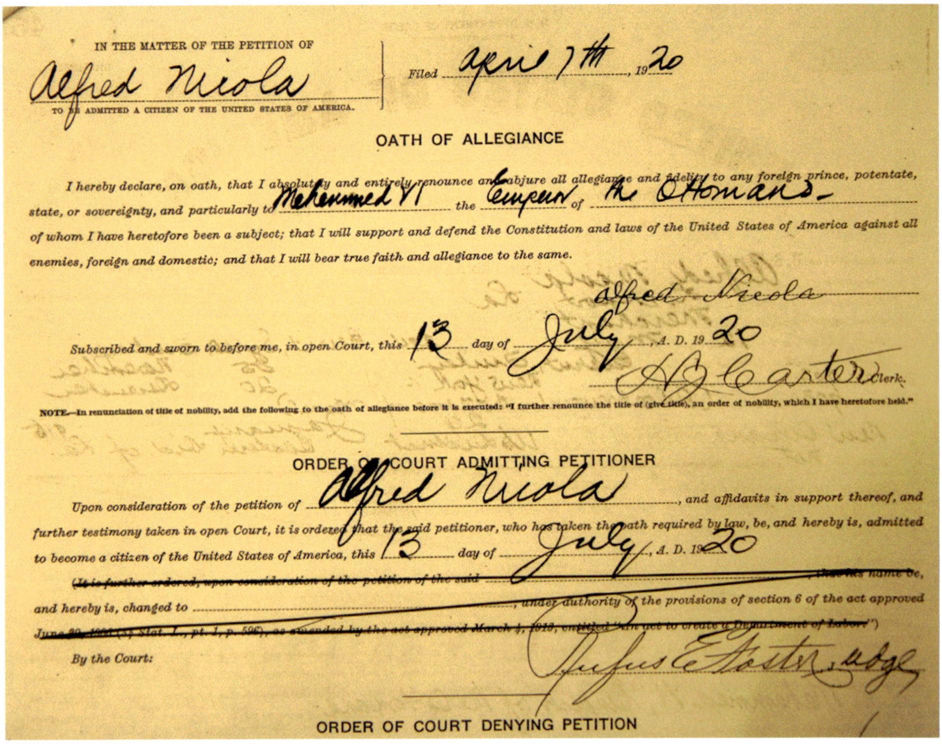

IN THE MATTER OF THE PETITION OF

Alfred Nicola

TO BE ADMITTED A CITIZEN OF THE UNITED STATES OF AMERICA.

Filed April 7th, 1920

OATH OF ALLEGIANCE

I hereby declare, on oath, that I absolutely and entirely renounce and abjure all allegiance and fidelity to any foreign prince, potentate, state, or sovereignty, and particularly to Mehemmed VI *the* Emperor *of* the Ottomans *of whom I have heretofore been a subject; that I will support and defend the Constitution and laws of the United States of America against all enemies, foreign and domestic; and that I will bear true faith and allegiance to the same.*

Alfred Nicola

Subscribed and sworn to before me, in open Court, this 13 *day of* July*, A. D. 19*20

H. B. Carter, *Clerk.*

NOTE.—In renunciation of title of nobility, add the following to the oath of allegiance before it is executed: "I further renounce the title of (give title), an order of nobility, which I have heretofore held."

ORDER OF COURT ADMITTING PETITIONER

Upon consideration of the petition of Alfred Nicola*, and affidavits in support thereof, and further testimony taken in open Court, it is ordered that the said petitioner, who has taken the oath required by law, be, and hereby is, admitted to become a citizen of the United States of America, this* 13 *day of* July*, A. D. 19*20

~~(It is further ordered, upon consideration of the petition of the said ... that his name be, and hereby is, changed to ..., under authority of the provisions of section 6 of the act approved June 29, 1906 (34 Stat. L., pt. 1, p. 596), as amended by the act approved March 4, 1913, entitled "An act to create a Department of Labor.")~~

By the Court:

Rufus E. Foster, Judge

ORDER OF COURT DENYING PETITION

23. The same clerk admits Alfred Nicola to become a citizen of the United States on July 13, 1920.

24. Aerial view of Bayou Lafourche. The only way to go is "up the bayou, down the bayou, or across the bayou." Alfred Nicola walked the towpaths on either side and sold the contents of his valise to the eager families who made a living from fishing.

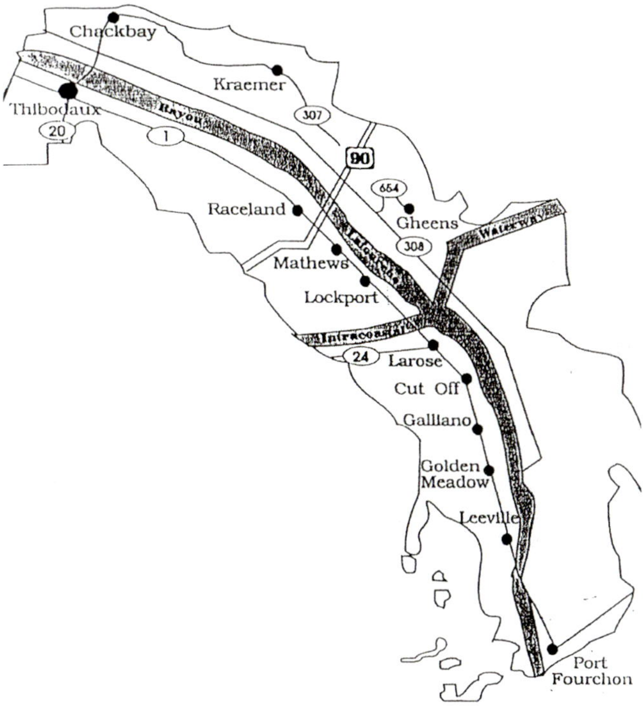

25. Lockport proved to be a strategic location, at the junction of navigable routes, then important economic arteries.

26. Beyond New Orleans and across the Mississippi in the days before the Crescent City Connection was built, Alfred Nicola crossed by ferry to Gretna and Algiers to do business.

27. In Leeville, in the southernmost part of Louisiana, Alfred Nicola was fondly remembered, mostly by the shrimp fishermen, to whom he sold work clothes.

28. Walking along the Gulf of Mexico before the days of weather forecasts was certainly hazardous for peddlers like Alfred.

29. In Lockport with my great-cousins, Fred Joseph Jr. (*fourth from left*) and Al Joseph (*first on right*), and their families. Al was named after Alfred Nicola. Also in the picture: Rosemary Ortlieb (*first from left*), Global Fellow for Lebanon at SUNY and my partner in researching this book, and Brent Joseph (*second from left*), Fred's son and a successful filmmaker.

30. In Lockport with (*from left to right*) Jay, Mary, Gail, and Becky Joseph, grandchildren of Habib and Zahia Joseph.

31. The grave of Habib and Zahia Joseph in Lockport. We ended up jumping the fence of the cemetery, understandably an offense, but one that may be excused given the honorable intentions of this Lebanese from Hadath who came to pay his respects to his great-aunt so far away from home.

32. With Fred Joseph Jr. and Glen Pitre, a producer and director who captured the Cajun culture in celebrated films.

33. When the Constitution was drafted in 1926 and Lebanon was recognized as a republic, the appellation given by the French in 1920—*Grand Liban*—fell out of usage. Here, it was simply crossed out from stamps and substituted with "République libanaise."

Part II

Alfred in Louisiana

4

From Lebanon to Louisiana

Ellis Island

The Statue of Liberty had been standing on her pedestal for sixteen years when Alfred Nicola first laid eyes on her. She must have seemed sturdy, cold, and certainly haughty to the impressionable seventeen-year-old beardless boy who had been at sea for a month and a half. Sleeping in steerage in the creaking hulls of vessels, squeezed and pushed by the overwhelming crush of travelers, all immigrants like him, he must have felt tired, vulnerable, and perhaps a bit scared.

His journey started at the port of Beirut, where seaport agents and middlemen had some control over passengers. In previous times, when the Sublime Porte oversaw emigration, a whole class of smugglers and human traffickers had emerged, shameless profiteers who knew how to circumvent the regulations. Typically, they bribed port officials and used fishing boats to transport clandestine passengers to steamboats at discreet collection points along the coast. Sometimes their boats were intercepted by the Turks, and the hapless emigrants were dragged back to shore and thrown in jail. At others times, when money was short, many would-be travelers ended up in Cyprus or Port Said, penniless and lost. Passengers renegotiated over and over again their fees, what was to be paid to the traffickers, what was to be paid to the crew on the vessel, and often ended up paying manyfold what they had originally agreed upon. Many migrants saw their destinations changed because they had been swindled of so much of their money or simply because unexpected events dictated they sail a different route.

Most of these abuses ended after 1898, when Sultan Abdul Hamid II was forced by circumstances to open up to the Europeans and ease up on his own nationals' ability to immigrate. Travel documents were given to whomever wanted to travel, notwithstanding the occasional hassle from greedy bureaucrats. The cost of the *tezkere*, the identification document, was set at fifty piasters. Still, despite this radical change, the agents and middlemen at the port remained active and were still there a few years later when the Turks ceded Beirut to the French.

Alfred Nicola had his papers in order, but he was still forced to pay a few piasters for the *nawlun*, a bribe that became normalized over time, paid on top of the harbor fees. Deeply hidden in the lining of his vest, he kept the twenty-dollar bill he knew he had to show to the immigration clerks when entering New York. That was one of the conditions imposed on immigrants to the United States; the assurance of enough personal capital to see oneself through the first weeks after arrival, pending the search for gainful employment.

I suspect his mother Helena had sewed the bill into his vest herself and given him clear instructions on how to retrieve the money upon arrival. He only needed to pull a certain thread and the lining would yield the treasure while his vest remained intact. The watery eyes of the dexterous and loving Helena while at work must have weighed on the mind of Alfred. He took extra care to hide away the other money he had procured for the travels, buying different currencies from one of the *sarrafs* who swarmed the harbor. There were French francs to use on the French liners taking him from Beirut to Marseille and later from Le Havre to New York. Francs also paid whatever expenses he incurred traveling inland from Marseille to Le Havre. He also had American dollars to spend once he arrived in the United States, and Ottoman coins, of course, low-value piasters and paras, to use at the port in case of an unexpected expense. And unexpected expenses there would be! In total, he must have had the equivalent of thirty-five dollars, a small fortune for the time, an amount he had earned through weeks of hard labor and privations. He did not want to take money from his father, what little money his father had left from the mortgage of the house, and he knew that if his enterprise were unsuccessful, if America failed him, he would have wasted an opportunity for his family to still earn a living here with his hard-working hands.

But the money in his vest and pockets was only part of what his journey had cost. Alfred bought his tickets to France and on to America from a shipping agency in Beirut. Many companies at that time offered this service, ever since travel picked up with the softening of regulations by the Sublime Porte and the refurbishment of the port by the French in 1894. Agents rented offices near *Bab Dabbagha*, across from the harbor, and sold tickets to practically every destination on the Mediterranean, wherever commercial liners had regular routes, and also tickets to the Americas. The agents provided precise schedules, had correspondents in major cities, and sometimes booked train tickets and hotel rooms. Every agent had a correspondent in Marseille to help voyagers with the next stages of their journeys, Marseille having developed into a major hub for travels and exports ever since engaging in the silk trade with Beirut.

Alfred Nicola bought his tickets from the Pharaon Agency, one of the reputable travel companies of the time. He bought tickets for the two liners but decided not to buy train tickets or book hotel rooms. The agents offered high-end hotels, which were not for the likes of Alfred, an immigrant forced to exile himself to earn money. As for the train tickets, he pondered whether it would be cheaper to buy the tickets in Marseille, or even travel overland by some different means, if it meant saving money. Alfred paid $12.50 for his tickets for the liners.

Marseille harbor was a bustling hive. Through nowhere else across all the Mediterranean countries did so many people and so much merchandise pass. Alfred Nicola made his way through customs on April 13, 1902, admitted on the evidence of his intention to travel on to America. He took a coach from the harbor to St. Charles train station, traveled on the PLM (Paris-Lyon-Marseille) train to Paris, a journey of no fewer than twelve hours in those days. Once in Paris, he took the one-year-old Metro to the Gare du Nord to catch a train to Le Havre.

Having time to kill, his train to Le Havre departing hours after his arrival to Paris, Alfred stretched his legs, walking around the city of lights at the height of its *belle époque*. Which sites did he visit? Did he explore the area around the Gare de Lyon, where he disembarked from his first train? He might have walked the Rue de Lyon and seen the Colonne de Juillet at the Place de la Bastille, a monument to the memory of the 1830 revolution that brought Louis Philippe to the kingship "of the French" (as opposed to kingship "of France," marking a modest move toward constitutional monarchy). Did Alfred stay overnight in Paris? The area around the Gare du Nord abounded with cheap lodgings, many owned by the train companies themselves and advertised inside their compartments. However he spent his time, he eventually made the five-hour trip to Le Havre on a train run by the Compagnie des chemins de fer du Nord. Once in Le Havre, and after a night or two at another travel lodge, Alfred boarded the *Lorraine* on April 16, 1902, en route to New York.

Once aboard, Alfred heard people talk of America. He heard the good and the bad, stories of people who struck it rich and of others who returned home penniless. He heard a story about two industrious Syrian brothers who had made four hundred thousand dollars that year selling gloves in Gloversville, New York. It was enough to give any fortune-seeker shivers down the spine, let alone a seventeen-year-old charged with the overwhelming responsibility of saving his father's home and sustaining a family. Alfred was on the *Lorraine* for three weeks, three long weeks, a floating community of strangers who came from all around the world, united in their mission of starting a new life.

No picture could better depict life in steerage class aboard these vessels than a 1902 photograph I saw in the Alixa Naff collection, when Rosemary Ortlieb and I did research at the Smithsonian Archives in Washington, DC. I include this picture for the strength of its impact and because it was taken the same year Alfred Nicola sailed to New York (see plate 12 in the first gallery). The odds that this picture was taken aboard the same vessel that carried Alfred to Ellis Island are not very high; however, I would not be totally surprised if one of the youngsters with their backs to the camera turned out to be him. In a way, I view all of them as Alfred Nicola.

Alfred also heard many Arabic-speaking passengers talk of Little Syria on the Lower West Side of Manhattan in New York. Many were going there to learn more about America and make use of any help they could get from their better-established compatriots. The talk of Syria stirred vivid emotions of home, of his mother, whom he worshipped, and of his siblings, for "Syria" at that time was the generic term given to the entire crescent-shaped area that extends from the eastern edge of the Sinai to the mouth of the Tigris on the shores of Iraq toward the Persian Sea. It is bounded by four rivers—the Tigris, the Euphrates, the Litani, and the Jordan—giving this part of the Middle East the appellation "the Fertile Crescent." In short, Syria included modern-day Lebanon, Syria, Iraq, Jordan, and Israel/Palestine. These countries did not exist then, and all the nationals of this area were referred to as Syrians. They were also called the Turks before 1899, *Turcos* in Latin America, because they came from the countries of the Ottoman Empire. A joke from these days tells the story of a Syrian in New York spending the night before Thanksgiving Day running for his life after hearing the farmer who employed him tell his daughter that he planned to kill a turkey!

Alfred always referred to his hometown as Hadath in Mount Lebanon in Syria, a region of the Ottoman Empire. He would not know it any other way. Was not today's American University of Beirut known back then as the Syrian Protestant College? Lebanon was not an entity yet, no more than Jordan, Iraq, Syria, or Israel/Palestine were.

The *Lorraine* docked at Ellis Island on May 7, 1902. Passengers rushed to line up by the gangways, but although the vessel was moored, there was no sign of anyone disembarking, and the excited passengers broke the lines and went back to their corners waiting for a signal. The signal came a day later. The immigration authorities were overwhelmed with new arrivals, and the processing of the *Lorraine* was deferred to the following day. Alfred spent his first night in America on the deck of a French vessel, docked at Ellis Island. He sat among the crowds, the odors of the sea mixing with those of sweat and dirty children, speechlessly conversing with Lady Liberty, whom he could see through the glow of the stars. She seemed stoic, imperturbable in her might, superior in her posture, regal in her style.

Above all, she seemed so silent.

The next day, Alfred Nicola was led into the immigration hall, a large square space paved with brick-colored stone, having a high ceiling and a continuous wooden balcony on all sides. Two large flags hung at an angle from the main walls, giving the large crowds—some sitting on wooden benches, others standing in lines in front of the immigration clerks—their first lesson in the country of the stars and stripes. Alfred pulled the thread on his vest lining and took out the twenty-dollar bill. He clung to it fervently, hiding it in the inside pocket of his jacket. By now, his total funds had dropped to under twenty-five dollars.

When Alfred's turn came, he stood facing an immigration clerk who sat at a high desk and looked down at him. Alfred was a tall young man, but the clerk sat so high up that he was forced to look up at the man at the desk, who was scribbling notes in haste in a large accounting-style ledger. Alfred could not speak English but could answer simple questions, such as "Name?" and "Origin?" probably because he had had time to rehearse them aboard the *Lorraine*, taking advantage of any help he could get from talkative travelers. This is when the real name of Habib Shwayri got lost, for when questioned about the name of his father, Alfred said "Nicola," stressing the *o*, anglicizing in his own fashion the Arabic pronunciation of Nicolas. For whatever reason, the clerk retained this name as the new arrival's identity.

As for the first name, Ellis Island saw new ones every day, often chosen from among the names of a clerk's relatives or the clerk himself. Perhaps on May 7, 1902, all new immigrants who faced this same high-seated clerk were to be called Alfred! Newly named, Alfred was admitted to the country, but he still had to go through medical exams similar to the one in Francis Ford Coppola's classic *The Godfather, Part II*, in which the Corleone child is placed in quarantine in a cell at Ellis Island. Luckily, Alfred, after a painstaking physical examination, was assessed to be in good health.

Free to go, he took the ferry, a free shuttle courtesy of Ellis Island, to lower Manhattan. On the way, he saw the skyline bursting with high buildings and the Brooklyn Bridge to his right.

Some say life begins at seventeen.

A forerunner Moujaes: Ann Murray

Amin Merhi Moujaes, a native of Shwayr, traveled to New Orleans with the first flow of immigrants from Mount Lebanon, when economic conditions there had become intolerable. In 1870, disease ravaged the silkworms and mulberry trees, leaving cultivators with no options. And since misfortunes never come one at a time, the demand for silk also fell abruptly. The main buyer, France, had been defeated by the Prussians at Sedan in 1871, a situation that brought business in Marseille and Lyon to a standstill. At the same time, competition in the silk industry was growing fierce: with the opening of the Suez Canal in 1869, a ship could travel from

London to Bombay in half the time. Imports of silks from the Far East rose sharply, while production in Mount Lebanon plummeted. Extremely low prices forced many cultivators out of business; of these, many had borrowed from moneylenders and now simply could not repay their loans. Amin was one of them.

So Amin crossed the Atlantic in 1876, probably disembarking at New Orleans directly. Sailing to New Orleans was easy and Syrian hostels there welcomed immigrants as early as 1875. The Crescent City became a favorite point of entry for Arab immigrations. The port of New Orleans had become very active, and communications with the northern and western states were improving. Amin liked New Orleans and stayed. He changed his name to Amin Murray, trading his Lebanese Merhi for the Irish-sounding Murray, and became known to later generations as Uncle Murray.

Amin was one of many—too many—Syrians who were infected with immigration-to-America fever. The fever began when a rumor spread around Mount Lebanon at the same time as the economic upheaval caused by the collapsing silk market. According to the rumor, the "king of Amirka" was giving land away for free. The rumor was immediately accepted as fact and emigration soared. In fact, the popular rumor was based on Abraham Lincoln's Homestead Act of 1862, a few years delayed, but still in time to offer an alternative to Amin and his like.

Amin's sister, Spa'iah Merhi Moujaes, was next to emigrate. She was the second wife of Youssef Shwayri, whom we met in part 1, the son of our stonemason, Fares Bozeid Moujaes. When Youssef passed away, Spa'iah gathered her two sons and followed in the footsteps of her brother Amin. She was in her forties then, having been born around 1855.

By the time his sister arrived, Uncle Murray had established himself in Gulfport and owned a house in the French Quarter of New Orleans. He had started as a peddler and then opened a shop, a classic sequence for the Syrians of that era. Spa'iah passed through Ellis Island in 1892, changing her name to Ann Murray, a name more suited for the life she was about to lead in America. She went peddling in New Orleans, living in the French Quarter at 916 Bourbon Street with her sons, who became peddlers too. I visited the house where they lived in the company of Fred Joseph Jr., my cousin and the great-grandson of Ann Murray. The house is still there, but attached to a larger estate next door and converted into the dwelling for the wealthy Creole owner's in-laws. It is graced with a swimming pool, concealed in the angle of a sumptuous inside courtyard that sits under a New Orleans–style balcony.

Ann Murray was a strong woman, that's clear, but was she unique? The sturdiness of Syrian women and their propensity to work would have been no surprise. In the heyday of the silk industry in Mount Lebanon, it was women who worked in the mills, at the *ker-khanat*, and when the industry slowed, they were first to lose their jobs. Used to hard labor, to thirteen-hour workdays at the mills, to the suffocating heat of the khanat, and to the nauseating odors of the dead chrysalides and gluey cocoons, peddling in America may have seemed, if not a walk in the park, at least less demanding than the work they were used to, and probably a little more rewarding. In fact, no fewer than a third of the Syrian emigrants who came to America were women. One illustrious example is the mother of Khalil Gibran, famed author of *The Prophet*, a prophet in his own right as well as a philosopher and a painter. Kamila, his mother, left her alcoholic, bullying husband and took her children to Boston, reaching Ellis Island in 1893. I marvel at the serigraphy print from 1892 (see plate 11 in the first gallery), which expresses the tenacity of these strong-willed women.

In previous decades, many people had emigrated from Mount Lebanon to Egypt, where exciting opportunities beckoned. But the rebellion led by Ahmed Urabi in Egypt in 1879 that culminated in the British occupation in 1882 closed Egypt to Syrians, and America presented itself as a replacement destination. This presaged a large flow of Syrians to America, a movement that saw no less than one-third of the population of Mount Lebanon leave for the Americas (some historians say one-half). By 1900, Syrian immigrants were sending home around one million dollars every year. According to Philip Hitti, by 1924 Syrians in the United States of America numbered around two hundred thousand, eighty percent of whom were from Mount Lebanon.

After setting foot in lower Manhattan, Alfred Nicola searched for the train station where he would embark for New Orleans. Having existed on smoked meats and eels for three weeks, he certainly needed a proper meal, preferably something from his own country. He saw a number of Syrian people being met at the docks, and he joined the multitude that was walking toward Little Syria. He was hungry. He was curious. And it was funny how religious divisions and tribal differences faded as soon as one left the scarred topography of Mount Lebanon. Now they were all Syrians from Mount Lebanon, and they meant to look after one another. Alfred walked with them to Washington Street beneath a skyline of buildings under construction that seemed to defy the law of gravity.

And there it was, Little Syria, the smells and sounds of home, a soothing anchor for all Syrians like him who had disembarked into the unknown, a remedy for homesickness and nostalgia. People in suits and others in charwals walked side by side, wearing Borsalinos and fez. "Queer Costumes" read the title of one piece about Little Syria in the *New York Daily Tribune* of October 2, 1892. For Syrians, modernity and tradition all too often proved difficult to combine, torn as they were between their conservative demeanor and the urge to conform to the larger group. Two restaurants, the Nile and Ibn El Sheikh, rather awkwardly named under the circumstances, offered traditional meals and Middle Eastern bread ("like Scotch scones," commented *Harper's Weekly* of August 3, 1895). Ice cream makers sat in their shops beating chilled cream with mortars and pestles. Water pipes added to the surreal ambiance, and backgammon players sat next to barbers giving hand and neck massages to their customers as part of the service.

By the time Alfred arrived in America, two major world fairs had taken place, one in Philadelphia in 1876 and another in Chicago in 1893. The Ottomans sent representatives to both, people from across the empire undoubtedly including a number of Syrians from Mount Lebanon. Americans were much taken by this eccentric breed "from Jerusalem," as they were sometimes said to be, a misconception that left the mercantile Syrians with no shortage of money-making ideas, immediately peddling rosaries, incense, and icons from the Church of the Nativity! Another fair would take place in 1904, in St. Louis, two years into Alfred's American life, advertised in the *Daily Picayune* on July 10, 1904, as "fun on the pike" and offering sightseers "a collection of types of various Nations from all parts of the world"; Arabs, Egyptians, and Turks came first on the list, before the Sinhalese, Eskimos, and Cliff Dwellers, and finally "Syrians Etc., Etc., Etc." But Little Syria was not just some oriental fantasy where American sightseers came in droves, intrigued by the stories they had heard or presentations they had seen at fairs. Washington Street was also the location of booming businesses, including a garment factory owned by a member of the family Traboulsi that produced no fewer than one-third of the sweatshirts worn in New York (which, admittedly, were not as popular then as they are now).

Syrians on Washington Street mingled their homes and businesses. In an October 2, 1892, article entitled "A Picturesque Colony," a *New York Tribune* reporter observed that they stored everything a peddler "can carry in his pack or find a market for in his wanderings." The ground or first floors were used for displays and where bargaining took place and business was done. Upper floors were where families lived and slept. The houses were generally very old and weather beaten, sometimes unhealthy to live in. Usually coming from a peasant background, Syrian immigrants were disinclined to work in industrial settings, and peddling became the trade of half these newcomers to America. The *qasheh*, or peddler's pack, became the symbol of Syrians in America.

A visit to the Tenement Museum on Orchard Street in New York City provides a sense of what an immigrant's home looked like in those days. The museum, for example, tells the striking story of Natalie, a woman who raised four children on her own after her husband deserted her. She supported her family working at a sewing machine she installed in her small one-bedroom apartment. The toilet, used by all tenants, was outside. The bathtub concealed under the kitchen table was used once weekly, and the one small bed that filled the bedroom slept all five of them. Natalie and her once-responsible husband had come from Germany, searching for a better life.

Washington Street was also home to the first Syrian bank, which opened in 1891, as well as the *Al-Hoda* newspaper, founded by Naoum Mokarzel, who originated the Arabic linotype machine in 1912 in the cellar of his home. Mokarzel was called "the guide" of Washington Street (*al-hoda* means "guide"), and he is said to have served the best *arak* (an anise-flavored alcoholic spirit) in America. Syrian immigrants were prolific writers of news and gossip from home. A number of papers were in circulation from early on. *Kawkab America* (The Star of America) was published by the sons of Dr. Joseph Arbeely, said to be the first native Syrian to come to New York; the *Syrian Review* had eminent writers, such as Philip Hitti and Khalil Gibran; *Al-Mohajer* (The Emigrant) published Gibran's first works—*Al-Musica* (Music), *Al-Ayam* (The Days), and many others. Some publications echoed the religious differences from home, *Miraat Al-Gharb* (The Mirror of the West) voiced Greek Orthodox opinions and was countered by Mokarzel's *Al-Hoda*, expressing the views of the Maronites. The most refreshing was *Al-Kalima* (The Word), which I discovered in the Alixa Naff collection at the Smithsonian, edited by the priest Raphael Hawawini, who brought news from home and included a twist of religiosity to keep readers' spirits from going astray.

Alfred asked for directions to the train station and was read the details from one of the newspapers lying around. It would be Grand Central Station in midtown, off Park Avenue. As he walked north, his small valise filled mostly with gifts from Hadath for his cousins in New Orleans, he realized he was beginning to like his new home.

South to New Orleans

At Grand Central Station in New York City, Alfred climbed aboard the Pennsylvania Railroad train bound for Washington, DC, planning to connect there with the *Vestibule* to New Orleans. His tickets cost him most of his remaining money, so he had to watch his expenses during the forty-hour journey. He passed Atlanta, then Montgomery, and made it to New Orleans two days later. In all, he had been on the road and away from home for nearly a month and a half. He had one spare shirt in his valise, which he changed into every other day, washing the soiled one with a bar of soap and whatever water he could find, hanging it to dry overnight while sleeping on the floor, his head on the valise. His bar of olive-soap was his connection with home, the scent of Hadath, land of mulberry and olive trees, the land of his fathers. He enjoyed the sensation it awoke in him—the warmth of home—and it reassured him in his venture.

Ann Murray's sons were great-cousins of Alfred. They were twelve and eleven years older than him. Alexander, the older brother, had married Alfred's sister Julia in 1895. It was customary then to marry one's niece, and the Shwayri were no exception. By the time Alfred reached Louisiana, Julia had borne two daughters and a son. They lived with Nicolas and Helena at their home in Hadath.

For Alexander, life in America was only for work; his real life was in Hadath, with his family. He traveled to America to make enough money to provide the standard of living he thought they deserved. Not so for Habib, the younger brother, who had different ideas. He had come to stay, and although he knew he would go back at some stage to marry a girl from home, he intended to make a life in America and had plans of his own.

From New Orleans Union Station, Alfred walked a few blocks to 916 Bourbon Street in the French Quarter, the address he had for his cousins. Ann Murray and her sons had already lived there for ten years and knew the area well. They spoke some French, the lingua franca in the French Quarter, a kind of French that has certain consonants rooted in the different cultures and origins of its peoples. Arriving in 1892, they started as peddlers-on-foot, buying their merchandise on credit from a large grocery store on Decatur Street owned by Kareem Abboud, a Lebanese immigrant. Very soon, they grew independent and each went a different route in the morning, meeting in the evening at home to tell stories of the day.

Eventually the brothers acquired a horse and wagon, purchasing fruit and vegetables at the St John's market each morning and selling the load along the way up to Jackson. Ann kept walking, often taking the streetcar to rural areas, where she sold her buttons, fabrics, and domestic knick-knacks.

The reunion was jovial. Alfred was officially in America and with his relatives. What a relief to reach the end of his odyssey and finally have the chance to put his hands to worthwhile work. He could not wait to start earning enough to save his family's home—the clock was ticking—and a month and a half of enforced idleness had been hard to bear. Worn-out though he was after all the traveling, he was ready to start right away. He had not slept in a bed for a long time, though, and the thought of a good night's sleep was tempting. He bathed behind a curtain in the kitchen, borrowed a shirt and pants from Habib, and sat at the table with his three relatives to share the first family meal he had had in quite some time.

After dinner, he gave Ann the soaps he had brought for them from Hadath, the olive oil he kept in a sealed bottle, and the dried jasmine from the garden of his father's house. Still at the table, he regaled them with tales of his fantastic voyage, his stopovers in Paris and New York, his visit to Washington Street, and the people he saw along the way. They talked of Ellis Island and his unexpected name change. The name "Alfred Nicola" prompted a few laughs and stirred memories of their own arrival in 1892, when Alexander and Habib exchanged *Shwayri* for *Joseph*, their deceased father's first name (Youssef). And although it was his first evening in the Crescent City, they also discussed his prospects for work. His occupation, of course, was a foregone conclusion: He would be a peddler and would accompany Ann for a few days to learn the business.

The next morning, Alfred Nicola borrowed an old belt from Habib and strapped it around his empty valise. He then took this improvised peddler's pack and threw it onto his back, holding the belt firmly with two hands, clutching the strap-end to his chest. Habib smiled and said in Arabic, "Nobody ever wore a pack like this. You'll be the first!" Alfred used what he had, the valise that he brought with him from Beirut, rather than spend whatever he had left to buy a pack. A valise and belt would have to do for now.

That morning he went out with Ann and they walked for the day. He followed her and shadowed her moves, heard the cries she shouted, her pleas for customers, which she chanted in perfect harmony and with varying pronunciations: "Achète de moi, lay-dee, linges et accessoires . . ." Long hours for little return, Alfred noted, yet Ann went on and on, laying her pack on the ground whenever a customer showed interest. She often pantomimed, for her French was very basic, and she often did well, selling the contents of her small pack to the passersby. Alfred trailed her the second day and the third, and then was ready to go alone.

On his first day alone, he packed the valise with an assortment of dry goods that he sensed could sell and took the streetcar on Canal Street with Ann, getting off at Napoleon Avenue, where they separated. From there, he walked down St. Charles Avenue southward, calling at every house on both sides of the street, until he reached the Mississippi River. He stopped at the beautiful mansions along the way only to have doors slammed in his face. For the sugar cane planters and other wealthy homeowners on the street would have no dealings with a peddler with a pack; they made their purchases at the elegant department stores of the time, D. H. Holmes, Godchaux, and Maison Blanche.

Farther south, Alfred managed his first sale at the Irish Channel, one of the roughest neighborhoods of New Orleans. It was settled first by the Irish, who fled the potato famine in the 1840s and then grew into a mixed community of Germans, Italians, and African Americans. There, on Tchoupitoulas Street, he sold an Irish-accented housewife a blouse for herself and socks and work shirts for her husband. That was his first sale in America, and it came after a whole day of rejections. As he walked away from that house to reunite with Ann for the streetcar journey home, he came away with a most important lesson: persistence.

Having no fixed workplace, Alfred did not need a license to peddle. And so he went, day in and day out, selling door-to-door, making customers, changing routes, developing his cries, looking for new opportunities. He learned quickly and had a flair for business, an asset that would serve him well in the coming years.

At this time, New Orleans was a much divided city. The Vieux Carré, or French Quarter, was largely inhabited by Creoles, now an appellation used for anyone with Latin ancestry. Originally, *Criollo* referred to those who were born of Spanish parents in Louisiana, when Spain took over the territory from the French in the eighteenth century. Louis XV of France, hoping to prevent La Louisiane from falling into English hands, ceded the territory to his Bourbon cousin in Spain, and overnight, Spanish Louisiana was born. Spanish architecture still adorns the city, including the lacy ironwork facades that pleased Alfred so much.

When Napoleon Bonaparte came to power forty years later, the Spanish were coerced into ceding Louisiana back to the French, and soon afterward Napoleon sold it to the new United States. Thomas Jefferson, the president, was overjoyed. Who would expect so much territory for so little investment and no military engagement? The French emperor needed money, though, for his wars, and Louisiana counted for little in his eyes. In the meantime, displaced by the war of attrition declared by the French on Saint-Domingue (well resisted by the inspiring Toussaint Louverture), many Haitians fled to New Orleans and enriched the ever-evolving Creole population even more. As for the English speakers, they came after the sale of the territory in 1803 and settled beyond the French Quarter to the north, reinforcing the ethnic divisions of the city.

So Alfred explored a city that was much influenced by the French, although certainly American, too! As he worked, he began to realize that the older parts of the city did not offer him many economic opportunities. By 1902, most wealthy Creoles had moved away, to the Faubourg Marie for instance, leaving the older city to those who struggled to earn a living. Alfred realized that he would have to change territories to earn good returns. And he did; out into the various faubourgs at first, then north into the English-speaking communities, and farther north toward Jackson and the Lake Pontchartrain. He even took a ferry across the Mississippi and peddled in Jefferson Parish and Gretna, and as far as Algiers.

The farther Alfred traveled, the more money he made. He would walk for days, his strapped valise hanging on his back, throughout the wider New Orleans region, identifying the areas where his wares were in demand, and he didn't return home until the valise was empty. Then he bought more merchandise, items that he knew would be marketable in the region he intended to visit in the coming days. At first, the young peddler bought from grocery and clothing shops in the French Quarter, the quantities he needed being relatively modest. Then, as sales picked up, he looked for sources of better-quality goods at cheaper rates. At the New Orleans docks, he was directed toward the wholesale markets along Tchoupitoulas Street.

He bought supplies there and tried other markets too, some offering good value, others not. He was learning fast, getting to know the land, the people, seeing how to do business and get ahead in life.

Eventually Alfred made two acquaintances who had a lasting impact on his retail operation: Lucien Bonck, the owner of the B. Bennett Clothing Company, and Julius Cohn, a wholesaler who owned a number of outlets on Tchoupitoulas Street. These two men were deeply associated with Alfred Nicola's business, and, in time, became his close friends.

Earning good money, Alfred moved to a separate apartment in the same house at 916 Bourbon Street, although he was hardly ever home. His remote peddling made returning at night impossible, and he often slept on the side of the road. His valise serving as a pillow, he slept on oyster shells and bare ground. On better days, after opening his valise to the marveling eyes of some farmer's wife and, making a good sale, he might also earn a night's sleep in the guest room of the house, a natural thing to offer a stranger in rural Louisiana. Alfred ate at many tables and befriended many of the farm families and well-to-do people, too.

The money kept flowing in, so much so that after six months in business, Alfred had saved enough to pay off the mortgage of his father's house. He went to the Hibernia Bank on 812 Gravier Street and opened an account. He deposited all the bills he had been holding and also handed the startled clerk a paper bag filled with change he had collected. Alfred Nicola now had his first bank account, and his mother Helena would be proud. The twenty-dollar bill she had sewn into the lining of his vest and watered with her tears had sprouted and grown. Now it was ready for harvest. Alfred wired the money to his father's account in Hadath, ordering the bank to send the total amount, less a minimum balance to keep the account open. Then Alfred walked to the telephone office and sent a telegram to his father to advise him of the transaction. The mortgage was paid!

I visited the Hibernia Bank in 2012. After surviving the Great Depression, it had grown to be the largest bank in Louisiana before being bought by Capital One in 2005. Yet the building was much the same as it was in 1902, especially the grand entrance, a high door made of reinforced steel and marble, signaling the power of money in an industrious country during an industrial era. Alfred must have felt proud walking out that door with his valise still on his back. Looking back at the bank with a sigh, he said to himself the words he would repeat the rest of his life: "America, you land of plenty, you land of generosity."

His father Nicolas paid the mortgage and saved his home, but he was weakening by the day as his heart condition worsened. It stopped beating a few weeks later.

5

A peddler on foot

On the bayou

Nothing can teach you better how to overcome the whims of nature in the swamps of Southern Louisiana than years of being attuned to the whims of the Turks and the "Turkicized" Syrians of the Ottoman Empire. Alfred had endured his share of Ottoman whimsy, so he was fairly prepared for his new life down in the bayous. The landscape was harsh and inhospitable in this part of Louisiana, and few people ever ventured there. Those who did either had a good reason to go or were compelled to live there, forced into exile and not admitted anywhere else. One million acres of swamps, of flooded forests of cypress, of oak trees draped with moss, of marshlands, of bayous, and of alligators—killing machines that were a constant threat. So were the frequent outbreaks of yellow fever and Spanish flu, floods along the Mississippi, breaks in the manmade levees, and devastating hurricanes.

Yet, the pirate Jean Lafitte found value in this less-than-ideal environment and established his headquarters in Barataria on Grande Terre, beyond the swamps and out in the Gulf, across the Grande Pass. It seemed like an ideal hideaway for a pirate—or "privateer," as Lafitte called himself—and a good location for the hit-and-run operations against the Spanish that he took every pleasure in perpetrating. Lafitte ended up being idealized as a Louisiana hero when he took up arms with the future president Andrew Jackson against the British in their last colonial war in the New World. But this was ancient history for Alfred, who had only heard of Jean Lafitte after walking past a barroom where the privateer was said to have hung out. Alfred also heard about the hunt for Lafitte's treasure, a make-believe treasure that Lafitte pretended existed but that was still on everybody's minds eighty years later. No treasure was ever found, however, and it is doubtful whether the barroom drinking joint that bears Lafitte's name today ever saw Jean or his brother Pierre drink or gamble.

I have been to the Grand Isle, southwest of the Pass, probably the most beautiful island in the archipelago. I went there with Fred Joseph Jr. and Rosemary Ortlieb in the chill of a February, after the British Petroleum oil spill, at a time when the company was mounting a grand media campaign to redeem its good name. Alfred Nicola had walked with his valise all the way down there, all the way to the Gulf Coast of Mexico.

With his unique sense of geography, one that served him very well later in life, the uneducated and nearly illiterate Alfred decided Bayou Lafourche was the place to be. New Orleans was too competitive, the number of peddlers on the streets growing by the day, and although he had found some success north of Lake Pontchartrain, and an equal measure of success in the Faubourgs and on the eastern bank of the Mississippi, he still searched for more fertile ground to secure better returns. After all, the work he did was not easy and not always safe either; peddlers were looked upon with disdain by many and often brutalized.

I spent some time at the Louisiana National Archives, reading newspapers from the epoch on microfilm, and came away with a surprising number of clippings that reported on Syrian peddlers being assaulted, robbed, and killed. To say the Syrian peddlers were despised would be an understatement, as this passage from the *Times Picayune* of September 3, 1904, makes clear: "But the most objectionable of all the immigrants are what are termed the scum of the Levant, made up of Syrians, Armenians, Greeks and Turks. The inspector declares that the physique of these people is very poor, and the percentage of loathsome and contagious diseases among them is very high."

For his first trip south, Alfred went with Habib and Alexander, both of whom traveled to the bayou regularly to buy farm produce to sell in New Orleans and further north in Jackson and on the banks of Lake Pontchartrain. It was a summer day in 1903. The three men took a streetcar from Canal Street, crossing the Mississippi on a ferry at Audubon Park. At Harvey Canal, they boarded the Barker barge. The barge was docked on the west bank of the canal, in a cluster of narrow steamboats standing belly-to-belly, all specifically built for Louisiana and suitable for traveling along the river and on the bayous, canals, and swamps.

The cousins took the *Climax*, a steamer operated by the Barker Barge Line that ran from New Orleans to the southernmost points on the Bayou Lafourche once a week. It was an eye-opening experience for Alfred, who was venturing out into the swamps for the first time. Their visit came just before a flood destroyed the sugar plantations in the Lafourche area, the man-made levees unable to withstand the water pressure and giving way.

Alfred had heard about this region and its inhabitants, the Cajuns, who lived in the bayous and down in the swamps. A people with strong traditions, he was told, who lived by fishing in autumn, trapping in winter, crawfish hunting in spring, and trawling for shrimp in summer. He knew that the Bayou Lafourche area was a land of many dangers, but he also felt it was a land of plenty, and he wanted to see it with his own eyes.

The Mississippi draws sediments from thirty-one states, cutting its way from Canada to the Gulf of Mexico and creating fertile land for agriculture along the flood plain with the passing of time. The river, swollen by countless tributaries along its path, seems to crawl so peacefully, so quietly, even lazily at times, with a nonchalance that seems consistent with the simple way of life of the southeastern Louisiana Cajuns. Across the bayous, the current is weak and water seems not to flow, as if sitting stagnant. Locks had been recently installed, at Donaldsonville and elsewhere, to divert the excess flow of the Mississippi in springtime, a measure that slowed the current in other seasons too. The resulting stagnant water made disease more prevalent, especially in the summer heat, when infections were carried by the real inhabitant of the waters: the ever-present mosquitoes.

Many residents of New Orleans spent their summers south of the city at Grand Isle, the most beautiful island in the archipelagos, and a fast-growing vacation resort. Many of the vacationers hoped to escape the contagions that often plagued crowded New Orleans at a time when sanitation was poor. Was Alfred contemplating selling goods to the vacationers down at the Gulf Island? Many Creoles were wealthy, and he already had met them and sold to them at their homes and farms around New Orleans. Following them south in summer would make economic sense and helps explain the choices Alfred made.

Whatever his reasons, Alfred went down the Mississippi and its tributaries, very much like those early adventurers who came down from the north on homemade flatboats to sell goods in New Orleans, stopping en route sometimes to sell at small settlements along the river. When the load was sold, the flatboat itself was disassembled and the wood sold to pay the steamboat fare back home. One of these adventurers was Abraham Lincoln. He came down the Ohio River to the Mississippi twice in his teens, on flatboats he had built, and was deeply impressed by the trading he saw in New Orleans, particularly that of slaves. The route Lincoln sailed and that Alfred was sailing now was the trade highway of the nineteenth century and made New Orleans the sixth largest city of the Union. Also through the markets of New Orleans came all the consumables exported from Caribbean islands, among them, to quote the Cajun-born filmmaker Glen Pitre, "the first take-away packaged meal in history: banana."

With his keen business acumen, Alfred knew that the New Orleans markets were a unique trading hub, offering a tremendous variety of supplies for him to sell. He also knew that there were no stores on Bayou Lafourche and people there hardly ever traveled. The longest journeys they took were at Christmas or New Year's to greet friends, visits that usually extended for days, spent discussing fishing, trapping, houses, boats, and the daughters to marry. Alfred had a hunch—Bayou Lafourche was the opportunity he had been searching for—and he pursued it.

He might have had other reasons for moving out of New Orleans. One was the city itself, the so-called city of sin, where prostitution was legal and had a whole district for itself (it would be more accurate to say it was disallowed elsewhere in the city). The city's new music was said to be "devilish," with bands of African American men sitting at pianos playing something called *jass*. By contrast, down in Bayou Lafourche, the fishermen and trappers led quiet and structured lives, just as people did back in Hadath.

Like him, Alfred's father had been a hard worker and his mother was a righteous woman who always looked out for her children, warning them about the *banat el hawa*, or "girls of wind," who practiced the world's oldest profession. Alfred was still seventeen going on eighteen, and the teachings of his parents were still uppermost in his mind; what's more, the money he earned came with many hardships, and he intended to save it. As for music, he only knew the Byzantine hymns from the church next door to his father's home, Mar Elias, and he was not prepared to trade them for anything.

Habib and Alexander got off the boat at Raceland to meet their suppliers at their farms, leaving Alfred to enjoy the voyage across both sides of the bayou. They all planned to ride back together with their purchases when the Barker Barge Line steamer returned a few hours later. It was cheaper for the brothers to use the steamboat to transport perishable goods than to drive their horses and wagons, and certainly quicker. On passing Cut-Off, Alfred could see the canal that had been built fifty years before as a means to contain the overflow of the river in times of flood, though to no avail. North from that point, people lived solely by agriculture, sugarcane and cotton being the main crops. Ever since a Creole from Haiti discovered a technique to crystallize juice from sugarcane, rice cultivation had been practically abandoned for sugarcane fields.

South of Cut-Off, where the steamer was now headed, people were fishermen and trappers. Named to mark the point where the overflow was cut off, Cut-Off ended up marking the point where agriculture gave way to fishing and trapping. And here was Alfred, floating on the waters where he would spend the next eighteen years of his life. Did he decide this instantly? What was on his mind, looking at the houses along the Bayou Lafourche that seemed to stand side by side like a regiment in review, with him as the commanding general, riding the waters in their midst?

When the French took hold of La Louisiane, they instituted a system of measurement from Roman times that was still in use in eighteenth-century Bourbon France. The measure was the *arpent*, a unit of length roughly equal to 192 feet.

The French divided land along Bayou Lafourche in "ribbons," granting each less than four arpents of bayou frontage, but ten to fifteen times as many arpents in depth. When land was distributed, the owners had strips of land with the bayou in front, swamps in the back, and a long stretch of fertile land in between. These settlers all built their homes on the frontage, "with their feet in the bayou," and so houses stood in a line, neighbor after neighbor, as one passed along the bayou. Boating across the bayou was to sail by practically all the inhabitants of the bayou. What better marketplace could an entrepreneurial spirit such as Alfred Nicola ask for his peddling?

The situation could only get more favorable with each generation, as all children had an equal share of the inheritance from their parents, again following French tradition, which meant that the strips got slimmer as the land was divided longitudinally among the heirs. All siblings were given access to the fertile lands toward the bayou as well as the less important lands toward the swamps in the back. In a few years, areas on the Bayou Lafourche came to be known by the names of the families who lived side by side, houses nearly touching: la cote Guidry, la cote Laffont, la cote Terrebonne, la cote Pitre, and so on, and on. A common joke that portrays the close proximity of houses along the bayou tells of the return of a young soldier from the European front. Cruising on a petrol boat down to his parents' house, he salutes an old-timer on the porch of his house upstream on the bayou and shouts, "The war is over!" A half hour later, nearing home, the soldier is greeted by his brother, who waves his arms excitedly and shouts, "La guerre est finie!"

Closeness and intimacy characterized the habitations along "the longest street." Houses were built by the inhabitants themselves, with the help of neighbors, all with small wharfs on the bayou and small boats for fishing and commuting. The fields behind the houses were planted with potatoes and okra; citrus trees dotted the landscape, cows were raised for milk, and beef cattle grazed everywhere. Traditionally, a parent bought a calf for his child when he was in puberty, to grow with the child and to serve him when he came of age and settled down.

Steaming farther down the bayou, Alfred reached Grand Isle where the memory of Lafitte was still very much alive. There, Alfred saw trappers setting bait for the alligators, the nasty breed that had to be contained to keep families safe. Alligators were a constant danger, and with food supplies limited in the swamps, they could show up at one's doorstep. A season for crocodile hunting was decreed, one month at the end of summer, when trappers were authorized to shoot a certain number of alligators; sold for their skin, the larger specimens were the most valuable.

The steamboat made stops along the way, loading and unloading people, while Alfred stood on deck, staring at and analyzing the locale and its residents. He liked what he saw, although he did not understand much of what the local passengers were saying. They spoke a language that did not sound like that of the French-speaking Creoles he had befriended in New Orleans. Nevertheless, as the steamboat sailed back to the pier on Harvey Canal across from New Orleans, Alfred knew he had hit upon a very good venture.

But who were they, he wondered, these Cajuns?

"Up the bayou, down the bayou, across the bayou"

For a while, Alfred came down to the Bayou Lafourche area for one week every month to test its sales potential. During the previous six months he had developed a market in New Orleans, had carved out a route for himself, and it was too precious to give up before he had the assurance of success down south. Habib and Alexander Joseph were doing well, each had his own horse and wagon. They sold a number of things, each with a captive market, and they had no problem switching from vegetables and fruits on Monday to clothing on Tuesday and then back to produce on Wednesday, changing routes and taking orders as they went. Rolling stores they had become, while Ann Murray was still walking or jumping on streetcars to reach the few destinations she knew and where she was awaited by loyal customers.

Alfred too was walking, the valise still on his back, but a larger one now with a more suitable strap. He also used streetcars extensively, riding from the French Quarter to the various suburbs, wherever there was a clientele to satisfy. And once a month, with his valise full of treasures, he boarded one of the many steamboats churning the waters toward Bayou Lafourche and southward to Grand Isle, and disappeared for a week or so. In time, he learned to choose the articles that sold best, getting to know the people and their needs, befriending many of them and becoming a sympathetic figure much awaited by the people of the bayou.

It was Alfred who introduced the first ready-to-wear garments in Bayou Lafourche, and the gingham dress was one of his popular sellers, as were *pantaloons* (pants), *chemises de travail* (work shirts), and *cravats* (ties). Yellow rubber slicker suits were also popular among the harvesters, though these were heavy to carry. White gloves for women were in demand, worn to mass on Sundays; also in demand were the fashionable wedding sets, earrings and necklaces, and they were much easier to pack in the valise and lighter on the shoulder.

The word *Cajun* is a corruption of *Acadian*, the name of the people who once lived in what are now Canada's Maritime Provinces, primarily Nova Scotia. Founded as a French colony in the early seventeenth century, Nova Scotia became an English colony as a result of the peace accords that ended the Seven Years' War, known in the New World as the French and Indian War. The original inhabitants of the island were French, mostly from Normandy and Brittany in the north and northwest of France, a people who had emigrated during or after the religious wars that wracked Europe in the sixteenth century. Coming from a fishing region where oysters and seafood abounded, these French speakers brought their culture, religion, and traditional skills to their new home, only to be expelled three generations later when the English took over.

Many found their way back to France, an alien country to them by then, living on aid graciously supplied by the king. Others went south looking for a hospitable land to settle but were turned away wherever they went, from Connecticut to the Carolinas. Eventually they reached the coast of southern Louisiana, where they settled and put down roots, adapting to an environment that, although hostile in many ways, lent itself to their fishing culture.

Louis XV, getting weary of his unexpected guests from North America, a burden on his treasury more than anything else, shipped the recent immigrants to Louisiana with the promise of viable land and a prosperous future. Settling there, they rejoined their cousins, and today, Cajun is the generic term given to one people with heterogeneous roots. It has been acknowledged as denoting a multicomposition that eventually brought together Germans, English, Irish, French, Spanish, and escapees from the French and Spanish dominions. In a way, this is true. All nationalities have contributed to the formation of a hybrid people that is unique. I find the definition given by Bob Hamm, quoted in *The Longest Street* by Tanya Ditto, very accurate: "A Cajun likes fiddles and accordions in his music, plenty of pepper in his courtbouillon, shrimp in his net, neighborliness in his neighbors, and love in his home."

Alfred's peddling journeys in the Bayou Lafourche area began at Lockport, an ideal location to start walking. It was the only settlement that had the real features of a town back then. Located north of Cut-Off, surrounded by farms, it was the gateway to the lower Bayou Lafourche area, which was populated by fishermen and trappers. Alfred dressed well, a white shirt and an elegant bowtie that matched his jacket, and he was careful to button the jacket whenever he was in the presence of customers. That would be his attire, with the occasional addition of a Panama straw hat, throughout his years in Louisiana. His father always said, "A man should look as good as the materials he is selling." And hadn't his father been a successful trader?

Like his father before him, Alfred was an early riser and spent time getting prepared, taking good care of his appearance, shaving closely and brushing his beautiful dark hair. In the beginning, he brought all sorts of items in his valise, from pillow cases to candies, and earned himself the name of *vendeur de paquerettes*, the peddler of daisies, a nickname he would soon exchange for a weightier one when the inhabitants of Bayou Lafourche got to know him better.

Whenever he came to Bayou Lafourche, the contents of his valise sold quickly. He understood the seasonal nature of demand down there and the different needs that arose at different times of year. He started early on to sell trappers their winter vests and fishermen their waterproof boots, buying them on Tchoupitoulas Street from Bennett Clothing, the first wholesaler in New Orleans to import Levi's jeans from San Francisco and sell blue chambray shirts. Before long, he became friends with the owner, Lucien Bonck, a self-made Creole of French descent. Alfred also bought from Tulane Clothing, a line that suited laborers on farms and sugarcane plantations, and he made friends here too, including the owner, Julius Cohn, a hard-working New Orleanais of German extraction. Both company owners lived in the French Quarter, minutes away from his apartment, one on Robert Street in the Upper Garden District and the other on Dupré, near the Fairgrounds Racetrack. Their relationships grew strong as Alfred became a regular customer, always paying for his purchases in cash and never asking for credit.

Down along Bayou Lafourche, Alfred was building a name for himself. At a time when people made their own clothing, Alfred had the original idea of introducing ready-to-wear outfits. He brought dresses for brides, First Communion outfits for children, and jewelry, which he kept in a wooden box hidden away in the valise. If people did not have money to pay him, he often left an item with a customer and collected the money on the way back, and many times did he not collect. But that was Alfred, a genuine character and a loving heart. Becoming part of everyday life along Bayou Lafourche, the young man from Hadath saw the Cajuns as his alter egos. He loved their simplicity and integrity and identified with their lifestyle. He walked down one side of the towpath, the narrow trail on both sides of the bayou used to tow boats, and up the other, entering homes where he was usually welcome and expected. He often ate at his customers' tables, simple seafood from the bayou. One familiar dish was fried shrimp on a French baguette, with tomato, lettuce, and lots of mayonnaise. A po'boy it is called, a poor boy's meal, and he loved it. He also ate raw oysters with the oystermen, shucking the bivalves open with his bare hands; he liked crawfish, too, and took pleasure catching them along the muddy ditches.

Back in Hadath, the death of Nicolas had left Helena very fragile. He had always dealt with everything, and Alfred's mother did not know how to manage her property and finances on her own. Thankfully, Tanios, Alfred's trusted uncle, was living with them at the house and had been for as long as Alfred could remember. Tanios had helped out during the dark years, when his brother Nicolas was in debt, contributing all the earnings from his shoe-repairing business. Now Alfred turned to Tanios and entrusted him with his mother and sisters. Though not the eldest of Nicolas's sons, Alfred Nicola had been thrust into the position of the family patriarch, a role no one contested and all seemed relieved to have him assume. He sent money to Uncle Tanios with the clear request to spend it on his household and keep his mother and sisters from any need. "Spend graciously," he wrote. "I want my mother and sisters to live as they did in my father's house during the days he was a success."

Then Alfred's brother Alexander came out to Louisiana, entering through Ellis Island in 1904 under the name Alexander Nicola. He lived with Alfred at 916 Bourbon Street, next door to Ann Murray and her sons, Habib and Alexander. If one remembers that Alfred's real name was Habib, changed at immigration in 1902, one might observe that in two neighboring apartments now lived two Alexanders and two Habibs! Alexander Nicola was well read and not inclined to do manual work. Nevertheless, Alfred had him work with their cousins at first, wanting him to try the strenuous work of peddling. So the newcomer rode with them on their wagons for their daily sales. After a while, however, he chose to stop this demanding work, and though he would work as a peddler later on from time to time, Alexander Nicola searched for an office job.

Alfred's life was increasingly focused on the bayou country. The simplicity of life down there matched the area's undeveloped terrain. Bayou people did not need complicated directions to reach a destination. You either went up, down, or across the bayou. Life had a simple matter-of-fact quality, as illustrated in more recent times by a Cajun farmer who drove his lorry to downtown New Orleans to sell his potato harvest. Found sleeping on board his truck, literally atop the potatoes, he was questioned by the police. The Cajun replied, "Don't sleep on ya pota'oes, next mornin' there will be no pota'oes!" Alfred was also a simple man and had slept many time on the gravel-covered ground, his valise for a pillow. So he understood well the world view of his new Cajun friends, and he admired it; that, and their sense of tradition.

A people of extremes

What we term today as French Creole is a hybrid language formed from three different French dialects: colonial French, which came with the early inhabitants of New France; Acadian, which came with the refugees from Nova Scotia; and Haitian French, a colorful speech that stretches letters, rounds vowels, sings phrases, and makes up vocabulary as needed for everyday life on Hispaniola. When Alfred left Beirut, Lebanon was far from being the French colony it would later become. French was not spoken widely there, mainly being used by the business elites who had ties with the French companies that controlled the local economy. In Hadath, on the property of Mar Elias Church, a Russian missionary had started a school where Russian was taught. But Alfred did not speak French when he came to Louisiana, nor English, nor Russian, only the vernacular of his hometown, an offshoot of classic Arabic, a language that was not written, only spoken: Lebanese.

In Cajun country, the local dialect was also only spoken (a patois is hardly ever written or read), and only a handful of people could read or write anyway. Isolated as they were, the Cajuns developed their own culture independently from the English-speaking peoples in the north. In fact, they only started trying to use English during the First World War, when many were drawn into the world crisis. Their speech include many colloquialisms that seem funny to outsiders: They said "Je vais naviguer" to mean "I am going out," probably because sailing on a pirogue canoe was the most common way to get around; "Ça grimace dehors" meant "It is drizzling outside," *grimace* meaning "to make faces." And their language made free use of alliteration, repetition, and onomatopoeia: *tac-tac* meant "popcorn," *Maw-maw* for "grandma," and *Oo-ye-ye* for "I am sad."

The simplicity of Cajun beliefs, and their superstitions, did not escape Alfred either. For example, the Cajuns believed that werewolves lived in the bayou lands. *Les loups-garous*, a terrifying species with big red-eyed wolf faces, could not be destroyed with weapons; the only way to hurt them was by throwing frogs at them! Fear and superstition seemed omnipresent in the life of Cajuns. People along the bayou slept with their windows tightly locked, their houses practically airproof, even in the height of summer, for fear of the night air, full of germs that could incapacitate a man. The recovery of a sick child was readily attributed to the Virgin and her intercession, following a stream of prayers and devotions that might even lead a mother to dress her sick boy in blue and white robes, the colors of the mother of Christ.

To an outsider like Alfred, the superstitions must have seemed strange. Cajuns ate sand and charcoal when they had indigestion; to make their hair grow, they cut off a lock on Good Friday and buried it; for a sore throat, a cup of tea made of dried dog manure was a remedy; to secure a husband, a Cajun woman might carry a picture of Saint Joseph in her purse for six months; to get rid of a neighbor, kill a black chicken and throw it over his house.

Many Cajuns carried *gris-gris*, placing them on the doorsteps of unwelcome neighbors, or in the fields to chastise demon spirits that ruin crops. In one case, a woman planted a cypress branch in the form of a crucifix in the mud, sprinkled salt on it, and wondered why the rain did not stop as promised. She went away in the rain, irritated at herself for having made the amulet incorrectly. Some people took advantage of the Cajuns' superstitious nature. Some pseudo-doctors, more commonly referred to as *traiteurs*, garnered money and power by selling worthless medications made from animal skins and body parts. These potions, if not endangering the lives of the suffering, certainly did them no benefit. Fortunately, certified doctors—and there were a few: Lockport alone had two doctors and a dentist in 1902—gradually gained influence, and many took leading roles in the management of their parishes, becoming sheriffs and elected officials.

Alfred also saw that Cajuns were a spirited, red-blooded people. If two were having a fight, instead of jumping in to separate them, other Cajuns grouped around in a small circle and shouted to egg them on. They even proposed bets instantly, waving their money in the air. What was sure was that Cajuns were always up for fun! The bayou-side dance halls on Saturday night were packed, some walking there along the towpaths and others sailing in on their pirogues. Glen Pitre's film *Belizaire the Cajun*, starring Armand Assante, presents the spectacle of a Cajun Saturday night gathering, complete with lively dancing and Cajun music. It also paints a fair picture of the hot-blooded and high-tempered inhabitants of the bayou. Fiddles and accordions are their instruments of choice, and their songs mix their melancholic and humorous tendencies. Yes, the music, the food, and the people were rough, just as rugged as the bayou itself, and that's why the rugged Alfred liked it. For him, rough and rugged meant genuine, and he felt close to genuine people.

So on Alfred went, spending long days in the bayou, only surfacing in New Orleans when his valise was empty. He learned Cajun French along the way, drank bayou water from the jars of his hosts, and, when invited, stayed on for the *fais-do-do* evenings, the dancing merriments whose name derives from *fêtes de Dieu.* On occasions Alfred also took part in a *boucherie*, a social event when a pig was slaughtered, cut up, and distributed among the attendees. In a time before refrigeration, people had an informal agreement to share the meat of the animals they butchered so that it would not spoil and go to waste. Neighbors took turns at hosting the boucheries, which often developed into hours-long celebrations.

Alfred also saw the showboats, floating theaters that dropped anchor along the Bayou Lafourche occasionally and mounted entertainments, everything from stand-up comedy to Shakespeare, large and small productions, singers and magicians. One common magic show on the Bayou Lafourche, which Alfred must have seen, featured a snake pointing to the correct time of day on a large cartoonlike face of a clock. The secret of the trick lay in the food bait that the magician skillfully held behind the correct number; this bait was seen only by the snake who flexed his body toward the number to get it. A simple trick, but one that gave the enthralled audience something to puzzle over all night.

There were also marriages and charivari that Alfred took part in, as a provider of suits and wedding dresses at first and later as a guest of friends of many along the bayou. Marriages were arranged in a distinctive way. When a girl in a house was ready to marry, the house's chimney was painted white. Interested parties and would-be grooms showed up in turn and introduced themselves to the household. If a visitor received signs of encouragement from the girl and her family, the family of the groom-to-be appeared next to speak on his behalf to the bride. If a woman was marrying for the second time, the ceremony would be less formal. After the wedding, it was customary for guests and friends to raise a noisy ruckus, not stopping until the newlyweds promised to give away something, usually a free meal. That was charivari.

Cajun people were known by their nicknames, rarely by their real names. In obituaries, newspapers always listed the nicknames next to the real names. One Cajun told me he only learned the real name of his own cousin after he passed away, reading the obituary and seeing it juxtaposed next to his nickname. A common Cajun joke tells of a man talking to a reporter and mentioning the name of his wife, Clementine. She interrupts angrily and states, "My name is Armandine!" Perplexed, the reporter turns back to the man only to hear him say, "We have been marr'd for twenty years and I always call'd my wife Miz Joe!"

The people along the lower part of the Bayou Lafourche did not keep secrets from Alfred. He knew them all and saluted them by their nicknames. He also knew every house and could tell the difference between a bungalow and a shotgun, an oysterman and a trapper. They were simple structures, easy to build with local materials, cypress planks for walls and roofs, and *bousillage*, an effective insulation made by mixing dried moss, mud, and ground-up oyster shells.

Alfred was also profoundly sensitive to the pious attitude of the Cajuns. They were Roman Catholics and did not miss a Sunday mass. They dressed in white gowns and suits—Alfred was a major supplier of these—and sailed their boats along the Bayou Lafourche to church. Many went barefoot, a common practice of the Cajuns, and some had never bought a pair of shoes in their lives. Religion was part of their daily lives and occupations. The archbishop of New Orleans came every August to bless the shrimp fleet and mark the opening of the season, and the boats and trawlers were sprinkled with holy water during the crowded open-air service on the bayou. And of course there was Mardi Gras, marking the beginning of Lent and the abstention from meat and other pleasures of life for seven weeks. What has become today a wild celebration in New Orleans was a pious Catholic demonstration of faith in Bayou Lafourche, with children wearing masks and going door-to-door, soliciting coins, gumbo, and *gâteaux*.

In Hadath, Alfred had gone on similar quests on Saint Lazarus commemoration days. One child would play Lazarus, lying lifeless on a stretcher, covered with a papyrus bearing the words of the Gospel. Later, standing alive and wearing a hideous mask, he visited every porch, asking for coins and candies while the accompanying group chanted in one voice the hymns of the occasion.

But the land of dancing and singing, of boucheries, weddings, and showboats, was also the land of the yellow fever. Ignoring the quarantine at New Orleans in

June 1905, a ship carrying bananas brought the germs of yellow fever to Louisiana, and the ever-present mosquitoes in the bayous soon transmitted them to people. Alfred had never seen anything like it and was terrified. During the outbreak, he limited his peddling and stayed at his apartment on Bourbon Street, locked up with his brother, Ann Murray, and his cousin Habib. (Alexander was in Lebanon at the time, visiting his wife and children.) The epidemic soon struck New Orleans and the death toll was stark: 452 dead in a few days. Dead bodies lay in the streets, and in his stifling apartment, Alfred worried about his friends down along Bayou Lafourche. He now carried every single one of them in his heart. By August, the threat had subsided, thanks to the sanitizing efforts of New Orleans. The city was fumigated and the water cisterns were covered to destroy the breeding grounds of mosquitoes. As soon as it was safe, Alfred Nicola went back on the road, down to Bayou Lafourche to reunite with his Cajun friends.

"Sweet Papa"

His sales route along Bayou Lafourche, first peddling north among the farmers and then south among the fishermen and trappers, led Alfred to use the centrally located Cut-Off as a base of operations. He opened an account at Citizens Bank there to deposit the cash he earned on each leg of his route. Although he felt safe among the Cajun homeowners, he worried about falling prey to bandits, who were known to target peddlers. For not only did peddlers carry money, they also had packs filled with items, some expensive, which could easily be fenced in the city. Alfred was especially vulnerable during the frequent naps he took along the towpath.

When first heading out for a week's peddling trip, Alfred spent time in the morning carefully packing, arranging, and rearranging every item in his valise. In a 1970 recording, Alfred's young nephew, Fred Sr., Fred Joseph's father, recalled watching him pack his valise and spoke of the extensive time he spent at it, and the precision and diligence that characterized the operation. (This made such a lasting impression that in later years Fred named his second son after him.) Alfred was up very early, well before the Louisiana sun started its ascent over the river, had a morning chicory coffee, dressed, and opened wide his valise on his bed. Choosing items from the piles of clothes and jewelry in his apartment, he layered them carefully into the bag, mentally tracing his whole route, from Lockport to Thibodaux and back, then to Grand Isle, visualizing the farms and houses he would stop at to fill orders and laying down the items in the valise in the order he would need them. He worked meticulously, taking every care to fold the shirts and dresses in a way they would not wrinkle; at the same time, he used his limited space effectively, packing as much as possible but keeping the weight manageable enough to carry.

Alfred's apartment on Bourbon Street looked like a warehouse, filled with all the stock he had bought at the many markets in New Orleans, from the docks directly, and from his two good friends on Tchoupitoulas Street. When he had an order for three chambray shirts for a customer in Leeville, say, Alfred would buy twelve from Lucien Bonck and earn a discount on the total. He would fill the pending order and keep the remaining nine shirts in his apartment for a later sale. From Julius Cohn, he bought seasonal dresses and work clothes in quantities that he stored, from season to season, building a consistent stock of materials that gained in value with the passing of time. A year into his business, Alfred was doing rather well. He was sending money to Hadath regularly, rented his own apartment, and owned a relatively large stock of dry goods and jewelry.

Along Bayou Lafourche, he felt free, happy to be among people he felt so close to. He would start his trek at Thibodaux, visiting the farms and filling the orders that were placed on his previous visit and calling on other possible customers, some familiar, some new, to propose purchases of clothes and accessories. He had a keen look in his eyes and an expressive face, a prominent forehead, thick eyebrows, and luxuriant hair that became disheveled during the day. That gave him the look of an exotic Persian, sprung from some popular romance novel or fabulous tale, or the leading man of one of the melodramas presented on the showboats along the bayou. People loved him and, more importantly, they trusted him. He was known to be a man of his word and this, for Cajuns, was the ultimate test of honor.

The cry Alfred shouted along the Bayou Lafourche became his trademark, and many came out to greet him and look at the marvels he carried when his voice resonated along the towpath, reverberating over the waters of the Bayou. "Achetez mes robes, portez-les le jour, lavez-les le soir," he repeated in a closed loop, chanting in the local patois. "Buy my dresses, wear them in the day, and wash them in the evening." He would drop the valise off his back, lift it onto a high surface, take the lid off, and show his wares, one by one, to the admiring audience of grandmas and daughters, farmers and fishermen. Those who had placed orders the previous month received their long-awaited purchases with much excitement, especially if they were destined for a special event such as a wedding or a first communion. Others were just mesmerized by the opening of the valise, a shop on their doorstep that broke the monotony of their days.

Well dressed, well mannered, good-looking, serious, and honest, Alfred was also generous to the Cajuns, never denying his merchandise to those who could not pay. "Take it now and pay later, if you can," he told them, and in return they called him "Sweet Papa," a nickname that demonstrated their affection and attachment. He had sweetness in his heart, sweetness in his looks, and sweetness in his show of solidarity and brotherhood. Alfred was also Papa, a friendly and intimate appellation that the Cajuns used respectfully, much as I might call my ten-year-old son *vieux*, in French, meaning "old one," projecting myself onto him in a game of role-playing. Sheer affection, genuine affection from the heart, simple and uncomplicated; that was what the people of Bayou Lafourche had for Alfred Nicola.

A week passed quickly but, as Alfred delivered merchandise, his valise emptied more quickly, often before the week was up. He needed to have more merchandise on hand to keep going and maximize sales, especially now that he was expected further down in the Caminada Bay area and the swamps. But he only could fit so much in one valise. His solution to this problem was to bring two valises on the barge, leave one at Cut-Off, and come back for a refill as he walked from the farmers up the bayou to the fishermen down the bayou, then back again for another refill before riding the steamboat down to Grand Isle. And so he went, crisscrossing the bayou, up, down, and across, always coming back to Cut-Off to deposit money and restock his valise. On the steamboats, Alfred met all sorts of people. There were many Cajuns, but also Creoles from New Orleans and the Faubourgs going down to the island for a vacation. He did not waste time presenting his merchandise to them though; more often than not they turned him down, preferring to buy from the fashionable stores along Canal Street in New Orleans.

Back in New Orleans, Alfred's cousin Alexander was excited. He had just returned from Hadath and had news of his family back home. As is always the case no matter what the nationality, immigrants would listen to reports from home with the excitement of a five-year-old awaiting a candy treat. Helena, his mother, was living decently, and his uncle Tanios was taking care of everything. But tension in the streets of Beirut was mounting, probably due to the turmoil in Istanbul caused by the revisionist parties rising up in defiance of the weakened Ottoman Empire. Something was about to happen, but neither Alexander nor those living in Hadath could be sure what it was.

And there was another thing to discuss, now that Alfred had taken the leadership role of his family. Habib, his cousin, wanted the hand of Alfred's sister Zahia in marriage. Alfred could not think of a better husband than his great-cousin and friend Habib, a serious, hard-working, and very ambitious man. He smiled when he thought of the proposal, however, thinking that his two sisters would now be wed to the two Joseph brothers, Alexander and Habib. A happy turn of events, he thought, and he gave his blessing, saying he would relay his decision to his mother.

It was then that he spoke to her, for the first time since he had left Hadath for Louisiana. He sent a telegram giving the precise time for his mother to walk to the central telephone switchboard of Hadath and await his call. They spoke for the first time in eighteen months, a long time that had seen the passing of his father, the payment of the mortgage, and his creation of a successful business with income enough to pay expenses in Hadath. What they talked about remains a secret the two of them have carried into eternity, yet it would be simple to guess some of the substance of a conversation a mother might have with her son after so long a separation.

At first, Helena would hardly be able to contain her weeping, and the first minutes would be hard on both of them. He would be reassuring, soothing, caring, and as loving as ever. She could count on him. She would thank him for being so responsible, a man who had done his duty every step of the way, a man who would "make his father so proud were he still with us today." She might say Alfred's voice had changed, that his speech sounded different. Helena surely gave him her blessing and invoked Allah on more than one occasion, that He keep Alfred in health, that He keep him from harm, that He give him strength, and that He keep him for her, for his loving mother who missed him and his presence so much. Eventually, Alfred told Helena that he approved of Habib and that, if she blessed the union, he would consent to Habib and his sister Zahia marrying.

The marriage took place in Hadath in 1908 at the Mar Elias Church, where all the generations of Shwayri, ever since Fares Bozeid Moujaes first settled in Hadath, have worshipped and prayed and married. Zahia wore a beautiful white dress and walked to the church next door to her father's house. Habib wore a Louisiana-cut suit. They dined, danced, and rejoiced, with Alfred often on their minds. It fell to him to pay the expenses of the wedding ceremony of his sister Zahia, which he fulfilled to the last piaster. He sent money from his account in New Orleans to Uncle Tanios to cover all the costs and to pay the dowry. There was also a request for Tanios to buy the best available bouquet of red roses in his name, to have it delivered to Zahia at home, and, after the wedding, to place it on the grave of his father Nicolas. These wishes were executed to the letter. Days after the wedding, it was Zahia's turn to leave the house and Hadath. Helena would now live with her son George, her brother-in-law Tanios, and Julia and her children. The separation was hard. Alfred, Alexander, and Zahia, all three, in the *mahjar*, in the land of immigration.

Habib and Zahia reached America in 1908, coming through Ellis Island, where Zahia kept her first name and took the surname Joseph after her husband. They traveled down to Louisiana, where Alfred was expecting them. The reunion was affectionate and ushered in a new era for the Joseph and Nicola families. Zahia lived with Habib, Alexander, and Ann Murray in their apartment at 916 Bourbon Street in the French Quarter. She brought with her a refined taste and great skill at preparing traditional Lebanese cuisine that she would put to good use throughout her life, to the contented hearts (and stomachs!) of her husband, brother, mother- and brother-in-law, and children and grandchildren to be.

That same year, 1908, radical change came about in Istanbul with the establishment of the second constitutional era (*ittihad ve tarakki*), forced by the fast-rising Committee of Union and Progress (CUP), a precursor to the movement that would bring the Young Turks to power in coming years. Adding to the uncertainty, Sultan Abdul Hamid II was deposed the following year. As the Ottoman Empire dwindled, and territories once under its sovereignty broke free, a new epoch loomed on the horizon. Although its outlines were still uncertain, one thing was clear: the ever-greedy colonial powers were waiting to prey on it.

For the time being, however, events in Istanbul seemed to have little effect on Alfred. He was rising at his normal early hour, exemplifying his half-Cajun, half-Hadathi philosophy: "Your day is like your mule. Wake up before it, and you lead it. Let it wake up before you, and it will lead you." That credo was passed on to me by my father, who learned it from his father before him, from Alfred, the wise young man who lived to meet the needs of others, a "sweet papa" who was fondly remembered for over a century. His memory lingers on to our own day, as I found out when I investigated his odyssey in Louisiana and heard accounts of his loving soul that were passed down the generations in the lands of the Cajuns.

"Achetez mes robes, portez les le jour, lavez-les le soir." Echoes of his cry seemed to resound through the unspoiled Bayou Lafourche countryside that I skimmed over 110 years after him. Sweet Papa was my sweet grandfather. And I am a proud grandson.

6

A shotgun house, a wagon, and a horse called Mac

Lockport

Zahia had been in New Orleans for just a year when she bore Habib his first child, a son, which was considered the appropriate gender for the firstborn of a conservative Middle Eastern Arab. Isaac was born in 1909, and his father, feeling melancholy for Mount Lebanon, gave him a second, Arabic name, Aziz, which is listed on the census of 1910. The apartment on Bourbon Street was getting small for the large family living there—Ann Murray, her two sons, Zahia and the newborn—but times were hard and moving into a larger apartment was not an option for the moment. Their days were much the same as before, peddling on foot or on wagon, but they now had Zahia, who, like her mother, was an assiduous homemaker. The house had to be impeccable at all times, and the meals had to be delicious and in copious quantities for the men when they got home from work.

Zahia walked to Decatur Street each day, carrying her newborn son, to buy her groceries at a shop owned by Kareem Abboud, a fellow immigrant from Mount Lebanon. Kareem was a close friend of Alexander and Habib and spent long evenings with them sipping arak, the national drink with the famed Damascus anisette, a precious nectar processed in home-owned alembics in most villages in Mount Lebanon. Kareem sold arak and other delicacies, which he imported from Beirut, out of his home. At Kareem's, Zahia found all the ingredients she needed to prepare her dishes, bulgur and spices being first on her list. Soon her culinary skill became known to the Syrian community in New Orleans, many of whom dined at her husband's and brothers-in-law's table and very much appreciated her tabbouleh, kebbeh, and various oil-based vegetarian dishes that are prepared during Lent in Mount Lebanon. So did Alfred, a regular invitee at the table, who particularly enjoyed the kebbeh nayeh, a mutton tartar, eaten raw, with bulgur, spices, and citrus zest, a meal she prepared on Sundays that the men ate hungrily while sipping arak.

The political news from home was getting worrisome, especially the abdication of the sultan of the Ottomans, Abdul Hamid II, and the sequence of events that brought the Young Turks to power. After four hundred years of Ottoman rule over Mount Lebanon, no one could believe the empire was falling, and no one even speculated on the repercussions this event would have on Mount Lebanon and Hadath in particular.

Alfred was now spending more time along the bayou, going for two weeks at a time, surfacing in New Orleans with his empty valises, filling them with more merchandise, and going back to the region and lifestyle he had chosen for himself. As the years passed, his ties deepened with Lucien and Julius, the merchants on Tchoupitoulas Street, and they introduced him to many jewelry wholesalers. Now Alfred would sell watches down in the Lower Lafourche area and bring them back for repair when necessary. Lucien and Julius cosigned as his guarantors on the purchases he was sometimes forced to make on credit. Alfred did a particularly good business with Hiller Jewelry, which supplied him with Illinois pocket watches. These sold well and were of good quality, seldom needing repair. They came in solid gold for the better-off and silver for the more cost-conscious customers.

Alfred decided he needed to move closer, down to the Bayou Lafourche area, and expand his work there. He did not have to wait for long, either, for in 1911 Zahia and Habib had a second son, Fred. Habib, still in an Arabophile phase, also gave this son a second, Arabic name, Fareed. (He discontinued this second-name trend when faced with the prolific progeny Zahia would bear him in the coming years.) As it turns out, Fred is short for Alfred, a hint to the close relationship that united the two cousins and brothers-in-law. The apartment on Bourbon Street was now definitely too small for the Josephs, and when Alfred announced his decision to move to Bayou Lafourche, the Josephs decided to go with him.

Two months after the birth of Fred Joseph Sr. in 1911, the Josephs and the Nicolas moved to Lockport, to a shotgun house "in the back of town," that accommodated all of them. Ann Murray stayed behind on Bourbon Street, continuing the work she knew with the customers who knew her. The house in Lockport was airy enough, with two large living spaces that connected through a door in the middle, a kitchen area with no running water, and a wooden outhouse in the back. Cooking was an ordeal for Zahia as it meant burning wood in the stove and dealing with smoke in the house.

The shotgun design was an indirect consequence of the practices of the Spaniards when they made law in Louisiana from 1763 to 1803. Back then, Spanish law imposed real estate taxes that were based on the total floor area of the living space. So people had every reason to eliminate corridors in order to reduce the floor area and also the tax. Hence the shotgun design; the name simply meant a shot fired from one end of the house would exit the other end if the doors across the rooms were left open. And so they lived, Habib's family, Alexander Joseph, and Alfred and Alexander Nicola, in a town that Alfred already knew well.

For Alfred, the move meant he could resupply his valise more quickly, since he had a large stock close by to draw on. He still traveled back and forth to New Orleans for buying his stock, but now he bought in greater quantities, relying on Lucien Bonck and Julius Cohn to consign the shipments on trains and barges. Lockport was roughly halfway between Thibodaux, where he supplied the needs of a large community of farmers, and Cut-Off, where he had his bank account. With logistics simplified, he could now spend more time on the road, mixing with the people and doing his work, which he had come to view as a mission. The move also meant that he himself was now a bayou dweller, a Cajun among the Cajuns. This realization brought him comfort and he took pride in repeating it to all his friends along Bayou Lafourche, up, down, and across the bayou. This made Sweet Papa even more of a fixture in the region, a distinctive presence with his signature valise dangling from the strap over his shoulder, which obliged him to walk with his back bent forward.

One day, Alfred's youngest brother George sent important news: he too wanted to be useful and come to Louisiana. And so he did, the same year Alfred and the Josephs moved to Lockport. Landing at Ellis Island and entering as George Nicola, he was the fourth of the clan now living down in Lockport. With George gone, Helena grieved for her loss but found comfort in the large family Alexander Joseph had left in Hadath: her daughter Julia and Julia's children, especially Edmond, the youngest, a promising young man. Tanios was still there also, dear Uncle Tanios, and his new bride, for he had married late in life and was unfortunately not given the joy of paternity. She wrote to Alfred via telexes that were read to him by Alexander, and letters she dictated to her granddaughters Adma and Najla, for Helena could neither read nor write.

George left Hadath in a hurry, due to a quarrel that had degenerated into a knife fight, in which he was said to have injured his rival. George was known for his hot temper and, being the youngest of five children, was rather spoiled by his mother. So he jumped on a steamboat to France, lingered in Paris for a while, and then sailed to America. He lived in the house in Lockport and took up peddling, the family trade. Alfred taught George the basics and directed him to routes that no one else traveled, across Bayou Terrebonne into Bayou Cane, then southward into Pointe-aux-Chenes and the Ile de Jean Charles area. It was there that George met the Sabines, a racial mix of white, black, and Native American peoples, who never had an opportunity to buy ready-to-wear clothing. George did especially well in Houma, a town inhabited by descendants of Indian tribes (Houma, Biloxi, and

Chitimacha) and Cajuns who had settled there toward the end of the eighteenth century. Living in proximity to the French-speaking Acadians, the Indian tribes spoke French and gradually abandoned much of their own culture and language. George filled his valise from Alfred's stock in Lockport, sold the contents in the marshlands of Terrebonne Parish, and then paid Alfred for the merchandise at cost, keeping the profits for himself. In no time, George was making a good living as a peddler, tiring work of course but rewarding in all aspects. He took after Alfred in his love of people and felt very much at ease among the Indians and Cajuns. Alfred told him, "All people are good and are a blessing; all people are *ḵhayr* and *Baraḵa*." In the years they spent together in Lockport, Alfred passed on to George a sense of the mission that supported all his peddling down in the Bayou Lafourche.

Alfred Nicola saw people as equals, whatever their creed, race, or religion. All of them are a source of khayr and Baraka, all have been endowed with a role to play under the sun, and together, they stand as one in their diversity. This credo grew out of his own rich experience. He had gone to work early in his life, toiled hard for a living, experienced separation in his teens, sailing far into the unknown, suffered a change of identity, and ended up peddling with a heavy valise on his back. He was well placed to understand human suffering. And suffering had no creed, nor race, nor religion.

On war and peace

Najibeh was twelve years old in 1912 when the Italian navy moored at Beirut and fired cannons at the capital city. The race for territorial concessions was on and the Italians were seeking their share of colonial spoils. If Lebanon was not Italy's real target, it served its purpose as a decoy and sent a message to the Sublime Porte and the CUP, the Committee of Union and Progress, now the real governor of the Ottoman Empire. The Italians were actually after Libya in North Africa and took advantage of the Turks being at war in the Balkans to attempt a diversion by shelling Beirut. Much of the old town was destroyed and many people perished. Najibeh was at her grandparents' house in Gemmayzeh, which overlooks Beirut Harbor, across from Hamidiyyeh Square, which was renamed Place de la Liberté when Sultan Abdul Hamid was dethroned. Not only could she hear this Armageddon, she could see it through the large windows of the Mamluk-style residence.

Najibeh's father was Abdallah Meshrek, an educated man who studied law in Cairo and played a considerable role in the governance of his hometown, Shwayr. He was the *mudir-nahia*, the district director of Shwayr, an all-powerful figure, and a position that was only granted to people from the landed gentry, well educated and known for their impartiality and righteousness. And Abdallah Meshrek was just that, a man of many virtues and very much a conflict resolver. His house in Shwayr was known to people as the *qarakun*, the police station, for he was looked upon as a firm judge, a preserver of the peace, and the authoritative director of the area.

News of the shelling of Beirut reached America with lightning speed. Alexander Joseph brought the news to the large household in Lockport and soon had all four Nicola children worried about their mother. Was Hadath a target? Was their mother all right? It was not long before the answers came and the worries subsided, but an underlying fear remained, amplified over the coming weeks and months by the mobilization of the European empires. In addition, 1913 saw the radicalization of the Young Turks with the coup that brought three despotic generals to power, one of whom, Jamal Pasha, would play a particularly bloody role in the history of Lebanon. The idea of bringing his mother to Lockport crossed Alfred's mind, and he may well have suggested that to her. But Helena would not want to part with her house, the only bond she still had with her late husband, whose memory she cherished. Besides, Helena had Julia and her five children to look after, and she certainly felt responsible for them in the absence of Julia's husband in Lockport.

Alfred had an innate understanding of politics, as he did for commerce, both based on his knowledge of people. He knew Hadath would be in the line of fire if Baabda became a target, the nearby town where most of the governors under the mutasarifiya resided. Yet he let go of his fears as soon as he was out with his valise, peddling down Bayou Lafourche, living to the rhythm of the peaceful, slow-moving river. The once wide and sometimes raging waterway that could flood its banks and wreak havoc on towns and houses was now tamed by new locks that dammed the bayou at Donaldsonville, near Baton Rouge.

Something about the bayou was comforting and reassuring. It taught Alfred patience and gave him scope for reflection, a way to make peace with himself and control any anxiety arising from the disturbing news from Lebanon. The fun-loving and always hospitable Cajuns also helped Alfred forget his worries. They didn't know where Alfred came from, and most didn't know him by his name. To them he was just Sweet Papa, and they didn't care that he spoke that very marked French language of theirs with a very marked accent. And in time he managed to speak Acadian French fairly well, so well that he could pass for a Cajun in the eyes of anyone who had not met him before.

In March of 1913, Woodrow Wilson was inaugurated president of the United States, the third president—after Theodore Roosevelt and William Taft—since Alfred's arrival in Louisiana. On the continent, a second war loomed in the Balkans, and the tension was high in the Levant. From Spain to Russia, nations were keeping their powder dry and guns ready. Then came the spark from Sarajevo that ignited the blaze. Najibeh was with her family in Shwayr, Helena in Hadath, and Alfred along Bayou Lafourche when an infernal sequence of events culminated in the outbreak of World War I.

In New Orleans the bubonic plague was spreading, and citizens waged a war on rats. A year later, a devastating hurricane hit southeastern Louisiana, the eye passing over Grand Isle, its storm surge so powerful that it flooded the entire island before moving northward across Bayou Lafourche to New Orleans and further up to Lake Pontchartrain and Maurepas, with gusts as high as 120 miles per hour. In Lebanon, the British navy imposed an embargo on all products entering Beirut, while the locally grown products were seized by Jamal Pasha to feed the fourth army stationed in Beirut and Mount Lebanon. To make matters worse, an invasion of locusts decimated the land, stripping it of any possible source of food not yet confiscated by the Turkish army. In Louisiana, the sheer anguish of wrecked homes and lost plantations; in Lebanon, famine and death. In many ways, 1915 was a year of total desolation.

Lockport suffered a good share of the damage the hurricane wrought on Cajun country. Hurricanes back then were not rated or given a name, but the storm of 1915 must have had a high magnitude. The Nicolas and Josephs took refuge in their little house, sealing the windows and doors with tape. The Deep South did not have professional meteorologists until 1951, so in the time of Alfred, there were no warning systems; there were not even any radio stations along Bayou Lafourche then. So people relied on their experience of past storms, noting when the winds picked up and the squalls threw sheets of rain. Most people didn't take these early signals very seriously, but Alfred and Habib did, and they prepared themselves for a major storm.

A few days later, after the hurricane had passed, Alfred went down the bayou, this time without his valise. It was the first time in thirteen years that Sweet Papa wandered along Bayou Lafourche with no weight dangling from his shoulder. He walked where he could, some towpaths being completely inundated, then climbed onto pirogues with local residents, hurrying from house to house to help those who had suffered the full fury of the storm. He lent his hands, his strong and rugged hands, to those who needed help, as others in the bayou did, neighbor to neighbor, each pained by the misery of the other. Never before had Sweet Papa been sweeter to the hearts of the people than that day and every day of that week that Alfred stayed on to help his friends recover. One can imagine the resilience of Cajuns and their joie de vivre when, like Alfred, one experiences their resolve that first evening after the storm—roofs gone, boats sunk, possessions unaccounted for—families sat and sang together. They sang for Mary, hymns of joy and hymns of thanks; then they switched to the Cajun music, some even dancing; and despite their damaged homes and shattered kitchenware, some offered pots of gumbo and bottles of beer to their guests. Only after a week had passed did Alfred return to Lockport, where he dug into a large portion of kebbeh nayeh that Zahia had prepared, only the bulgur was not there.

The bulgur was not there because Kareem Abboud had been unable to import any from Lebanon since the beginning of hostilities and had been out of stock for some time. Lebanon was as desolate as Bayou Lafourche, not by a storm but by famine. Children were dying with bloated bellies, and adults looked like walking skeletons. Najibeh, now fifteen, was encouraged by her father to help out. She dug up their garden in Shwayr searching for roots and helped her mother improvise new recipes that used the found ingredients. Long-forgotten recipes were soon back in fashion, and to feed the hungry, Najibeh distributed a kebbeh made of nameless roots and chickpeas, which very much resembled meat. She went out with a large tray of pseudo-kebbeh cakes, still steaming hot and dripping with olive oil, and went round her village distributing what she had. She did this every day and every night, for as long as her garden bore fruit, cooking in a frying pan over a wood fire, for the starving multitude.

Later in 1915, the agents of Jamal Pasha managed to obtain a list of the names of people who favored Lebanese independence and had close relations with the French. Possibly, the dragoman of the French embassy, a certain Philippe Zalzal, played the snitch. Eleven intellectuals paid the price for their determination to end autocratic rule and plea for independence; they were left hanging from ropes on the Place de la Liberté, which would eventually be renamed a fourth time, Martyrs' Square, in their honor. At the same time, political assassinations were a common occurrence, with men taken from their homes and left hanging from trees or thrown on the ground, their bodies riddled with gunshot wounds.

During this time, Helena did not leave the house in Hadath. Loyal Uncle Tanios provided for everything. Julia and her children kept Helena company, and she cooked for them, ingenious preparations she concocted with whatever ingredients she had on hand. Indeed, it remains a fact that much of today's traditional Lebanese cuisine was inspired by such hungry moments across our tormented history.

Alfred sat on the porch in Lockport; it was night and the sky over Cajun country in Indian summer was clear and dotted with glowing stars. He leaned back in his rocking chair and stared at the peaceful heavens, using the stars and constellations to interpret the singular meaning of his own life's history. For a man of little education, he possessed great culture and wisdom. Suddenly he saw himself transported on a bed of stars to Hadath, to his mother Helena, who stood with open arms awaiting his embrace.

Najibeh sat on the balcony of her home in Shwayr. The night was dark, although the moon was shining behind the dense forest of pine. A cacophony of night grasshoppers, owls, and wolves sounded all around her. She fixed her eyes on the sky and dreamed of the day when people would live lives of justice and righteousness.

The day would soon come when Najibeh would befriend Alfred and when they would look at eternity together with the assurance of the bayou dweller and with the heart of the "lady with the lamp" (the nickname given to another angel of mercy, Florence Nightingale). But for now, there was only a moon, and stars, and the dark cloak of the night to keep them together, two lonely souls, hungry for peace, hungry for life.

A peddler by wagon

By 1916, a valise or two were no longer enough for Alfred's fast-growing business. The time was right for him to purchase a horse and wagon to maximize his sales. That would be like driving a store on wheels, with enough space to carry a wide diversity of goods, clothing, jewelry, and special orders for his friends along the bayou. With a horse and wagon, he could travel greater distances, further south to the islands, where he was always expected.

By then, Lockport had developed into a lively commercial town serving the Lower Lafourche delta. So Alfred bought the wagon from Toups Brothers, a wheelwright shop, and the horse from A. A. Scott, the principal livery, both in Lockport. Behind the house the Josephs and Nicolas shared stood a barn, where Alfred parked the wagon and tied the horse whenever he was back from the bayou. In a place where animals often got their names for a reason, it was not hard for Alfred to figure one out for his new peddling companion, who took the heavy weight off his shoulders. He named his horse Mac, short for macaque, the sturdily built short-tailed monkey, probably because it was so lively and didn't stay in one place for very long. Alfred took good care of his horse, bought the best feed from the livery stable on Main Street, washed him regularly and curried his brown coat while humming the Byzantine hymns from Mar Elias Church in Hadath.

As Alfred's purchases in New Orleans expanded, he was no longer able to carry them himself, and the distance from Lockport was too far to take his wagon. He used the Barker Barge Line steamboats that plied the canals and lakes that connected New Orleans and Lockport to ship his merchandise. During one of his visits to New Orleans, while busy unloading a cart full of merchandise on the docks, a young man approached and offered to help. Alfred was happy to accept the offer, noticing the man seemed honest and had a jovial look. So Alfred hired him, a proud moment, for it was the first time that Alfred had employed anyone, a major milestone. Of course, the job was a brief one, nothing involved, but Alfred always needed a hand while in New Orleans and the man needed a small job to supplement his income. Johnny was the worker's name, an African American whose father had been freed from slavery after the Civil War. Johnny liked to read and could write, too, but what he excelled at was music, and he played divinely. He called himself "the banjo man" and played jazz with a pickup band every night on Basin Street in Storyville, "the city of vice," as it was known to some, but also the birthplace of jazz, a music that would soon conquer the world.

Following a well-organized routine, Alfred saw his business grow and grow. He went down to the bayou almost every week, disappeared among the islands, returned to Lockport to restock, and then left for another week of peddling. Every fortnight, Alfred went to New Orleans for a couple of days, met Johnny, who would hire a horse-driven cart for his visit, stop at Lucien Bonck's and Julius Cohn's for his regular purchases, wander around Tchoupitoulas Street in search of bargains, and travel back the next day with enough merchandise for two weeks. At times, his brother George accompanied him, although he relied on Alfred to purchase the items he sold in Terrebonne with his valise on his back.

Due to its location, Lockport was becoming a major hub for travelers. The locks installed on the bayou at the end of the nineteenth century meant that ships traveling in both directions on the Mississippi were funneled into the town. And with the rise of American industry, traffic on the river was heavier than ever. In addition, oil rigs were making their debuts on the landscape down in Grand Isle, furthering Lockport's importance along a busy commercial route. Alfred and Habib had expected these developments when they decided to move to Lockport from New Orleans, and they wanted to be in a position to benefit from the boom in commerce.

After nineteen years of peddling, first fruits and vegetables and then clothing, Habib and his brother Alexander had decided to "settle down" and open stores in Lockport. Habib Joseph opened his clothing store on the canal side of town, on Main Street in Lockport, and the entire family gathered one day in 1916 to witness the moment when the name "H. Joseph and Sons" was unveiled on the front of the store. Even Ann Murray was there for the occasion, and she must have felt immense joy and pride at the sight of her son's name over the store, the same name that had been her husband's. Many years had passed since she fled Beirut, when that city was still part of a wilayat under Ottoman rule, when she had been smuggled out with her two sons and come to New Orleans. Did she weep that day, standing in front of the store with the name freshly painted for everybody to see? The Moujaes are known to be stubborn and tough but also highly emotional. Which emotion won out that day? I have not been able to find out.

Alexander Joseph soon opened his own store in the same business district, renting space in Dr. Price's building, a few doors down from his brother.

The year 1916 was also when Alfred Nicola signed a declaration of intention to become a naturalized American citizen. "It is my bona fide intention to renounce forever all allegiance and fidelity to any foreign prince, potentate, state or sovereignty, and particularly to Mehmed V, Emperor of the Ottomans, of whom I am now a subject . . . it is my intention in good faith to become a citizen of the United States of America . . . so help me God," read the declaration. Unable to write, Alfred signed it with an X in front of a clerk at the Eastern District of Louisiana. It was a Thursday, January 27, 1916. Lucien and Julius took him out for the evening, and the three men dined and drank at Antoine's to celebrate Alfred's forthcoming citizenship. The peddler from the bayou now appeared to be a well-to-do young man wearing an all-cotton blue-and-white-striped seersucker suit, a fashionable hat, and a pocket watch and chain of solid gold. This was their first night out since Alfred had arrived in New Orleans, and the three men decided to visit Storyville, probably on the suggestion of Lucien, who had already frequented the city of joy a number of times. Johnny was playing there that night, as every night, and he had repeatedly invited Alfred to come and listen to him play.

To be sure, Alfred was not a man for such escapades. His seriousness and the hardships that forged his character were framed by a certain righteousness inculcated long ago by his mother and the next-door church. Yet they went, Lucien, Julius, and Alfred, across Canal Street and into Basin Street, passing closed houses and brothels, for a casual night out that the successful young men felt entitled to. On Alfred's suggestion, they went to Minnie White's where Johnny played, much to the astonishment of "the banjo man," who never expected Alfred to show up at his cabaret or in Storyville at all. The music sounded strange to Alfred but pleasant and catchy, with drums, piano, saxophone, and banjo. Johnny also sang as he played, songs like "Down the Lazy River" and "Basin Street," colorful music that was unique, a melding of different styles of music and different cultures, spiced up to the chili heat of New Orleans.

Although he didn't know it then, Alfred was witnessing the birth of jazz and may have encountered Sidney Bechet or Louis Armstrong, both of whom started off at Storyville before going on to fame elsewhere. In 1916, Armstrong, who later took his distinctive voice and trumpet-playing up to Chicago, was five years younger than Alfred and made his living in Storyville. Back then jazz was seen as a vice equal to more familiar sins and was fought by those who considered this part of the city as a cancer that needed surgery. And Storyville did soon disappear, when World War I reached a fever pitch and the United States started recruiting soldiers.

Jazz brought together a mix of races and cultures from the broad palette of Louisiana. White and black, French from all three derivations, Spanish, English, and even an Asian Pacific blend of Filipino and Chinese. Storyville gave a certain libertine aroma to a blend-in-the-making, lifting all taboos so anything could emerge from the strings, drums, and tubes. That was the magic of jazz and the no-less impressive magic of Storyville, a part of town that ironically took its name from an evangelical judge who had intended to stamp out prostitution altogether. Johnny played his banjo with zeal and excitement, his friend Alfred there to watch him, possibly the first and only guest he had ever had. I recently had the chance to connect with this traditional Louisianan music that was played in the early part of the twentieth century and that has a unique venue in New Orleans today starring Fritzel's jazz band.

Later that year, only a year after the hurricane and two years after the yellow fever epidemic, Lockport was struck by disaster once again when a fire engulfed much of the town, practically devastating the entire business district. Habib and Alexander worked frantically to move their stock to the bayou side, and by a stroke of luck, their stores were unscathed. Alfred was in the islands when the disaster occurred, and he only learned about it when he saw the charred ruins while driving his wagon home.

The significant changes occurring in Europe and the Levant were hard for anyone to grasp, let alone Sweet Papa, whose lifestyle was now in harmony with the easy-going ways of the bayou Cajuns. Yet, at this moment, history was being written—in the blood of the innocent no doubt, but written all the same. In 1917, Alfred enlisted in the army in Thibodaux, the county seat of Lafourche Parish, and was issued a mobilization number on his draft card. Alfred was in the first generation of Americans to be subjected to the Selective Service Act of May 18, 1917, which authorized the president of the United States to temporarily increase the size of the armed forces, and it was his patriotic duty to serve, now that he had declared his intent to become an American citizen. The war ended before he could serve, but his enrollment document is still there to bear witness to his growing devotion to the land of America.

"I lift my lamp beside the golden door"

While war raged across Europe, Syria was also witnessing a moment of change. The Sharif of Mecca, the protector of the Holy Muslim shrines, called for a rebellion against the Ottomans and was supported by the British, who captured Jerusalem by the end of 1917. The sharif's son, Faysal, entered Syria and was proclaimed King of the Arab Republic, one that extended across all of natural Syria, which until now had been a continuous spectrum of land and peoples that lived across the Fertile Crescent. But this understanding was not to the taste of the French, who had earlier, in 1916, secretly negotiated with the British the Sykes-Picot agreement.

The agreement outlined the two empires' proposed spheres of influence should the Allies defeat the Ottomans in World War I.

In the end, the Arab Republic only existed for three weeks. The French sent troops to Beirut under the command of General Henri Gouraud and evicted Faysal, whose army took a blow at Maysaloun, at a mountain pass across the anti-Lebanon. (After defeating Faysal, General Gouraud is said to have stood on the grave of Saladin in Syria and taunted the twelfth-century empire builder with "Saladin, we are back!") The British, who had previously supported Faysal, turned a blind eye to all this and went about appointing kings to the new kingdoms they had masterminded: they gave Faysal the territory of what is now Iraq; while the Nadjaf, and with it the holy shrines of Mecca and Medina, went to the house of Saud, which would establish their Kingdom of Saudi Arabia in place of their previous ally, Sharif Abdallah. For consolation, they gave the latter the desert lands on the east bank of the Jordan River, the future Hashemite kingdom of Jordan. The British had made too many promises during the war to gain the confidence of a large base of local princes, promises that they now could hardly keep. One such promise was in the 1917 letter of Arthur Balfour to Baron Rothschild, in which the British foreign secretary confirmed to the leader of the British Jewish community the support of his government for the establishment in Palestine of a Homeland for the Jewish people ("from Dan to Beersheba").

Circumventing a resolution backed by President Woodrow Wilson, which stipulated "the right of people for self-governance," the French and British dressed up the colonization of the newly created five countries as "mandates," pretending disinterested assistance to the nationals in their quest for self-determination. The mandates were endorsed by the newly formed League of Nations, and although an international inquiry, the King-Crane Commission, formed exclusively of Americans came to the Levant and recognized the indigenous people's rejection of the mandates, the Wilson administration played along. (Interestingly enough, one of the commission's findings was that the Arab majority had actually requested an American mandate with a democratically elected constituent assembly.)

The framework of the Sykes-Picot agreement was revisited by the Allied powers at the Liguria seaport of San Remo in 1920. It placed Jerusalem under direct British rule instead of remaining an open city with an international status. It also gave France an upper hand on Syria. From his residence in Beirut, the French high commissioner Gouraud declared the birth of the "Grand Liban," a territory comprising Mount Lebanon; parts of the previous Sandjaks of Beirut, Damascus, and Tripoli; the coastal cities; and the fertile plateau of the Bekaa. The flag of Grand Liban was raised over the government building for the first time: a French tricolor standard with a cedar tree in the middle.

While all this was happening, Habib and Zahia Joseph were busy raising children—Isaac, Fred, Isabel, Joe, and Celima. The house in Lockport was crowded, with the three Nicola brothers, the three Josephs, and their five children. Alfred was doing so well that he was considering going home to Hadath for a visit to see his mother, invest some money, and, most important, get married. He was turning thirty-five and wanted to start a family of his own, and his mother had told him, on their occasional phone conversations, of a young, well-bred, and educated girl from a good family, Najibeh Meshrek, the "lady with the lamp." Back in those days, marriages were often arranged ceremonies, in which mothers were very active. Coming from matriarchal ancestries, Arab societies empowered their women this way, and they still do today. Mothers searched around for the perfect match, and potential brides had to have everything: education, looks, manners, a good reputation, youth, and propriety ("the lips only brushed against by the mother"); furthermore a likely bride had to be from a good family and, if not wealthy, at least reasonably land-owning. In these regards, Najibeh Meshrek was a good catch, and Helena worried that she would slip through her fingers and be taken by some other candidate, not Alfred.

This was also the time when Alfred took more time for himself, was out more often, came down to New Orleans every weekend to meet with his friends, as if he were discovering the world outside of Hadath and the bayou for the first time. He wanted to catch up on the many things he had neglected in past years. First on his list was learning how to read and write. In addition to wearing seersucker suits and gold watches, he needed to sign his name with a real fountain pen. In a way, the stratified society of Louisiana provided benchmarks. He was never indifferent to the ostentatious caste of the Creoles, who owned beautiful estates in New Orleans and in the Faubourgs, and Alfred wanted to be like them. He had saved money and had a few ideas on how to multiply this seed capital, but for now, he took the time in New Orleans to learn from Johnny, the banjo player, the vowels, consonants, and magic of words. With his rough hands, Alfred would never master the art of writing, nor would he ever be an accomplished reader, his literacy limited to basic sentences. Yet he gave himself wholeheartedly to the task, working as hard as he could, and was soon able to say that he was a wealthy, literate, and cultured man of his era.

This Alfred had a chance to demonstrate on July 17, 1920, standing in front of a judge at the United States District Court for the Eastern District of New Orleans, when he signed his full name on the certificate of naturalization. Back in 1917, on the petition for naturalization, he had only drawn a shaky X. Three years later, he proudly signed his name with bold solid assurance. Again he renounced in writing his allegiance to the emperor of the Ottomans, now Mehmet VI, and took the oath "to support and defend the Constitution of the United States of America." His two witnesses and signatories to the act were none other than Julius Cohn and Lucien Bonck. Alfred was now an American citizen. He had earned it and he felt himself equal to anyone else in the generous land of America; he even felt he was the "brick that was ignored by the masons, and which turned to be the cornerstone of the edifice." Storyville was no longer there for the three men to celebrate, as it was demolished in 1917 after the decision was made to eradicate vice from the Crescent City. So they dined in the French Quarter and spent the evening listening to jazz, the "evil" music that had thankfully survived Storyville.

The Spanish flu hit Louisiana the same year, in 1920. It ravaged the city but did not stop Sweet Papa from going down to Bayou Lafourche to see his friends and customers. He even tempted Johnny to come and work with him now that his earnings from music were curtailed by the demolition of Storyville. Johnny made the trip with Alfred occasionally but was not suited to life on the bayou. This was not the case with George, who loved the bayou and whom Alfred had chosen to replace him while he was away in Lebanon; for that was his plan: return to Hadath, marry, and bring his new wife back to Louisiana.

Alfred needed George. He did not want to inconvenience his friends down the bayou, especially south of Leeville and in the islands, who relied on him for clothing and accessories. At the same time, he did not want to leave his peddling territory open for some competitor to steal. George could fill in for him in the interim, and George would do it, for Alfred had always looked after his younger brother, counseled him, and helped him with stock and money. Moreover, the bayou people took to his younger brother, and Sweet Papa made sure to introduce him to every house and plantation along the route.

I can only imagine what the last ride down Bayou Lafourche must have been like for Alfred, before he left for Hadath. Hardened by years of labor, he was nonetheless as emotional as any of the Moujaes and Shwayri that preceded him. I can see Alfred giving away as many gifts as there were people, shaking hands and eating last meals with the fishermen—po'boys, jambalaya, stuffed crabs, and etouffées. I can also see Alfred teaching George the tricks of the trade, his younger brother next to him in the wagon, pointing at houses and impressing on George the knowledge he had gained in eighteen years of peddling. Finally he took George to the bank at Cut-Off and signed over his account to him, appointing him as a signatory. He did the same at the Hibernia Bank in New Orleans, giving him control of the account there.

Alfred also turned over his stock to his brother George, as well as the horse Mac and the wagon. George was hesitant to take the horse, as he was happy peddling with the valise on his back, a habit he would never lose, using the wagon only occasionally, mainly to transport stock while on his travels down to the southernmost part of the parish and Grand Isle. What both men did not know was that George would eventually make his mark on the route that had been traveled exclusively by Alfred; that he would be known as "Sweet Papa" in his own right, sliding into Alfred's shoes and perpetuating a legend that is still alive in people's minds.

Sweet Papa George would continue traveling with a valise for several more years, until peddling was no longer needed and distances seemed to shrink with the popularity of motor vehicles. Even then, there are many stories of George driving the fanciest car, peddling with a car trunk full of clothing, stopping by the side of the road to sleep in his car, just as he and Alfred did along the towpaths in previous decades. Apart from the wagon, horse, and merchandise, Alfred also gave George a valuable possession he acquired from the same Hiller Jewelers in New Orleans, a pinky ring with a precious diamond. George wore it all his life.

As for Habib and Zahia, they would have two more children, Josephine and Emile, during the next three years. The last of their children would be christened in Lockport, and Kareem Abboud, the grocery owner in New Orleans and their friend from the early days, would stand as godfather. In the absence of a Greek Orthodox Church, this generation of Joseph children would be baptized in the Roman faith, the principal faith of the Cajuns of Bayou Lafourche. Ann Murray, the Moujaes who had come first to Louisiana, would pass away in 1925, which would also be the year of the passing of Helena, Alfred's mother.

Comfortable that George would take care of his business, Alfred went to a travel agent and bought two tickets for Hadath, one for him and one for his brother Alexander, who had never really taken to peddling in America. As if to settle scores with destiny, Alfred and Alexander boarded with first-class tickets. They traveled in the wagon from Lockport, driven by Johnny, crossed Bayou Lafourche one final time, and alighted at the railroad depot at Rita to catch the train to Raceland and then the Southern Pacific to New Orleans. Alfred had a large green trunk with metal locks. In it, he folded and arranged his last order, one destined for his mother and his uncle Tanios, and for himself a stock of shirts, cotton underwear, and suits from his beloved Louisiana. As the vessel left the dock in New York, Alfred looked at the Statue of Liberty, the lady he had encountered on his arrival in America eighteen years before; back then she seemed to snub him with her profound silence and haughty looks. Now when he looked at her, she looked back, smiled and raised her eyes, shook her torch, and spoke words that he alone could understand. The keeper of the golden door had spoken to him as she had to millions before.

Here at our sea-washed, sunset gates shall stand
A mighty woman with a torch, whose flame
Is the imprisoned lightning, and her name
Mother of Exiles. From her beacon-hand
Glows world-wide welcome; her mild eyes command
The air-bridged harbor that twin cities frame.

"Keep, ancient lands, your storied pomp!" cries she
With silent lips. "Give me your tired, your poor,
Your huddled masses yearning to breathe free,
The wretched refuse of your teeming shore.
Send these, the homeless, tempest-tossed to me,
I lift my lamp beside the golden door!"[1]

As the ship made its way out to sea, Alfred stared back at the skyline of New York, now crowded with skyscrapers. His eighteen years in New Orleans swam before his eyes, people and places, friends he had made, and customs he had lived by. The smell of fried oysters and the shouts of trappers ecstatic after a good hunt, the elegantly dressed and barefoot children on a barge crossing the bayou to church, the Cajun music that played no matter what, the superstitions and the simple conversations. It was all there before him as he departed. "America," he said to himself, "you land of plenty, you land of generosity."

When Alfred and Alexander sighted Beirut, they weren't sure what to expect. They knew their mother and uncle would be there on the dock waiting for them; they also knew that the city they were about to enter would be very different from the one they had left. When Alfred had left eighteen years earlier, the regime in Mount Lebanon was the mutasarifiya, and the Ottomans ruled Beirut. Since then, there had been many changes; cut off from news during his month-long journey home, Alfred did not even know if the French were still supporting a "Grand Liban." In reality, the principle of "Grand Liban" would not have meant much to the two men who had been half a world away for so long. From the mutasarifiya to the rule of terror under the Young Turks government; the depredations of Jamal Pasha, the famine and desolation throughout Mount Lebanon, the fall of the wilayats, and the various events dictated by generals Allenby and Gouraud; the Arab Republic under Faysal and his defeat by the French, the forced mandates, the announcement by a French high commissioner of a Grand Liban: all these were drastic changes, changes that occurred during Alfred's absence and hard to fathom by a bayou-dweller who had lived to the rhythm of the lazy river. Nevertheless, Alfred was in for a few more political changes and surprises!

1. Excerpt from "The New Colossus," by Emma Lazarus, engraved on a bronze plaque and mounted inside the monument.

Part III

Alfred's legacy

7

Returning to a country in total upheaval

In his absence: The dismemberment of an empire

Back in Hadath, Alfred struggled to make sense of the changes that had occurred in his absence. True, he had heard about some world events, but down in the bayou news traveled slowly, especially news from distant continents with no particular relevance in Bayou Lafourche. The years he had been away were certainly critical to the shaping of a new world, and even more so for the remapping of the Middle East, the name that was now in vogue for the region. It was introduced in 1902 by Alfred Mahan, an American naval officer and historian, to denote the region between Arabia and India, and it became a figure of speech in the diplomatic corridors of the British Arab bureau in Cairo during the First World War.

When Alfred came home, the times were uncertain, not only for the Grand Liban that had been declared by the French high commissioner the previous year but for the whole region. He left for Louisiana holding a travel permit with the thugra of Sultan Abdul Hamid II, when Mount Lebanon was under the mutasarifiya regime and Beirut a wilayat of the Ottoman Empire; when Europe was governed by Romanoff Russia, Habsburg Austro-Hungary, Hohenzollern Germany, Third Republic France, and Saxe-Coburg–Gotha Britain. He returned to Greater Lebanon, an entity that was new in every respect and governed by the French. Europe too had totally changed. Russia had fallen to the Bolsheviks, the Austro-Hungarian Empire had been dislocated, and Germany had been subdued by the victorious allies. Only France and Britain preserved their territorial integrities and traditional governance (the English monarchs cannily dropping their German surname, Saxe-Coburg–Gotha, in favor of the more appropriate Windsor).

In addition, new entities had emerged from the belly of the defunct Ottoman Empire, turning the familiar four-colored map of Europe that Alfred had known into a mosaic of nations, some confirmed and independent, others in-the-making and still dependent on other nations. Alfred knew that America had taken part in the war effort and that President Woodrow Wilson had drawn a line to contain the victors who were hungry for spoils, affirming the right of every nation for self-governance and independence. The League of Nations had been formed, again as part of Wilson's Fourteen Points, announced in 1917, when the United States entered the war.

War was over and peace conferences multiplied. (I have counted no fewer than thirty between 1918 and the day Alfred Nicola set foot in Beirut again.) War was over, yet instability, uncertainty, and chaos shaped the underlying mood on the streets in Egypt, Mesopotamia (Iraq), Afghanistan, Persia (Iran), Anatolia (Turkey), Arabia, Palestine, Syria, and, of course, Grand Liban. Under the pressure of their electorates and their faltering economies, the prime ministers of Britain and France were quick to disband the large armies that were stationed in the Middle East during the war, a decision that weighed heavily on the ground. This decision also impacted the outcomes of the peace conferences that dragged on for over two years and lost momentum with the demobilization of the one million British soldiers who had been on duty in the Middle East.

This was an incredible number of soldiers for the era—Britain had around forty million inhabitants back then—and it's not surprising that the British made the laws and surpassed their allies in their mastery of the region, France in particular. Now that this overwhelming British force was gone, it became nearly impossible for London to prevent the new countries in the Fertile Crescent from falling out with one another, especially since the former European allies were conniving to outmaneuver one another in the region. Uprisings occurred everywhere, and the British, their interests endangered, turned to their Indian regiments for help. As a result, Saad Zaghloul of Egypt was time and again exiled to Malta, followed by Amanullah Khan, the young amir of Afghanistan who threatened the integrity of the British dominion in India. These men ended up planting the seeds of independence for their countries that would bear fruit in the coming decades.

Unable to contain the turmoil, whether due to real nationalism or simply outbreaks of violence encouraged by rival European nations, Britain ended up relinquishing many of the gains it had secured in previous agreements entered during the war. Supported by the Arab Bureau in Cairo, Reza Pahlavi, a colonel in the Persian army of the Qadjar sultan, marched into Teheran with his Cossack followers in February 1921 and seized power, ushering in a new dynasty that was to last some six decades. In 1923, the leader of the Turkish National Movement, Mustafa Kemal, defied the established order and moved the capital of Turkey from Istanbul to Ancyra (Ankara), away from the British navy moored in the Dardanelles, and placed himself at the head of a newly elected Turkish parliament. Greece, under the combative and highly spirited premier Eleutherios Venizelos, had received the

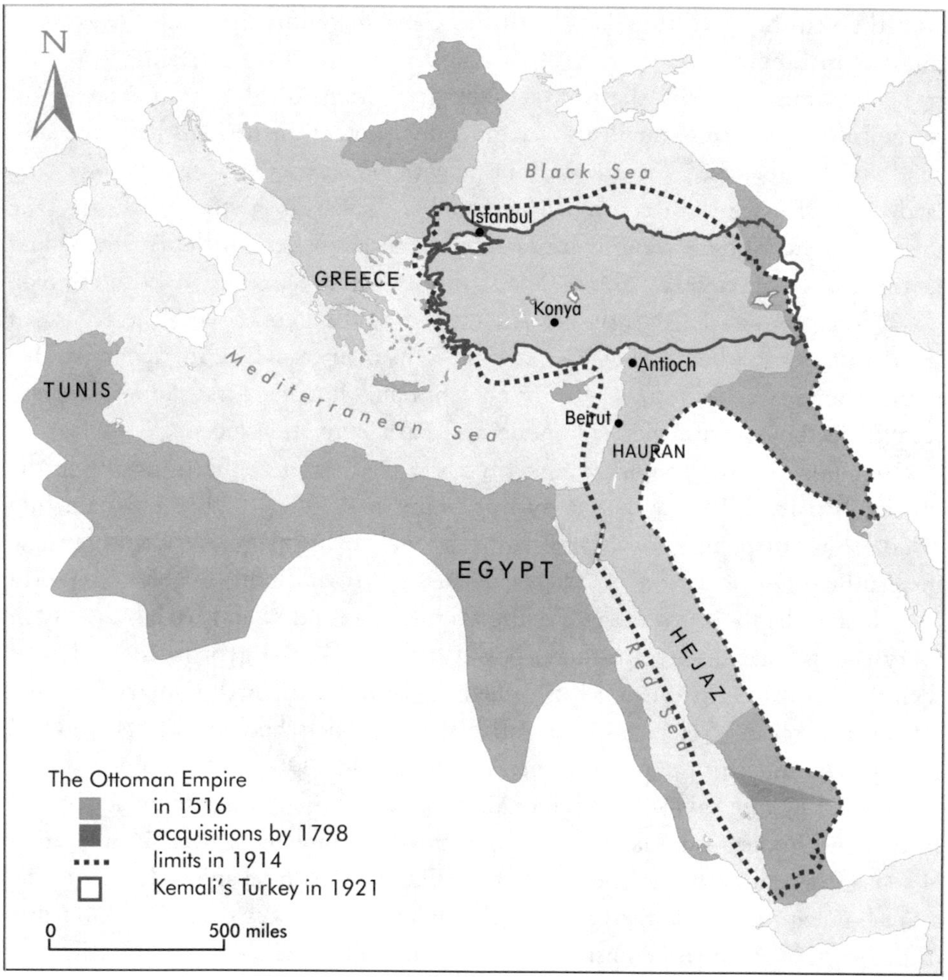

Map 6. The Ottoman Empire: Four centuries of rising then shrinking tides

go-ahead from the British to conquer the Aegean coast of mainland Turkey around the region of Smyrna (Izmir), restoring Hellenism to its former territory. Fighting there was in progress when Alfred returned to Hadath, and it took another two years before the Greeks were soundly beaten by Kemal, who in 1934 was granted the surname Atatürk, the "father of the Turks."

When war started in 1914, no one expected it would last long or cause the agonies and disarray it did. Within a year, the breadth of the conflict was obvious, and it was clear to the Allies that any solution would be found outside the trenches that were devouring soldiers by the thousands, to no avail. Early on, the Ottomans realized that their only chance to keep their empire together would be to oppose the French and British, nations that would tear the empire apart if they won the war. So the Ottomans joined the German camp, alongside the Austro-Hungarian Empire.

With their forces in the west at a standstill—the Allied forces unable to cut through German lines—the British sought a diversion in the Dardanelles, the water conduit that connected the Mediterranean with the Black Sea, an area long coveted by the Russians but controlled by Istanbul. The British strategy was to take the war to the Ottomans and, with Istanbul in their pocket, hit the Austrians and Germans on their eastern flank. When it was executed, however, in 1915, the plan was a complete disaster. Nearly nine months of fighting ended with the retreat of the British army, which left behind 250,000 of its own casualties and a comparable number among the Ottomans. Winston Churchill lost his First Admiralty as a result, and the governments of London and Paris both succumbed.

Gallipoli, as the conflict is sometimes referred to, after the peninsula in the European part of Turkey, was a turning point in the war. It thrust Britain into Middle Eastern politics on a large scale, if only to justify to the British people the crushing loss of personnel. Thereafter, since 1916 and until the Second World War, Britain had a new strategy for the Middle East and would have some say in every change that took place there, however banal, from Egypt to India. It was then that the Arab Bureau was established in Cairo, staffed with military and civil intelligence, mostly from the Conservative Party, public-school aristocrats who had strong connections in the political corridors in London. Of these, two figures were to leave lasting imprints on the region: Mark Sykes, whose shuttle diplomacy earned Britain and France—and later Russia and Italy—an agreement over the allocation of spoils from future dismemberment of the Ottoman Empire; and T. E. Lawrence, a much-eulogized yet conflicted personality whose ascendancy over the Arab tribes in the western Arabian Peninsula made a lasting difference.

Unlike Sykes, a wealthy Tory Catholic who sat in the House of Commons, Lawrence was an exception in the Arab Bureau, for he had a modest background. The Arab Bureau, then a section of the Intelligence Department in Cairo, often relied on intelligence operations behind enemy lines. The Ottoman Empire was vast and had become very porous by this time, controlled by the Committee of Union and Progress (CUP), whose leadership was increasingly nervous. Since the coup in 1913 that gave them control over the government, the triumvirs at the head of the CUP did not have a plan of action to disengage from the Europeans who held much of the empire's debt and had clear aims on its dominions. While Enver and Talaat led the government from Istanbul, Jamal Pasha had control of all Syria (with Lebanon part of it). This he ran from Damascus as his private dominion, commanding the ruthless Fourth Army that would leave indelible scars on the region.

Jamal Pasha's goal was to contain the British in Egypt and, if possible, flush them from Syria. Containing them meant making sure that snitches in consulates and fifth-column informants among the populations were neutralized. His first measure when taking control in Damascus was to open a martial court in Aley, a short distance from Baabda, a court that passed judgments summarily and to Jamal Pasha's liking. He also organized his own circle of moles and had spies everywhere, many of them middle-class citizens seeking to please the overlord and better their social and economic positions. Many succumbed to dishonesty and had blameless people indicted for trivial reasons, sometimes their business competitors or long-time personal foes, in a land marked by generations of social cleavages. For Jamal, whoever was suspected of dealing with the enemy was systematically liquidated, as illustrated by the thirty-three hangings that took place in 1915 and 1916, showcased on the main city squares of Beirut and Damascus.

Greeks and Armenians were deemed highly suspicious, especially the Armenians who lived on the eastern side of Anatolia, on the border with Russia, with whose citizens they had Christianity in common. Tsarist intelligence agents found receptive ears among the neighboring Armenians, who had begun their own underground operations after the inception of the Dashnak, or the Armenian Revolutionary Federation, in 1890, and they used this channel to infiltrate Anatolia. Or at least this is what Enver and Jamal later claimed they believed. In any event, the reaction became one of history's greatest human tragedies. Mass deportations and unscrupulous killings were ordered, events referred to today as genocide: half the population of Turkish Armenia perished in 1915, a million and a half people. The tragic genocide of 1915 gave a *laissez-passer* to the Allied forces, the British in particular, allowing them to leverage public opinion at home to get an endorsement for the major resources they were committing in the Middle East.

One person who was adept at committing these resources to native tribes was none other than T. E. Lawrence himself, the so-called Lawrence of Arabia, known as "the man with the gold" by the Bedouins. Gold sovereigns were sent from the Arab Bureau in Cairo across the desert, whole cases on camel back, for Lawrence to spend building the army of Prince Faysal, second son of Sharif Hussein. A one-time favorite of the British armed services, which had provided him the means to exert an overarching grip over the Arab tribes, Sharif Hussein was soon to reveal the actual measure of his reach. A revolt brokered by the Arab Bureau in 1916 to give Arabs a head start at precipitating events turned out to be a flop for Hussein, who could not gather more than a thousand men. As a result, Hussein, a privileged correspondent of the high commissioner in Cairo, Henry McMahon, whose letters relayed the promises of a caliphate and of leadership over a unified Arab dominion, was downplayed in favor of Faysal. (McMahon had replaced Lord Herbert Kitchener in 1915, when the latter was called to London to sit as the head of the War Office at the beginning of the war.) The elegant prince, whose refined taste and stoic posture contrasted with a high nervousness, was ready to play the part that the Arab Bureau and Lawrence gave him, as long as he was given a throne.

Well before the war was concluded, the British were eager to remap the Middle East and reach agreement with the other Allied nations on the distribution of dominions. That task was assigned to Mark Sykes, who had assumed many positions within the Arab Bureau throughout his career. His counterpart on the French side was François Georges-Picot, the son of a hardliner colonialist, who founded the Comité de l'Afrique Française, delegated to enter in negotiations concerning the division of spoils after the war was ended. A series of meetings took place in London in January 1916, leading to the Sykes-Picot agreement, a framework for the allocation of territories. France received the region from Syria to Mosul in today's Iraq, while Britain appropriated all the southern territories. The agreement remained secret, unknown to foes and allies alike, and was only revealed, to much confusion, late in 1917, when tsarist Russia was toppled and the Bolsheviks found the document in Saint Petersburg. When Sharif Hussein got wind of the agreement, he certainly felt double-crossed, as the agreement was contrary to the promises he had received from High Commissioner McMahon in the famous letters known as the Hussein-McMahon Correspondence. Besides, the agreement was concluded with such secrecy that it seemed unlawful and had the taint of a backroom deal. While keeping communications open with the British, who replenished his coffers, Hussein tried for a while to reestablish contact with the Young Turk triumvirs, hoping to keep his options open.

To add complexity to a situation already intricate, Herzl's ideology of a Zionist state was back on the agenda. Looked on favorably now by Sykes, who had been indifferent earlier if not totally opposed, Zionism found its way to the decision rooms and gained the enthusiastic backing of British diplomacy, thanks to skilled advocators such as Vladimir Jabotinsky, who founded the Jewish Legion under the British army; David Ben-Gurion and Itzhak Ben-Zvi, leaders of the Labor Zionist movement; and Chaim Weizmann, president of the Zionist Organization and a respected scientist who lent his skills to the war effort (he would later become the first president of Israel). The result was a half-hearted declaration on November 2, 1917, by the foreign secretary, Lord Arthur James Balfour, committing to the establishment of a Jewish homeland in Palestine.

The strongmen of the war were Britain's David Lloyd George, France's Georges Clemenceau, and Woodrow Wilson after the United Stated was drawn in. The men were very different. While Lloyd George favored Britain's expansion, Clemenceau was known for his anticolonial positions. Concerned about the ongoing German threat, he believed France's troops should be fighting at home, not in some distant land. Wilson, for his part, had gained from his father and grandfather before him, both Presbyterian clergymen, a deep sense of duty and was not directly

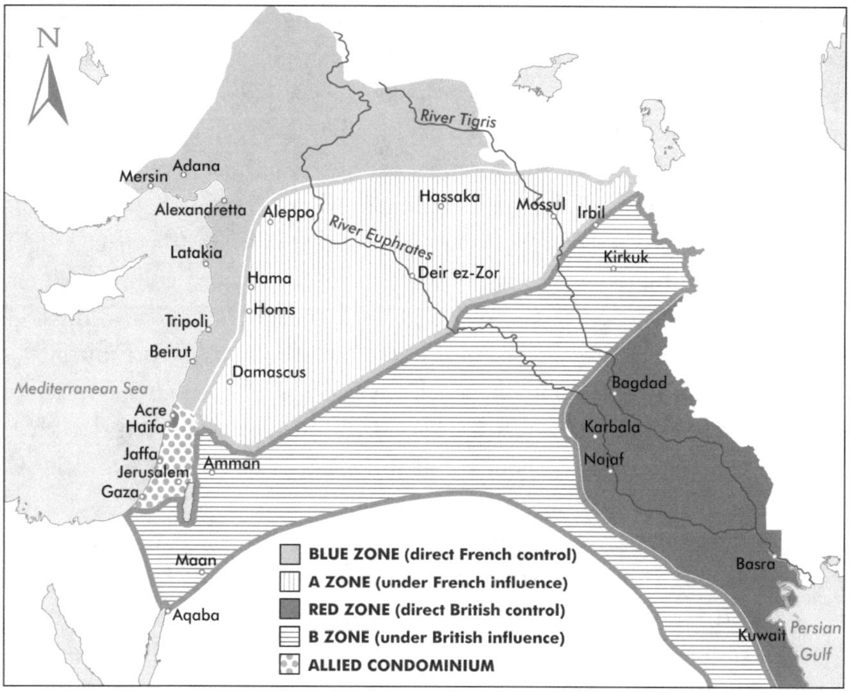

Map 7a. The plan of partition of the Middle East in 1916 (Sykes-Picot)

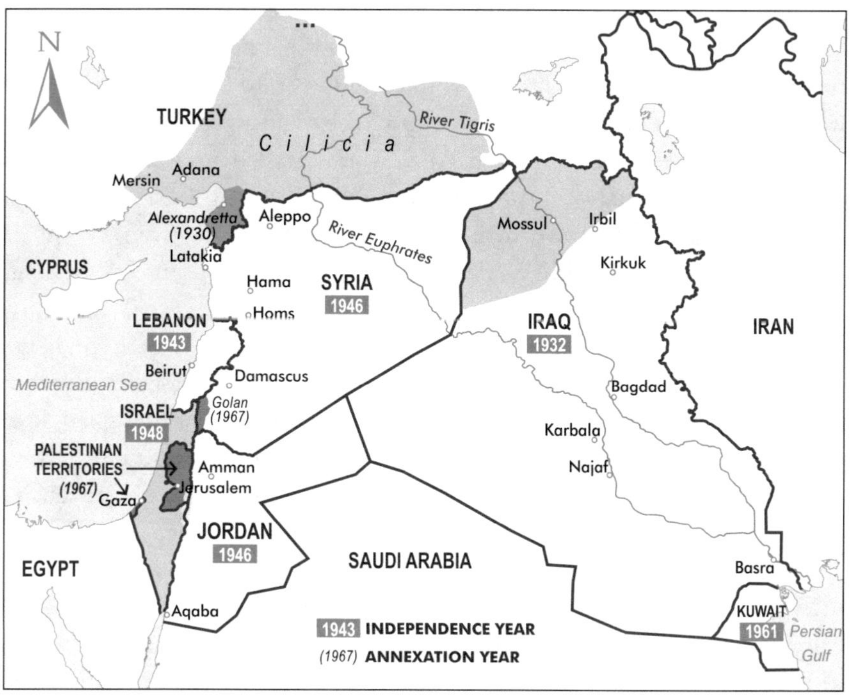

Map 7b. Implementation of the Sykes-Picot agreement (1920, San Remo) and later permanent territorial annexations

concerned with the Middle East, only the missions that were carried out by Americans there. The Syrian Protestant College, for example, represented an American interest in Beirut and could not be overlooked, especially since the chief financial supporter of President Wilson, Cleveland Hoadley Dodge, was closely associated with the college. Dodge was the founder of the Near East Foundation and was related to Daniel Bliss, a Christian missionary from Vermont and the founder and first president of the college, through marriage. His son (Bayard Dodge) and grandson (David Stuart Dodge) were also presidents of the college, which was renamed the American University of Beirut in 1920. There were also missionaries to look after, and the concerns of American philanthropists who funneled nearly one million dollars every month in aid to Syrian and Armenian populations. So Clemenceau and Wilson had a restrained and circumspect approach to the Middle East; Lloyd George was expansionist and intended to be first to plant the Union Jack on a subcontinent waiting to be taken.

While the trenches were filling with blood in Verdun and British soldiers were falling by the thousands (sixty thousand in one day, on July 1, 1916, at the Somme), Lloyd George sent Field Marshal Edmund Allenby to the Middle East with the clear order to "conquer Jerusalem by Christmas." Earlier, the battle for Aqaba, on the nodal tip of the Red Sea, was fought by Faysal, and the region was secured from the Turks. Lawrence later took credit for the fall of Aqaba, though it remains unclear what his role was precisely in the battle. The Sinai cleared, Allenby advanced from Cairo. Like a house of cards, Palestine fell in no time, and Allenby and his armored cars were in Jerusalem in early December 1917, a good two weeks before the deadline that had been given to him by Lloyd George.

Syria came next and, although Allenby was stalled for six months when a number of his regiments were called back to the Western Front, where the Battle of Verdun was raging, the field marshal was in Mesopotamia (Iraq) by the end of the year and was able to establish a liaison with the Indian contingents. Throughout his long march, Allenby was careful to coordinate with Faysal, so as not to give the impression he led an invading army, especially in large towns where the majorities of the population were Muslim. The entry into Damascus was a particular moment of glory for the Arabian prince, who raised the Sharifian flag (designed and produced by the Arab Bureau under the directives of Mark Sykes). This flag would also be raised in Beirut the following days, to the consternation of the French, who wanted Syria for themselves (as specified by the Sykes-Picot agreement).

Georges Clemenceau left office in 1920, ceding the seat of president of the council to Alexandre Millerand, who, unlike his anticolonial predecessor, did not intend to leave Syria to the British. With a small contingent, mostly Senegalese, General Henri Gouraud entered Beirut and chased Faysal to Damascus, defeating his army at a mountain pass. Though they had been allies throughout the war, the British and the French were less enamored with each other when the time came to settle scores. The French, for example, negotiated the terms of the surrender of Hungary without their British ally (or any other), while the British negotiated the surrender of the Ottomans without the French (or any other), signed onboard a frigate named *Agamemnon* (English humor knows no limits), which was moored in Moudros harbor at the Greek island of Lemnos.

With Winston Churchill back in frontline politics, appointed by Lloyd George to the War Office and later to the Colonial Office, events moved at a quicker pace. Faysal was given the Kingdom of Mesopotamia, renamed Iraq, while his brother, Abdullah, was given the lands on the eastern side of the Jordan River, which the British called Transjordan, today's Hashemite Kingdom of Jordan. The Saud, a client tribe of the British who held a knife against Hussein's Hashem tribe, gained new recognition and was given a kingdom of its own to be managed under the banner of the strict Wahhabi sect. This would become in later years the Kingdom of Saudi Arabia. With only minor changes, the Sykes-Picot agreement was put into practice, and the final settlements were confirmed at a summit that brought the victors together in San Remo, Italy, in April 1920.

In Beirut and across Mount Lebanon during World War I, Jamal Pasha had imposed conscription under the Turkish banner on every able-bodied man aged twenty-five to fifty years, except those who paid the *bedel*, an exonerating tax of forty-four Turkish pounds in gold. Fearing an Allied invasion of Syria across the Lebanese coast, Jamal ordered the destruction of all carts, wagons, and livestock that could be used by an invading army. As a result, food was scarce and distribution networks were disrupted. The meager agricultural produce was confiscated by Jamal to feed the eight thousand men of his Fourth Army, and what little was left was managed by commissions for food rationing, whose central offices were located in Hadath of all places. Bread and basic commodities were sold on black markets by unscrupulous clerks, and profiteers from Beirut and Mount Lebanon with access to storehouses multiplied their gains by mixing grains with dirt to trick the populace. What Jamal did not appropriate and the commissions did not confiscate an invasion of locusts ravaged in April 1915.

With famine rampant and thousands dying of starvation, Jamal Pasha, who fancied the climate of Mount Lebanon, was well received by the local gentry, who luxuriated in the riches they managed to hold on to and acquire, many deriving wealth from the deregulated and chaotic circumstances. Jamal Pasha made many visits to Sofar, a holiday retreat on a scenic hilltop near the Damascus Road. By then, the mutasarifiya had been suspended, and although governors were still appointed, their role was undermined by the Turkish military until the Administrative Council was finally abrogated in June 1916 by order of Jamal. The last two mutasarif would be Muslims, in total opposition to the Organic Statutes agreed upon since the origins of the regime and throughout the successive amendments.

A year later, the German military appeared on the streets of Beirut, under the command of Lieutenant-General Otto Liman von Sanders, who planned to invade Egypt from Syria to loosen the British grip on the European front—Gallipoli reenacted, in a way. Eventually local civilians took hold of the administration from the Turks, and Jamal Pasha left for Istanbul. Beirut was again the theater of retaliations from Allied marine forces.

By the end of the war, one hundred thousand people had died in Beirut and Mount Lebanon, mostly from the famine. Victims were collected in municipal carts and dumped in collective graves at the al-Raml quarter.

Alfred in Hadath: From mandate to independence

Away in Bayou Lafourche, Alfred Nicola did not have to live through the ordeal inflicted on his countrymen by Jamal Pasha and did not experience the suffering of the thousands who fell to famine. Najibeh, on the other hand, endured every episode of the agitation imposed by a dying empire that fell prey to insatiable colonial whims. The sour taste of hunger was still in her mouth years later, when a Second World War was at the doorstep, as were her memories of the corpses of children, victims of famine in a land that ironically had served as the "granary" of previous empires.

When Alfred came home, Tanios was still living there, his loving uncle who had looked after his mother and family all those years. His wife had gone to Brazil, where she had family, and stayed there, sending news every now and then. Nothing is known of her long years in Brazil, for she only came back in old age, a short time before Tanios passed away. He took her back at their home, next door to Alfred's, which Alfred had rented for him when he got married. With the income Alfred provided while in Louisiana, Tanios did not need to keep his shoe-repair workshop after he developed eye problems. Instead, he locked the shop, plastered over the door that opened onto the street, and fashioned a more private opening from inside the house. He redid the interior, painted the walls, and installed bedroom furniture—all to accommodate Alfred upon his return.

Julia and her children had relocated next door to a new home that Alexander Joseph purchased a few weeks before Alfred's arrival. Throughout Alfred's years in Louisiana, Julia and her children had lived with Helena and Uncle Tanios. Alfred had provided for them all and was happy to support his sister, who had married at fourteen, herself a child when she gave birth the first time. She was still very young—thirty-four years old—when Alfred came home, in 1920, although she had already borne Alexander Joseph five children. The youngest one, Edmond, would study medicine and become a specialist in urology, ushering in generations of new doctors as a professor at the American University Hospital (including my sister Roula and her husband, Michel). He lives in North Carolina today, retired, with his wife and adopted son.

The home in Hadath must have seemed silent and almost empty to Helena, with Julia and her five young children having moved out, replaced only by Alfred and his brother Alexander. From the first day of Alfred's return, Helena nagged like never before for Alfred to take a wife and give her grandchildren to cry and shout in the large empty house. She feared she would not have much longer to live, and like all Lebanese mothers, she wanted to see her son settled and the head of a large family before she parted.

Helena told him about Najibeh Meshrek, the young and dazzlingly beautiful girl of good stock from Shwayr, whose father was a notable jurist and whose brothers were medical doctors and lawyers. Najibeh was born in 1900 and had almost turned twenty when she and Alfred first met. He was fifteen years older, rough in manners and in the hands, but elegantly dressed in a Louisiana-cut seersucker suit; he was ambitious and a little pompous, probably like all successful and self-made men. Najibeh was highly educated for the time, having studied at the British School, an uncommon path that her father had encouraged; she was the youngest in a family of eight, all highly educated.

Alfred fell under her charms from the outset. She fell under his, the charm of an uncomplicated man whose sharp eyes spoke of wisdom and simplicity, of love of people and generosity. They met at her father's house in Beirut, in the presence of her mother and Helena, who made many visits to the kitchen to give the young people a chance to talk. She told him about herself, the war she had witnessed, the school she went to and her studies, and about Shwayr, the village of both their fathers.

Alfred spoke only a little, expressing more with his profound gaze than with words. He spoke of Louisiana, of its natural beauty and the goodness of its people. There is no doubt he spoke to her about his intention to go back in due course and make a life in Louisiana, and there is no doubt that she took in this information without giving her thoughts away. For what was definite for Najibeh was her intention to stay and build a life in Lebanon. It would take three whole years before Alfred and Najibeh finally swore an oath to one another, three years during which Alfred was not ready to turn his back on Louisiana, unwilling to distance himself from the land that had welcomed him with open arms and given to him so generously.

Najibeh was resolute, however, and the strong-willed and decisive young woman finally got Alfred to agree to her terms. They married on July 23, 1923, at the church next door, under the auspices of St. Elias, the patron saint who had blessed every step Alfred had undertaken. Najibeh was twenty-three; Alfred was thirty-eight.

Najibeh's strong character was a stroke of luck for Alfred, for she played a role in every decision he made when investing the money he had saved while peddling in Louisiana. His own business flair may not have been enough when closing deals and buying property, for Alfred was a bit too sentimental. Behind the sturdy exterior and bushy eyebrows beat a big heart that gave generously at will without always anticipating the consequences. Many times in the bayou he had gone unpaid for goods that he had left with customers who had promised to pay but who never did. Najibeh was the perfect match for him because she was inflexible even before the most polished; moreover, she could spot the one-in-a-million deal, holding Alfred's hand firmly, selecting properties, setting prices, settling accounts. Later, when the properties he bought appreciated in value, she would rein in his unsophisticated impulses, his readiness to sell when a promoter came to the door with some heartbreaking tale or too-good-to-be true offer. "I will not let you sell the properties; they are for our children, not for us," she told him.

Najibeh had her first child in 1924, a year into the marriage, a girl they named Emily. A year later, a son was born, whom Alfred named after his father, Nicolas. They had two girls after that, Nada in 1928 and Lodi in 1930, and then, in 1935, my father, whom Najibeh chose to call Nadim, which means "close companion" and was used in previous centuries in nomadic Arabia to designate the merry friend and the confidant; Nadim was a bit of all of that to his mother and to his fifty-year-old father.

As the youngest, Nadim was the mascot of the house, coddled like no other by his sisters and brother, who covered for his excesses, interceding with their authoritarian and conservative father. They were not alone in doing this, for another Helena joined the household in 1934, a nanny whom Nadim held high in affection and esteem and whose photo still adorns his private study at home next to those of Alfred and Najibeh. "I would break the hand that dares to rise against him" (*tenkesir l'eed elli temtad a'lee*), she said about her young protégé, and it would not bother her at all to jump out of bed in the middle of the night to make him a sandwich if he so much as suggested it. Unable to repress his sudden whims of going out at night to play in the garden, she had a large basin filled with sand and hid away under his bed for his nightly leisure. Anything Nadim wanted, Nadim was certain to obtain. He would have his sister Lodi pinch a cigarette from their father's pack to smoke under the bed, and when there were no packs at hand, he would have her roll a leaf of molukia and puff all the same.

Alfred first had him attend the Christian Brothers' School, a French-language religious institution that offered an excellent education and was known for its strict discipline. Perhaps it was for the latter that Alfred chose this particular school for Nadim, thinking to curb his son's capricious behavior. The school was in Gemmayzeh, within walking distance from Martyrs' Square in Beirut, which Nadim reached by riding the tram from Hadath, a trip that took nearly forty minutes each way. The day always started with a religious service in the school's chapel and was followed by long hours of methodical teachings in the sciences, languages, and the art of rhetoric.

The school uniform was compulsory, and students were regimented in symmetrical lines every time they moved from chapel to class, from class to refectory, and back to class. Silence and abstinence were the rule of the all-boys school, and extracurricular readings were restricted to the Christian Brothers' magazine, which conveyed the teachings of the congregation—all that was needed to be known, in other words. It was during this time that Nadim developed his aversion to gray, the overwhelming color inside the school and on its uniform. Instead, he preferred cheerful colors when, in time, he went about building the institutions of Al-Kafaàt. He particularly favored yellow and orange.

Next to the school in Gemmayzeh, as he came in the morning and walked back to the tramway in the evening, he was taken by the sight of elderly women living in a sort of shelter, badly dressed, neglected, and indifferent, chain-smoking and drinking. Viewed with disdain by the Brothers, who did not succeed in their efforts to keep the women out of sight, Nadim learned early in his teens the misery of man's fate. The end-of-the-line prostitutes, who had once enjoyed the glitter of nearby Mutanabby Street, the red-light district of the time, were condemned to a life of misery in the backstreets of Gemmayzeh under the scornful eyes of most passersby.

The eyes of Nadim, however, were full of sympathy. His mother Najibeh was a good listener and very much a mentor in his young age, spending long hours reading the Old Testament with him, particularly the hymns of David and Solomon, discussing their full import and connecting their meanings to his own experiences. Nadim learned a good literary Arabic from these readings, a language Najibeh spoke eloquently; also, a high sense of duty and responsibility came from his long discussions with his mother. She was revolutionary in many ways, having been among the first girls in Shwayr to ever go to school and living in a house where tolerance and people's rights were advocated by an exceptional father. Najibeh relayed these strong values to her son and encouraged him to break away, as she had and her father before her, from the restraining yoke of conservatism and social divides.

Alfred was less proactive and, in that sense, less present in the life of Nadim, undoubtedly due to his reclusive nature and advancing age, and perhaps also because of his intimidating personality, austere and serious, speaking little and uncomfortable about sharing his personal feelings, let alone his history. Scarce were the moments the two of them bonded beyond the casual interactions of a filial relationship, yet the impact Alfred had on his son was considerable. Nadim would understand and assimilate the rectitude and morality of his father in time, by observing him, analyzing him, listening to his silence, and filling in the words. The simplicity with which Alfred confronted all of life's problems, whether big or small, his undifferentiated love of people, were traits that Nadim would also embody. Walking with his father one day, or behind him, rather, beating the bushes with a stick, Nadim spotted an electric wire dangling in front of his father, who had his eyes on the uneven pathway. Quickly, he jumped to Alfred's side, reaching him in time to prevent the accident. Alfred took him in his arms in an embrace that nearly choked him and kissed his forehead. My father told me it was the only affectionate gesture Alfred ever made toward him.

Born into wealth—the value of Alfred's properties and resources having soared considerably—Nadim was led by his contemporary mother and righteous father, and by his early independence and evolving experience, to view money as a means to an end, as a mere necessity in service to a higher cause, one that he could not identify yet, although it had been in gestation since his schoolboy years. Caught reading the *An-Nahar* newspaper in school, not the compulsory Christian magazine, Nadim was brought before the disciplinary panel of Brothers and, rebel that he was, relieved himself of years of frustration, spoke his mind, turned his back, and walked out of the door.

At home, it took lots of pleading and the intervention of his mother to talk Alfred into letting Nadim register at the American School, the precursor of today's International College, an institution that grew in the shadow of the American University of Beirut. Worlds apart from the ultraconservative religious school, the American School—and later the American University—would become a liberal and liberating melting-pot to which Nadim brought all the ingredients he earned from his family and seasoned them with a mix of the cultural and political changes of the day. By the time he entered university to study business administration, Lebanon had come a long way in building itself as an independent nation. Born more by C-section rather than natural birth, the new country was torn between colonial interests and regional conflicts, its unity impeded by an ambivalent identity that thwarted the country's potentials.

France had enjoyed strong ties with Lebanon, and though these were usually couched in cultural terms, the economic nature of the bonding, particularly the net returns to the French treasury, was what always really mattered. By the time World War I began, France literally owned all there was to be owned of public projects and operating companies in Lebanon. Classified into two groups—statutory (or concessionary) and of public utility—the French companies controlled all the sectors of the Lebanese economy and undertook most, if not all, of the infrastructure projects. The French web was well in place at the turn of the twentieth century when the declining Ottoman Empire was coerced into ceding its vital economic interests to the French. This was a paramount concern to François Georges-Picot when the 1916 negotiations with the Arab Bureau were at their zenith.

So it was no surprise to anyone when, during the war, France's president Raymond Poincaré referred to Lebanon as "Little France," or when the leader of the French Syria Movement in the senate, Pierre-Étienne Flandin, spoke of her as "France of the Near-East." French dominions across the world were seen as mere extensions of mainland France. The Colonial Exposition, which took place in Paris in 1931, brought together the riches of all the territories France had power over: Indochina, Morocco and Algeria, Pondicherry in India, Guyana and the Islands, several regions in West and Central Africa, Syria, and Lebanon. Lined up in the spacious Park of Vincennes for the public to admire were life-sized models of each colony's indigenous architecture. That of Lebanon was a Moorish-style building meant to replicate the Grand Palace of Amir Bashir in Beiteddine, where Fares Bozeid Moujaes had toiled early in the nineteenth century.

Ever since General Henri Gouraud expelled Faysal in 1920, gaining the permission of the British, who were willing to relinquish Syria for other interests, Beirut was his to manage. Now high commissioner with plenipotentiary powers, one of his first decisions was to organize a colonial exposition in Beirut itself, which took place in 1921, a year after Alfred Nicola returned to Hadath. It was the occasion for Gouraud to inaugurate in great pomp the Place de l'Etoile, the new square built in Beirut's northern marketplace, which copied the design of Haussmann's square of the same name in Paris (although the star in Beirut was truncated on one side because St. George's Cathedral stood there). New streets were opened, all named after generals in the French and British military—Gouraud, Weygand, Allenby—morphing the bazaar-filled Arab city into a western-style French capital with a twist of local architecture. The 1921 exposition took place on a section of Allenby Street that since has taken the name Maarad, which means "exposition" in Arabic, named for the event that was no doubt intended to endear the locals to their colonial overlords.

President Woodrow Wilson's belief in the right of nations to self-determination, the basis of a resolution adopted by the newly established League of Nations at the urging of the US president, was a thorn in the side of the French, for colonization was contrary to the resolution. The British had the same dilemma to deal with regarding Palestine. Circumventing the resolution, they both went away with a "mandate," approved by the league in 1920 and ratified in 1923; this was meant as a sort of "support to the indigenous populations to gain autonomy," supposedly in accord with the wishes of the population, never mind the findings of the King-Crane Commission that showed this was not the case.

On September 1, 1920, General Gouraud announced the inception of Grand Liban, formed by the reunion of Mount Lebanon, the coastal towns, and the Bekaa valley. The boundaries were roughly drawn along the hillcrest of the Anti-Lebanon Mountains to the east, the Akkar in the north, and Ras Naqura in the south. This one-sided declaration was received with mixed feelings and precipitated an identity crisis that has afflicted the Lebanese ever since. Bringing Tripoli into the fold, with its active harbor, was seen by the new business elite in Beirut as a potential threat to its privileges; moreover, the population that came with the coastal cities, mostly Muslim, equaled that of Mount Lebanon proper, and although Christians were still in the majority, they no longer enjoyed an overwhelming preponderance across Greater Lebanon.

In a way, neither Christians nor Muslims were at ease with the new entity, and a number of political formations started to crystallize around dogmatic principles. In short, three main visions were advocated: one called for a Christian entity centered on Greater Lebanon, excluding certain regions that had Muslim predominance, such as Tripoli (Sunni) and Jebel Amel (Shi'a); another looked at Syria as one undivided entity that encompassed Greater Lebanon, based on economic dependability; a third looked at the Fertile Crescent as one nation, the entire Bilad Sham, based on shared traditions and a common language. These conflicting views echoed throughout the Middle East, with King Abdullah of Transjordan pushing for a larger Syrian annexation under his tutelage, and his brother, King Faysal of Iraq, looking at an even larger Fertile Crescent under his, a project that would be perpetuated with zeal by his prime minister Nouri Said.

Whatever the vision and no matter who espoused it, the French had their minds made up about the general shape of the region, and they intended to see it through. The question at the Quai d'Orsay was how to control the region better and keep it subdued to the authority of its high commissioners. Should it be splintered into small cantons, as Robert de Caix of the Ministry of Foreign Affairs suggested, or broken into larger states, "which would allow us to divide and rule at will," as General Maurice Sarrail, the high commissioner, proposed? The debate took six years to settle, during which Organic Statutes were proposed and others counter-proposed by various high commissioners and other committees, raising the question as to whether Syria should be unified or broken up into smaller states, and more importantly whether Greater Lebanon should be part of it or independent. The trial period eventually gave way to the government of the Alawis, the government of the Druze Mountains, and the government of Syria in two regions—Damascus and Aleppo. (The Alawi confession is a splinter from Muslim Shi'a that was mainly present, as today, in western Syria, with Lattaqieh as its regional capital. It is a minority group in Syria today, with Bashar Assad its most prominent figure.) Revolts erupted and were harshly repressed by the hardliner Sarrail before he was replaced by another high commissioner in 1925, Henri de Jouvenel, who navigated in troubled waters to calm the partisans of a united Syria and to deliver by the due date, September 29, 1926, the statutes for Syria and Greater Lebanon, whether they would be united, federated, or independent.

The September date was set by the League of Nations in the charter that empowered France with the mandate, and the rebel agitations and harsh repressions so close to the deadline had raised tensions. It was in this atmosphere, while revolt in Syria was still raging, principally in the Druze Mountains and in Syrian towns—which spilled over into Lebanon—that a constitution was drafted for Greater Lebanon and announced on May 23, 1926. The constitution recognized the authorities of a parliament and a senate and regulated the relationships between judicial, legislative, and executive powers, vaguely implying the supremacy of Christians in state affairs. The constitution also relinquished many personal affairs to the religious bodies, giving authority to the religious courts in matters such as marriage, legacies, and disputes, perpetuating the ascendancy that the Maronite Church had gained over the secular administration in the times of the muqataaji system.

Independence was granted, but under tutelage, as was stipulated in Article 102, which placed the Constitution "under the safeguard of the French Republic by virtue of its mandatory role given her by the Society of Nations." Be that as it may, the 1926 constitution announced the genesis of the state of Lebanon and granted the new republic its French tricolor standard with a cedar tree in the middle. Upon ratification of the Constitution, a president was appointed (by the French commissioner), the first for the Republic of Lebanon: Charles Debbas. A Greek Orthodox notable who worked in the Department of Justice, Debbas was a compromise solution, approved *de improvisio* by the Maronites and Muslims alike; a Maronite contender would have been provocative to the Muslim unionists, who saw in the creation of Lebanon a fantasy for an all-Maronite homeland. For compensation, the leading Maronite figure of the day, Émile Eddé, himself the candidate of the Church, was bestowed the Légion d'Honneur by the president of France.

The constitution was soon amended, just a year later, reducing the parliament from a bicameral formation to a single chamber, but the spirit remained. Lebanon was to be a liberal nation that upheld the liberties of individuals; it was to be republican, democratic, and parliamentary; and it was to recognize the religious groups as "constituting the power-structure of the State." The first two principles were largely inspired by the model of France's Third Republic, probably introduced by the French commissioner himself; the last was particular to the Lebanese context, a reminder of three centuries of intricate religious provincialism. This last principle would later prove to be lethal when demography and regional politics upset the precarious equilibrium of earlier times.

Another bone of contention was the primacy of the president over the government. The constitution gave such weight to the position of the president that it entrusted him with the overall executive powers, relegating to an advisory role the cabinet ministers whom the president appointed himself. He was a "parliamentary monarch," as a contemporary judge once said, but this was in the interests of the drafters, especially those who represented the pressing interests of a "merchant republic," to use the description of Fawwaz Traboulsi. The committee brought together by the French commissioner to draft the Constitution, the "Committee of 13," as it was known, was composed of all the religious groups of Lebanon but was boycotted by the Muslims. Spearheading the movement of Syrian unity including Greater Lebanon, the Sunni, Druze, and to a lesser extent the Shi'a (who would only be given a legitimate position in the power structure of Lebanon with the National Pact, in 1943) could not be part of a committee that advocated separatism, certainly not when it was masterminded by the Maronites and their French protectors. The real mastermind was in fact not a Maronite but of Chaldean and Greek Catholic extraction, a bank owner and prominent businessman who belonged to the establishment that had been nurtured by the French concessionary companies, a Francophile philosopher and columnist who was close to the mandatory powers, a man called Michel Chiha.

As a result of the Constitution, not only was Lebanon's sociopolitical identity to change but equally so its economy, deeply rooted in sericulture, agriculture, livestock, and citrus and olive trees. Mount Lebanon was largely dependent on the Syrian hinterland for agricultural produce and on Beirut harbor for exports, and by separating the two—Mount Lebanon from the deep rural countryside—a major shift was precipitated, one that was to establish Lebanon in her new vocation as the trading post and banker for the Gulf countries. Except for the fertile plateau of the Bekaa, whose inclusion was intended to meet the needs of the population for crops and livestock, Lebanon was led to develop into a service economy and break away from the agrarian system that had been its source of wealth under the mutasarifiya. In this new economic role, Bechara Khoury held center stage for nearly three decades. Not just part of the establishment, but the very heart of it, Khoury shared a lineage with most of the aristocratic families and business clans that owned or sat on the boards of highly lucrative banks and businesses. His rival for the first office, Émile Eddé, was the favorite of the French commissioner and the Maronite Patriarch, but he was no match for the power of Khoury's financial oligarchy.

When the term of Charles Debbas ended in 1932, Eddé and Khoury ran for the presidency, as did a Sunni mufti from Tripoli, a precedent the French high commissioner could not possibly allow. When Eddé realized he was running behind Khoury in the polls, he cleverly stepped down in favor of the Muslim candidate, a maneuver that prompted the commissioner to unilaterally call off the elections, disband the parliament, and suspend the Constitution. As a reaction, Bechara Khoury started the Constitutional Party, a political party that called for the restoration of institutions and the return to constitutional rule.

Émile Eddé also organized a party, the National Bloc, which was particularly concerned about the demographic trends in Lebanon that had brought Muslim populations to parity with the Christians, as reflected in the census carried out by the French in 1932 (which would, in fact, be the last that Lebanon would ever carry out, lest the fragile ground of the Constitution be undermined). Eddé suggested treating Tripoli, the coastal town of northern Lebanon, as a city with special status, where the Christian population would have Lebanese nationality and Muslims would be treated as Syrian nationals. He went on to propose similar measures for the Bekaa and Jebel Amel, measures that aimed at reinstating the predominance of the Christians to eighty percent of the population. In geographic terms, Eddé was simply proposing the restoration of the mutasarifiya with a minor adjustment of borders; however, instead of a non-Lebanese Christian governor under Ottoman control, there would be a Maronite president under the mandate of the French.

One reaction to Eddé's proposition came from Riad Solh, a prominent Sunni figure who went in the opposite direction, advocating the reunification of Lebanon with Syria. Lebanon's identity crisis was peaking, higher than ever before, and took a radical turn in the swirling antagonistic currents. The spectrum of ideologies went from one extreme to the other—Arab nationalism, pan-Syrian unity, Christian Lebanon—and each current had its supporters and many resources. In Europe, fascist movements were on the rise, and this trend soon influenced the Lebanese political parties. Paramilitary uniforms, personality cults, party anthems, emblems and flags, marches, parades and salutes—no party was immune from them.

The Syrian Nationalist Social Party (Parti populaire syrien, or PPS), established in 1932, called for the regrouping of the Fertile Crescent into a single nation, on the basis of socioeconomic and societal continuity. This position was opposed in 1936 by the Kataeb, proponents of a Christian Lebanon; that same year, the Najjada, a Sunni formation, advocated for Arab nationalism. The Syrian Protestant College, a bustling campus that drew students from across the region, became a nest of political activism and saw more than one political formation organize. It is there that Constantine Zreik and Nabih Fares, two Christian political thinkers and professors, spoke of Arab nationalism. It is there also that Charles Malek, founder and chair of the philosophy department, spoke of a Christian Lebanon under the banner of the Lebanese Front (which he cofounded with Pierre Gemayel and Camille Chamoun). It is also there that Antoun Saadeh found fertile grounds for his PPS, and where his underground was nurtured under the nose of the French and the local authorities (for a while, members of the PPS organized clandestinely). The times were also ripe for rewriting history to accommodate political platforms and create some legitimacy for one faction over another, such as the claim by the Christians to have had their origins in a historical Phoenicia. The argument was patently absurd, yet it served its purpose and still survives to our day, many Christians claiming to be the descendants of Phoenicians and not Arabs, as if the Phoenicians were a race that lived in a vacuum and were not affected by the Arab appropriation of the Bilad Sham.

Not only was emancipation from the pan-Syrian and Arabist ideologies an incentive for this Phoenician role-playing, another goal was reinforcing the image of the Lebanese as a seafaring people who lived at large, the famed traders who held commercial enterprises at every harbor across the Mediterranean. A constitution that liberally supported trading and banking would resonate more loudly among the people if associated with the one-time trading civilization that gave us the alphabet and ventured out to sea guided only by stars and constellations. Some truths about the Phoenicians were wiped from memory or recast to polish their reputation. The myth of the phoenix, which rises from its own ashes, was revived and revisited; so were those of Princess Elissar-Dido in Carthage; of Zeus's abduction of the Tyrian Princess Europa, who would give her name to a whole continent, and of her brother Cadmus, who gave it modern language; and many others. Even the name Phoenicia, which means "the region of palm trees," was said to derive from the name of the legendary, epic, and heroic phoenix. These efforts were part of a campaign mounted by literary magazines and daily newspapers, mostly controlled by Michel Chiha and Charles Corm, another political philosopher and columnist of the day, to help forge a separate identity, however chimerical, that distanced the Christians from their Muslim fellow citizens.

The identity crisis reached the point of no return when France signed a treaty with Syria in 1936 that ended the debate about the incorporation of Lebanon into a Syrian unity, to the dismay of a large population of Lebanese, mostly Muslim. The streets erupted, and clashes between Christians and Muslims in the suburbs of Beirut became the norm. The decision to sign the treaty was precipitated by a general unrest that spread across the Middle East, from Egypt to Iraq. The Egyptian political parties united to call for full independence in line with the agreement signed in 1923 and were granted that by the British, who kept their interests nonetheless in the foreign policy of the country and the strategically important Suez Canal.

In Palestine, the implementation of the promises of the Balfour Declaration by the British was proving segregationist, with the influx of Jewish immigrants in great numbers from Poland and Russia, and later from Germany after the rise of National Socialism, while the Arabs, overwhelmed by the circumstances, were not given to organize as a nation. The Arabs of Palestine constituted ninety-three percent of the population in 1918 and Jews only seven percent, but the British downplayed the rights of Arabs to form a nation in Palestine while maintaining a permissive immigration policy favorable to the Jewish Agency, which hoped to settle more Jews before government institutions could be addressed. The establishment of a legislative council in 1935, the basic instrument for governance, was not approved as long as the Jewish population was still a minority, since democratic institutions would affirm the population mix that gave precedence to the Arabs. Disenfranchised in their own land, the Arabs of Palestine revolted in 1936, but internal rivalries coupled with empty promises brokered by Iraq and Transjordan defused the popular uprising. With the signing of the French-Syrian treaty in 1936, "the Arab world that was in a deep sleep for long years had finally woke up," opined the Turkish-language newspaper the *Republic*. That same year, Émile Eddé was elected president of Lebanon.

By the time war broke out in Europe in 1939, the establishment that governed the Lebanese economy, though mainly Christian, did not want the French mandate any longer. By then, the thirty or so governing families had stakes in every industry, and they intended to bring under their own control the French concessionary companies and the companies of public interest. Banks, utilities, public transport, road construction, the port of Beirut, the post office, tobacco companies, insurance, importing companies, hotels, ski centers, airlines (Air Orient used seaplanes, landing in waters off Minet al Hosn, until the Beirut airport was opened in 1938), and many other lucrative industries were all in one way or another controlled by the establishment, although many were owned by French companies. The establishment had become strong and independent, highly active in communications and politics, and the wealth of its families was estimated to be fifteen times the size of the national annual budget.

The position of Lebanon as a trading post between the Gulf countries and the West brought these families a golden opportunity when the princely kingdoms in the Arabian Desert struck oil. Beirut became the gateway for American and European companies who traded in the Gulf, emancipating Lebanon from the French monopoly that had characterized previous times. Strong with this new economic manna, the establishment saw itself in a position to bid for the French companies that controlled most of the Lebanese economy, and even oust the French altogether. The umbilical cord was cut the moment France was no longer the sole provider of services, as it had been under the mutasarifiya. A new business elite, versed in trading and banking, was playing the middleman between large Western corporations and petrodollar states.

The resentment of the Lebanese toward the French mandate was exacerbated by greedy policies adopted by some French-owned companies, which imposed substantial costs for public services, such as water and electricity. Some of their practices were even fraudulent and were widely publicized by the newspapers that were owned or controlled by members of the establishment. Resentment rose further after the outbreak of the war in Europe, when the high commissioner suspended the Constitution and, dissolving the parliament, took power into his own hands. When Charles de Gaulle visited Lebanon in 1942 to inspect the Free French regiments in the Levant, he admonished against any form of independence for Lebanon outside the control of France and reaffirmed the authority of the high commissioner.

The situation was profoundly tense, but it certainly was favorable to Bechara Khoury and his friends, who saw independence in reach and knew it was simply a matter of time before they held it. The treaty signed in 1936 with Syria, which was followed by another with Lebanon (of "friendship" only), favored new strategic alliances in local politics. After an initial period of resistance to the independence of Lebanon from the Syrian unity, Riad Solh decided to work with Bechara Khoury on the elaboration of a common understanding for Lebanon that respected the individualities of all religious groups. It was in Cairo, in 1943, under the auspices of the Egyptian prime minister Nahas Pasha, and after two visits during which Bechara Khoury committed to economic partnership with Egypt, that a pact was entered between Khoury and Solh. The National Pact, as it became known, was an unwritten agreement between the two men, representing the wishes of their respective Maronite and Sunni caucuses, one that defined the codes of power-sharing among the constituent groups. It was never written into the Constitution (until the entire constitution was discarded in 1989 and, under the auspices of the Saudis, replaced by another, bringing a seventeen-year civil war to a close), which meant there were now two founding texts to abide by, one written and the other oral, a unique situation across the world's democratic landscape.

The pact concluded by Khoury and Solh gave rise to a series of understandings, the most important being the religious labeling of government seats and the renunciation by both of any foreign loyalties. In that sense, Riad Solh discontinued his support for pan-Arabism and Bechara Khoury committed to break with the French, an opportune pledge, for he had intended to do so anyway, albeit for more lucrative reasons. The political thinker and columnist George Naccache commented on the pact with a twist of irony, saying that "two renouncements don't add up to a nation" (*deux négations ne font pas une nation*). The other important aspect of the pact, locking all the functions of government in the grip of religious provincialism, reserved the seat of president of the republic for a Maronite and that of prime minister for a Sunni. As for the parliament, it was expanded to fifty-five seats and divided between thirty Christians and twenty-five Muslims, a ratio that would be respected until the new constitution prevailed in 1989. It was also to be presided over by a member of the Shi'a denomination, ushering that all-too-often undermined community into the political arena.

With the National Pact solemnly approved by the chamber, Lebanon requested the end of the mandate and a transfer of government from France, which the latter refused on the pretension that it would be up to the League of Nations to discharge a mandate that it had itself consigned. On November 8, 1943, the chamber met and unilaterally declared Lebanon's independence, a provocative move that, not surprisingly, met with hostility from the high commissioner. He ordered the arrest of the self-proclaimed government members and consigned them to prison in Rashaya, in Wadi Taym, at the southern end of the Bekaa plateau. Arrested were Bechara Khoury, Riad Solh, Camille Chamoun, Adel Osseiran, Abdel Hamid Karameh, and Pierre Gemayel; three members remained at large—Majid Arslan, Sabri Hamadeh, and Habib Abi-Chahla—and took the fight in their hands, assuming the interim "government of free Lebanon." Such was the political pressure after the arrest that Paris ordered the men's release and recalled its commissioner. The detained were freed on November 22, 1943, a date proclaimed as Independence Day and commemorated yearly to this day. Independent, yet the French would take another six years to evacuate their military personnel; in the meantime, the Lebanese government took control of the public interest and concessionary companies.

The first president of the Lebanese Republic was none other than Bechara Khoury, and the prime minister, Riad Solh. The republic was in motion, yet the liberal momentum that was encouraged by its new patrons left the country in thrall to the financial interests of the Lebanese establishment. The termination of the mandate did not mean that Lebanon and its business families aborted economic relations with the French. On the contrary, these blossomed and had no better advocates than the president himself and the government at large. Long before the establishment of a central bank, the state budget and finances were handled by a private bank (Banque de Syrie et du Liban) that also issued money and bonds, owned by notable families and French companies. The latter were part of a larger consortium that had control over a large financial empire that siphoned much of the country's economic output back to France. The new parliament itself was mocked as "the assembly of notables" (Fawwaz Traboulsi), whose role was to foster, by way of legislation, a climate that suited the business transactions of the establishment. The entire system was there to serve the notable families. In the words of Traboulsi, Michel Chiha had "set up an interesting bifurcated model for the relationship between economic power and political power."

If the political oligarchy were soon to be supplanted by a coalition of local forces that stood in opposition, the model that Chiha had masterminded would remain in place, used and abused by all the political factions that existed or were to come. "One always takes off the rider, never the horse," observed a political figure of later days, Raymond Eddé. In the end, Bechara Khoury stepped down in 1952, toward the end of his second term in office, having succeeded at coalescing most political formations, formerly each other's enemies, against him. Riad Solh, for his part, got worse treatment, gunned down by a commando of the PPS, who held him accountable for conniving with Syria to detain and condemn arbitrarily its founder, Antoun Saadeh.

In 1947, during the term of Bechara Khoury, the United Nations charter for the State of Israel partitioned Palestine between the Arabs and the Jews. It was also during his tenure, the following year that the annexation of land allotted to the Arabs under the same UN charter ensued. Jewish militias perpetrated atrocious incursions and committed hideous violence against the Arab population, who fled their homes and took refuge in Jordan, Syria, and Lebanon. In this way, at the expense of the Arabs, Israel gained territory equal to half the territory originally approved by the United Nations, annexing Galilee, the Negev, and a corridor to Jerusalem. The Arab countries quickly organized a liberation army to fight against the incursion, Lebanon contributing a symbolic force. The command of the Arab army was divided, and it was soon incapacitated.

The Palestinians who fled to Lebanon were assigned temporary shelter in tents and in prefabricated tin cabins at ten different locations across the country. In time, these would grow to twenty-two locations and transform into permanent camps, where three generations have so far endured under often horrendous conditions. Nearly half a million people crowded into them before the outbreak of the Six-Day War in 1967. The Palestinian camps remain a stamp of shame on the forehead of many nations, Lebanon among them.

Alfred Nicola lived through Independence Day much the same as any other day, not realizing the importance of the event, there having been so many radical changes during the past half century. From the Ottomans to the Young Turks, to the French, and now independence, and with them all came different borders—sometimes united to Syria, at other times unlinked—and different local overlords. For the simple man who had traveled across the wide landscape of Louisiana, down along the bywaters of the Mississippi River, all the political agitation must have seemed too complex and unnecessary. I can imagine him questioning the need for so much tergiversation when all life needed was a bit of common sense and much goodwill. He lived on, taking to the new governance, adapting to the prevailing new structures, much the same as he always had, rising for an early coffee on the porch, dressing neatly in tailored suits, shaving twice a day, and spending much of his time on the moss-laced chair greeting the passersby.

Najibeh kept her eyes and ears open to restrain Alfred's tendency to be overly generous, especially when she sensed a questionable affability on the part of some visitor. However cautious, though, she was not always able to contain her husband's donations, which in the end added up to a small fortune. The plight of the Palestinian people caused him great distress; he had met many Palestinians in America and across Beirut in the souks where, when still a child, he had walked with his father on business. Many camps would engulf Hadath, in Sabra and Shatila, and in Chiyah across from the airport; new neighbors who came in pajamas with nothing to wear or eat, newborns in their arms and elderly in their care. The skirmishes on the southern frontier of Lebanon with Palestine, an area now annexed by the Israeli forces, brought many peasants to settle at the southern entry of the capital, running away with their families. Farmers originally, these Shi'a families were hosted by landowners and employed to work the lands west of Hadath, and most ended up staying.

Helena, Alfred Nicola's mother, did not witness the agonies of an entire people in exile. She didn't even live to see the independence of Lebanon, having passed away early in 1925, followed by Alexander Joseph in 1931 and Uncle Tanios in 1933. At least Helena got to see Alfred settled with the woman she had chosen for him, and she was there to hold in her arms his first three children. Alfred grieved for Helena and Tanios intensely, as well as for his cousin and brother-in-law Alexander, his close friend in Louisiana. He refrained for months to hum the Byzantine chants and wore a black symbol on his hat.

With the end of the tenure of Bechara Khoury, who was eased out of office, and the election of Camille Chamoun as president of the Lebanese Republic in 1952, a new period began. The coming years would see the further polarization of the Lebanese identity and terminate in the civil war of 1958, a period that would bring grievances to the house of Alfred Nicola. After the Second World War, the world became a theater for a new form of confrontation, between the United States and the Soviet Union: the Cold War. The race for armaments and for having satellite client states was on, and the Middle East was a particularly important region for both powers. Lebanon, in the middle of the region, stood out as an important gateway and, at times, a bridgehead for struggles between the East and West. The world economy had been Americanized, the United States succeeding at imposing the dollar as the baseline currency instead of gold at the summit of Bretton Woods in Massachusetts. Meeting in 1944, while war was still raging, the leaders of forty-four industrial powers agreed to the change. By that time, the United States was producing nearly fifty percent of the world's gross domestic product, half the wealth produced worldwide.

The USSR, for its part, remained a "riddle, wrapped in a mystery, inside an enigma," as Winston Churchill once described it. The Cold War could not have had any better expression than what the 1950s offered in terms of the alignments of nations between those favorable to the United States and the others who fell into the orbit of the USSR. The Baghdad Pact, modeled after NATO, brought together a number of countries (Iran, Iraq, Pakistan, Turkey) that feared communism and endeavored, with the support of the United States and the United Kingdom, to contain the USSR by drawing a strong coalition of states along its southern border.

Not standing idle while this was playing out, the USSR went fishing for client states within the Middle East and found a good one. In 1952, a coup in Egypt overthrew the monarchy in favor of a military regime that brought three men to head the state, soon to be supplanted by just one of them, who would hold the stage for two decades: Gamal Abdel Nasser. For having accepted weapons and ammunition from the Czechs, Nasser was punished by John Foster Dulles, secretary of state in the Eisenhower administration, who cancelled previously agreed-upon funding for Egypt to build a dam in Aswan.

This move pushed Nasser further into the arms of the communists, having already recognized the People's Republic of China. By 1956, the chips were all down when, as a response to Dulles's asset freezing, Nasser, a much-lauded leader in Egypt and the Middle East and a master of mass communication, nationalized the Suez Canal. The move came as a surprise, swamping the French-governed channel with Egyptian troops, and marking a major turn in regional politics. At a secret meeting in Sèvres, France, the British, French, and Israelis agreed on a combined strike against Nasser in the Sinai; the Israelis would start it off, the other two assuming the roles of supporters rather than perpetrators. Followed across the Middle East with great interest, the combined strike routed the Egyptian forces with relative ease but was soon halted by Eisenhower and Khrushchev, who feared the consequences.

With the retreat of the British, French, and Israeli armies, and despite suffering a notable military defeat, Nasser was afterward eulogized as the father of Arabism, the true leader of the whole Arab nation. In every capital across the Middle East, Nasser was praised to the skies. Did he not stand up to imperialism and win the day? Momentum grew across the Arab countries, and the old aspirations for a united pan-Arab state were renewed, especially among Nasser's coreligionists, the Sunnis, who constituted the great majority of Arabs in the region.

In Beirut, the situation was different and, to say the least, critical. With a Christian head-of-state and a Christian majority in the parliament, the call for pan-Arabism was hardly unanimous, especially with a president like Camille Chamoun, who was a Westerner at heart and who did not shy away from an ostentatious Western model of governance as soon as he stepped foot in the Qantari Palace. The location of the presidential palace back then was on the Qantari hill, a short distance away from Hamra Street and the hotels quarter of Minet al Hosn on the marina. It also was a short distance away from Mazraa and Musaytbeh, the Sunni strongholds of an eminent personality, Saeb Salam. Chamoun had adopted in the first part of his term a particularly repressive policy toward the Lebanese establishment that his predecessor, Bechara Khoury, had built meticulously. Despite undermining the oligarchy of the past, however, Chamoun did not build the capacity of the government but instead substituted one consortium for another. He hurried to institute the bank secrecy act, a move that would earn Lebanon the repute of a safe haven for risk-free money laundering and capital deposits. By a master stroke of political maneuvering, he managed to rid the chamber of influential personalities, including Saeb Salam and Kamal Jumblatt, the leader of Lebanon's Socialist Progressive Party and a descendant of the notable Druze overlord Bashir Jumblatt.

Salam and Jumblatt were particularly fond of Nasser and saw in his growing popularity a possibility of change that they hoped to take full advantage of, if only to subdue Chamoun, the powerful president who loved hunting, spoke English eloquently, and graced his guests with such *dolce vita* that subsequent presidents thought such shows of grandeur were part of office protocol.

Salam, an inveterate cigar smoker, would not make any public appearance without a Churchill in his fingers. He spoke English eloquently (with a heavy Beirut accent) and was a success story in his own right, having engaged in the airline business with the Kuwaitis and earned fame and fortune (Salam founded Middle East Airlines in 1945). Jumblatt, the beneficiary of a longstanding history of muqataaji rule that went back to the Ain-Dara clan struggle in 1711, was a highly educated francophone who dealt with politics and managed his armed tribesmen while practicing Hindu-style meditation in his Shouf retreat. Jumblatt was not agreeable to the "consensual" democracy that restricted the first office to a Maronite Christian and, in fact, made it his life's mission to occupy the position himself.

After the 1956 Suez debacle that brought Nasser to the pinnacle of his political career, events in Lebanon moved quickly. Mazraa and Musaytbeh became rebellious, inflamed by Salam, who smarted from his exclusion from the parliament at the hands of Chamoun. The Druze Mountain was on a war footing as well, encouraged by Jumblatt, who had been equally undermined by the president. Salam literally detained Chamoun in his Qantari Palace while Jumblatt threatened the occupation of the airport. By exaggerating the role that was given him by the Constitution, Chamoun downplayed the spirit of the National Pact, the oral understanding that was an equal founding text, and ended up causing a schism in the heterogeneous composition of the republic. Nasser did the rest, giving moral support to his coreligionists to undermine the very essence of the pact and take direct aim at a president who did not think twice about appropriating government and the tools of government. The result was explosive.

As all this was happening, more news arrived, not surprising in the ever-changing Middle East. Another coup, in Iraq this time, brought down the monarchy in favor of yet another military government. King Faysal II, the grandson of the Hashemite king who played along with the British Cairo Office and befriended Lawrence, was lined up with his retinue and family against a palace wall and shot dead in the back. Nouri Said, the acting prime minister who worked under both Faysals, was disfigured and also killed. In 1958, Iraq was to become the turf of two activist military men, Abdul Karim Qasim and Abdul Salam Arif, who ushered the Ba'ath Party into government. The Ba'ath Party of Iraq, as we shall see, would surrender the reins of power to none other than Saddam Hussein.

A second event that same year, of equal and far-reaching importance, was the union proposed by Nasser between Egypt and Syria under the appellation of the United Arab Republic, or UAR. A genius at the art of provocation, Nasser made the announcement so unexpectedly that it energized the masses who, after the 1956 nationalization of Suez, now felt invincible. The first to rejoice were the Palestinians, the hundreds of thousands of refugees in Jordan, Lebanon, and Syria, who saw in the UAR the promise of an Arab awakening that would restore the lands and properties of Palestine to their rightful owners. Some of the Sunni partisans in Beirut were similarly euphoric and demanded the annexation of Lebanon by the UAR.

President Chamoun was overwhelmed. He appealed for international support, American in the main, based on the Eisenhower doctrine to intervene militarily whenever an independent nation was threatened by communism. Awaiting an occasion to curtail Soviet expansionism, the United States did not need to be asked twice, and in less than twenty-four hours, the US navy had reached Beirut. No fewer than seventy-seven American warships, already present in the Mediterranean and on high alert, found their way to Beirut, the carrier *Saratoga* among them, fitted with nuclear warheads. Fifteen thousand troops were landed on the shores of Beirut and did a good job at containing the civil war that was raging, coordinating with the Lebanese army that was equally disciplined and impartial despite the repetitive calls of the president to quell the Sunni insurrection pockets, Mazraa and Musaytbeh in particular. The army was led by an exceptional commander-in-chief of the era, Fouad Shihab, himself the scion of the Shihab family of Wadi Taym, whom we met early on in this book.

Chamoun viewed the landing of American marines on the shores of Beirut as a feather in his cap and campaigned for the forthcoming election, anticipating a second term in the high office. The intentions of the Americans were just the opposite, however, and the election went to another, a man of military integrity as the times dictated, General Fouad Shihab himself. The parliament saw new members elected while the American troops were still on the ground, many historians testifying to the role they played in the election outcomes. A coalition of circumstances had brought Chamoun down, a coalition of circumstances that included Saeb Salam and Kamal Jumblatt.

In the house of Alfred Nicola, much had happened in this decade. Habib Joseph, his cousin, brother-in-law, and friend in Louisiana, passed away in 1950. Alfred wore the customary black ribbons on his shoulder and hat and refrained from humming the Byzantine hymns. For a few days, he lost his appetite and looked beaten by the loss. He must have relived his early days in Louisiana when Habib took him in. It was Habib who gave him the good-luck belt he used to hold the suitcase on his back, the improvised peddler's case that had brought him fortune. He organized a funeral service in Habib's memory at St. Elias Church next door, where Habib and his sister Zahia had married forty-five years before. After Habib's came the death in 1953 of Alexander Nicola, Alfred's brother who had followed him to Louisiana. Same ritual, same lump in his throat, same anxiety. On the brighter side, George, Alfred's younger brother, who had taken up his peddling route and become "Sweet Papa" himself, came to visit in 1955 with Isaac, the son of Habib and Zahia Joseph.

By then, Alfred was ill, showing early signs of dementia, though the diagnosis was unclear given the shortcomings of medicine in those days. Alfred had been hospitalized with severe respiratory problems, and he also suffered from serious sores on his feet. At home, his youngest daughter, Lodi, looked after him, massaging his swollen feet and bandaging his heels, until he regained some of his strength. When George and Isaac visited Alfred in 1955, he was hardly himself anymore, done with the striped suits, stylish hats, and cologne. In his final months, he practically lived in his pajamas, struggled to get out of bed, dressed carelessly, and only shaved occasionally. He was losing his passion for life, too tired to carry the weight of the body he had taken along so many routes and down so many towpaths. Although he could not bear to have his picture taken, he did make the effort to stand for a last picture with George and Isaac. A legacy of the Creole culture, Alfred equated still photography to still existence, to staring at people of the past, to passing away, and he did not want to be counted among the kingdom of the missing. I tried to find pictures of him in Louisiana; I could hardly find any of him in Hadath.

The last days were painful. Alfred could no longer stand on his feet or move his legs. He was paralyzed. For a man who had lived in harmony with nature, following unfamiliar paths, sleeping on the ground, relying solely on his own strong physique, the prognosis was very poor. For six months, Alfred could not move, confined to bed or a long chair, nursed by his daughter Lodi, who was his last companion. He passed away in 1956, the year Nasser nationalized the Suez Canal and two years before the outbreak of the first civil war in Lebanon. His last words were for Louisiana, the country that gave him so much, the land of plenty and generosity.

As it happened, Zahia had started off on a trip to Lebanon just days before her brother Alfred passed away. She had not seen him since 1920, when he left Louisiana, and she came with her daughter Isabel and son Fred, not knowing he was dying. When they arrived, he was already gone. Zahia would outlive her younger brother, George, who passed away in 1959, departing herself in 1965. When I went with Jay and Mary Joseph, the grandchildren of Habib and Zahia, to visit their memorials in Lockport in 2012, the gate was closed and we didn't have the key. So we jumped the cemetery fence, admittedly an offense but one that may be excused given the honorable intentions of this Lebanese from Hadath who had come to pay his respects to his great-aunt so far away from home.

What was Lebanon at the close of the Chamoun era? I am tempted to quote two great men who delved into Lebanese culture and identity and spoke with wit of the country of the cedars. In 1942, General Charles de Gaulle likened Lebanon to a mercantile counter saying, "Lebanon is no nation; it is about bartering" (*Le Liban n'est pas une nation, c'est du négoce*). Much later, in 1997, Pope John Paul II said in Beirut that "Lebanon is a mission." By that, he meant the country was a collegial, interdenominational, multicreed melting pot that served as an example to the world and hence was endowed with a singular mission. So which is it, bartering or mission? A bit of both, I would say, a testimonial to democratic life in the midst of storming theocracies, yet a life bound by elitist aspirations of wealth and power. The constitution and National Pact were ephemeral snapshots in time of an ever-changing identity, and they faltered as soon as the internal demography changed. And the pressures of foreign involvement, the Palestinian issue in particular, would play a major role in the breakup of the country.

8

On true resilience

Nadim Shwayri

Nadim was twenty-one when Alfred, his father, passed away. He was still in college, completing a thesis in economics for the master's degree he would earn a year later. He chose to study the Litani River for his thesis, the one tributary that was of vital importance for the Bekaa plateau, the main agricultural region of Lebanon. It was of such importance that during the days when the French and British were drawing the borders for the states they created, the British pushed the northern borders of Palestine to encompass the Litani itself, which is twenty-five miles into Lebanese territory to the lowest stretch and twice that much to the valley, where the Qaraoun Dam now lies. This border was advocated by the British at the urging of the Zionist Organization, whose leadership understood the importance of water in the region.(The Zionist Organization's president, Chaim Weizmann, said: "[We] consider it essential that the Northern Frontier of Palestine should include the Valley of the Litani, for a distance of 25 miles above the bend.") Along with the Jordan River, the Euphrates and the Tigris, the Litani was a main confluent that configured the Fertile Crescent–shaped region of the Near East, from the Sinai to the mouth of Shatt al-Arab on the Persian Gulf.

With his understanding of regional economics, Nadim saw the Litani River, with its yearly flow of nine hundred million cubic meters of water, as a cause for conflict in the region. The important waterway, which has its source in the northern Bekaa, runs south and then arcs westward before it empties into the Mediterranean, north of the ancient city of Tyre. Nadim was proven right when, in 1978, Israel invaded southern Lebanon and took control of the Wazzani River, a fresh water stream feeding the Jordan River, as well as the Hasbani River, where it installed pumps and pipes to divert the waters into Israel. In 1982, the Israeli army went back to annex the south of Lebanon on the pretext of establishing a buffer-zone free of *fedayin*, the Palestinian vigilante combatants who made armed incursions into northern Israel. While occupying the south of Lebanon for eighteen years and giving the Shi'a populations living there reason to organize into a liberation army (as in the case of Hezbollah), the Israelis tapped into the Litani River at the level of the Qaraoun dam and continued to access Lebanon's water resources until their evacuation in 2000, despite Security Council Resolution 425 (fulfilling, three decades later, the recommendations of Weizmann). The National Water Carrier of Israel, the country's largest water project, did not wait that long to lay hands on the water and funnel it to irrigate the waterless Negev: it had started early on, since 1948, to drain lakes (as in Huleh) and tap Syrian and Jordanian resources (Banias and Yarmouk to name but two large tributaries), despite the incessant UN resolutions (as in Security Council Resolution 92, in 1951).When you visit Jordan today and walk along the once fast-flowing Jordan River, where John is said to have baptized Jesus, you cannot but feel disheartened by the thin trickle of water it has become. At the source, the Syrian Banias and Lebanese Hasbani tributaries were tapped into extensive canals that circumvented the natural riverbeds to supply the Israeli pipes.

Although he never engaged in political debates or even went as far as giving his opinion, Nadim was the most clairvoyant political thinker I have ever met. Perhaps his impassive personality, his nonpolitical mission in life, made him a unique political analyst. A skilled economist and an equally astute social worker who explored welfare programs all his life, Nadim knew the dynamics of government and of society at large. The difficulty for him was to keep his logic to himself and accept the wrongs that were done against the nation, against the institution that he would create and nurture, against his family, against his person and inner beliefs, and keep going. In many ways, Nadim was an uncommon person, an exceptional man who defied the order in extraordinary times, who devoted his wealth and life to a cause, a singular cause that has grown over the years into a far-reaching organization.

During my intimate discussions with him, on our Saturday afternoon drives along the forgotten mountain trails of Mount Lebanon, I always told him that he would always be one step ahead of me. With a somewhat defiant attitude, common in filial relations no doubt, I used to give him the measure of my own achievements at Al-Kafaàt and speculate on those to come, concluding that whatever I did, there would always be the first step that he held over me. "Had I been in your shoes in 1956, at age twenty-one, having substantial wealth, would I have given it all up for a life of philanthropy?" I mused to him on numerous occasions. In a way, I was conditioned to the life I have chosen today, but for him, it was a different story. He made the choice of his own accord to exchange his well-to-do, comfortable lifestyle for one that was very atypical. In this, he has always been my source of inspiration and model in life. In my first book, *Nadim, un Liban généreux*, which I intended as a tribute to my father on the fiftieth anniversary of his creation, Al-Kafaàt, I likened him to Jean Valjean, the stoic character in Victor Hugo's epic *Les Misérables*.

Life for Nadim was no joke; it was not meant for leisure and certainly not pleasure. Life was hard work and, in quite an existential interpretation, a punishment for the fall of man. That was a subject that always arose in our Saturday afternoon discussions, Nadim's theologically profound sense of existence, of life and death, of the duties that fell onto man to fulfill, in return for the forgiveness of the Father. Al-Kafaàt, in that sense, was Nadim's expression of surrender to the divine will, his statement of redemption, as he inscribed it in the Cypriot-made mosaic icon that adorns the chapel he built on the campus of AL KAFAAT UNIVERSITY, which reads: "To Thy feet I rest Al-Kafaàt, my Lord" (*A'la ḳadamayḳ Al-Kafaàt, Rabbi*).

Nadim always remembered his encounter near his school in Gemmayzeh with the aging women who had fallen from grace. By 1956, he had already found work at the largest bank in Lebanon, Bank Intra, and was sought by a large corporation called Iqtisadiya, which had a reputation for savvy financial speculation, mainly in property in Lebanon and abroad. Graduates with master's degrees in economics were hard to find in those days, and corporations chased after them. Nadim's college tutor introduced him to Michel Zeidan, the owner and managing director of Iqtisadiya, who hired Nadim to look for opportunities in real estate while managing capital for investment. Back in those days, communications were slower and investment decisions often needed to be made away from the office and independently, a situation Nadim confronted while in Brazil and Quebec, two markets that were of interest to his company and where Nadim worked for over a year. In Quebec, he bought land at bargain prices along the St. Lawrence, real estate that gained in value and brought Iqtisadiya and Michel Zeidan substantial profits.

Zeidan had once lived in Egypt, where he came across a congregation of sisters who were active in Lebanon and who owned a convent there, in Salima, in the Metn area of Mount Lebanon. When he heard about Nadim's social ethos, he introduced him to the Lebanese chapter of the congregation, not realizing he was starting Nadim on a course that would take him away from the investment business. The French Catholic congregation, Notre-Dame des Apôtres, had its headquarters in Lyon at the time but held on to the convent in Mount Lebanon. The convent was large and had two floors; the lower was used by the congregation, but the upper was empty, closed-up since the novitiate school that once occupied it was transferred to Egypt. With his imaginative and entrepreneurial spirit, Nadim did not have to think twice. He proposed immediately that the congregation house a school for underprivileged young girls, thinking particularly of children born to parents who lived or dealt in drugs and prostitution.

The Chamoun era had completed the predestined course chartered by Bechara Khoury and the Lebanese establishment, fostering the tourism industry in Lebanon, which had overnight become a favorite destination of the international jet set. With the economic boom of tourism came the sordid low life of drug users and prostitutes, equally dazzled by the "oriental mirage" but often doomed to sad endings. The memory of the elderly women near the Christian Brothers' School was vivid in Nadim's mind when he confided with his tutor and friend at the university, Said Takieddine, about his proposed project. Rich in experience and just two years from retirement, Takieddine advised Nadim to devote his attention to children if he wanted to make a difference, not their elders.

Nadim took his mentor's words to heart when he went to Salima to find the French congregation. There, he met with the assistant superior of the convent, a fine Egyptian woman named Sister Athanasia. She was to become Nadim's personal friend and lifelong colleague through Al-Kafaàt until her passing in 2002. Their first encounter was in 1956, but the school opened a year later on August 15, 1957, a date we observe as the founding day of Al-Kafaàt.

While continuing his work at Iqtisadiya for another few years and closing more profitable deals for the company, Nadim also focused on the school on the second floor of the convent. From just seven students in 1957, it grew in a few short years into the iconic catering school in the Middle East. Over the next eight years, Nadim divided his time between Iqtisadiya and Salima, earning money from the first and spending it at the second to nurture the school he had founded. At one point, he bought for his company a large stretch of woodland in southeast Beirut and was later in charge of subdividing and selling the property. By selling to them their estates in this area, he befriended the politically engaged poet Said Akl and the composer Assi Rahbani. The latter married the cantatrice Feyrouz, whom Assi propelled to fame with his popular songs and musicals.

These friendships would develop and strengthen in time, especially after Nadim chose his new course in life. I remember the Sunday lunches at my father's house with Said Akl presiding over the family table, eating little (as he always did) and speaking in poetic metaphors. He spoke of "ten bounties that Lebanon had given the world," Europe and mathematics coming in at first and second place (the rest, I am ashamed to say, I don't recall).

The times were not easy for Nadim, who feared for Lebanon, a fragile entity as he sensed ahead of his peers and rife with agitations on the street that would lead to the civil war of 1958. He passed people in arms, civilians who took to weapons on the orders of their party leaders, parties that resembled pseudo-tribal and religiously marked militias where the cult of the leader counted more than the allegiance to an all-empowering state. Anybody with a conventional outlook would have clung to his lucrative business, would have lain low and stuck to the status quo, would have looked for ways to save money for the day of need, at a time when the future seemed most uncertain. But that was not Nadim. Instead, in 1964, while the fast-growing school in Salima was as busy as a beehive, Nadim made the decision to leave Iqtisadiya and devote his life to social welfare. Not that he had anything specific in mind, just ideas and a mission, a burning mission that drove him so passionately, irrespective of the vagaries of politics and everyday life.

A few years earlier, the sisters at Salima had informed him of an awkward situation they were facing: two wheelchair-bound young girls who would have been ideal for the program at the convent could not be admitted because the location was not accessible. They were denied entry. As always with Nadim, this human suffering was not ignored; then and there he decided to move in a different direction. First-class travel and money-mongering with Kuwaiti clients were no longer for him—they were never really his thing—and a first-class life would be one spent helping others. About that time, he had a dream that he interpreted as the expression of his true calling: "I heard someone mumbling and I came close. I saw a monster in the dark. Closer, the monster seemed human and it spoke to me. Closer still, I could see a person in distress and I held out my hand. When we crossed eyes, I realized I was looking at myself."

Always the economist and successful entrepreneur, Nadim took it upon himself to prove that any person with a disability could be an equal contributor to society, and, given the chance to perform, "he too could be a taxpayer." As proof, he invited three young men, one in a wheelchair and two deaf, to join him in starting a company that would only hire people with disabilities, one that would produce leather goods at a profit. They held regular meetings at the Ronda Café in downtown Beirut until the four of them, "all handicapped," as Nadim used to say, started their factory in a slum of Beirut on an eastern slope of Achrafieh called Karm Zeitoun. There, Nadim rented a three-bedroom apartment where he started production; later he added a second adjoining apartment to his factory, and a warehouse area in a next-door building. He managed the operation, from procurement to production, designing to packaging, accounting to shipping, with an extraordinary ability to view a business from all angles and to manage sleepless nights. Nadim's early colleague, Ali Saleh, a handyman who made himself useful in all facets of the business, recalled the long hours Nadim put in, staying up so late that he practically collapsed onto his ledgers and Ali covering him for a night on the factory couch.

The factory in Karm Zeitoun not only made a profit, it soon became a rallying point for local people with disabilities who wanted to prove themselves, to get employment, to take part in the active world as "potentials, not handicaps." This slogan was used from the beginning: it was short but telling, concise but powerful. During an evening of brainstorming with his friends Said Akl and Assi Rahbani,

Nadim searched for a name to express the mission of his enterprise; at one point, *Al-Kafaàt* came up, a word meaning "abilities" in Arabic. As a name, it said a lot about Nadim's philosophy. Al-Kafaàt it would be, and the name was soon on a shining sign high on the factory, recruiting one by one other potentials awaiting their chance to grow and contribute to the country.

One day, Said Akl came to the workshop unannounced with a young man who had cerebral palsy. He was ambulatory but physically challenged, spoke with difficulty, dragged his feet while walking, and made abrupt gestures including a bouncing of the head. Said introduced the young man to Nadim and asked with the spontaneity of a close friend to give the newcomer "something to occupy his days." Nadim took the man in and, after a couple of days, realized he had a good eye for spotting production defects; so Nadim appointed him quality controller of one line of products, and then, a few weeks later, the quality controller of the whole factory.

When Said Akl came back a few months later for a visit, he found his protégé busy controlling the production of an enterprise that was, by then, employing some forty workers. He stood speechless, overwhelmed by the scene, probably a little humbled for having labeled him as handicapped. For the young man was all but that, an extraordinary potential who only needed Nadim and Al-Kafaàt to come to light. Said was stunned even more when he learned the new quality controller was earning double the minimum wage, a considerable amount for the time, yet it only represented, as Nadim said, a small percentage of what he was saving for the factory.

Said Akl was an eminent public figure of the time, highly acclaimed and well known for the eponymous prize that he awarded yearly to people who distinguish themselves by their service to society. How surprised Nadim was when Najibeh called him from his room next morning to announce what she had just read in the newspaper: Said Akl had bestowed his prize upon Nadim "for his realization of Al-Kafaàt, an iconic institution that promises to become a cornerstone of world rehabilitation."

The election of Fouad Shihab to the presidency in 1958 ushered in a new form of governance that was in many ways controversial, yet it represented the only period of tranquility and real nation-building that Lebanon would ever witness throughout its short existence. While Bechara Khoury had ridden the wave of the Lebanese establishment, an oligarchy of some thirty families that sapped the country's resources for their own benefit and for whom state and politics were just a means to that end, and while Camille Chamoun had merely substituted his own cast of characters for Khoury's, Fouad Shihab went a separate way.

Shihab despised politicians, a character trait he shared with many military men who have taken on official state functions, such as Charles de Gaulle, of whom the Lebanese president was very fond. Shihab did not fight politicians, as

Chamoun had, and he would not play along with their petty connivances; instead, he decided to live and let live, bringing into his cabinet of ministers a plethora of members of provincial families, giving them status while depriving them of their ability to oppose him. While these one-time contenders were happy to sit in government, Shihab went his own way, establishing a parallel government where true power lay, composed of palace advisors and police intelligence officers, the *deuxième bureau* as it came to be known, the real engine that Shihab relied on to hold the politicians in check.

The deuxième bureau had the upper hand in public life, manipulated elections, made arrests at will, managed corporations and banks, paid under-the-table money, and orchestrated real politics while the politicians were only playing at their roles. Whatever the deuxième bureau really was, it remains that Fouad Shihab governed for real and his intentions were honorable. With a unique understanding of the people gained by commanding the army, a heterogeneous body of young men from across the entire Lebanese landscape, he understood how to reach their hearts and minds. The real Lebanese people for him were from the peripheries, the less fortunate of Akkar, the South, and the Bekaa, and these did not view favorably the practices of previous presidents, who had focused on the wealthy in Beirut and enriched themselves along the way. Their regions, their families, their children had rights too, and Fouad Shihab recognized this.

Masterminding a resignation after two years in office, at a sensitive time when his governance was undermined by the traditional politicians, Shihab was acclaimed by the people and brought back to power a strong and uncontested man. Politically, Shihab broke the unilateral position adopted by Chamoun, which oriented Lebanon to the Western powers, and made it a point to meet with Nasser a short time after his election, choosing to convene in a tent on the border of Syria, which was part of the Nasser-controlled UAR by then. Economically, Shihab recalled resources to the state treasury, back from the usurers of the early establishment and the Chamoun-era hangers-on, who enriched themselves to the people's detriment. Socially, Shihab initiated policies that still improve life today, building vigorous public systems, such as the Social Security Fund and the Office of Social Development.

The style of governance that Shihab encouraged, and his considerable accomplishments in so short a time, led to a new political formation called *Nahj*, which means "the conventional pathway," a program just in the title. A circle of intellectuals, not part of the muqataaji landed-aristocracies or the business bourgeoisie of the establishment, the Nahj gathered such men as Elias Sarkis, a court of accounts official who was Shihab's chief of staff during his term and who would serve as president himself in later times.

Not surprisingly, the Nahj would face vehement opposition from all the parties that saw their roles, missions, and interests dwindling. Christian parties reacted negatively to the renewal of relations with Nasser, dreading a departure from the isolationist ethos they craved for Lebanon; the business elite, of course, was not ready to give away its privileges for whatever state was under construction. Added to these was a silent opposition that materialized in Muslim caucuses and that felt sidetracked by developments, as in the case of Saeb Salam, who was shelved in favor of the Tripoli politician Rachid Karami, appointed prime minister in the latter years of Shihab's tenure. In addition, Muslim conservatives such as Salam were already questioning the UAR and fearing it would absorb Lebanon. These opposition forces coalesced into an alliance that turned the foes of yesterday into blood brothers, ready to stand up to the constitutional ogre. Saeb Salam, Raymond Eddé (the son of Émile Eddé, who was president of Lebanon before independence and who played cat-and-mouse with Bechara Khoury), and Camille Chamoun became a triumvirate, each resenting for a different reason the governance of Fouad Shihab.

The reign of the general came to an end, but Shihabism was alive and well in the Nahj, who held a large majority in the parliament and would remain in office after the election of Charles Helou, another partisan of Shihab, to the presidency. Although "Helou had the heart of Shihab," Charles Winslow noted wittily, "he did not have his teeth," and teeth were much needed at the time, for the region was about to witness a new cataclysm. The Palestinian refugees in their camps had been organizing into militias, some supported by Nasser, others by Syria, receiving military training and weapons. Shihab had contained the camps by imposing strict regulations and policing them, but with only a moderate grip, in keeping with his policy of rapprochement toward Nasser. Helou, by contrast, practically ignored what was happening in the camps, turning a blind eye to the militarization of the Palestinians. When he finally decided to reimpose police control, it was simply too late.

Nasser supported the establishment in Egypt of the Palestine Liberation Organization (PLO), whose early leadership was entrusted to Ahmad Shukayri but was soon spearheaded by Yasser Arafat, who used the camps in Lebanon as reservoirs of fresh recruits and as staging grounds and retreats for his fedayin operations against Israel. Arafat did the same in Jordan, where Palestinians represented nearly seventy percent of the population, hoping to have a pincer effect on the Jewish state by hitting its flanks across southern Lebanon and along the Jordan River.

Two events took place in Beirut in 1966 that had the unfortunate effect of radicalizing the Palestinian refugees: the assassination of a critic of the PLO freedom of action in Lebanon, Kamel Mrowa, the founder and publisher of the daily paper *Al-Hayat*; and the collapse of the largest bank in Lebanon, the Palestinian-owned Bank Intra. The fall of Intra was definitely orchestrated by outside forces as the bank, part of a giant empire managed by Youssef Baydas, had enough assets to cover its liabilities when word hit the street that the bank was insolvent. The

Lebanese central bank refused to backstop the sudden run on the bank, and Intra collapsed. No doubt the Lebanese establishment, with its family bankers and business bourgeoisie, was the principal beneficiary of the fall of Intra, but it was also a political faction that wanted to curtail the Palestinian influence in Lebanon.

The plot thickens when one learns that the perpetrators of Mrowa's assassination were linked to Intra, not just the gunman but also the masterminds, and that Intra had dealings with the deuxième bureau of a financial nature that were not always legal. There have been many interpretations given for the sudden and unexpected fall of Intra, and whatever the real story, Baydas did not survive his escape to South America and passed away before he could give his own version of events. With Intra gone, the moderate Palestinian presence in Lebanon was ushered out, leaving the country wide open to the fundamentalist groups that revolved around the camps: the PLO of Yasser Arafat; the Popular Front for the Liberation of Palestine (PFLP), led by George Habash; and the Saeka, the Syrian-backed militia, to name but three.

Nasser was dealt a serious blow when the UAR disbanded in 1961, mainly for having supplanted the Syrian administration, who viewed the union as a mere annexation by the Egyptians. The breakup was a bad omen for Nasser's pan-Arab projects, and his star started to wane, even in some Sunni quarters in Lebanon that had suffered from the interference of Nasser in their local politics. A more decisive blow came in 1967 with the Six-Day War and the annexation by Israel of the West Bank and East Jerusalem (from Jordan), the Sinai and the Gaza Strip (from Egypt), and the Golan Heights (from Syria). The Six-Day War was decisive, not only because it broke Nasser and gave Israel preeminence in the region, but also because it brought about the demise of a moderate form of Arabism, giving rise to a fundamentalist and sectarian form of religious expression that thrust the Muslim Brotherhood of Hassan Banna to the forefront.

The Middle East and the world at large would thereafter suffer the morphing of Arab nationalism into a call for arms, and one can find some roots of present-day fundamentalisms in the Six-Day War of 1967. As with every turn of fate in the region, Lebanon received the spillover of violence and soon found itself trapped between the Israelis and Palestinians, with the latter harboring military hardware in their camps under the nose of the incapable host country. The hijacking of an El Al flight by the PFLP of George Habash and its detention for a month-and-a-half on the tarmac of Algiers, and the firing at another a few months later in Athens killing an Israeli passenger, called for severe retaliations. The Israeli air force bombed the airport of Beirut in December 1968, destroying thirteen aircraft, eight of which belonged to Middle East Airlines. This operation was called "Gift," and it certainly came just before Christmas. The message was intended for the Lebanese government in general and Charles Helou in particular:

contain the Palestinian militias on Lebanese territory or expect the retaliation of the Israeli armed forces.

Easier said than done, however. With the Palestinian militias becoming more organized, while Lebanese politics faltered under untimely divisions between the Shihabist Nahj and a new tripartite coalition that opposed it, the *Hilf*, composed of Camille Chamoun, Raymond Eddé, and Pierre Gemayel. (When he stepped down from office, Chamoun started his own political movement, the Liberals, or *Ahrar*, which he supported with a militia, a trend in those days. Gemayel had his already, the Phalanges, or *Kataeb*. Eddé was the exception with his National Bloc, refusing to allow it to drift into a paramilitary formation.) While the times called for unity in the face of the mounting threat, and with Lebanon at the brink of implosion, with Palestinian guerillas armed to the teeth and wandering around freely, the politicians and the interested Lebanese establishment found nothing better to do but to outwit one another for petty political gains. The climax of this tragedy came a year later, in 1969, when Nasser called for a meeting in Cairo between the Lebanese government and the PLO. The Maronite Charles Helou and the Sunni Rachid Karami, the president and prime minister respectively, laid low, fearing the disapproval of their caucuses. In a last-minute decision, the commander-in-chief of the Lebanese army, General Emile Bustani, unprepared for such talks, was sent to attend.

The Cairo agreement stemmed from this meeting, recognizing Palestinian guerillas and giving them rights for military training and free commuting across Lebanon. It was signed by Bustani for Lebanon, a death warrant that was ratified by the Lebanese parliament a few days later, boycotted only by Raymond Eddé, who understood clearly the dangers. A year later, in 1970, Nasser passed away. King Hussein of Jordan then undertook the most courageous act of ordering his army, which was totally faithful to him, to annihilate the PLO presence in his kingdom. Black September, as it would be called in Arab history, rid Jordan of an imminent danger, only to dump it on a country that was incapable of managing itself in times of crisis. All the escapees from Jordan and their armaments found refuge in Lebanon, now a powder keg that only needed one spark to burn to ashes.

I was born in December 1968, two weeks before the bombing of the Beirut airport by the Israeli air force. We lived in Hadath, in a large penthouse apartment that my father rented and that had an exceptionally large outdoor play area, a mega-balcony that connected to all the rooms in the house. Nadim's factory in Karm Zeitoun was doing well, now producing designer leather bags and fashion poufs that immediately became popular. For his logo, Nadim used a caricature of an elephant, a mammal whose sturdy virtues he emulated in all his leather products. Entrepreneur at heart and having great experience in international business from his time at Iqtisadiya, Nadim stepped up his travel abroad to find new markets for his products. He found one receptive customer in Uke Thumbert, the owner of a shop in Stockholm called INDISKA. The shop was small and could not afford an entire shipment of leather bags, but Uke was confident the products would sell. So Nadim did what any goodhearted adventurer would do and sent Uke the shipment without payment, with the understanding that Uke would settle the account once the bags were sold. (Nadim was a remarkable businessman in this way, for I have not met any wholesaler who would give you even a sample product without payment first!)

Uke was successful in selling the shipment, and many more followed, all paid in time by the growing Swedish shop. Yet Uke Thumbert never knew the story behind the bags—that they were produced by people with handicaps—until he came to visit Nadim a few years later and saw with his own eyes the atypical factory. He was in tears. Later, with Lebanon devolving into civil war, the two men lost touch with one another. Nearly thirty years later, I was in Stockholm on Al-Kafaàt business and I recalled the story of Uke Thumbert that I heard from my father. On arrival, I asked the receptionist at the hotel if he knew of a shop called INDISKA, which, to my total surprise, he did. It turned out to be just around the corner from where I was staying. The "Beirut bag," as it was called, was on display, although it was now manufactured in India. I asked to see Uke Thumbert, not knowing if he was still alive. The shop manager said I would find him at the central office and gave me the address. The building I found was immense, imposing enough to make me question the story my father told of a small shop that could not pay for a shipment in advance. I announced myself and waited in the reception area, only to hear the name "Nadim" shouted at me by an aging man with thick glasses, who rushed out like a child leaving school after a long day. Uke thought it was Nadim coming back after so long. He took me into his large office and gave me his account of the Beirut bag, a product that had made him a fortune, enough to open a hundred shops across Sweden and turn INDISKA into a lucrative company.

By 1970, Nadim had reasons to relocate his factory into a new facility designed to suit his growing business. He called on his lifelong friend, Samir Khairallah, the architect who had given the American University of Beirut one of its most critically acclaimed buildings, Nicely Hall, to design a center on an estate that Nadim inherited from his father, Alfred, which Alfred had bought with the seed capital he had earned peddling in Bayou Lafourche. Samir was himself a founding trustee of Al-Kafaàt and produced a unique design, which he undertook to execute to high standards. It was an iconic, barrier-free structure, and is still vibrant forty-five years later.

When Nadim moved the factory from Karm Zeitoun to its new location in Mreijeh, at the western edge of Hadath, there were 140 workers, all handicapped, who shared the dream of the social entrepreneur whose mission was becoming well known. The new center was all-inclusive, encompassing a factory where people with disabilities worked, a mainstream school pledged to include the handicapped, an interdisciplinary therapy center, and a large workshop for the production of orthotics and prosthetics. Nadim had understood that, if disability is not always a restraining factor for work, the lack of education is. This was the reason why he decided to start a school where children with disabilities (mostly polio survivors) and children with no particular handicap from the neighborhood of Mreijeh could sit side by side and receive a proper education. Educated and fitted with the appropriate braces or orthotics, people with disabilities could hold jobs and be able to assume responsibilities as well as, if not better than, others.

About this time, Nadim made an unusual acquaintance that brought Al-Kafaàt a new advocate and an equal partner in the struggle for the welfare of the people with disabilities. Ramez Aouad, a young orthopedic surgeon who had just returned home after seven years of medical specialization in Boston and Chicago, joined Al-Kafaàt as its medical coordinator. Nadim and Ramez would do such marvelous work developing rehabilitation services that Al-Kafaàt was called on two occasions, in 1972 and in 1978, to train technicians in orthotics and prosthetics for the Arab World, the sessions funded by the World Rehabilitation Fund in the United States and the US Agency for International Development (USAID). The common bond the two men shared from the very start has borne tremendous good for Al-Kafaàt. Their continuing struggles to realize the rights of people with disabilities despite the hardships of the time were inspiring. Ramez sat as dean of the faculty of medicine at the Lebanese University in later years, and, as president of the board of trustees of the Al-Kafaàt Foundation today, he continues to serve Al-Kafaàt with undivided passion.

A particularly moving and quite expressive example of the mission that Nadim had chosen for Al-Kafaàt is the story of Charlie. Born in Palestine in the late 1930s, Charlie was twelve when his village of Bassa, in the region of Acre, was assaulted in 1948 by the Haganah and its population forced to flee. He lost most of his family there and then; only an aunt was left, and she took him on a three-day walk to Beit Jala, near Bethlehem, and left him at the door of an orphanage before taking her own life, having lost her husband and children during the assault. The orphanage was a home for children with vision impairment, and Charlie was blind. What is more, he was struck with amnesia following the harsh episode he had endured.

Charlie lived and studied at Beit Jala until the Six-Day War in 1967, when he happened to be in Jerusalem at the moment when East Jerusalem fell to the Israelis, and he, like so many others, was deported. He rode the bus to Lebanon and ended up a refugee at the camp of Ain Helweh near Sidon. Life in the camp was insalubrious, and Charlie was mocked and pushed around, enduring the prejudices and ignorance of militias who governed the streets. One day, a goodhearted neighbor told him about a factory he had heard about in Beirut that employed people with disabilities. Charlie had been given so many empty promises since his second exodus that he was not expecting much when he met with Nadim at his workshop of Al-Kafaàt. What a surprise when Nadim immediately took him in, gave him a job, and arranged for his lodgings.

The home in Beit Jala where Charlie had lived between 1948 and 1967 was managed by a British charity, the Bible Lands Society. The charity had a shop in London on Museum Street, minutes away from the British Museum, where it sold for charity items collected from across the "lands of the Bible." Bob Clothier, the director, had met Nadim on a previous trip to Lebanon and was buying the Beirut bag and other leather items for the shop on Museum Street. He had known Charlie well from Beit Jala, had been his mentor and stand-in father. Clothier in fact gave him the name Charlie, after his own adopted son, when the amnesiac child first came into his care. Bob lost track of Charlie after 1967, though, despite the search he conducted, and was deeply saddened about it. In 1970, while touring the workshop with Nadim, Clothier spotted Charlie. The reunion was as emotional and magical as one can imagine.

Charlie continued to work at the factory until civil war struck Lebanon in 1975 and he was again forced to flee, but he stayed in touch with Al-Kafaàt and would return to work at a later occasion. I found this story so compelling and expressive that Charlie was the main character of my first book. Nadim and Bob Clothier became close friends and together organized several projects that have endowed Lebanon and the Lebanese youth with rehabilitation and development services. The charity continues to this day, renamed "Embrace the Middle East" in London, and coordinates with Al-Kafaàt to serve the populations most in need.

In 1972, Lebanon's president, Sleiman Frangieh, having heard about Al-Kafaàt's phenomenal achievements in securing gainful employment for people with disabilities, decided to bestow on Nadim a presidential distinction. Frangieh designated the prime minister to deliver the award, none other than Saeb Salam, who came with a large contingent of journalists and local politicians to visit the center. A sensitive and elegant man, Salam was truly moved by the suffering of people, and he stood speechless "in front of the miracle of Al-Kafaàt," as he publicly declaimed in a speech he gave after the visit. When the time came for Salam to decorate Nadim with the National Cedar, it was Charlie (everyone having agreed to this beforehand) who walked toward Salam and received the high distinction on behalf of all the workers. There would be two other occasions when the republic reached out to bestow on Nadim such distinctions, and both times he humbly abandoned the honor in favor of Al-Kafaàt workers and children, who were, as he said, the rightful candidates for such tributes. With his social enterprise, Nadim had convinced civil society and government that people with disabilities were creative partners, able to provide wealth to the country and be responsible citizens. In Nadim's own words, which he delivered in 1972:

> Every man, irrespective of the degree and severity of his handicaps, remains a reservoir of potentials, a source of life, of hope and joyfulness. The human being transcends every limitative definition which confines him to any aspect or status.
>
> The human potential is an invitation to action and creation, the "handicap" acting as the propulsive force. To limit the interest to the "handicaps" and build up custodial care centers to institutionalize the impaired is an injury to God, a depreciation of the human being, and a misuse of material and human wealth.
>
> This leads to the vital importance which should be given to the concept and practice of *rehabilitation*. In its processes, the "handicapped" could become an enriching factor, and an indispensable element in those developing countries with limited resources, where auto-financing would be the only means to implement and realize a sound and overall social policy to the scale of the country as a whole.

Najibeh was proud that her son's undertakings had received such recognition. She was present at Al-Kafaàt's opening ceremony and knew that Nadim, whom she had taught human values by reading the Old Testament to him while he sat in her lap, would live up to her teachings. She was an aging woman who still lived in the same house in Hadath with her two daughters, who would remain single, Nada and Lodi. I remember the medlar tree at my grandfather's house in Hadath, with the orange-colored fruit that Najibeh picked and gave my sister Roula and me to eat, and the fountain in the garden where we used to run around and splash water as she ran after us. She went to Shwayr with her daughters on occasions and stayed there all summer, away from the heat of the coast. It was there one morning in 1973 that she rejoined Alfred in the kingdom of the living.

The elections of 1970 brought Sleiman Frangieh to the presidency, a choice that says much about the political deadlock that Lebanon was enduring at this critical time. The Hilf of Camille Chamoun, Pierre Gemayel, and Raymond Eddé weighed in strongly against the Nahj candidate, Elias Sarkis, who was then the governor of the central bank. With a divided parliament, the only alternative was to look beyond the two traditional party formations to the Centre Block, which brought Sleiman Frangieh, Saeb Salam, and Kamel Asaad, the head of a Shi'a Party in Jebel Amel, to power. This was a coalition of convenience more than anything else, and one that had the virtue of belonging to neither the Nahj nor the Hilf. Lebanese politics are governed by interest groups, each with a large caucus and most with the fire power of self-owned militias; appointing a provincial like Frangieh, who had neither a caucus nor a militia, was a recipe for weak governance in the country. And that was exactly the point for the establishment, who dreaded the return of Shihabism, for their economic interests demanded a certain looseness in state relations and definitely less control on the part of government. Frangieh had his stronghold in northern Mount Lebanon, the region of Ehden that had been home to Youssef bey Karam, whom we met earlier in this book, and like his ancestor, he engaged in simplistic politics where lawmaking was a vague notion that depended on the type of relations he had with people. As expected, Frangieh nominated Salam to preside over a cabinet of ministers from outside the regular channels, all young and most not members of the common political formations or the establishment.

A government of "technocrats" we would call it today in Lebanon, with a twist of irony, and one that did not last long. Ministers dropped out one after the other, simply unable to stand up to the practices of the Lebanese establishment and those of the traditional politicians, who undermined any reform they tried to implement, particularly those that threatened their own turfs. So the five years leading up to the all-out war were spent in erratic cabinet appointments and resignations, some ministers lasting only two months; the chaos was presided over time and again by prime ministers who had no leverage and who were unable to even understand the complexity of the situation.

In the areas of the military and intelligence, Frangieh took the initiative of substituting key personnel with his own partisans, who were inexperienced and who lacked knowledge of the commands they were given. Shihabist operatives were practically expunged from the deuxième bureau, and the commanding officers of the Lebanese army were reassigned. In short, Frangieh did an excellent job of denuding Lebanon of its executive, military, and administrative structures. No wonder that Lebanon stood idly by when the Palestinian guerillas swamped the country after their expulsion from Jordan following Black September: there was simply no one competent to respond!

On the domestic side, Lebanon faced "housekeeping" problems. The rampant greed of the oligarchic establishment meant that all the gains from the sound economy—which paradoxically was at its best in the early 1970s—were siphoned off, providing little to the treasury for public spending. The strong economy did lead to a rise in the cost of living, and most people were confronted with a growing inability to make ends meet. Riots and demonstrations erupted across the country when the cabinet was unable to respond to people's needs; instead, ministers were caught in a vicious cycle of power-sharing that dramatically revealed their shortcomings.

When the "Palestinian question," as it would be known for decades thereafter, became an armed conflict, Lebanon was already in turmoil, badly managed and split into pieces by self-interest groups for whom the nation and its resources were merely the guarantors for their businesses. Assassinations, abductions, car bombs—Beirut was the stage for such aberrations with a frequency that was untenable and that targeted the army, civil society activists, and civilians equally. What little leverage the government and the armed forces still had over the situation was lost unequivocally when General Emile Bustani defected to Syria; the former commander-in-chief of the army and head of the deuxième bureau, Bustani signed the Cairo agreement in 1969 that gave Lebanon to the Palestinian guerillas on a silver platter. The man in charge of intelligence, who had firsthand information about the most sensitive topics, was now a guest of Syria, the country that harbored a number of Palestinian guerillas itself, some even headquartered in Damascus.

Palestinian groups were not aligned with each other, as one would think, but in opposition most of the time, each with a separate agenda and a different leadership. When Saeb Salam negotiated with Yasser Arafat, the other factions made sure to send a message to the prime minister to say they did not feel bound by the discussions, usually by way of a car bomb parked on a street busy enough to cause many casualties. While Palestinians were undermining the already frail Lebanese government, the Israelis piled on by targeting Palestinians and Lebanese alike. The commando raid led by Ehud Barak in 1973 to assassinate Mohammad Najjar and two other PLO operatives in the Verdun area was highly professional. Barak and the other commandos, some of them (including Barak himself) disguised as women, were in and out of Verdun in no time, the Lebanese army not realizing what had actually happened until much later.

At the same time, the Palestinian fedayin were taking up positions in the south of Lebanon, across from Israel, their numbers reinforced by the incoming troops from Jordan after 1970. As a result, many Shi'a villagers left their homes and lands and sought refuge in Beirut, settling down in the southern suburbs, across from Hadath. Clashes between the Israelis and Palestinians on the southern border intensified in 1975, the year a total Armageddon began.

Lily

On a visit to the showroom of the Stephan Company, Nadim encountered a young woman who made a strong impression. She had grace and beauty, and her stunning green eyes contrasted with her dark hair and soft white skin. She dressed elegantly and walked with lightness, spoke softly and politely; the perfect woman, Nadim thought—these were his own words—from the moment he set eyes on her. Nadim was thirty-one and was no novice at making the acquaintance of women; he was a known Don Juan who made no effort to hide his interest in the opposite sex. The high-spirited young man, intelligent and good looking, seemed miles away from falling for the nineteen-year-old who was busy filing papers in the office. Yet before they even spoke, he knew it would be her, the one who would walk by his side, his inspiration and companion in Al-Kafaàt, who would bear his children and nurse him in old age. Don't ask how, he just knew it. He told me so on every occasion we spoke of my mother, occasions when he used profound language pronounced in clear and bewitching tones. Lily.

She was the daughter of John Stephan, the owner of the company where Nadim purchased the presses for the leather factory at Al-Kafaàt, a self-made man who had studied at the American University and made his way in trading, eventually becoming the regional representative across Arab countries for a number of worldwide companies. A hard worker, strict and disciplined, he spoke little, was generous and kind, liked to garden when he wasn't at work, and enjoyed sipping tea or drinking coffee in the afternoon while puffing his English tobacco. His travels to Europe on business were always occasions for him and his wife, Mary, to spend a few days at big hotels; enjoying five o'clock tea at the Park Lane Hotel in London was a routine that my grandmother would remember fondly in her old age. John and Mary made their home in Beirut, on Bab Idriss, one of the high-end streets of the old souks, where John had his offices. Lily was born there in 1946. When war threatened them in 1975, John took his family to Mansourieh, in the Metn region of Mount Lebanon, where he owned a second residence. They ended up staying there, their house in Beirut succumbing to the fate of all the souks, devastated by the spiraling of violence in 1976.

Nadim met Lily at her father's offices in 1965. They got engaged relatively quickly and married a year later in 1966 at the Church of Bhamdoun in a village resort on Damascus Road. Both John and Alfred, the fathers of the bride and groom, had properties there, although they had never met before their children's wedding. My mother bore four children, but she always confided, repeating what my father said, that she brought five into the world, Al-Kafaàt being the eldest. On their first date, Nadim took Lily to the convent in Salima, of all places, to visit the school he had started with the congregation there; on their second, he took her to the leather factory, still in Karm Zeitoun. Not romantic venues, one might say, but they had the benefit of giving Lily an intimation of the life she could expect with Nadim, and she took to it instantly.

For half a century, Lily supported Nadim every step of the way as he built center after center and put together program after program. She gave Al-Kafaàt much of the wealth that she inherited from her father, and more so of her time and devotion as she delved into the daily operations of an institution that was constantly growing. In time, she gave Al-Kafaàt a heart, while Nadim injected a soul with his unique philosophy, the two of them balancing a life of dedication to others with a normal family life where emotions were abundant.

The couple that my parents formed was atypical in many ways. I can't remember an occasion when just the two of them went out to the movies or to a restaurant. Their evenings were extensions of the long days they spent deciding which program would serve better this or that population of children with special needs. For leisure, my father would pick a book from his well-stocked home, a book that spoke of human sufferings in one way or another, and often with a bit of existentialism, of which he was such a vehement advocate. He made the complex writings of Nietzsche, Sartre, and Kierkegaard, thinkers he often referred to, sound so simple, despite their harsh diatribes about the death of God and the "man of resentment." A friend of Albert Schweitzer, with whom he had a sustained correspondence early in his teens when Al-Kafaàt was still a mission-in-the-making, Nadim also knew Helen Keller, whose signed photograph hung in his private study at home. Another friend was the French revolutionary abbot Abbé Pierre, whose call in 1954 in favor of the homeless during a particularly fierce winter made a deep impact. Yes, Nadim and Lily lived with the ghosts of great men and women.

As a teenager, I sat listening to my father talk of the reunions he attended at the Cénacle libanais, a think tank of intellectuals that looked at every aspect of the Lebanese condition, economic, social, political, and constitutional. Michel Asmar, the founder of this unique group, was a good friend of my parents and one who would follow them in their realization of Al-Kafaàt. My father occasionally took me with him to the Cénacle, seating me at one corner of the small meeting room in Asmar's office in Ashrafieh. I would be the only child in the room. I heard Yasser Arafat, the controversial Palestinian leader, speak there. I came across people who spoke of Lebanon from conflicting points of view, though I could hardly understand their discourses: Moussa Sadr, the imam who had started his own political party to plead for the inclusion of his community, the Shi'a, in the power balance; and, at the other extreme, Pierre Gemayel, who spoke of a Christian Greater Lebanon along the lines of the 1920 French arrangement, with Maronites as the dominating force. When my father published his first book, edited by the Cénacle libanais, Michel Asmar gave me a fifty-pound bill, the old Lebanese currency that still held some value in 1982, which represented the cost of the first copy he had sold. I still keep the bill, which has sentimental value for me. These were the only times my parents parted, if only for an afternoon, from their near-obsessive focus on Al-Kafaàt.

In my parents' house there was no small talk, no time for wasting, no parties to attend at friends' houses, or television programs worth staying up for; life had a purpose and was meant to be taken seriously from as early as possible. In this environment, one could only count on one's next of kin to enliven a dull afternoon, when, at age twelve, a ball game was the only existential debate that came to mind.

It was in those days that my relationships with my brother and sisters grew very strong. We knew we were the depositories of a very important mission, yet we did not know what to do about it. My brother Ramzi and I went as far as starting a charitable society, a two-member association that did not reach beyond the bedroom of two teenagers. In his free time, Ramzi was sent to work in construction at one or another of Al-Kafaàt's centers that was expanding despite the conflicts that marked most of the 1970s and 1980s. I was sent to work at the orthotics and prosthetics department, producing limbs for amputees and walking aids for the handicapped. The payment was a quarter of a lira, which my father awarded ceremoniously and which was enough to buy a bottle of Pepsi Cola.

I have so many memories of an epoch that was quite paradoxical: generosity and peace across Al-Kafaàt, all-out violence across the whole of Lebanon. When the 1976 conflict gained momentum, sliding Lebanon down to oblivion, life in Hadath became unbearable, for our house stood in the middle of the battlefield of the rival parties. As a child, I heard fabricated stories about Palestinian guerillas who killed little children, cutting off their genitals for prizes, and they certainly scared me at eight years old. However soothing my mother tried to be, I was frightened by those stories, and they came to mind whenever sporadic shooting broke the silence of the night, sometimes with such violence that we ran down to the basement that served as a shelter for all the families in the building. It was in this shelter that I handled an M16 for the first time, the American-made machine gun that was used by the Christian militias. War games would have been easy to slip into for the young and passionate boys, but my ever-present mother prevented that, at times overprotecting her children to such an extent that she seemed suffocating. But could she have done otherwise?

As the conflict intensified in 1976, it became necessary to evacuate our house. Hadath was on a demarcation line that divided the city into two parts, Christian on the east side and Muslim on the west, and our house became a target for both contending parties. What did not burn to ashes would be vandalized. So my father took us away to Shwayr, where we stayed at our summer residence, but even there, war was at the door. The countless cease-fires that were agreed to by the rival groups never lasted, and the cycle of violence went on, intensifying across all the regions. In the center of Beirut, destruction was complete. Days after we left, our own building in Hadath took a direct hit, and it became evident to my parents that a return to our old life was not possible.

With a new school year approaching, a different solution had to be found. While my father could not possibly leave himself, with Al-Kafaàt needing his presence more than ever, he decided to send the rest of us to Cyprus for a short time, suggesting we travel on to France if the clouds of war did not clear by the end of summer. Nearby Cyprus became the obvious escape for many Lebanese during the seventeen-year war, and I have counted nine occasions when our family went there for refuge. Although it was a short flight, only twenty-five minutes, the trip to the airport was hazardous in 1976, when as many as fifty militias and splinter groups, each with a different banner and all with very sensitive triggers, controlled the streets. Later, the demarcation line that split Beirut into denominational zones became so tightly monitored that we had no access to the Beirut airport at all.

My father drove us to Jounieh, then a small fishing town north of Beirut, where he saw my mother and the four of us onto a boat that took us to Larnaca in Cyprus. I remember the separation at the harbor, the heartbreaking moment when my father took each of us in a long embrace, and I remember my mother sobbing at the separation, though she made an effort to conceal her distress and worry from us. She had just turned thirty, and had four children to look after, the oldest, my sister Roula, nine, and the youngest, my sister Myriam, only three. Now she found herself at sea, sailing away from her husband and country into the unknown. The crossing to Larnaca was a debacle, with the two-propeller fishing boat losing one engine, partly because it was carrying twice the capacity it should have. Without enough water and food, the journey took forty-eight hours, a trying ordeal for my mother, who had a crisis to manage with four scared, hungry, and agitated children. In Larnaca, we stayed with George Markou, a friend of my father's and the director of the School for the Deaf in Cyprus, himself a victim of a recent war in 1974 that partitioned the island between the Turkish and Greek populations. He lost the school in the process, and his only son. Mela, his wife, was dressed in black when she settled Ramzi and me in the room of her late son.

Sensitive and highly emotional, Lily was also able to summon up enough strength to face any situation, and she had a unique sense of humor. In the middle of the torments we were suffering at this time, she would make comments that made even the most anxious among us burst into laughter. Having been educated at the British school, she did not speak a word of French when she arrived in Lyon in 1976 with her four children. I remember at a bakery once when she wanted to order a baguette and, not knowing the gender, whether it should be *un* baguette or *une* baguette, she ended up ordering *deux* baguettes, refusing to let herself rely on simple mimicking to communicate. She would learn to speak French within a year.

Some traits of Lily's personality are perhaps not so uncommon among people, but one of them I have always found unique. I took the measure of it in 1984, at another dramatic junction in the history of Lebanon. We were living then in a rented flat in Baabda, on a high promontory that overlooked Beirut, next-door neighbors of the French ambassador. At the time, my father was building our family home closer to the center of town in Baabda, opposite the Shihab Palace, which had been the seat of government under the mutasarifiya (it is the seat of the regional government for Mount Lebanon today) and across from the presidential palace. The construction would take six more months to complete—good timing, because that's when our lease on the rented apartment would be up. Then, one Sunday morning, quite unexpectedly, my mother woke everybody early. She insisted that we pack the house and leave immediately. The discussion was tense as we all argued her decision was arbitrary, that it would be impossible to pack a whole house and move in a single day, that our home-under-construction was far from complete. Our resistance did not matter, and despite my father's effort to reason with her, we surrendered, and spent the most hilarious day I can remember. We had no boxes, so we carried out filled drawers, and my father drove back and forth with clothes, chairs, kitchen appliances, books, and what-not piled onto the car seats or dangling from the tightly roped open trunk. Incredibly, we slept at our new home that night, on the floor, with a gentle breeze that came through the window openings, no water in the pipes, no electricity or lights. My mother dismissed the general disgruntlement by saying that we had finally gotten to go camping, something she had always promised us.

The next morning, my father and I drove back to the other apartment to shower, only to find ourselves at a battle scene. A rocket had fallen on the building the night before, leaving two people dead and injuring another two. At our apartment, glass debris and shrapnel filled the rooms, hitting every single bed but one—funnily enough, my mother's. That was Lily.

Shwayr, in a child's memory

War was raging all around us, and Katyusha rockets rivaled the intensity of M16 rifles fired in close-encounter street fighting. The year was 1976, and having vacated our home in Hadath just before it took a direct hit, we had driven to Shwayr, hoping to escape the lethal spiral of violence in Beirut. My father was at the wheel of his 1971 Plymouth, a large white car he had bought when my brother Ramzi was born and which drove him and my mother safely home from hospital after his birth. An important story to tell in my father's eyes, for whom symbols had importance. No less important was this story to Ramzi, who kept the Plymouth, now a vintage car, and drove his bride home from church in it some thirty years later.

In any case, there we were, squeezed into the Plymouth, four brothers and sisters in the back, my father in the driver's seat and my mother next to him. We drove out of Shwayr toward Bologna, a neighboring town, when the war caught up with us. Out of nowhere, a storm of rockets fell on Shwayr and its suburbs, and an all-out battle ensued. Taken by surprise, my father drove off the road and pulled over against a high wall, turning the car away from the streets where danger was most likely. I remember the scene vividly: the four of us lying low under the black leather backseat, my mother reaching out to each of us with her comforting hands every time a rocket was launched. She always had a unique capacity to turn a frenzied situation into a casual anecdote. "When you hear the whistle, you should not worry. It means the rocket is passing over us and we have therefore nothing to be scared about!" In this analysis, if we were to take a direct hit, we would not hear a thing, a thought that made Roula and I giggle. I remember my father sitting there debating what to do with my mother, speaking English so as not to alarm the four of us, who could not understand it, their whispers climbing in intensity every time a whistling rocket encroached on their conversation. And the radio, how can I forget the all-too-present radio, with its news flashes that kept one informed of the ever-changing fighting lines. News flashes would cut in with a jingle that sounded like the theme from *Starsky and Hutch*, the epic detective series of the disco era. The news presenter was a monotonous character with a grave voice that contrasted deeply with the stirring music that continued playing.

When the shelling intensified, my father made the decision to walk to a nearby hotel, the Bois de Boulogne, and have us shelter there. The distance was short, yet it must have seemed to my parents like the longest journey they had ever made. My mother had all four of us by the hands, holding us in pairs, while my father was walking ahead, covering his family with his body from any frontal threat, looking around nervously for any source of danger that would make him change his plans. Once in the hotel, we joined other people who were caught in the middle of the fighting. We stayed there a few hours, in the basement with everybody else. News flashes were mumbling in the background and there was a complete blackout due to a power failure, which was softened somewhat by the glow of a few candles set on coffee saucers and distributed around the large hall. We were waiting for a cease-fire to be declared so everybody could go home, but it never came.

Late at night, when the rockets seemed more sporadic and the machine gunners seemed to ease on their triggers, a priest who was among the sheltering party spoke out and proposed to lead a convoy of cars into Shwayr. In a religious country, a priest in full dress was expected to earn some respect from a combatant in arms if the convoy came to be intercepted. Or at least, this was what the priest believed. "God will protect us," he promised, and we all went. And the Almighty did. I remember the drive home in this convoy very well, as if it took place last night. I saw nothing, only the pitch black of the sky, from under the seat where my mother had us hiding. When the convoy reached the center of town, my father broke lines and drove us home, minutes away from the center of Shwayr. Power was restored as we came in and we prepared for sleep. That night, television aired an episode of *Columbo*, the highly spirited, poorly dressed police inspector. The next day we left Shwayr, crossing mountain passes into Jounieh harbor in the Christian zone and boarding a fishing boat to Larnaca in Cyprus. That was the last time I saw

Shwayr as a child. I was eight years old then and it would be another twenty-six years before I saw it again.

Land of my ancestors, Shwayr was also the land of my childhood fantasies, my wonderland, and the land of my innocent years. We lived in a beautiful house my father rented and where we spent our summers and weekends. It was our secondary residence and it meant holidays for me and for my older sister Roula, away from our Beirut school and its drab uniforms. We climbed down a long stairway to get home from the main street, a flight of no fewer than forty stairs, which made the height from the access point of the stairway to the lower ground approximately twenty feet. All too often did I stand at the top, climb out onto a short wall that also served as a flower container, and jump all the way down—some twenty-four feet—to a corner of the garden below. Just the thought of it makes me dizzy today!

The stairway led down to a central space that served two houses, ours and that of the Nassar family. Their son was my friend, and on many occasions we lit bonfires in this space and spent evenings playing around it. The top item on my play list was jumping across the bonfire without getting caught by the fire; throwing firecrackers in it was another favorite. Sometimes, we would combine the two and jump across while firecrackers were exploding. Somehow, I always ventured to take the first turn at this. Playing with firecrackers was fun and other pyrotechnic stunts were on the list, like holding a skyrocket in your bare fingers and lighting the wick with the other hand. Given that the Chinese-made rockets would explode on the ground sometimes instead of climbing high in the sky to display their magnificent colors, the risks we ran of serious injuries were certainly not negligible. But did we know? I remember my mother chasing after me and giving me the rules to abide by, yet I would go my own way as soon as she turned her back.

My obliviousness led me once to an old woman by the name of Afifeh, who lived alone deep in the woods across from our home and whom we affectionately called *teta*, for grandma. My father was always supportive of her and brought her food and sweets occasionally. Alone, I once took the footpath to her home without telling my mother and stayed late, enjoying her generous hospitality, which came with lots of candies and homemade marmalade. Hours passed and I was taken for lost by my parents, who mobilized friends and neighbors to look for me in every possible place all over town, until my father finally found me at Teta Afifeh's. It was evening already and my parents had spent a whole afternoon looking for me. I was severely punished.

Another time, my mother took me to town to buy a pair of ranger boots, the type of shoes the soldiers wear and which I wanted wholeheartedly. I must have seen someone wearing them and developed a fixation on them, for I made my mother promise to buy me a pair. I remember the shop we went to, across from the municipal building, a bazaar for anything and everything made of rubber, from raincoats to garden boots. But not ranger military boots for six-year-olds! Despite the seller's assertions that military boots didn't come in small sizes (for good reason!), I went on whining and demanding. I was not willing to go home without them and that was that. My mother next took me to the only children's shoe shop in Shwayr, where the answer was the same. Back home, I would not get out of the car, locking myself in from the inside and pushing the lock down every time my mother tried opening it with the key. Finally it was late in the afternoon and my father came home from work. He stood there glaring at me through the window, and with shivers running down my spine, I opened the door and surrendered to his punishment.

Shwayr was the land of toys, or at least that is how I viewed it as a child, a town that harbored Qaysar Amer, the large toy store where plastic, steel, and wood took the forms of cars, swords, and machine guns. This is where we bought firecrackers and where we chose outfits for costume day, a yearly religious feast that has a Halloween-like atmosphere but celebrates Saint Barbara, a third-century convert to Christianity. We dressed up as all types of characters and ate the Saint Barbara sweets, the alms of the occasion given us by the people on whose doors we knocked.

Barbara was not the only saint of the region who called for a yearly celebration. Every July came the anniversary of Saint Elijah, and grand ceremonies were staged around the eponymous convent of Mar Elias. The narrow street leading to the convent was crowded with sweets vendors and carnival-style game stands, their yellow lights dangling from an improvised installation of electrical cables and bulbs. The sight was awe-inspiring to us children, especially at night, when the street was busiest and the smell of fried *zlabieh*, crusty honeyed dough balls, invaded the air.

The convent was well known to me because my parents took us there practically every Sunday for the liturgy. I was a devoted church boy, assigned to walk one of the candle posts across the church, in rehearsed steps that most certainly had liturgical significance but were hardly comprehensible to me then. There were two candle posts and one cross that were carried by children in processions that started behind the hand-carved iconostas and wound around through the church. The cross stood higher than the two candles and was carried by a bigger boy, and all three trailed the bishop, who held the Bible in the procession while his archimandrite preceded the group with an incense burner, spreading the enchanting scent across the small four-hundred-year-old church.

One day, I asked to carry the cross, the higher post among the three, but was put off by the older boys who took turns doing it. I insisted and my insistence paid off; the archimandrite standing nearby looked me in the eyes, pressed the post against me, and said, "It is bigger than you but I will trust you with it!" Proudly, I walked in the middle between the two candles, behind the incense burner and the bishop, who held the Bible, the sacred book, encased in golden leaves and adorned with colored cabochon caps. As the group passed the nave under a magnificent chandelier that hung from the ceiling, I walked straight, filled my chest with air, raised the post as high as I could, eager to show that I was capable of carrying the cross, and slammed it right into the chandelier. The shattering of crystal was mesmerizing. As I write, I can still see the fragments on the floor, lying on the red carpet for everyone to see and contemplate. I stood there speechless, unable to move a muscle. How the mess was cleared and whether the liturgy went on as usual, that I do not remember. What I do know is that this incident did not put me off showing my prowess at tolling the heavy cast-iron bell in the churchyard, a demanding task that only the hard-muscled and well trained could do. I would stand on a stepping stone while gripping firmly to the rope that dangled from the bell tower and pull with all my bodyweight. I was never as impressive as the big boys who stood still, not moving an inch, the rope gripped in one hand, their ties undone and dark-colored suits spotless, shaking the big bell so hard that it tolled out the much-desired four repeated gongs.

I saw my first movie in Shwayr. My mother drove Roula and me to the Rex, the only theater in town, to see *The Sound of Music* with Julie Andrews. She left us there and took the younger two, Ramzi and Myriam, with her to the nearby town of Bikfaya, where she drove every day to shop for fresh fruits and vegetables. There, she always bought each of us juice that came in a triangular pyramidal-shaped carton that we punctured with a pointed straw that came with it. I don't know if it was the juice I liked more or the ritual of all of us going to town, the children sitting in the back seat of the two-door Morris Marina, our second car. Sitting in the dark theater as the movie was playing, I could only think of the drive to Bikfaya that I was missing, so I decided to jump out of my seat and run home to my mother; perhaps she was still there and I could still take the ride. Roula chased after me, shouting like mad (she was enjoying the movie), and we were both at home when my mother returned an hour later, worried to death after not finding us waiting at the cinema.

On one visit to Bikfaya, as we were waiting for her in the car at a grocery shop, my mother slipped and fell to the sidewalk, breaking her right leg. Responsible and stoic, she jumped in the car and drove the manual transmission Marina back home despite the agonizing pain she must have felt. I remember her in a thick plaster cast resting her leg on a chair and wonder today how she managed to drive in her condition. "God gives strength," she would say.

This was the period when my parents first let me go out on my own. Once I went to my aunt Lodi's house to return a Pyrex plate on which she had brought us rice-stuffed sheep intestines, a meal she alone could prepare to perfection. As I walked with the plate, a car ran into me, an old-style open military car that was used by a driving school. The driver was eager to leave, scared to see a boy bleeding under his wheels. I stood up and was feeling fine, although I had many bruises on my hands and feet. The Pyrex plate was broken, however, and that was my real worry: I had failed in my mission, and I was ashamed. I walked on to my aunt's door and when she saw what a state I was in, she took me inside and gave me enough hugs to make me realize how unimportant the Pyrex plate was after all. Later, she bought another plate and brought *mughli* to us on it, a cinnamon-based sweet that she prepares with equal skill. She still has this plate, which she calls the Raif-Pyrex.

In Shwayr, I learned to ride a bicycle. Who doesn't remember the first bike and the first ride? At first I was confined to the square area at the foot of our outside stairs, the square with the bonfires; only when I convinced my father that I could stay on the bicycle seat without difficulty did he let me ride on the roads. Beyond a certain distance, he would drive the car and trail me, apprehensive, as he would claim, about the driving abilities of others (never mine).

In winter, my father had a stove installed in the living room, an oil-fueled stove that looked like the mask of a deep-water diver. It had a window through which you could gaze at the flame, a tube to monitor the level of fuel in the tank, and a circular stovetop, which we used for grilling chestnuts and potatoes. I can smell the room still, with delicacies grilling (they sometimes included onions and garlic) and the odor of fuel oil, which I always found quite sweet.

Nuts were a frequent delicacy, and pine fruits that we picked in season were cracked open with a hammer to get the tiny nuts inside; these were delicately placed one by one to fill my mother's glass jars. For meals, my mother cooked all sorts of stews, all containing the precious pine nuts we had spent hours collecting.

Snow always fell in Shwayr in winter. Overnight, the town turned into a gigantic playground for the children. My favorite activity was coasting down the numerous hills on a sled, a sport we usually enjoyed with our friends, the children of the Mrowa family, whose parents were our parents' friends and who lived just minutes away. I now take my own children sledding on the same hills. There, I tell them stories about their ancestors, of Fares Bozeid Moujaes, the stonemason who was first to come to Hadath, of his lineage, of Alfred Nicola, and of their grandfather Nadim and his achievements. All these years, and the taste of the snow remains exactly the same.

A cry in the wilderness

The radicalization of the Palestinian presence in Lebanon occurred when Sleiman Frangieh headed a government handcuffed to an unworkable constitutional framework, impeded by the self-interest groups that formed the Lebanese establishment and undercut by the rival political parties who did not shy away from taking seats as ministers on many occasions. While Lebanon's economic outlook seemed rather bright, the management of the country was appalling.

Regional changes added further tension to Lebanon's fraught situation. In October 1973, Egyptian president Anwar Sadat undertook to regain the Sinai, which had been occupied by Israel since 1967, following the Six-Day War. He orchestrated a surprise attack on the Jewish holiday of Yom Kippur, which he coordinated with the Syrians, who fought a second front, going simultaneously after the Golan Heights, also annexed in the Six-Day War. The first three days brought euphoria to the Arab World as the Egyptian and Syrian armies advanced, avenging as they went the affront they suffered in 1967. However, Sadat did not win the day during what has come to be known as the Yom Kippur War, for Israel managed to curtail the Egyptian and Syrian threats and force their armies back, even going on the counterattack and threatening, for a while, Damascus and Cairo.

Fiasco or not, the military operation had immense consequences on the power relations across the Middle East. Egypt was an ally of the USSR, as was Syria, while Israel was an ally of the United States. Coming during the time of the Cold War, the incursions and counter-incursions in the Sinai and the Golan Heights had serious repercussions and could have degenerated into a clash between the nuclear titans. Thankfully, this did not happen, yet shifts in alliances were to follow. It would take Sadat four more years before he made a complete transition to the American camp, which would be sealed at Camp David by the peace accord with Israel in 1978, but the initial steps came fairly quickly after the debacle of Yom Kippur. If the failure of the combined Egyptian and Syrian armies brought despair to the Palestinian guerillas in Lebanon, news of Sadat "eloping" to the American side made them realize that their chances of massing Arab support for their cause were dimming, at least under the Egyptian banner. In fact, while many of the Arab states were giving lip service to the Palestinians, they were pushing the Lebanese to rid themselves of the imminent danger they represented and went as far as suggesting in half words that they orchestrate their own Black September.

The Palestinian problem was becoming a burden to many, especially some of the Arab countries, whose economic interests brought them closer to the United States and to the Western Hemisphere. That the Palestinian leadership got wind of this general feeling did not help. By this time, there were as many as twelve different factions widely dispersed around Lebanon, reinforced with the incoming personnel and equipment from Jordan, and well funded with money from Libya, Iraq, and Syria. All that and a dysfunctional Lebanese government and military made the country a powder keg awaiting a spark.

It came at a rally in Saida, in 1975, while fishermen were demonstrating against the establishment of a large fishing company that they believed would monopolize their industry with its more modern techniques. The fishermen were especially unhappy that this Arab company was partly owned by none other than their previous president, Camille Chamoun, now minister of the interior. The rally was interrupted by government forces and the clash rapidly escalated; bullets were fired and a prominent Sunni figure, Maaruf Saad, an outspoken opponent of the Palestinian military presence in Lebanon and leader of the Popular Nasserite Organization, was killed. Later that year, an attempt on the life of Pierre Gemayel, the leader of the Christian Kataeb, was avenged by his militiamen in the massacre of a busload of Palestinians driving from one camp to another. Twenty-seven people on the bus were butchered, and the civil war was ignited the same day, April 15, 1975.

The first year of the war seemed almost surreal. As many as thirty different militias, most with specific agendas and with foreign involvement and financing, took part in the hostilities. Equally surreal was the attitude of the Lebanese leadership itself, with leading politicians going around organizing their own militias and so further undermining the capabilities of the central government. While sitting as the minister of the interior (which controlled the police), Camille Chamoun, the former president, had his son Dany organize his militia, the so-called Tigers. Even President Frangieh, in disagreement with his cabinet, retired to Ehden, his stronghold in the north, abandoning Beirut for two whole weeks, during which time he had his son, Tony, organize his militia, the Marada.

Cease-fires were brokered by the hundreds and never respected, each of the contenders in turn sabotaging the peace efforts when the strategic reality on the ground was not favorable. Ironically, no one was willing to put down his weapons until the situation turned to his advantage: Pierre Gemayel aspired to his vision of Greater Lebanon, with a Christian majority and himself as president; Camille Chamoun wanted the presidency back for himself; Kamal Jumblatt, the Druze leader, wanted no less than a totally new constitution. It was a dialogue of the deaf, and the contenders did not seem to be bothered about the outcome of their actions as long as they could walk away with the ultimate prize at the end.

Coalitions of circumstance were formed and then reformed along opposite lines. Kamal Jumblatt started off opposing the Palestinian military operations and then changed sides to use their momentum to his own advantage. His National Movement would soon revolve around leftist groups and Palestinian commandos, particularly the PLO. In opposition, the Christian militias formed the Lebanese Front, which fought in the same ranks with the Syrians. War was raging in Beirut between the Kataeb and its allied groups against the Palestinian and the National Movement forces, turning the souks and the city center to rubble. While the Christian militias were ransacking the hotel district, the National Movement forces seized

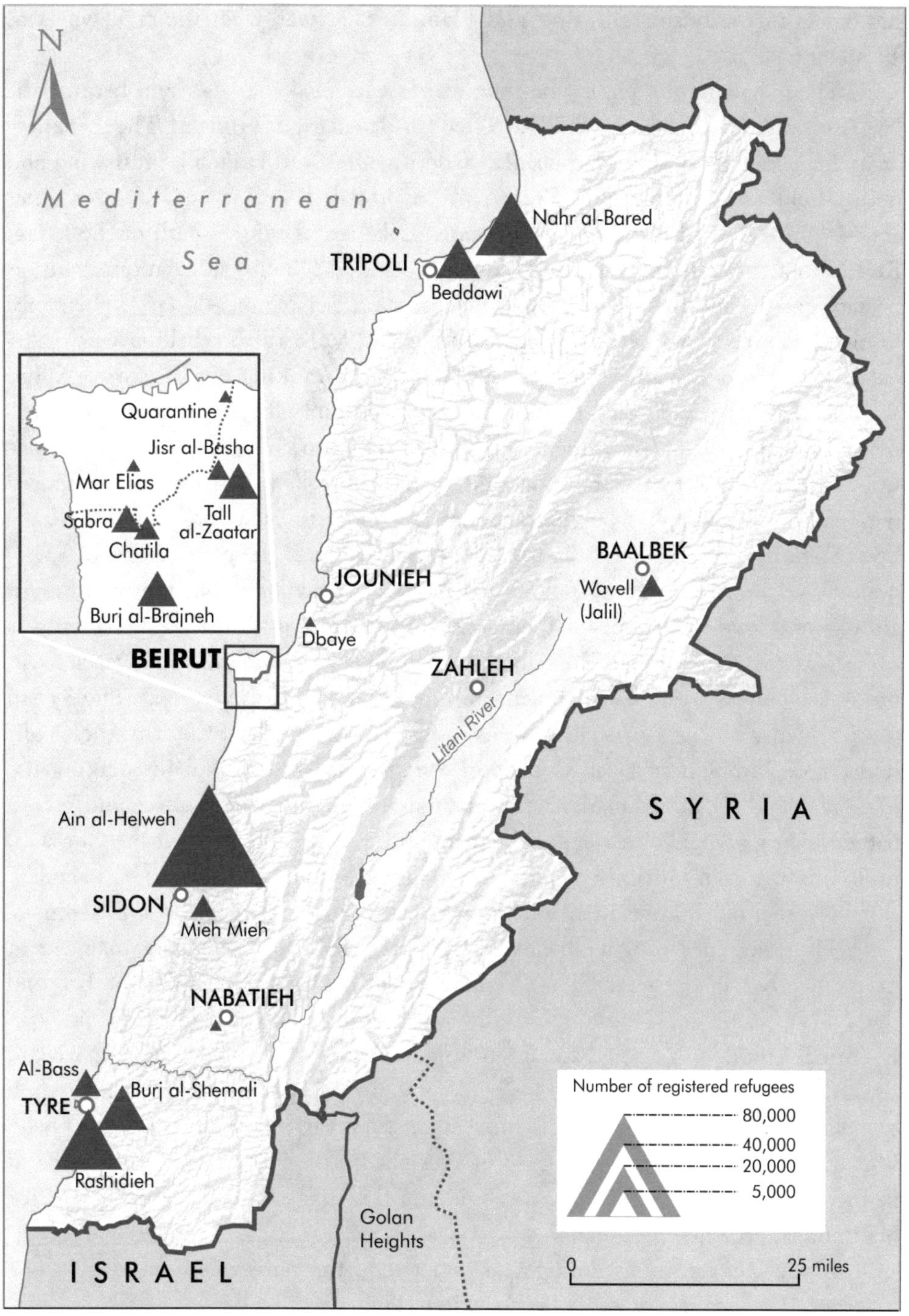

Map 8. Palestinian camps on the eve of Lebanon's war (1975)

the banks in the business district and Hamra. That was what the civil war was all about at first.

Then change took place when the war lost its local character and became the "war of others on Lebanese soil," as Ghassan Tueni rightly put it. The Lebanese army fractured, with one faction, under Commander Saad Haddad, mutinying and taking hold in the south. This Free Army, as it called itself, would in later times act as a bridgehead for the Israelis to annex Lebanese territory south of the Litani River. Another army mutiny saw Lieutenant Ahmad Khatib gather momentum as brigades across the Bekaa, Tripoli, and some southern regions declared allegiance to his Arab Army. A few days later, still in early 1976, a third rebellion was spearheaded by the commander of the Beirut area, a high-ranking officer named Abdul Aziz Ahdab, who went on television and declared himself the "governor of Lebanon." Like the army, government institutions had also collapsed, and governance was in the hands of the plethora of militias that controlled the streets and imposed their laws on the helpless populations that fell under their sway.

With the entry of the Syrian forces at the request of the government of Lebanon, the war took a different turn. It was no longer a civil war, one that was fought among local feuding groups for their perceived self-interests; instead, Lebanon was to become, as Muhammad Hussein Fadlallah, a Shi'a cleric and political activist, put it, the "lungs through which transpire the problems of the region." The Syrian troops sided with the Christian militias to fight Jumblatt, the PLO, and the Coalition forces. Jumblatt surfaced to support the army separatists equally, making use of Saad Haddad and Ahmad Khatib at times to heighten his chances and gain a better sniping angle. With weapons pouring in from Israel to support the Christian militias, some even fancifully conjectured that the Syrians and Israelis had actually sided together on this one, their self-interests outweighing their political differences.

The two sides fought all across Lebanon, their forces equally matched at first. Then Syrian president Hafez Assad massed fresh troops for the conflict, and the crisis became more complex, with other Arab countries providing aid, too. Eventually the Saudis called for a summit meeting, which took place in Riyadh toward the end of 1976, and brokered a cease-fire. It was also decided in Riyadh to dispatch a multinational Arab force to insure that the cease-fire was upheld. Mostly composed of Syrians, the Arab Deterrent Force gave Assad the upper hand in the game. He, in fact, went away with no less than an Arab endorsement for his military presence in Lebanon.

If you went away assuming you understood the crisis in Lebanon, said one observer, it means it was explained poorly to you.

In 1976 Al-Kafaàt suffered more than her share of destruction. The center in Mreijeh that was honored by Premier Saeb Salam four years earlier fell under the control of the PLO. It was occupied and looted. The machines and presses that once gave employment to 140 people with disabilities were all stolen and sold for scrap. Whatever could not be sold, because it had no significant value or because its use was not known, was destroyed and left in piles of debris and waste. Anything of value—tiles, electrical fixtures, plumbing—was ripped out and sold. The chapel at the center was desecrated, and the icon of Mary that adorned the iconostas was torn to pieces. A fine mosaic, it was created for the opening of the center in 1972 by the School of the Deaf in Cyprus and presented in person by George Markou, who came especially for the ceremony. So much had happened in four years in the lives of the two friends, George and Nadim, both living to witness their creations, fruits of elevated inspirations and deep commitments, trampled on by ignorant people with machine guns.

The PLO had adapted and installed a rocket-launcher on the roof of the building, a Russian-made Katyusha, which can shoot a number of missiles in a very short time with noise that resembled that of a long stick beating the wind, which earned the device its nickname, "the organ of Stalin." With every launch of rockets, the building vibrated to its foundation, and it suffered from structural flaws thereafter. But the damage done by the PLO was hardly the problem; the real destruction came from the fire power of the opposing militias, who returned the favor and gave tit for tat.

The PLO held the ground for six months, during which the Al-Kafaàt center served as a depot for ammunition, a retreat for the fedayin, and later a detention center. Yasser Arafat came once to visit his combatants in person and is said to have stayed overnight. With the arrival of the Syrian army under the banner of the Arab Deterrent Force and the deployment of its troops across Beirut, the PLO evacuated, but by then the center was completely devastated. As soon as Nadim was cleared for return, he headed for Al-Kafaàt and was stopped, questioned, and searched at military checkpoints along the way. His first act after he arrived was to enter the chapel and dust the altar. Then he toured the entire facility to assess the damage. The next morning, he came back with engineers, technicians, and construction workers and began repairing the damage and rebuilding the spaces that were completely wiped out. With the leather factory lost, he decided to use the space to start new programs and designed new spaces with his architect friend, Samir Khairallah. Through his work in the factory, he had met many people with hearing impairments and others with cerebral palsy, and he decided to use the space from the defunct factory to accommodate education and rehabilitation programs for them.

An extraordinary turnaround at an equally extraordinary time! It takes a person of exceptional character with nerves of steel and a resolute mind to take a blow so hard, stand up again, analyze the losses, and start afresh. Who would even dare to entertain so big a challenge and budget great sums at a time when destruction and violence were the stuff of everyday life? History abounds with accounts of valiant people who stood for high principles, such as nonviolence, people who followed the command to "love your enemies and pray for those who persecute you." We totally admire their stories and beliefs, even wearing some of them on our T-shirts, but how many of us actually live up to them? Nadim Shwayri could and did, and the renovated center reopened six months later, with new facilities and programs.

The Al-Kafaàt center was now a large institution that served children with special needs, an oasis of hope in the midst of an ocean of cruelty, a cry in the wilderness. Maintaining the operation was a daily challenge, as was providing for the needs of the populations in the care of Al-Kafaàt. Nadim had partnered with public administrations since the early days of Fouad Shihab's presidency, when social services were outsourced by government to service-providing organizations. He had never lost faith in public service and always believed it to be his duty to stand by the government, however weak it might be, and he contested the legitimacy of parallel structures that undermined the "government of the people." In his partnership with public administrations, Al-Kafaàt took on delivery of specialized services and care to children with disabilities, providing social, educational, medical, therapeutic, and community support. Government, for its part, resigned from all rehabilitation efforts and restricted its role to a financial contribution, which it disbursed on a nominal basis for services rendered.

If the terms of this arrangement were erratic, the implementation was worse. Payment delays were permanent, rates were low, and the administration of contracts was extremely complex, slow, and tedious, intertwined in a number of ministries that were dispersed across the city, on both sides of the dividing line. Each administration had to sign and rubberstamp before a simple procedure could be cleared: approval from the Office of Social Development at the Ministry of Labor, the Ministry of Finance, the Court of Accounts, as well as the Council of Ministers whenever there was a need for amendments, ratifications, and extension of financial periods when accrual payments were still outstanding. Not only was this bureaucracy an annoyance, a long chain of mostly unnecessary public offices, but the interference of militia-governed politics in public services had the most demeaning impact on the integrity of the government structure. One could not deal with a public administration from the standpoint of rules and regulations, rights and obligations, but rather from the position one occupied within the complex sociomilitary system that ran parallel to—and all too often as a substitute for—a government of law and order. And in that system, a third-line commander of a given militia in a minor town district had more influence and power in the corridors of the ministries than the rightful advocate of people's rights at Al-Kafaàt.

There were also the physical dangers and the humiliations one had to live with when crossing from one part of Beirut to the other. The Office of Social Development was on one side, at the Christian-dominated *Sharqiyeh* (East), while the Ministry of Finance was in the Muslim-dominated *Gharbiyeh* (West), and crossing over took place only at specific points, along stretches of no-man's land, scorched earth where snipers held everyone in their sights. At night, these zones turned into a smuggler's paradise, where business deals were done: fuel for bread, cigarettes for whisky, anything that was scarce on either side and could be sold the next day during the intermittent cease-fires. With the development of a new society of contraband smugglers, cease-fires followed the beat and frequency of their business transactions: hostilities were halted at night for as long as was needed for smuggling across the lines, and again in the morning to keep a semblance of ordinary life for people to attend to their daily occupations. The crossfire resumed in the afternoon. Profiteering was a common activity of the militias, if not from contraband then from illegal taxes on people who fell under their sway, and most of all from the misappropriation of government resources. The Kataeb, for example, scooped up much of the port's activities by controlling its fifth basin, earning the Christian militia in excess of two billion dollars within a few years.

Nadim crossed over the dividing line regularly, going from one administration to the other, from Sharqiyeh to Gharbiyeh, walking on foot through the checkpoints and catching a car on the other side. Edouard usually drove, a close companion from the heyday of the leather factory, a hairdresser who changed careers, taking charge of customs operations for the factory. (The son of Armenian refugees, Edouard himself had a life worth writing a book about.) The supreme irony of this period and no doubt the peak of humiliation were the impositions that Palestinian militias made on the local populations: crossing westward from Mreijeh, where Al-Kafaàt had her center, Nadim passed along the PLO-controlled districts, which subjected him to the whims of their people in arms. He was given an identification card bearing the colors and name of the Palestinian Liberation Organization, with his picture and details, to use on crossing. He was allowed to circulate on the lands of his father and his forbears for five generations, on the soil of the Republic of Lebanon, by Palestinian militia teenagers in arms. This he also endured in silence, no doubt profoundly disturbed, yet taking the blows as they came with resolve and strength of mind. The roads to His Grace are painstaking, but it falls on us to never question His Will, he always said. Knowing this is equally as important as knowing what Al-Kafaàt is and stands for today. Building institutions in developing countries is tricky by definition, with overwhelming logistical limitations and administrative and financial constraints. Building institutions where social reformers are subjected to the ugliest forms of repression, bullying, humiliation, and physical threats, while having to endure the other constraints, is almost a mission impossible.

I remember my father coming home from his long days of crossing military checkpoints across the demarcation line, hurrying in to embrace each of us so tightly as if encountering a loved one after a long absence. No doubt he wondered every day, going from one side to the other, witnessing the level of barbarity that prevailed, whether he would get home safely. His days were like odysseys, which he discussed with my mother at length, keeping us children away in the make-believe realm of Walt Disney and his like, as if we did not see or understand.

From 1977 onward, the Lebanese war was simply out of hand. No one could tell what was going on or who was behind this or that car bomb or assassination. There were key players, each with different agendas, all beholden to the interests of regional powers or worldwide groups of nations. Someone once said that nations don't have friends, only interests, and Lebanon in the wake of the internationalization of the war on her soil certainly bears testimony to that. Syria's Hafez Assad was now at home in Lebanon, his army large and well equipped, holding strategic positions after the National Movement fell into disarray. Kamal Jumblatt, the Druze leader and the driving force of the movement, was assassinated in the early months of the year, ceding the spotlight to his son, Walid. For revenge, the Druze took it out on Christian villages in the Shouf, inflicting unnecessary bloodshed that left many people dead.

Free to do as he pleased, Hafez Assad ordered his troops into West Beirut, the principally Muslim part, which he occupied without resistance. The east side of the city was a different story. There, the sons of the activists of the previous era who had stood up in defiance to the French in the time of the mandate, Bashir Gemayel (son of Pierre) and Dany Chamoun (son of Camille), were holding their ground. Bashir managed to escape the overwhelming presence of his father, who controlled the Kataeb, and started his own formation by reviving the Lebanese Forces, a moribund consortium of Christian militias (of which the Kataeb was the main constituent). With the support of a thousand men, the younger Gemayel spoke a bellicose language that excited the young Christians who lived in the suburbs, immigrants in their own country, having been pushed out of their homes by one or the other religious militias, the Druze assault on the Shouf villages being only one of these episodes.

When Assad's forces went after the Christian fiefdom of Ashrafieh on the east side of Beirut, pounding it for three consecutive months, Bashir resisted the attack and soon saw his star rise when Assad, under outside pressure, called off the assault. Bashir then went on a personal crusade with a clear objective—that of becoming president and "bringing a nation to the state," as I recall having heard him say in one of his frequent televised diatribes. To do that, he had to build his reputation, morphing from the singular East Beirut militiaman into a nationwide presidential candidate who spoke to all groups, whatever their background or religion. He orchestrated this transformation in three acts, earning support from other players whose pathways collided with his. Of these, and probably the most important at this stage, was Menachem Begin, the new prime minister of Israel and a hardliner who saw in the Lebanese debacle an opportunity. While the Arab countries (other than Lebanon) were all governed by single-party regimes that gave their presidents unequivocal decision-making power about waging war, Israel was a democracy and Begin, however influenced by past militia practices at the Irgun, had to justify his actions to the people of Israel. Possibly the best communicator of his time, he knew how to take full advantage of a situation, however distressing, to justify his dubious decisions.

On March 11, 1978, a Palestinian commando managed to hijack a bus and drive it almost to Tel Aviv, where a gunfire exchange with security forces ended in the tragic deaths of thirty-five passengers. This was one incident too many, one that could well override the pressure exerted on Begin by international opinion, and by the United States in particular, after the historic visit by Anwar Sadat to Jerusalem in 1977. If the Arabs were taking a step toward Israel, one that could usher in peace to the region, shouldn't Israel reciprocate and show goodwill toward the Palestinians? No, not this time.

Never had Yasser Arafat been as helpful to the Israelis as on the occasion of the bus hijacking, a nonsensical act. Israel's response was a full-fledged annexation of a large territory in southern Lebanon, an operation that received the green light on March 14, three days after the hijacking, which had nothing to do with Lebanon in the first place. Although the argument for the incursion in Lebanese territory was to contain fedayin activities against Galilee and northern Israel in general, the more important reason was to tap into the Litani River, a water source coveted by Israel since her inception in 1947. The name given to the event, "Operation Litani," said it loud and clear.

A few days were enough for the Israeli army to dislodge the Palestinian fedayin and annex the territory south of the Litani, stationing their client rebel army that had splintered off under Major Saad Haddad across the occupied zone and withdrawing their own troops in compliance with a UN resolution. Begin had Haddad and his South Lebanon Army to control the buffer zone that his army had just carved out and that would even receive international policing from a United Nations Interim Force in Lebanon (UNIFIL), a peacekeeping force that took up positions across the border that same year and that is still stationed in South Lebanon to this day. With territories under his sway in Egypt (Sinai), Syria (the Golan Heights), and Lebanon, and with the Palestinians divided, their rival militias doing a good job at earning themselves international condemnation for petty terrorist acts, Begin had enough cards up his sleeve to thwart any negotiations over a return to the pre-1967 borders.

For the second act of his dramatic sequence, Bashir Gemayel set out to establish his supremacy in the Christian regions, taking on the potential contenders, one after the other. If one can learn anything from this book, it is that politics in Lebanon is a family business, some political figures having ancestors who sat in ministerial seats during the age of cedars! It would not be surprising then if I added another name to the list of potential candidates to succeed yet another former president, Sleiman Frangieh: his own son, Tony. Young and bright, courageous and spirited, Tony Frangieh had stature in the Christian antechambers of politics, himself the architect of the Marada militia that was close to Syria's Hafez Assad, and was therefore a rival to Gemayel. On the pretext of avenging the murder of a partisan who fell at the hands of the Marada in Tripoli, Bashir ordered a battalion to eliminate Tony Frangieh. The battalion did a professional job of taking Frangieh's life at his home in Ehden, not sparing his wife, his three-year-old daughter, and a large contingent of aides and security people. Tony's son, Sleiman, named after the former president, was at his grandfather's house when the massacre took place; today, he is the heir of a "political house," as we call them, a member of parliament, a local dignitary, a close ally to Bashar Assad, and a candidate for the presidential seat. Though Bashir declined responsibility for the assassination of Tony Frangieh, his close aide and later minister and president of the Kataeb, Karim Pakradoni, said, "By appointing Samir Geagea to this mission, Bashir knew well what he was doing."

Geagea was later indicted and imprisoned for eleven years for a series of assassinations of prominent figures, one of whom was a sitting prime minister, Rachid Karami. He was released by presidential pardon after the retreat of the Syrian army in 2005; heads today a parliamentary faction, the Lebanese Forces; and sits in the parliament opposite Sleiman Frangieh. Geagea would become a candidate in the presidential elections of 2014.

With Tony Frangieh out of the way, Bashir Gemayel took aim at his previous friend and ally, Dany Chamoun, and tried to eliminate him in the same way in 1980, ordering an assault on the headquarters of the Tiger militia and taking the life of some two hundred partisans. Dany himself escaped and, ironically, threw himself into the arms of the leftist militias in West Beirut, whom he had fought against with Bashir Gemayel in the past. Realizing his loss of power and hoping to preserve what was left, and perhaps also looking to protect the life of his son, former president Camille Chamoun swore allegiance to Bashir.

Nine years later, Dany Chamoun would not be so lucky. With East Beirut overrun by Syrian troops, he was killed at point-blank range in his apartment, still in pajamas, along with his wife and two young children. There would be many more assassinations and internecine bloodletting, including Bashir's young daughter in 1980; there were also attempts on Bashir's life, his father Pierre's, and on Camille

Chamoun. Despite those attempts, by the end of 1980, Bashir Gemayel had sole control over Christian Lebanon.

As part of the second act of his dramatic tragedy, Bashir moved to link Christian East Beirut with the no-less Christian capital city of the Bekaa plateau, Zahleh, halfway to Damascus. Was it to extend his supremacy to Zahleh that Bashir went on this folly, sending bulldozers to clear a path across the Metn Mountains to allow his army to attack Zahleh's back door, or did he hope to provoke the Syrians in hopes of triggering a response from a particularly itchy Menachem Begin? A bit of both most certainly, but probably more of the latter, as he could not possibly have cleared Zahleh of the overwhelming Syrian presence. The fighting dragged on for three months with no clear outcome; Assad's army ultimately forced Bashir and his militia to turn on their heels and go back the way they came, but in the meantime, Bashir had won his tactical battle: Hafez Assad had deployed Soviet-made SAM II missiles across the Bekaa and earned the reprisals of Begin, who considered this to be a breach of the "red line."

Until Bashir Gemayel disrupted the status quo, an unspoken accord had been observed between Israel and Syria over their respective maneuvers in Lebanon. In a way, they both had similar interests in their contentions with the countless factions in Lebanon, and so could be of use to one another. When Israel infiltrated Lebanon in 1978 and later, in 1982, reached Beirut itself, Syrian troops simply gave way. Bashir Gemayel knew this, appreciated the tactics of Menachem Begin, and maintained good relations with him. Begin called Gemayel "my son," and the Israeli leadership considered him "one of theirs." Bashir also knew about the plans that were concocted in Tel Aviv and that were discussed at length with the American administration, plans that would reconfigure the region, redistributing populations like pieces on a chessboard. Under these plans, the West Bank would be permanently annexed to Israel, as would the Golan (where the Banias River has its source); Palestinians would be housed in Jordan, the Sinai would be returned to Egypt, and Lebanon would be unified under the command of a strong Christian leader. And that would be none other than Bashir Gemayel!

The president of Lebanon at this time was Elias Sarkis, a weakened and isolated leader who had been an aide to Fouad Shihab but who lacked his charisma and vision. Sarkis had been the candidate of Hafez Assad when Assad had good relations with the Christian militias, but when those relations grew strained, Sarkis saw himself sidelined by both, unable to project even a semblance of authority. Furthermore, the Lebanese army had been largely divided, and the brigades answering to Sarkis were mostly Christian, discrediting him in the eyes of the Muslim communities, who also began ignoring him.

Sarkis, unable to achieve things on his own, turned to Bashir Gemayel, whom he saw as the man of the hour. For some reason, Sarkis, a believer in Shihabism, bred on such principles as institution building and upholding the government of law and order, decided the methods of the leader of the Lebanese Forces were worthy of his support. Sarkis's term was coming to a close that year, 1982, a turn of affairs that suited the plan of Israel and the Lebanese Forces. The plan to reconfigure the region, or at least the Lebanese portion of it, was plotted in detail and the military tactics were all specified, consisting of a pure and simple invasion of Lebanon to lance the Palestinian abscess and bring Bashir Gemayel to control.

The two trajectories were finally coinciding, that of Israel, which was seeking a permanent solution to the Palestinian problem (outside of Palestine), and that of Bashir Gemayel, who was seeking to bring his Lebanese Forces to govern Lebanon. Begin, however, had again come under pressure from the American administration, from Ronald Reagan and his secretary of state Alexander Haig but also from the former presidents Gerald Ford and Jimmy Carter, who had met with him on the occasion of the funeral of Anwar Sadat, shot in 1981 by the Muslim Brotherhood, whose power he had endeavored to curtail. The king of Saudi Arabia had taken a step toward the recognition of Israel, and the late Anwar Sadat had signed a peace treaty at Camp David in 1978. It was now for Israel, the Americans pleaded, to make a move in the direction of the Palestinians.

Begin was not prepared to concede territory to the Palestinians; more than ever he wanted to implement his plan of action in Lebanon. But to do that, he needed a spark, a creditable excuse that would justify his action before the Knesset, his own people, and world opinion. In other words, he needed Israel to be provoked, as in 1978 with the bus hijacking. To help stir Arab animosity and bring about the awaited provocation, Begin decided, fourteen years after its occupation, to announce the permanent annexation of the Golan. The news was received with much anger, yet there were no reactions on the ground that could justify the unleashing of the annexation of Lebanon.

The shooting of the Israeli ambassador in London by Abu Nidal's Fatah group, though an isolated incident, provided an acceptable *casus belli* for Begin to commit his troops to "Operation Galilee." Three days after the attempt on the life of the ambassador, the Israeli army moved across the borders of Lebanon. Led by Ariel Sharon, then the defense minister, the army went beyond the twenty-five-mile limit that Begin had asserted was necessary to contain the fedayin. In a few days, the Israeli army was in Beirut, closing in from the Christian (east) side of the capital, which it entered without opposition, establishing a base to pound mainly Muslim West Beirut, where the Palestinians had retreated.

Yasser Arafat was trapped, as were all the Palestinian militias and those who fought on their side among the Lebanese. In the pitch dark, water and food supplies cut off, pounded with heavy firepower, West Beirut was easy prey. Sharon did not blink an eye at the suffering innocents, who fell by the hundreds. He went as far as using cluster bombs on the densely populated hostage city, a city that his army had surrounded on all sides, aided by Bashir's Lebanese Forces. In Washington, DC, President Reagan took the matter to Congress, stopped further shipments of bombs to Israel, and sent his special envoy Philip Habib to negotiate the evacuation of the Palestinian military. Within days, a multinational force composed mainly of American marines arrived in Lebanon to ensure the safety of the Palestinian civilians staying behind, as Yasser Arafat and the Palestinian militias boarded American ships for Tunisia. The date was August 21, 1982.

The multinational force was quick to disband, leaving the Palestinian civilians to their fate, now living in the open and with no protection for their camps. As expected, Bashir Gemayel was "elected" president of the Lebanese Republic by reluctant members of parliament, many of whom were coerced into attendance and voting. If his predecessor, Elias Sarkis, had been ushered into the first office in 1977 by the Syrians, the commanding force of the time, Bashir Gemayel rode the Israeli Merkava to the presidency, completing the third act of his ascension drama. Within days, Bashir and Begin met in Natanya, Israel, one of numerous behind-the-scenes meetings between the Lebanese Forces and their Israeli patrons.

Begin pressed his protégé to play his assigned role, now that he was president of the republic, urging him to sign a peace treaty with Israel. Bashir equivocated, playing for time on account of the Muslim constituency, which would not go along with such a treaty without the needed preparations. The meeting having gone sour, Begin sent a communiqué to the press, revealing information about the meeting to put pressure on Bashir. The young, impetuous, and Machiavellian playwright had not planned his fourth act properly, the what-comes-next scene that reveals paybacks and responsibilities. Perhaps it was the appeal of power that caused Bashir to stall and hold Begin in check. Shying away from his earlier commitment to impose a Christian Lebanon by coercion, the new leader now sought to play according to the traditional rules of Lebanese politics.

To do that, Bashir issued multiple declamations that spoke of pluralism, making symbolic visits to prove his intentions to Sunni figures, such as Saeb Salam and even to the Kingdom of Saudi Arabia itself. Twenty-one days into his term, not even officially sworn in, Bashir Gemayel was himself eliminated. At a meeting at the militia headquarters in Achrafieh, he was blown to pieces with members of his politburo, so completely mutilated under the rubble of the building that he could only be recognized by his hexagonal wedding ring.

The reaction on the street was dire despair in East Beirut and general euphoria in most quarters of West Beirut. As a response, two days later, a horrendous act of barbarity was committed against the Palestinian civilians in the camps of Sabra and Shatila. Under Israeli cover, hardliners of the Christian Lebanese Forces entered the camps and went through the narrow streets, killing whoever appeared, mostly women, old men, and children. Commanded by Elie Hobeika, the head of security for the Lebanese Forces, they went methodically into every house, raping and killing at will, defenseless children and pregnant women alike, using daggers when they ran out of ammunition. The carnage went on for three consecutive days, September 16, 17, and 18, 1982, less than one month after the Israeli incursion into Lebanon. At nights, Sharon ordered flares launched over the camps to assist the men of Hobeika in their assaults. More than one thousand corpses were counted; more than two thousand people were missing.

Afterward, the Knesset-appointed Kahan Commission spoke in half-truths about the explicit role of Ariel Sharon, who "was found to bear personal responsibility for ignoring the danger of bloodshed and revenge." In John Boykin's *Cursed Is the Peacemaker*, Philip Habib, Reagan's special envoy who oversaw US diplomacy in the region at the time, is quoted as saying, "Sharon was a killer, obsessed by hatred of the Palestinians" (Boykin's book sheds light on the events of 1982 and the intricacies that led to the massacres at Sabra and Shatila). Sharon stepped down as minister of defense, though he kept a seat in government and was later to serve as prime minister of Israel between 2001 and 2006. On January 8, 2015, interviewed in the Israeli newspaper *Haaretz*, Ehud Barak related the following: "[David] Ben-Gurion once told Sharon, 'If you cure yourself of your habit of lying, you will be a great leader.' Sharon, when he related that conversation, said the quote was incorrect, that Ben-Gurion told him, 'You will be a great leader during a crisis.' The evil gossips in Likud say that once Ben-Gurion told him that, Sharon not only waited for the crisis but worked to create it. Do you see?" His funeral in 2014 was an official state event, attended by the vice president of the United States, Joseph Biden, who gave a eulogy to the "historic leader." Elie Hobeika would become Lebanon's minister of social affairs in 1993, in the postwar period, then minister of energy, before being assassinated in 2002. His car was blown up on the eve of his planned flight to Brussels where he was slated to appear before a Belgian court about Sharon's role in the 1982 massacres. He died wearing a bullet-proof vest under his shirt.

In 1982, my family still lived in the heights of Baabda, at the same apartment that my mother forced us to vacate so precipitately on a hunch the day before it took a direct hit. Our building buzzed with activity at times because the French ambassador resided next door, but more important because a senior military officer close to the power circles of the time, Colonel Michel Aoun, had his offices on the ground floor. Nadim and Aoun soon became close friends, meeting regularly for long dinners during which the whole debacle of Lebanon was debated until late at night. I enjoyed those evenings, which were occasionally attended by the French ambassador, and I found it exciting to have firsthand information before television aired it. Early one August morning that year, Michel Aoun called Nadim and informed him that the Israeli army was closing in on Beirut and that he had but a few hours to evacuate his center in Mreijeh, which was at risk since it was located a few yards over the dividing line into West Beirut.

Nadim hurried out, calling on friends along the way to secure transportation, and soon a dozen cars showed up at the center, to the amazement of Athanasia, the nun from the congregation who worked with him at the school in Salima and who had devoted her life to working at Al-Kafaàt. In extreme peril, the cars crossed back over the line just minutes before roads were blocked and West Beirut was isolated by the Israeli army and Bashir's militia. In the cars were some fifty children, staff, and nuns; all others had gone home to their families when the Israeli incursion started.

How does one fit such a large company of people into a regular-sized apartment? The old joke about how to fit five elephants in a VW Beetle—three in the back seat and two in the front—makes people laugh, but I can assure the reader that it works. I saw it with my own eyes, how Lily managed to care for everyone in our apartment, for long weeks, with simplicity and grace. The soft-hearted and delicate Lily turned into an army general and had me, my brother, and my sisters take out our sleeping bags and go in a corner, assigning four children with disabilities to each of our beds. The situation was funny in a way, almost like a sitcom, with one child jumping out of the bath looking for his crutches, another using the crutches as a pretend gun to fire at a third, who couldn't hear and was unable to respond to the flooding of the toilet, which sent a blind child slipping and my mother running like mad. Her constant smile more than once gave me reassurance, as if it was all just a big fun party, nothing more (reassurances that were soon dispelled by the noisy firebombs falling on Beirut that we could hear very clearly). Lily hung bed sheets from the ceiling across one room to separate different groups of children. She borrowed plates and forks from the neighbors, who did not hesitate to lend a hand. Our sitting room had a large balcony, and we used to crowd outside, rushing to get the best seats on the swing, with a breathtaking view over Beirut.

Standing on this balcony I saw for myself the continuous pounding of West Beirut, a thick black swath at night that flickered in different spots with every blast, revealing buildings and streets that suffered damage. I can still hear the bombing and see the flashing over Beirut as I write these lines. During the day, I would use my father's binoculars to check the damages, spotting changes as children do today in activity books, sharing my discoveries with others. Death came close when a young woman who worked at Al-Kafaàt and stayed with us got news of the death of her brother, the only family she had left. She left sobbing, in a state of utter delirium, and I never saw her again.

In time, the full and lively house emptied, families finally managing to pick up their children, and it was just the six of us again in an apartment that seemed suddenly very spacious and extremely silent. After the departure of the Palestinian militias and the massacres of Sabra and Shatila, the pounding of Beirut reduced in intensity, and life resumed despite the omnipresence of the Israeli army and the new politico-military system that seemed to please all the militias. When Nadim learned that he could visit the center in Mreijeh in December 1982, he left hurriedly, anxious to see the extent of the damage. I insisted on going along, and off we went in his white Plymouth, passing Israeli tanks in Baabda and reaching Hadath before being stopped at a checkpoint on the old Saida road as we drove toward Mreijeh. I recognized the same hut at the checkpoint that had been used by the Palestinians, then the Syrians, then the Israelis and the Lebanese Forces, and now the Lebanese army, which controlled the area.

The checkpoint guards told us that driving farther was not possible because the sector was mined, no doubt by the retreating Palestinian militias. The army had drawn a white line along the way, a walking trail that had been cleared of mines and that we could follow on foot to reach our destination. I remember the tightrope walk, my father and me alone on that street, the white line under our feet, my father walking first and insisting that I follow in his footsteps, managing, however uncomfortably to hold my hand by stretching his arm across his back. I was fourteen, highly impressed by all the recent events, living in the moment, the half-exciting and half-distressing times.

When we got to the center, Abou-Ali was at the gate, the janitor who watched faithfully over the place and who learned in time to deal with the successive rounds of armies and militias from of all types. The damage was overwhelming, the center and its buildings completely shattered. The aluminum window frames had melted under the heat generated by phosphorous and cluster bombs. While walking across, my father touched something and had burns for weeks. What a sad sight! This vital center, which had seen so many happy kids running and jumping and limping through it, was now a desolate mass of fallen walls and broken windows. Even so, it would take more than that to stop a social entrepreneur, a man with a mission, from rolling up his sleeves and calling in the construction workers once again.

The damaged center was not Al-Kafaàt's only facility; in the years before 1982, Nadim had started another two. One opened in 1979, during a particularly harsh year when my mother took the four of us for refuge in Lyon via Cyprus. During our absence, my father slept at the center all that year, keeping company with the growing population of residents, nearly four hundred, all with disabilities. He started this unique project on land he inherited from his father, Alfred Nicola, minutes away from Mreijeh in Hadath. There, on a large estate, he tried to simulate a normal lifestyle for people with mental disabilities, where life in its entirety and diversity could be experienced but at a tempo that respected the residents' abilities to function independently. Nadim called it "the Village," and he wanted it to be simply that, a village where residents moved fluidly between work, leisure, culture, and social interaction, using a variety of workshops, multifunctional rooms, and shops set around a village center. Seemingly unconcerned with the disruptions caused by the war outside the Village, Nadim completed the first phase of his project and welcomed his first "villagers."

Having long reflected on the situation of children with hearing impairments who were denied education because they could not adapt to mainstream classrooms, Nadim decided to start a school that would advocate integrative measures. The building was completed in 1981, again on land in Hadath from Alfred Nicola, a school he named Our Lady after his eternal source of inspiration, the Mother of Christ. Children from all communities across Hadath and the region could meet at this unique hub of tolerance where Christians and Muslims sat next to one another, as did children with and without disabilities (or *apparently* without disabilities, for, as Nadim would often say, "We are all handicapped"). The school opened in September 1981 and grew quickly, employing highly specialized equipment that allowed students to perform normally.

A year after the 1982 conflict, which might have cooled the ardor of another social entrepreneur, Nadim went about building the second phase of his village. This new compound spread workshops around a central space, a theater, conceived ingeniously to express the true vocation of the Village in practical ergonomics and architecture. The building was still in progress, nearly finished, when violence, once again, began to spiral out of control.

Bashir Gemayel was buried in his hometown of Bikfaya amid an incredible outpouring of people who had come to pay their respects. All eyes now turned to Amin, Bashir's older brother, as a possible next president. Members of parliament cast their votes at the Fayadiyeh Military School, on the opposite side of Baabda across Damascus Road, where Bashir had been elected only a month before.

Menachem Begin needed to cash in quickly on the situation in Lebanon to keep on good terms with the Knesset and the Israeli people. He had pretended that Sharon's incursion into Lebanon would be a short "stroll of a few days," yet his army ended up laying siege to an Arab capital. Begin's countrymen were very sensitive to the visit of Sadat in 1977, which was followed by a full-blown peace treaty in 1978, and could not understand, however honorable the excuse of dislodging fedayin from their direct northern vicinity, why their sons, brothers, and husbands were fighting the Lebanese in Beirut. Moreover, images of the massacres of Sabra and Shatila broadcast around the world were not received with enthusiasm on the streets of Tel Aviv. In fact, the resentment and agitation of the people of Israel pressed the Knesset to convene the Kahan Commission.

If Begin could secure a peace treaty with Lebanon, he would at least keep the confidence of the people and justify his actions. What Bashir Gemayel eschewed,

Amin promised he would do. Before Bashir was even laid to rest, Amin confirmed this to a group of influential visitors at his "House of the Future," a cultural center for the Kataeb in Dbayeh, a Beirut northern suburb. Those visitors included Yitzhak Shamir, Ariel Sharon, David Kimché, Peter Nahum Admoni, and Menachem Navot (known to the Lebanese Forces as Mendy). The first two would become prime ministers of Israel; the others were Mossad spymasters.

There is an anecdote that portrays the office of Amin Gemayel, torn between Israeli and Syrian domination. A convict is given three punishments to choose from: walk on his knees for a mile, eat a pound of salt, or take a hundred lashes. He reckons the walk on his knees would be the least of the evils and manages to go three-quarters of a mile before collapsing, unable to finish. He decides to eat the salt instead, but is only able to take in three-quarters of the pound before gagging and surrendering to the hundred lashes. In the end, the man served his sentence three times!

So, too, did Amin Gemayel when it came to choosing the lesser of three evils, when seeking a resolution to the deadlock Lebanon found itself in. The first would be to complete the unfinished business between Begin and Bashir and sign the treaty; after all, the Israeli force was still in Lebanon and was not ready to leave yet. Amin was himself a partisan of a Christian Lebanon, a "Lebanonist" to use the term that is common among many historians, but he lacked the means to impose his vision. Unlike Bashir, he was not a military man at heart and did not enjoy the support of the men of his father's party, the Kataeb, nor that of his late brother's Lebanese Forces. He also lacked the hardheaded independence of Bashir, who cut the umbilical cord with the Kataeb early on and left his father to his party while he forged his own identity and style. Amin was the exact opposite. He was close to his father, with whom he shared the same vision and style, to the extent that, while he was in office, many considered Lebanon to have two presidents, not one.

The Israelis were happy to help further Amin's Lebanonist views, if only to push him into their fold, and they gave cover to the Lebanese Forces, who took the mountain roads of the Shouf, the stronghold of Walid Jumblatt. The incursion of the Christian militia into the predominately Druze region was aimed at protecting the Christian villagers from the aggression of the Progressive militia of Jumblatt. That, at least, was what was said in the briefing of the commanding officers of the men in arms. The consequences of this crusade might have been anticipated if anyone had read historical accounts of the wars of 1840 and 1860, which were partly fought on the same mountain.

When the Israelis retreated from the Shouf, probably to force Gemayel to close the treaty and pass it in parliament, the Druze and the Christians clashed in what would become known as "the war of the mountain." A peace treaty did come on May 17, 1983, but it was not well received by the Muslim communities and their militias, and it did not get ratified by the parliament. All it did was fuel further discord and escalate the level of engagement in the war, which was now being waged with new actors, each with a set of new interests.

After the Iranian Revolution of 1979 and the outbreak of the Iraqi-Iranian war, the Shi'a clerics of Iran took new interest in Lebanon. Khomeini's Iran found many supporters among the Lebanese Shi'a living in shantytowns in Beirut suburbs and in the south, a distressed population that saw the Palestinian fedayin leave their territories only to be replaced by the equally insidious Israelis. The Iranians met the distress of their coreligionists with military equipment and organization. US troops were in Lebanon at the time, the multinational force having reconvened after the massacres of Sabra and Shatila, but they were now seen in a different light. It was no secret that the American administration was supportive of Israel and that it had assisted the Israeli army in developing an overwhelming arsenal over the years. But now this arsenal was being used in Beirut against Palestinians and Lebanese alike. With Sabra and Shatila, the American administration was seen by many to have delivered Beirut on a silver platter to Sharon's army, who, in turn, gave cover to the mass murders of civilians in the camps. The United States therefore shifted from being seen as a neutral party to being seen as an enemy, especially since a large number of Shi'a who lived in and around Sabra and Shatila at the time were killed in the massacres. When President Reagan decided to bring the firepower of US warships into play and had them fire at Druze positions in the mountains, the nail was driven in the coffin. America was now seen by the Shi'a as taking sides with the Christians, and an overwhelming response came shortly thereafter. On April 18, 1983, a truck loaded with explosives drove into the lobby of the US Embassy and detonated, incurring a heavy toll of sixty-three deaths. Among them were eight CIA officers, including Robert Ames, a highly decorated operative who had the ear of President Reagan. Ames had managed to keep back channels open with the PLO in the 1970s and befriended the head of security and Arafat's second in command, Ali Hassan Salameh, a polarizing figurehead who was nonetheless an asset on the ground (he was invited to the United States for talks by the Carter administration on the suggestion of George H. W. Bush, then-director of the CIA, undoubtedly on Ames's recommendation). Salameh was taken out by Mossad in early 1979, closing the one channel that could have probably saved more unnecessary bloodshed and brought recognition of the PLO to the table much earlier. The tragedy continued later that year, on October 23, when marine barracks, located a short distance from the Beirut airport, were bombed, incurring another 241 casualties, mostly US marines. Within minutes, another bomb took the lives of fifty-eight French paratroopers.

It was Sunday, early in the morning, and I heard both explosions with my own ears. I remember jumping out of bed (so to speak, as it was only a mattress thrown on the floor of the shelter in the basement) and joining others around the radio to hear the news flash. Unable to leave, we spent all day assimilating the news reports as they came in. The visit of France's president François Mitterrand the next day was an occasion for a cease-fire and gave us a rare opportunity to come out of the dark and damp shelter in which we practically lived throughout the 1980s.

The Islamic Jihad, an Iranian formation, took responsibility for the explosions. In reality, and according to Kai Bird, the bombings were the doing of the Iranian Revolutionary Guard, orchestrated by General Ali-Reza Asgari, who was stationed in Baalbek at the time and the head of the Guard's cell in Lebanon. For the job, Bird says that Asgari chose among his fresh recruits a young Lebanese Shi'a by the name of Imad Mughniyeh. A combatant trained by the PLO and a member of Yasser Arafat's elite Force 17, Mughniyeh had grown disenchanted with Arafat's expulsion to Tunis and joined the Revolutionary Guard in Baalbek. He would later become the head of the armed forces of Hezbollah before he himself was taken out while on a visit to the Iranian Embassy in Damascus in early 2008 (the CIA and Mossad competed in claiming responsibility for the operation). Asgari would later become a brigadier general in the Revolutionary Guard and a deputy minister of defense in Teheran in the 1990s before defecting in 2007 to the United States, where he lives today. In later years, the Jihad and similar organizations, all supported by the Iranians, would multiply their actions against Americans, killing many (Malcolm Kerr, president of the American University of Beirut, a fine humanist and a distinguished scholar who was born and raised in Lebanon, was sadly assassinated in the early days of 1984) and taking others hostage (twelve in 1985 alone). The US administration did not sit idly by and had the CIA take a crack at car bombings, such as the attempt on the life of Muhammad Hussein Fadlallah, a spiritual leader close to the Jihadist movements, which took the lives of seventy-eight innocent civilians. That attack was in Bir Abed in 1984. Fadlallah's car was a minute late, held up by an aged woman who had stopped the cleric to question him. He survived.

The second less evil solution that presented itself to Amin Gemayel for putting an end to the war was not even his own prerogative. Having turned to the Israelis only to have them ratchet the chaos higher, he now had a Syrian peace proposal thrust before him. It came in the form of a tripartite accord, signed just after Christmas of 1985 by a most interesting trio—Elie Hobeika, Nabih Berri, and Walid Jumblatt—and under the auspices of Hafez Assad. Hobeika had commanded the militiamen in Sabra and Shatila in 1982 and earned the leadership of the Lebanese Forces for a time, before he was contested by Samir Geagea, equally ruthless, who had allegedly commanded the assassination of Tony Frangieh in Ehden in 1978. They fought a few battles, and Hobeika was driven into exile, only to surface on the side of the Damascus regime and earning the command of a splinter group of the Lebanese Forces. Berri was the commander of Amal, the Shi'a militia that was supported by Syria, and was himself opposed to the Iranian-supported Hezbollah that was formed around the same time.

The agreement the three men signed was a revision of the Constitution of 1926, which redefined the power-sharing balance between the different religious groups, giving weight to the Sunni prime minister and the Shi'a president of the parliament, and less power to the Maronite president. It also reviewed the count of members of parliament, arguing for parity among Muslims and Christians, and a set of other amendments. The Tripartite Accord would not have the slightest chance of going into effect, however, because on his return to Lebanon, Hobeika was defeated by Geagea and Gemayel, who combined their forces to crush his militia. The accord would nonetheless be revisited in 1989 and was used as the basis for the Taef Accord, which eventually stopped the war.

Amin Gemayel's first and second "sentences" had been impossible to pursue to the end; he hadn't succeeded at satisfying the Israelis or the Syrians, so the Lebanese president began surfing the waves of a new system in which *cantonization* became the watchword. Can't deal with Lebanon as a whole? Then break it to pieces and become king of your own canton! The events of the 1980s in Lebanon lent themselves to this development. The internal migrations of people had become permanent due to the ethnic cleansing that was perpetrated across every region, and populations regrouped according to a set of sociological parameters. Religious creed came first, but also political affinities and the adherence to this or that militia also determined where one lived. More than one million Lebanese had been displaced from their homes between 1976 and 1989, and another million immigrated to other countries.

Lebanon had become a mosaic of independent mini-states, each governed by a militia and inhabited by a homogeneous population. For a militia, the governance of a mini-state turned into a very lucrative affair, although it also fueled internal dissension and rivalries over power. Militias imposed taxes on businesses and households, controlled the food supply, and had a monopoly on fuel, which they smuggled into harbors, often sharing a shipment with rival militias. Militias started their own businesses, construction companies, hotels, jewelry, and alcohol and cigarette imports (and counterfeiting); in addition, they ran prostitution rings and dealt arms and drugs.

In the heyday of the business, nearly forty percent of the irrigated land across the Bekaa was devoted to hashish culture, controlled by the Syrians, who held the plateau under their sway. The processed hashish was sent to private harbors, mostly controlled by Christian militias, who shipped it to Cyprus where it was distributed to the rest of the world. In connivance with Saad Haddad's South Army, militias managed to import goods from Israel itself, rewriting the certificates of origin and selling the goods across the Arab countries. Weapons flowed in from Libya and were sold to Afghanistan and the Balkans; diamonds from Africa were laundered in cutting workshops and sold in Anvers.

While fighting the wars of attrition across a divided country, rival militias still managed to do business together. After 1984, the Lebanese economy began to falter with a loss in value of the Lebanese pound. This was partially due to an outflow of capital, money taken by the Palestinian militias, the PLO, and others when they departed Lebanon but also, and mostly, because of this parallel economy that was sapping the foundations of the country. The turnover of the militias in a one year (1986) was estimated at thirty billion dollars, which was twice the size of the official GDP of Lebanon that year. Business profits enabled the militias to buy ammunition and weapons to keep the war going (a necessary condition for the prosperous business to continue), profits that also enriched the warlords, who made investments in foreign financial safe havens. There is no doubt that at every junction, when a possible settlement was looming, militias fought it off. With the end of term of Amin Gemayel in 1988, the situation was too complicated to elect a new president. So Gemayel left control to an interim cabinet of six ministers and appointed the commander-in-chief of the Lebanese army, General Michel Aoun, to the seat of prime minister.

After the departure of the Palestinian militias from West Beirut, followed by the invasion of the Israelis and their withdrawal from the capital city, the Amal militia ("the movement," as it was called) became the de facto group that controlled much of the city, until it came to be challenged for territory by the other Shi'a rising star, Hezbollah, and the returning PLO operatives. At some time in 1984, when the programs at Al-Kafaàt were blossoming more than ever, its three separate centers helping beneficiaries thrive, a splinter group from the Amal militia commandeered the Al-Kafaàt center in Mreijeh and established in it the headquarters for its military operations. Known only by his *nom de guerre* Abou-Bayda, the commanding officer was a pompous, vacuous, and illiterate man, impossible to reason with. It was time to leave once again, this time with four hundred children with disabilities from Mreijeh and the Village. They all squeezed into the one center that fell outside the impounded area, Our Lady's.

There, in the five-story school building, all programs were reorganized, using one room to deliver multiple services simultaneously, employing stairwells for physical therapies, placing bunk beds in corridors for lodging, anything to keep the programs going and not surrender to the will of evil. Light prefabricated houses were installed in the courtyard to offer more services when, after a time, it seemed unlikely that a return to the other centers was in the offing. The school's ground floor was used for technical and vocational classes that were instituted by Nadim in 1977, and the catering school reconvened in the basement after it had been driven out by Jumblatt's militia from the convent in Salima. The eclectic mix of rehabilitation, training, therapy, and bartending *à l'anglaise*, all on the same corridor, with toddlers and parents waiting at the out-patient unit, was surreal in many ways. Yet it worked, and gave proof to resilience and tenacity, values that were core to every mission Nadim had ever undertaken.

A call from families who lived on the "other" side of the city came to Nadim in the early days of 1985, appealing for the reopening of the centers in Mreijeh and Hadath and the reintegration of their children, who were suffering from the forced disruption. A delegation of them went to meet the leader of the Amal militia, Nabih Berri, and asked for his intervention to drive Abou-Bayda out of Al-Kafaàt so that services could resume, for the sake of their children. By some game of give-and-take, Berri managed to make Abou-Bayda evacuate the center, which he had occupied for nine months, and sent a handwritten letter to Nadim asking him to "consider reopening the center that is delivering much-needed services to the people." As in 1976 after the retreat of the PLO, in 1977 after the retreat of the Forces of Dissuasion (Syrians), and in 1982 after the departure of the Israeli force, so it was in 1985 with the restoration of the centers in Mreijeh and Hadath, the return of the engineers and construction workers. I went with my father, as in 1982, on his first visit to inspect the damages, and was utterly sickened by the unexpected scene. In addition to the expected vandalism and thefts, there were foreboding messages on the walls, spelled in the blood of people who had been slaughtered there; rooms built to help children realize the joy of living turned into detention rooms, horror vaults for torture and killing. "Death to the Maronites," "Kill the Christians," and "Zionists shall perish" were a few of the slogans that covered the walls, dotted with bullet holes that told the stories of dozens of people who were killed at point-blank, their faces to the walls, shot in the neck. The stench was unbearable and it still enters my nostrils every time I remember that day.

The times called for the "cantonization" of Lebanon, and the Shi'a militias, as with all other religious groups, simply liquidated whoever they laid hands on who happened to be from a rival group. The Druze did the same to the Christians in the mountains, and Christians did as much against the Druze, Sunni, and Shi'a whenever the occasion presented itself. The drill had a name: "killing on identification cards."

As in previous times, Nadim had the center patched up and back in use in record time, having developed a particular skill at cleaning up after messy militiamen. Six months later, infighting within the same religious group caused Berri and Abou-Bayda to go separate ways, and the latter returned to invade Al-Kafaàt's two centers once again. That was one invasion too many, and Nadim thereafter refused to make repairs or reconvene programs before a final peace settlement was brokered, despite the constant invitations and later assurances from Nabih Berri.

With growing numbers of people in need of help, Nadim could not offer the necessary programs within Our Lady's center alone. So he built a fourth center, on yet another estate he had inherited from Alfred Nicola, on the eastern side of the line and just minutes from the town center of Hadath. There, he located the prevocational program that had grown to service 150 children with mental disabilities. They were taught in classrooms that surrounded a beautiful garden, covered by two aging rubber trees, which spread their branches elegantly over the central space. The colors were extraordinary, with a pointillist effect created by the soft light that traversed the branches and dappled the faces of the little children playing in the garden and around the pond.

Nadim and Lily reflected deeply on the governance of Al-Kafaàt, the institution they had built and which was growing rapidly. It rendered so many unique services to the most fragile and impoverished populations that its future viability needed to be assured. Al-Kafaàt had become an "Institution of Public Welfare" in 1980, a distinctive status bestowed by presidential statement, and about the same time Nadim organized the corporate governance around a board of trustees, marking Al-Kafaàt's shift from a personal initiative to an independent institution. Always concerned with the continuity of the activities and programs, Nadim's concern would grow in time with the further development of Al-Kafaàt.

During the harshest days of Lebanon's war, when two Al-Kafaàt centers were under occupation and while they were unable to ascertain if they would ever get them back, Nadim and Lily made what I consider to be the most profound commitment any person could make. They decided to establish a foundation to provide for the centers and programs, and to endow it with their personal resources, their family wealth. I remember very clearly the family reunion we had at the dining room of my parent's house, the six of us seated around the large table, my father presiding as he always did, my mother to his right, in her regular seat. Nadim was deeply emotional, spoke slowly and very affectionately, paused regularly, and used incisive words, simple yet profound, thinking to himself that an important part of the history of Al-Kafaàt was playing out that day. In his view, the four of us were the depositories of his mission, the disciples who had seen, heard, touched, and comprehended the ethos of his actions.

Beyond the act of giving that we were to witness there and then, Nadim projected a lesson in devotion, of total surrender to a principle, to a belief, not halfway measures, not partial commitments. He informed us of their decision to give away their inheritance, so that Al-Kafaàt could have a solid endowment, one that could take her safely into the future. He also said that they would leave a portion of their wealth for us to use, either to start a career if we chose one outside the realm of Al-Kafaàt, or to use as personal guarantees if we decided to plunge into the mission and the ocean of responsibilities that came with it. Then he held a *tour de table*, asking each of us to speak our minds and say whether we approved the decision they had made or contested it, for they would only proceed with their decision if we subscribed wholeheartedly to it. As part of the arrangement, we would have to relinquish our rights to our family inheritance, which we were guaranteed by Lebanese law.

Emotions ran high in the room as each of us acquiesced in order, almost instantly. I remember Myriam, my youngest sister, who was not yet thirteen, asking my parents why they had even bothered to ask. This happened in 1986, on my eighteenth birthday, and I remember telling my father that this was the weirdest birthday gift I had ever had! A month later, we held a similar get-together, but with a friend and a trustee of Al-Kafaàt, an expert legal advisor who would later become a government minister, Joseph Moghaizel. We signed the papers that day (they would become official five years later, with the coming in legal age of my youngest sister).

The relationship between President Amin Gemayel and the commander-in-chief of the Lebanese army, General Michel Aoun, was never good. Aoun gained popularity among the people for the good deeds and glorious actions that he purportedly had undertaken. He warned listeners about the Sabra and Shatila massacres before they took place, sounding the alarm when there was still time to avert the bloodshed. When he commanded the Eighth Brigade of the Lebanese Army at the strategic vantage point of Souk Gharb overlooking Beirut, Colonel Aoun valiantly fought off the Syrian assaults, refusing to surrender the position when ordered to do so by Amin Gemayel, the president and head of the armed forces. Politicians often had their reasons for doing things that Aoun, whose decisive actions earned him the amusing nickname "Napol-Aoun," did not accept, let alone understand. He was as stubborn as he was straightforward and sincere, a man of the people who lived, ate, and fought with his men. Michel Aoun came from a modest family and earned his position with sweat and honesty; Amin Gemayel was part of an oligarchic establishment that sapped the energy and resources of the country. He was nicknamed "Mister Twenty Percent."

The Syrian army was back in Beirut by 1987, to intervene in a conflict between the militias of Nabih Berri and Walid Jumblatt that were tearing West Beirut apart. The falling out of these two blood brothers came with the "war of camps," Jumblatt siding with the PLO returnees and Berri fighting them so as to bring all West Beirut under his sway. The Syrians silenced the feuding and ended up staying. On the East Side, Michel Aoun had started a campaign against militias, aiming first at the Lebanese Forces of Samir Geagea. Was he purposely making a show of force, thinking President Hafez Assad of Syria might support his candidacy to succeed Amin Gemayel as president? Probably, as later events indicated.

When the time came for Gemayel to leave the presidential palace, he had a hard time finding a successor. The candidate pushed by the Americans, Michael

Daher, was not to the liking of Hafez Assad, whose wishes Gemayel needed to consider. For some reason, Gemayel did not consider a second term for himself, perhaps guessing that the Sunni community would not hear of it (in fact, most Christians wouldn't have it either). In the end, Gemayel converted the office of president into a military cabinet headed by Aoun, which was instantly boycotted by the Muslims. The Muslim ministers in the cabinet all turned down their nominations, which left Aoun with only two ministers, both Christians, to manage an interim government.

On the other side of the city, in West Beirut, the exiting prime minister, who had worked under Gemayel, unilaterally revived his resigning government and proclaimed it to be the legitimate interim cabinet. At this moment in its history, Lebanon had no president but two governments. Realizing that Hafez Assad did not include him in his plans for the presidency of Lebanon, Michel Aoun went on a "war of liberation," as he called it, against the Syrian army in West Beirut, and he was aided in this endeavor by none other than Samir Geagea and his Lebanese Forces.

The six months of intensive fighting across the dividing line were the harshest Beirut had seen since the beginning of hostilities fourteen years earlier. Our own home in Baabda was hit on four occasions, direct strikes, while we were there, hiding in the shelter, power out, water leaking, the smell of powder and burning, and the never-ending radio news flashes that we used to keep informed (and pass the time). As this was playing out, some sixty members of parliament traveled to Taef in Saudi Arabia, where an agreement was signed in October 1989, much along the lines of the Tripartite Accord of 1985. Called the Taef Accord, it would enter the text of the Constitution and become the basis for a new republic; some referred to it as the Third Republic, after the 1926 and 1943 major milestones in the history of Lebanon.

If the Taef Accord succeeded at bringing the war to an end, it drew Lebanon into an ungovernable model in which a triumvirate exercised the authority formerly held solely by the Maronite president, who was now forced to share power with the Shi'a president of the parliament and the Sunni prime minister. Expanded representation in parliament, now 128 members, brought parity between Christians and Muslims (from the previous 6:5 ratio in favor of Christians).

Michel Aoun contested the Taef Accord violently in a spectacular television appearance during which he disavowed the accord and dismissed the parliament. A few days later, the parliament convened in the north of Lebanon at the Koleiat airbase, away from the firepower and influence of General Aoun, and elected a president in the spirit of the Taef Accord. A highly educated and enterprising figure, René Mouawad did not get the chance to govern, assassinated by a car bomb three weeks later on Independence Day, November 22, 1989. This came just a few weeks after the assassination, in similar circumstances, of the Sunni Mufti Hasan Khaled.

Days later, the members of parliament reconvened to elect Elias Hrawi, a representative for Zahleh, as president. The "war of liberation" that Aoun waged against the Syrians had not changed a thing (only adding another one thousand names to the list of dead innocents), and as soon as the general called it off without any explanation, he waged a "war of abolition" against the Lebanese Forces across East Beirut and the Christian regions of Metn and Kesrwan.

Aoun got his weapons and ammunition from Iraq, the natural enemy of Syria. The Sunni minority of Iraq governed a Shi'a majority, while the minority Shi'a (Alawi) of Syria governed a Sunni majority, a recipe for conflict. (This is one of the reasons why Saddam Hussein of Iraq and Hafez Assad of Syria governed with an iron fist, with single-party administrations and real military dictatorships that regimented their majority populations like silent flocks.) Saddam Hussein's seven-year war with Iran was finally over, and he had a large arsenal at his disposal (mainly American-made) and was happy to support whoever was at war with Syria.

When Iraq invaded Kuwait in 1990, the situation in Lebanon changed radically. With his instinctive political acumen, Hafez Assad condemned the invasion of Kuwait and took part in the force that was spearheaded by the Americans to subdue Saddam Hussein. Returning the favor, Washington approved the Syrian incursion into East Beirut and gave Assad a green light to topple General Aoun. Within days, Michel Aoun found himself in the custody of the French ambassador, going into exile in France, where he was to stay until his return in 2005. With Aoun gone, the Syrian army took total control over Lebanon, intending to keep the country of the cedar subdued by a *Pax Syriana*.

During the last part of the war in Lebanon, my mother and three of us escaped to Europe for a third time. While Lily stayed in Lyon with my brother Ramzi and my sister Myriam, I went to London, where I transferred credits from the American University of Beirut to pursue my degree in mechanical engineering at Kings College. My elder sister, Roula, stayed with my father at our home in Baabda despite the dreadful turn of events, as she was finishing her medical studies and could not transfer abroad with much ease. This was a time when cell phones and internet were not commonplace accessories of life, and we relied on landlines to communicate with one another, often having difficulties getting telephone connections with Lebanon. When I heard on the BBC that Syrian warplanes were pounding East Beirut, I figured out what was happening and got frightened. The presidential palace where Michel Aoun lived and worked was just minutes away from our home in Baabda, about one mile as the crow (or warplane) flies. My father was there with my sister, and although he never had anything to do with politics, he was nevertheless a personal friend of Michel Aoun, and I feared for their safety.

The news exchanged between Lyon and London was not comforting. We shared snippets we collected here and there, but nothing solid, and connections with Lebanon were simply dead. It was days after Aoun had fallen and Beirut reunited under the governance of the Syrian army that my mother managed to get through. "They are fine," she told me, "and they will come out for Christmas to Lyon." My mother prepared the kebbeh nayeh for the occasion, the meat tartar we always devoured with such gusto, and the Christmas tree was glowing as it always did in my father's house. He looked feeble and tired, and had lost all his hair overnight. The emotional shocks that Nadim had endured in the last fifteen years were terrible, and the weight that rested on his shoulders seemed simply unbearable.

I learned that Syrian soldiers had been to our house the day Michel Aoun was ousted, stolen a few belongings, and tried to intimidate my father and sister, but "God gives courage in such moments," my father said, "and the words to speak." One of the soldiers had a disabled brother and was taken by a picture he saw in Nadim's study that showed him with children at Al-Kafaàt. This unexpected turn of fate started a conversation that eventually led the unwelcome company to depart and both my father and sister to walk away unhurt.

But Christmas in Lyon was not a time for telling stories of the past. Nadim had plans for us, all four of us, and the family reunion was the occasion for Nadim to do what he always did best: plan the future of Al-Kafaàt. He had finished building a new catering school in Mansourieh, in the Metn region, on property that belonged to Lily and that she had brought to Al-Kafaàt as part of the endowment of the foundation. The catering school would follow the pattern Nadim developed early on in the leather factory, a dual approach that tackled education and production at the same time. This was his answer to the all-too-common question that organizations in developing countries have difficulty answering: how to finance education. In other words, how can any organization, however well intentioned, cover the costs of training when public resources for education are almost nonexistent? Also, how can education and training be practical enough to allow graduates to find employment, the bottom-line objective of development organizations in the first place?

Nadim's answer in 1964, when he first pleaded for the social integration of people with disabilities, was "self-financing" programs, as he demonstrated by his leather factory. In 1990, he addressed the issue by putting together a "school-enterprise" model, in which trainees were themselves workers. Kitchens and restaurants were businesses that lent themselves to on-the-job training. Training was kept to a high standard by highly qualified professional trainers, paid for by the returns from restaurant and catering operations. The school's opening in 1989, while Beirut and the Christian areas were subjected to the infighting between Michel Aoun and Samir Geagea, was well received; the turnout was so overwhelming that many people could not be served. This model of "school-enterprise" would become an underlying principle of education at Al-Kafaàt, and the foundation replicated it in countless applications in later years.

The catering school was not the only project that Nadim had established while we were away in Lyon and London. He also went ahead and moved the vocational and technical program, which he had started years earlier, to an independent campus. In order to position the Technical Institute a short distance from the major industrial areas of Lebanon, he bought an estate in Ain-Saadeh from the Maronite Bishopric of Mount Lebanon, in the Metn Mountains and a short distance from Beirut (which the campus overlooks). When we met in Lyon, a young and talented architect by the name of Nadim Abou-Rizk had already produced the blueprints for the campus, and the first building was under construction. Abou-Rizk was a senior partner of Samir Khairallah, by then the director of a reputable architecture firm, and sits today on the board of trustees of Al-Kafaàt. The campus soon became too small for Nadim's ambitions, and he went about purchasing two contiguous properties, only acquired after tedious negotiations that took him to the United States a few times, where some of the owners lived. Finally, he combined all three parcels of land into one large plot where the campus of AL KAFAAT UNIVERSITY stands today. While war was raging, the future uncertain, and his family in exile, Nadim more than ever was developing the capabilities of Al-Kafaàt to deliver more services.

Our family discussions in Lyon resulted in my going back to London with a clear objective in mind: I would prepare myself to attend to the needs of the Technical and Vocational Institute, whose first building would open in two years. Not only was I given my marching orders for the future, I was also given a timeline for the kick-off! My brother Ramzi also got his orders, as did my older sister Roula. He was to prepare, while studying economics and law in Lyon, to take charge of the catering school, and Roula, who was specializing in pediatrics, was invited to work at the centers that care for children with disabilities. Myriam, the youngest, was about to enter secondary school in 1989 and was spared for the time being. Each of us went away with clear missions in view, excited at the chance to finally roll up our sleeves and join Al-Kafaàt, to help Nadim and Lily make a difference in the lives of people.

I pursued my degree in engineering at Kings College London and moved on to the University of Wales to get an MBA at Cardiff Business School, choosing for my thesis "A Comparative Study on Vocational Training Systems across Europe," which brought me into contact with leading institutions in Britain and France. Ramzi, for his part, gained experience in the hospitality industry by working long hours with famous chefs while studying at the University of Lyon. When he graduated, he went to Bournemouth, in southern England, where he earned a degree in catering, making a little tour across Europe to experience work in five-star hotels. Roula finished her residency in pediatrics at the American University of Beirut and combined that with a degree in neurology, becoming a specialist in developmental disorders, just what Al-Kafaàt needed for her growing populations of children with mental and cerebral disabilities.

Ramzi and I flew from Paris to Lebanon in September 1992 to start work. The airport we entered on arrival in Beirut was badly damaged, pounded incessantly during the long war, a wreck through and through but adorned with posters of Syrian president Hafez Assad, glued in haste on the walls, many ripped and defaced, but there all the same to remind the returnees of who it was that now governed over them. Upon arrival in the terminal, our passports were taken by a Syrian soldier in arms who directed us, and most other young men, to one side for a thorough examination. Through the dirty window panels, steel bars, and slashed-open sandbags, I could see my father, mother, and Edouard, their close companion and driver. They waved at us with such excitement. The unfriendly reception we got at the hands of our Syrian "host" was ameliorated somewhat by the soothing smile of my mother and the apparent joy of my father. We were home.

9

A singular message in the face of continuing adversity

The peace of circumstance: And the failed state

The Taef Accord and the subsequent understandings that marked the swearing into office of President Elias Hrawi whither when analyzed under the light of true democracy. In short, all those who made war were given amnesty by the president, were all invited to sit in government, and were left alone to manage the businesses they had built during the war with the illegal earnings they had laundered along the way. The "liberal" Lebanon, so close to the heart of Michel Chiha, who wrote the Constitution of 1926, survived, but the Lebanese establishment had changed. The thirty families that formed the early oligarchy, mostly Christians, were complemented—in some cases replaced—by the warlords who had struck it rich by usurping the resources of the state. Equally, the "consensual" Lebanon, declared in the National Pact of 1943 between the Maronite leader Bechara Khoury and the Sunni leader Riad Solh, was preserved; only the power structure had evolved. The Maronites were coerced to let go of their political ascendancy and share power with the Sunni and with a third faction that had been totally overlooked in earlier years but that had grown in presence and regional politics, the Shi'a.

The three communities were to govern together in an intricate covenant that gave equal power to each, ensuring that the sum of their efforts would be a stalemate from the start. On paper, Lebanon still had a government and a parliament, an executive and a legislative branch, but these effectively were no more than remnants of a destitute parliamentary republic: the real power was in the hands of the feudal warlords, a new caste of muqataajis, much the same as it had been under the local amirs in previous centuries of Ottoman rule. Again, as in the early days of the republic, the concern of this neo-establishment was with growing its businesses under the protection of the state, whose government it was part of. In this "dummy" republic, the usurers could use the public resources for personal gains. Governments of "national unity" were and still are the pillar of this system, cabinets formed of the clans who stand at the antipodes and who could never blend into a cohesive unity. A salad bowl instead of a melting pot, the executive power was undermined and incapacitated from the onset by the clan leaders, who spoke a double language. These agreed to disagree on the affairs of the state, only they agreed tacitly to keep their channels open in a game of give-and-take to sustain each other's lust for business.

In the early 1990s, coerced by a Syrian force of forty thousand men, they all handed their weapons over to the Lebanese army. With Syria's blessing, Hezbollah alone kept its arsenal, on the basis that it was conducting a war of liberation of the southern territories annexed by Israel (as did the Palestinian groups in camps, now impregnable fortresses where the Lebanese government has no say). Then the militia leaders traded their military vests for Italian-cut suits and entered the government, recovered their innocence with the absolution that was granted for all past crimes (the famous slogan entered the annals of Lebanon's modern politics: *a'fa Allah a'n ma mada*, God had pardoned what is past), and went on indulging in their double-standard waffle. Until, that is, an atypical figure emerged, one who would govern the first part of post-Taef Lebanon: Rafik Hariri.

A Lebanese from Saida, Hariri rose from a simple clerk's position in Saudi Arabia, where he went seeking employment, to become a close confidant of the ruling family, having earned the trust of the Saudi king by conducting large-scale construction operations and businesses. Anxious to stop the bloodshed in his country, Hariri was an active organizer of the Taef Accord on the part of Saudi Arabia, where he was bestowed citizenship by the king, a rare honor reserved for exclusive servants of the kingdom. Later, with the elections of 1992, he entered the political scene in Lebanon actively and was appointed by President Elias Hrawi to form a government. With a few short breaks, Hariri would hold the seat of prime minister for thirteen years, until he was assassinated in a bomb attack in 2005. New to the ways of the Lebanese establishment, let alone one that brought together the warlords of yesterday, Rafik Hariri soon saw his authority undermined. His early moves to impact the economy by instituting open-air markets and organizing public transportation were opposed violently by most of the clan leaders who undercut his initiatives. So Hariri did very much what a previous president, Fouad Shihab, had done in his time and built a parallel government of advisors and close confidants to circumvent those who blocked his prerogatives. But if Shihab used his back channels to build government structures, Hariri used his to reposition Lebanon on the regional exchequer as an economic engine, a gateway to the Arab world.

In this, Hariri was probably unique. He must have looked at Lebanon and done the simple calculations that CEOs of multinationals do. It must have soon been apparent to him that sorting out the economic deadlock would start the country on the road to revival. The sheer size of Lebanon did not impress him. From the standpoint of GDP, which amounted to twenty billion dollars in 1992, Lebanon was one-fifth as large as a medium-sized construction corporation; from the standpoint of government spending, it was one-twelfth the size. And Hariri was adept at driving companies to succeed and make profits. With this for an agenda, he started Beirut on a course that would cause the city in the 1990s to become, after Berlin, the "largest construction site" in the world. In just a few years, Hariri rebuilt Old Beirut from scratch into a luxurious "downtown" that has been criticized by many for being a temple of consumerism for the wealthy Arabs and Lebanese.

To complete his projects, Hariri relied for financing on a joint-stock real estate company, which he founded and which drew Arab capital, forcing the landowners to sell their properties when they could not abide by the stringent regulations. A new airport was built to replace the old one, public buildings were restored, a network of roads and bridges was started (and continues today). Large public works, infrastructure, and even a stadium to accommodate the Arab games of 1999 and the Asia Cup in soccer the following year—all were Rafik Hariri's accomplishments.

Critics of Rafik Hariri complained that all the development was concentrated in the capital city of Beirut and that the cost was unaffordable: the size of the Lebanese debt soared to forty billion dollars in 2003, nearly 150 percent of the GDP for the period. Of course, debt does not frighten entrepreneurs and company owners, who are used to making financial projections based on economic returns, and Hariri had his own. But in his projections, he either downplayed or completely misinterpreted regional politics at a time when change was always likely. Syria was in Lebanon for the time, and although an "Agreement of Brotherhood and Coordination" had been signed by the two countries, pushed by Hafez Assad, the Syrian force became an army of occupation the moment it did not comply with the Taef Accord and withdraw its troops behind the Bekaa by 1995.

And Syria was not alone, for Israel still occupied the south of Lebanon and had a buffer zone controlled by its client army, now commanded by Antoine Lahd, the successor to Saad Haddad, who had passed away in 1984. Syria was turning up the heat on Israel across Lebanon by lending support to Hezbollah and closing in on the Litani River, in retaliation for Israel's continuing annexation of the Syrian-owned Golan Heights. The United States sought to bring the two contenders into negotiations and tried hard to keep channels open with Hafez Assad. He was, after all, the enemy of Saddam Hussein and would be a strategic ally to contend with in the future. Meanwhile the Labor government of Yitzhak Rabin had cleared the necessary hurdles and overtly addressed the PLO as the "representative of the Palestinian people," noting it was ready to "commence negotiations with it within the Middle East peace process." The famous handshake at the White House between

Rabin and Yasser Arafat, under the auspices of Bill Clinton, gave more than one viewer the sense that peace and tranquility in the Middle East was finally underway. But Rabin was gunned down at a peace rally in 1995, and the peace sentiment evaporated overnight. With the "artisan of peace" gone, Shimon Peres went on a military campaign against Hezbollah, probably to show the Israeli electorate that he too could be ruthless when the situation demanded. Bridges in Lebanon were targeted, and so were power plants, businesses, and other properties, in what seemed more like sabotage than a war on "terrorism."

Rafik Hariri multiplied his visits to decision-making capitals, harnessed his personal contacts among statesmen and people of influence (French president Jacques Chirac was a close personal friend), and even spoke in French on the French evening news, a language he had learned only after rising to the office of prime minister, exerting such pressure that Peres had to pull back, especially after the carnage in Cana. There, in the land where Christ is said to have performed his first miracle, Israeli warplanes pounded a United Nations compound where families had sought refuge. The result was a shameful loss of 105 lives.

The retreat of the Israeli forces and the high toll of casualties reinvigorated Hezbollah, which started to gather popular support, especially for its young and charismatic leader Hasan Nasrallah, whose speeches called for "liberating the South of the Israeli annexation." When, in the year 2000, liberation came and Israel withdrew from Lebanon, disbanding the South Lebanon Army of Antoine Lahd, Hezbollah and its secretary general Hasan Nasrallah were hailed as national heroes, especially when the detention center at the village of Khiam was revealed to the public. The testimonies of the torture and executions that were given by survivors and eyewitnesses there were shocking and only helped fuel the euphoria over liberation.

With Israel out of Lebanon, all eyes turned to Syria, which still occupied the country and meddled with the internal politics of government. Hariri had, in fact, more than once withdrawn from his office, preferring to resign than be coerced by President Elias Hrawi and later by General Émile Lahoud, the commander-in-chief of the army, who had stepped into office in 1998. They both were close to Hafez Assad, Hrawi having had his term as president extended by three years, overriding the Constitution, which had been amended by a near-quorum of members of parliament. Syria had more at stake in Lebanon than its simple tit-for-tat with Israel. After the dark hours of the war, Syria took a growing interest in Lebanon's vibrant economy, and the Assad administration looked at Lebanon as its own private fiefdom. Syrian personnel posted in Beirut and in the Bekaa had the upper hand in Lebanese politics, and the director of intelligence, Ghazi Kanaan, and later, Rustum Ghazaleh, acted as proconsuls in Lebanon. They hired and fired ministers at will and imposed their dictates on local politicians, whose two main concerns were to keep their seats and delve illicitly into the riches of the nation. It was only natural therefore that the neo-establishment counted among its members those pawns who served Syrian interests, both economic and political.

Hafez Assad passed away in 2000 and was succeeded by his son, Bashar, who earned no less than 99.8 percent of the votes, as president of the Arab Republic of Syria, a typical percentage for Arab democracies. If the young, educated president gave early signs of openness, signaling a long-awaited exit from the Cold War mentality that had governed Syrian policies, it only took a few months before what was bred in the bone came out in the flesh. The events following 9/11 changed everything. Iraq was invaded by a coalition of four countries spearheaded by the United States, and the Iraqi army was demobilized (an action many are still not able to comprehend). Instead of taking out Saddam and his retinue and empowering the Iraqi army to hold the country together and avoid chaos and civil war, the invading forces employed a scorched-earth policy.

The resulting disorder in Iraq had severe consequences on the whole region. Oil was an issue, but so was the sectarian strife that lay dormant under the claws of the authoritarian regime, namely, the Shi'a and Sunni schism. The porous borders of Iraq led neighboring Iran and Syria to maneuver for position, replaying there many of the scenes that had been seen earlier in Beirut during a previous war. The United States had become physically involved in the Middle East and Asia, no longer enjoying the comfort of intervening through proxies. In an earlier time, for example, Pakistan did much of the fighting for America in Afghanistan; after 9/11, American boots were on the ground, ushering in a shift in the geopolitical epicenter of the world.

The Middle East had become the center of attention, and the balance of power changed. Iran gained momentum, allying itself with Syria to ensnare Iraq and to hold in check the Sunni princedoms of the Gulf, pushing them further into the arms of the US administration. What Saudi Arabia has paid to develop its military capabilities—$80.8 billion in 2014, according to the Stockholm International Peace Research Institute, mostly to buy weapons from the United States, including F-15 fighters and top-of-the-line attack helicopters—looks indecent when one sees the poverty on the streets of Jeddah. The leaders of industrial countries such as France regularly visit Arab princedoms with delegations of industrialists to sell their products, military technology usually ranking first on the list. George W. Bush's policy of dividing the world into two clear sides, between those "with us" and those "against us," surrounding himself with such people as Donald Rumsfeld, Dick Cheney, and Condoleezza Rice, who had stakes in large oil conglomerates (Chevron named one of its oil tankers after Rice), made the lineup of nations easy to predict. Iran reaffirmed its presence in Lebanon by extending military support and training to Hezbollah, while the US administration reinforced its military presence in Turkey,

Israel, and some of the Gulf countries. More than ever, Syria needed to keep its foot in Lebanon, whose location was becoming ever more strategic as events unfolded, not to the displeasure of many members of the neo-establishment who moved and enriched themselves in Syria's shadows.

With his international stature and popular support, his constant concern for checks and balances, and his omnipresence, which somehow prevented a fall into chaos at a time when chaos might have served certain interests, Rafik Hariri was becoming too burdensome for some, and he was assassinated in February 2005. His assassination signaled the end of the one true state program that Lebanon had had since Fouad Shihab, contested perhaps, faulty in many respects when viewed retrospectively, yet a program all the same, and one that had a beginning, a road map, and a projected ending. In Hariri's program, the normalization of relations with neighboring countries, Syria foremost, was paramount and meant the withdrawal of Syrian troops from Lebanon. The revival of Lebanon's economy, the reorganization of its bureaucracy, cutting the gangrenous corruption that wasted state resources, and a clear intention to find a permanent solution to the Palestinians living in camps—these elements of Hariri's plan of action were undermining one too many agendas.

The reaction to Hariri's assassination was unexpected, certainly to the perpetrators. A popular uprising of unprecedented magnitude forced the Syrian troops to finally evacuate Lebanon, a posthumous reward for Hariri, who managed in death what he could not do in his short political life. Since then, Lebanon has been falling like an autumn leaf, propelled by the winds of regional change, ungoverned or badly governed, unable to organize, and increasingly undercut by the ever-grasping neo-establishment. Syria was driven out yet continued to influence many clan leaders, who still looked at Damascus for their marching orders. Car bombings have become a common spectacle across Beirut with no fewer than a dozen occurrences since 2005, targeting figures of the so-called opposition that formed around Saad Hariri, Rafik's son. Some of the bombings have been imputed to the Syrian administration, and the red-handed arrest of a former minister and Member of Parliament, Michel Samaha, transporting explosives from Syria in his own car, did nothing to weaken these incriminations, which still await investigation. Less charismatic as a leader than his father was, Saad Hariri would not benefit from the political momentum gathered by these tragic bombings, trapped by the general political stalemate that soon hit Lebanon.

The war of July 2006 between Israel and Hezbollah resulted, once again, in Israeli attacks on Lebanese bridges, power plants, and businesses (even an international award-winning dairy plant in the Bekaa that had no connection with Hezbollah), displacing more than a million people and severely damaging the country. The withdrawal of the Israeli army without completing a single objective, while bearing substantial human losses and incurring severe reprisals from Hezbollah, broke the spell of Israeli military superiority in Arab eyes and earned Hezbollah a new position of force in the country. With the Syrians out of Lebanon, Hezbollah turned to politics to cover its back, creating a political formation of its own that brought to its side General Michel Aoun, who returned from exile, and the leader of Amal and now speaker of the Parliament, Nabih Berri.

With General Émile Lahoud's term at an end, the tension between the two political formations was such that it proved impossible to elect a successor. The office of president was vacant for nine months until a summit in Doha was called by the amir of Qatar, under whose auspices General Michel Sleiman, the commander-in-chief of the army, was proposed as the "solution-president" in 2008. It is not unusual for the Lebanese to look for others to sort out their differences. The National Pact of 1943 was concluded in Cairo, under the auspices of Nahas Pasha, and the Taef Accord of 1989 in Saudi Arabia, both turning points in the making of modern Lebanon. Not only is the presidency a bone of contention, but government in general. The prime minister–elect Tammam Salam (son of Saeb Salam) took all of ten months to form a cabinet in 2014, and currently ninety senior offices are still vacant across the civil service, waiting for the neo-establishment to agree on the distribution of positions among the various clan leaders. Even today, at the time of my writing these lines, Lebanon is without a president, unable to elect a successor to President Sleiman a whole year after the end of his term.

The surreal politics of the country of the cedars are such that the presidential candidates for the two coalitions are none other than General Michel Aoun and Samir Geagea. The latter was imprisoned for eleven years, having breached the presidential amnesty that absolved the crimes of war by being indicted for the bombing of a church in Kesrwan. Even if Geagea was framed for this bombing, it was still cause enough to reopen his judicial record, which did not lack for substantial incriminations to send him to prison. Aoun is the candidate of the coalition that is close to the Syrian administration (which ousted him in 1990); Geagea runs for the coalition that structures itself around the specter of the late Rafik Hariri and is promoted by his son Saad. I suspect the impasse will be resolved at some summit in some Arab capital under some kingly augur and usher in some "solution-president," maybe the current commander-in-chief of the army, the one seat that seems to enjoy unanimity of support in recent times. A former ambassador to the European Union in Lebanon once told me, discussing the ways of politicians, that "Lebanese politics are incestuous." He argued that people walk deliberately in flocks to give themselves as living offerings to the militia converts, who are responsible for their destitution in the first place. I might not have put it this way, but I hear his point.

The Arab Spring, which started in Tunisia in 2010 and spread across Libya, Egypt, Yemen, Bahrain, and Syria, opened a breach for Sunni fundamentalism to penetrate. The better organized and most dangerous groups identify with Al-Qaeda and get their orders directly from its leader, Ayman Zawahiri, or from the Islamic State of Iraq and the Levant (variously referred to now as ISIS, ISIL, Daesh, or simply "the Islamic State"), a jihadist group led by Abu Bakr Baghdadi. These groups are present today across the Syrian landscape and have blended in with the sketchy opposition, partnering with one group and fighting another, exporting car bombs to Lebanon as a direct response to Hezbollah's intervention on the side of the Syrian regime. The longer the war in Syria lasts, the more pronounced the likelihood will become of the radicalization of the opposition and its crystallization around such dangerous and far-reaching fundamentalist groups.

In May 2015, shortly before this book went to press, Palmyra fell to ISIL, and its Roman theater was used to showcase the execution of twenty people, mostly Christians and soldiers from the regular Syrian army. With the fall of Palmyra in Syria and, the previous week, of Ramadi in Iraq, ISIL prides itself on having reunited the lands that were partitioned under the Sykes-Picot agreement and on having rebuilt the caliphate with Baghdadi on the throne. Stronger than ever, ISIL has even the luxury of keeping a step ahead, setting the order of the game: What happens after Palmyra? Will ISIL move on to Homs and stand at the doorstep of Lebanon, linking up with the fundamentalist groups in Tripoli and those hiding in Palestinian camps? The commander-in-chief of the Lebanese army, Jean Kahwaji, confided a few weeks ago to the French newspaper *Le Figaro* that ISIL is seeking to carve out an opening on the Mediterranean Sea. Would it be across Lebanon? It is true that the coalition of nations that has declared war on ISIL (by flying war jets over it) has only agreed on a mandate over Iraq, not Syria, which gives the ISIL command plenty of room to maneuver? Marching across the Syrian Coastal Mountain Range north of Lebanon is also a possibility, crushing in the process the stronghold of Bashar Assad and sprouting across the coast of Latakia. More questions tickle the imagination of any political analyst: Where does ISIL get the weapons, ammunition, and spare parts? Surely, these cannot be sold on black markets in such quantities; they need a steady supply only governments can ensure. Where does ISIL get the money to sustain its operations? The media is quick to say that the money comes from the sale of crude that fell under its control, in which case the question becomes where does ISIL monetize the oil? Surely not on black markets, for only governments could process such volumes. And who is supporting the other groups of fundamentalists, such as the Nusra Front, an Al-Qaeda splinter group present on the borders with Lebanon, off Baalbek in the northeast? What role are the Wahhabis of Saudi Arabia, Qatar, and Turkey playing in the region? What will happen if the Assad government falls and Nusra or ISIL step in to fill the power vacuum in the region? And while all this plays out, what is the Israeli administration up to? Is it pushing for more settlements, in the Golan Heights now, where a decision was made to settle a hundred thousand under the nose of Assad? These are questions that will only be answered as events unravel over time.

I wanted to include a map depicting the developments on the ground. But these are so rapid that it is hard to produce one today that could still speak of the deployments of fundamentalist groups by the time the book is out in bookstores. Here is a snapshot, however, at the time of publication (I must thank my friend and cartographer, François Eid, who indulged me with five reruns of this map in the last five months).

On June 4, 2014, much was happening. The Chinese were celebrating the twenty-fifth anniversary of their insurrection in Tiananmen Square, Barack Obama was in Poland to commemorate the fall of communism, France was making its best efforts to host the seventieth anniversary of D-Day, and Bashar Assad was elected president of Syria "by verdict of the barrel bomb and the ballot box," as headlined in the British press. In the evening of that eventful day, Secretary of State John Kerry chose Lebanon of all places, and the office of her prime minister more particularly, to address the press with an inspiring "[Syria's] elections are a great big

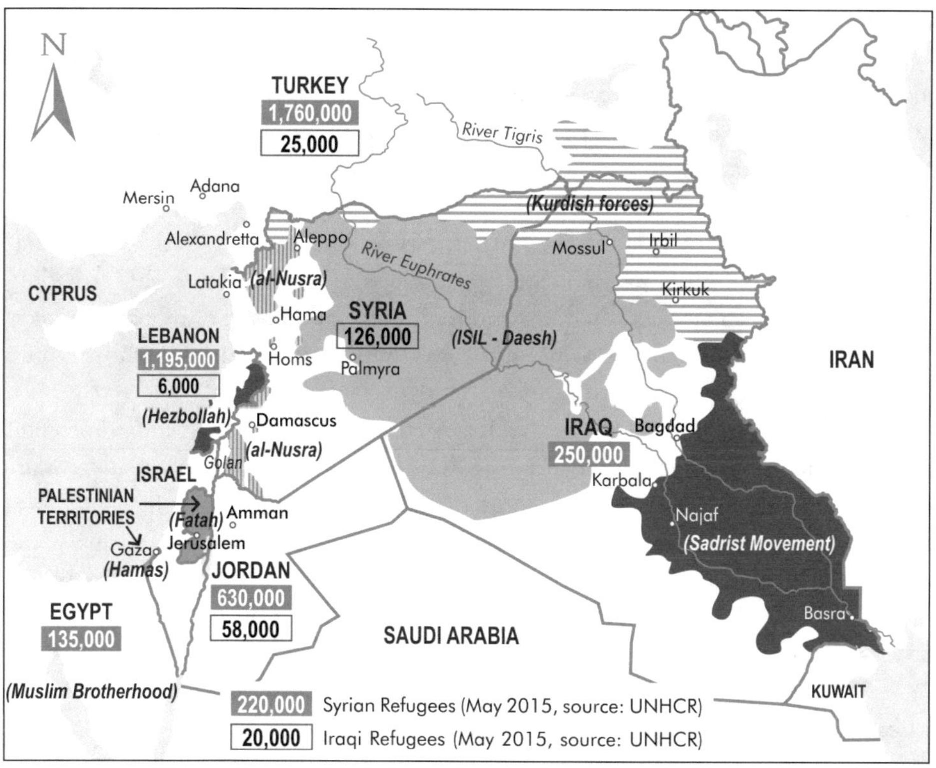

Map 9. Islamic movements: Forces in opposition and their respective areas of influence

zero." Voicing this opinion from Beirut instead of Washington carried diplomatic meaning, no doubt, but whatever the purpose and interests, it will definitely have a hammer-like effect on a country already torn apart by unbearable paradoxes and on the brink of collapse.

My first son, John, was born three weeks before the assassination of Rafik Hariri, at the same American University Hospital where the burnt corpse of Hariri was transferred. In Hariri's thirteen years in office, and despite the outbreaks of violence on certain occasions, his tenure was a time for reconstruction. Hariri's message was clear, and Beirut turned into a forest of construction cranes, with shops opening before streets were paved, people's magazines multiplying on newsstands, theaters reopening, and children's fairs surfacing again at Christmas markets on Martyrs' Square, around the high tree with sparkling garlands that regained its place after so long a hiatus. This period coincided with my return to Lebanon with Ramzi, in time for the plan that Nadim and Lily had outlined, and we began exploring the wide world of rehabilitation and education, working long hours to meet the increasing demand for the services of Al-Kafaàt. Ramzi turned the catering school in Mansourieh into an iconic training center and shares his knowledge with some five hundred graduate caterers every year. His expertise and devotion to his profession went beyond the limits of his catering school, showcasing itself in a daily cooking show broadcast on pan-Arab television and transforming him, still in his twenties, into the famed "Chef Ramzi" of world-class reputation. He was published on several occasions, and his encyclopedic book on cooking has sold well over a million copies.

Roula, for her part, started the Early Intervention Program at Al-Kafaàt rehabilitation centers, a program that caters to toddlers under five years old, providing them with comprehensive evaluations and follow-ups by a group of interdisciplinary specialists. She also organized a program for children with autism, which would later blossom into a pilot institution in Hadath that caters today to 150 people. Roula and her family decided to leave Lebanon in 2001, and she is today the chief of the division of developmental and behavioral pediatrics at the University of Massachusetts in Boston. She visits the center at Al-Kafaàt yearly, where she contributes her time and expertise training staff and educators. I was happy one day, while meeting in New York with a senior official of the organization Autism Speaks, to hear Roula referred to as an authority on autism. The official did not know of my relationship with her.

My younger sister Myriam finished her engineering studies at the American University of Beirut and took charge of the technical education program at Al-Kafaàt, which she managed with skill and dexterity before moving on to assume charge of the foundation's communications department. She also received a master's degree in communications at Syracuse University and has worked closely with the Antiochian Orthodox Archdiocese of North America and the late visionary metropolitan Philip Saliba to secure funding for the construction of a new center for children with mental challenges. That construction is in progress today, supported by the successor of Saliba, Metropolitan Joseph, no less of a man of wisdom and action. Myriam has also started her own social enterprise, along the lines of Nadim's 1964 leather factory, one that secures employment for people with disabilities and provides orders for products from artisans in rural Lebanon who struggle to make ends meet. Her company, Morus, contributes all its profits to Al-Kafaàt.

It has been twenty-three years since our generation, the sons and daughters of Nadim Shwayri, began its work at Al-Kafaàt. Today, the little school our father started in Salima in 1957 has transformed itself into a large umbrella organization that serves well over five thousand people of Lebanon daily, from all religious groups and regions of the country, on seven campuses that together employ roughly one thousand staff members. During the last fifteen years, Al-Kafaàt devoted much attention to developing higher education programs, founding AL KAFAAT UNIVERSITY and endowing it with buildings and grounds, and closing the deficits of annual operations. AKU is fortunate to have partnered since 2010 with the State University of New York on a project that received the endorsement of the Higher Education for Development (HED) and the US Agency for International Development (USAID). This first project allowed for sustained exchange programs between AKU and four colleges in New York State and has developed into a full-blown affiliation that was signed at the end of 2013. The affiliation is so close that a position was created in the SUNY system administration for a Global Fellow for Lebanon who now sits as a member of the board of trustees of AKU. My close friend and partner in researching this book, Rosemary Ortlieb, currently serves in these functions.

The realization of our goals during this period has been made more difficult by the political, economic, social, and security conditions in Lebanon. The exception has become the rule, and more than once we have had to organize humanitarian programs on the fly, hosting refugees in student dormitories, activating "meals-on-wheels" programs to feed the victims of sudden upheavals, staffing a mobile clinic to deliver orthopedic services and supply orthotics and prosthetics in war-devastated zones. Planning—producing a long-term road map and sticking to it—has always been an issue. How can one look to the future when, all around, uncertainty is the rule? During the last ten years, Lebanon has been governed with approximation, with no vision and no plan, without even a national budget. Spending has been ad hoc and uncontrolled, much of it through slush funds controlled by clan leaders, most government programs being milked for self-profit.

The absence of a national budget limits accountability measures. Between bad management and corruption, public service is very deficient and, in many instances, even lethal. For example, the number of shunt procedures currently performed on cardiac patients in Lebanon who have social security coverage is seven times higher than for patients with other insurance policies, although the population is much the same. The reason lies in the connivance of hospitals and public servants who do not mind sending healthy patients to the operating rooms to cash in on unnecessary procedures. Dealing with government is a daily confrontation, and since 2008 Al-Kafaàt has spearheaded a lobbying group that actively advocates for change, accompanied in this by a multitude of institutions, associations, and activists called the National Consortium for the Rights of People with Disabilities (NCRPD). The complexities of the socioeconomic and political background are such that bringing one additional brick to the edifice can be an overwhelming challenge. Still, I recall what my father used to say, with his unique courage and sense of duty, "that the mission beautifies when the weight becomes excessive." Also, it would not be a calling if it were just a simple walk in the park!

The message of Al-Kafaàt

We tend to read history today from the perspective of world events and impose a chronological order, sometimes looking for patterns and cycles, to understand the making of societies. We interpret other cultures and traditions through the prism of our own inherited values. Nowadays, we thrill to events that we learn about the minute they occur, on our portable phones and the ever-present social media. We comment on events with "like" or not, and we play reporters without borders by transmitting our video files to millions around the globe; we impact events, foster new events, and help some events take the giant leap to making history, a compilation of events that gives an account of our own past and present. Ever since I became acquainted with the readings of Fernand Braudel, the sociologist and political philosopher, I learned to distinguish between history that "agitates" and History that "breathes." One is events-driven, an assemblage of doings and defeats, of winnings and losses, of elections and coups, of partisanships, party politics and politicking. It is nervous, sharp-edged, short-lived, and vindictive, and builds on the interests of a few. The other is slow, resilient, natural, and righteous; it speaks of humanity and develops over the generations to the pace of nature and human evolution. All too often, "history as a series of events" overshadows the "History that serves humanity"; the former drags the latter through the mud, bullies it, mocks it, and tries to eradicate its very existence.

This book presents two narratives in one body, two histories of Lebanon that intertwine in measures of joy and sorrow. It gives the history of events that accompanied the making of a country, and the History of a family that toiled hard, lived and loved, had dreams and ambitions, and eventually endowed a unique institution that serves humanity and holds people's dignity at heart. The first history will continue in agitation and disquiet, torn between the lusts of an oligarchic few and the interests of administrations; the second History will go on breathing unabated, a skiff that sails across stormy torrents, drifting at times and occasionally taking on water, but one that always gets back on course after every blow.

Like the mutations in genomes that condition humans to their evolving environments, the power of nature extends to the evolution of humanity beyond the sequential events of our modern politics and builds a rich capital of human history. At the dawn of time, with human migrations from Africa to the northern lands, human genomes adapted to an environment of less heat and sun, and skin colors lightened. It took hundreds of thousands of years for this to occur, as it will take long generations for our system to codify and cure such diseases as cancer and Parkinson's and adapt to the new environments we live in (which we are regretfully altering today, through our overuse of fossil fuels). Unfortunately this is where the discrepancy lies; for the political, economic, social, and technological environment of our modern world is in constant agitation and outruns the slow pace of human-responsive History that breathes.

Nadim Shwayri was the repository of such a human History, one that breathed quietly down the generations of people who modified to infinitesimal measures the genome of their contributions to humanity. Nadim was a builder with Fares Bozeid Moujaes, an industrial entrepreneur with Habib Fares Shwayri, a family artisan with Nicolas Shwayri, and a peddler with Alfred Nicola. All these roles and more he enshrined in his creation of Al-Kafaàt, now the depository of a Human history that will continue breathing, an institutional culture that speaks to a multitude. Nadim's contribution to the shaping of the human genome and handing it down to the next generation was through Al-Kafaàt. He left a heritage that is awe-inspiring, a model and a testimony that can serve the world in many ways.

First, the socioeconomic model that Nadim fostered through his leather factory and many entrepreneurial schools supports a rationale that combines aggressive production and marketing policies with a paternalistic approach to social spending, a market economy scaled down to human size to meet the real needs of people. The message to the world, and to the developing countries more importantly, is that it is possible to provide such services as education and rehabilitation at a high standard, all while creating jobs and without incurring exorbitant costs.

Second, a belief in humankind, "all of Man and all of men" (*tout l'Homme et tout homme*), as another social entrepreneur, Grégoire Haddad, once said, was the cornerstone of Nadim's social endeavors. (Haddad, the archbishop of Beirut for the Uniate, or Greek Catholic, Church, fell from grace for embracing the real problems of people instead of the riches of the seat—and of the See. Haddad was a friend of

Nadim and an early trustee of Al-Kafaàt.) At the main entrance of the center in Mreijeh, which he built in the late 1960s, Nadim raised a wall-sized picture of a man who had polio holding the hand of a child equally disabled and helping him to cross a small ravine. Next to the picture, he had spelled out in the most beautiful Arabic calligraphy the bronze letters that told a parable from the Psalms: "The stone the builders rejected has become the cornerstone." In the midst of a broken society, with multiple social rifts along economic, religious, and tribal lines, Nadim gave testimony to a society that builds on respect, dignity, and love for one another, a plural community where everyone belongs, where everyone is a piece of a puzzle that is needed to form the whole, one in a multitude, whose togetherness gives a semblance of the image of the Creator. Whether Christian or Muslim, handicapped or handicapped differently (for remember, "we are all handicapped"), we are all called to live as one, building together a society of righteousness and equality.

The third lesson that Nadim taught through Al-Kafaàt was one of resilience, that "truth always prevails," not in words but in deeds and actions, by defying machine guns with a bare chest, by rebuilding clinics and workshops after every bout of gratuitous violence. Resilience also in holding on to one's mission, a pure and elevated mission, when all around speak of corruption, when public service is but a service to kleptocratic oligarchies that feast on the agonies of people.

In 2008, Nadim was diagnosed with Parkinson's disease. It progressed quickly, and in 2011 he fell and broke a hip. He is wheelchair-bound today and has become a shadow of his former self, frail and absent. A year ago, on one of his brief "awakenings," as I call them, he looked at me and murmured words that found their way into my heart and soul. He spoke the lesson of all lessons on true resilience: "I always thought I knew everything there is to know about disability for having devoted my life to serving its cause, but I still missed the feeling of being on the other side. Now I know and I could not have parted with life without knowing."

Alfred's legacy had more in its coffers than properties and golden Turkish liras. It had a human History to give, one that started early in time and was no doubt shaped on the towpaths of the bayous in Louisiana. This history continues today, seven generations after Fares Bozeid Moujaes, with my own children and those of my brother and sister, whether in Lebanon or in the United States. As Roula's daughter Zeina, a thirteen-year-old Bostonian who awakens to the genomes of her Human history, writes:

> I'm from the dulcet smell of pink roses and sugary sweet food in the air.
> From my Grandparents' house, where pictures are everywhere.
> Memories and love fill up the rooms,

as well as the humidity and smoke from the cigarettes Teta[1] Lily keeps.
I'm from a house full of children and toys.
Where the TV is always on, and nothing stays still.
I'm from dance, a world just for me.
Where I escape to my own land, my own thoughts, my own beliefs.
I'm from ballet shoes hung up on the wall,
next to the trophies and medals.
I'm from fear.
Fear of negligence, fear of being unloved.
From worrying about school and friends, to being care-free, living by the beach with family.
I'm from Orthodoxy, a family belief in God.
I'm from Al-Kafaàt, my grandfather's fifth child,
a school where handicapped children learn to grow.
From "Potentials, not handicaps," the words every child in my family is taught.
I'm from loving my brother, to fighting with him all through my childhood.
I'm from Lebanese cooking; hummus, merghli, and tabouli.
From the catering school my uncle owns, where we go by bicycle to grab a manouche.
I'm from puree de marron, the family's New Year traditional desert.
From Christmas Eve opening presents with the little kids,
and the Lebanese mountains in the summer.
I'm from cooking, dancing, and praying.
I'm from sadness.
From stories better kept untold.
From a long war that took my parents' childhood away.
From the stories told of horrible days and long nights.
I'm from a family's courageous escape to France,
a chance for survival, a second beginning for my mother.
I'm from loud bangs and crashes.
From bombs hitting the walls,
to children tripping on their laces.
From a fall that left my grandfather in a wheelchair.
From Parkinson's.
The disease spreading, eating away his thoughts and independence.

1. Granny.

I'm from regret.
Not saying goodbye to my great-grandmother, a month before we were all forced to.
From never forgetting the night it happened, to always remembering the times we spent together.
I'm from tears.
The ones on my Grandmother's face whenever it's time for us to leave Lebanon,
to the ones crawling down my Grandfather's cheeks when he's proud.
I'm from the way he looks at me.
Eye full of hope,
From hope for a better future, a better life, better health.
I'm from the love.
The love for family, the love for friends, the love for dance.
I'm from Phillip, Francoise, two Mayas, and an Isa,
the extended family I will keep forever.
From the first dance recital I can remember,
where lights hit my small face in every direction.
I'm from love, from hope, from care, from devotion.
From passion, hard work, faithfulness, and positivity.
I'm from Lebanon, and soon enough, Boston too.
I'm from family, from friends, and from God.

—Zeina Michel Fayad, "Where I'm From," 2013

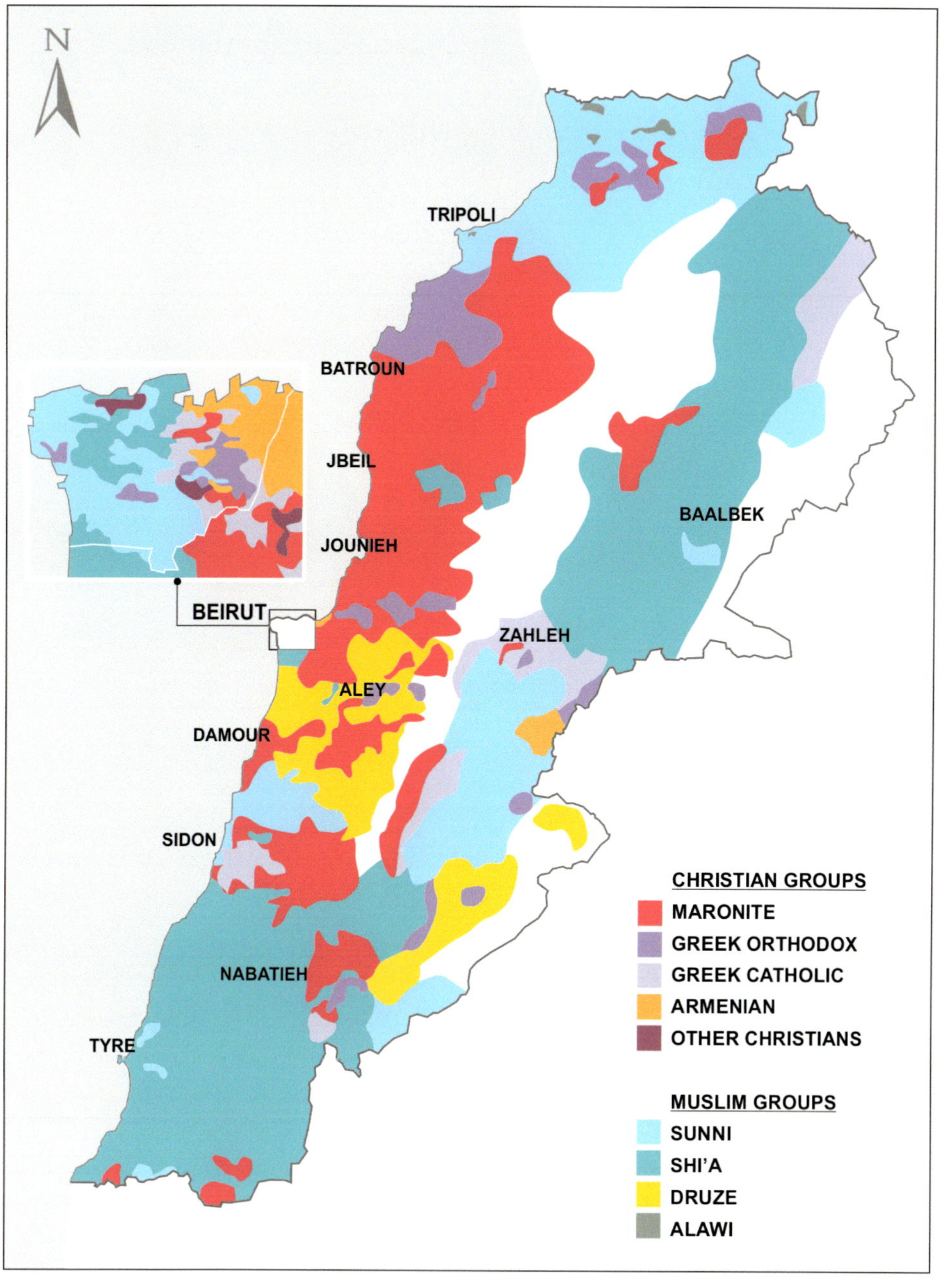

34. Lebanon's confessional mosaic as it stands today: Cultural diversity or powder keg?

35. Alfred Nicola and Najibeh Meshrek on their wedding day, July 23, 1923, three years after Alfred came back to Lebanon from Louisiana.

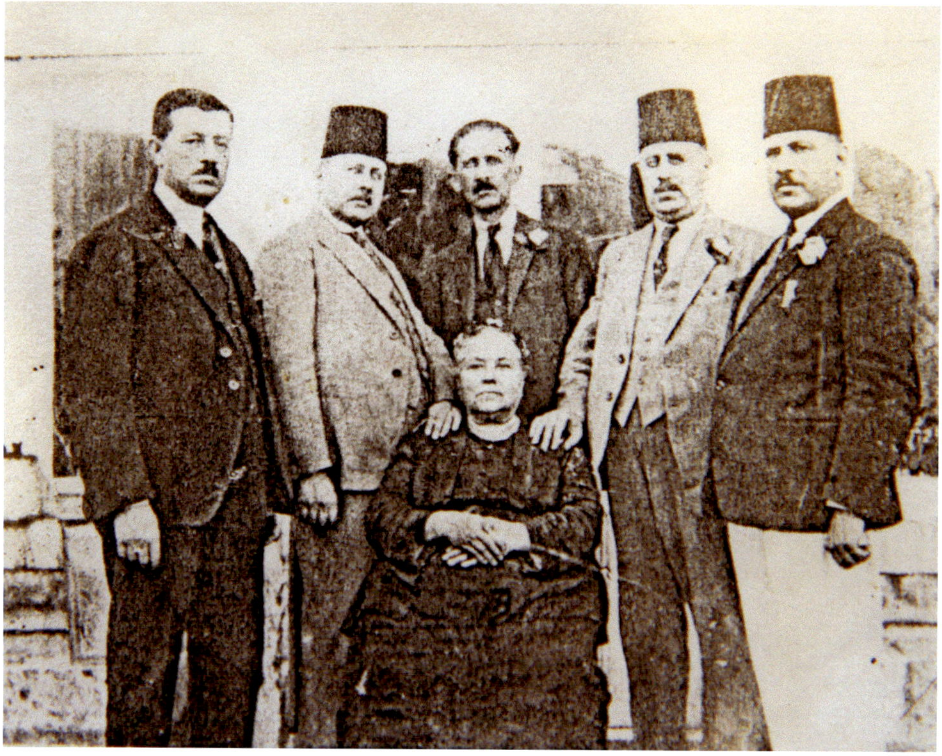

36. The successful Meshrek brothers wearing the Ottoman fez with their mother, Barbara Rahbani. The oldest brother was a businessman in Brazil, the second was a judge, and the younger two were medical doctors.

37. Alfred, Najibeh, and Nadim, my father, at their home in Hadath in 1948.

38. With my grandmother, Najibeh, at Alfred's home in Hadath in 1969. I wear the robe of my patron namesake, Saint Joseph (my second name).

39. With my sister Roula at Alfred's home in Hadath in 1972.

40. Alfred Nicola in 1955, a few months before he passed away. *From left*: My father Nadim, Alfred Nicola, George Nicola, and Isaac Joseph.

41. Alfred Nicola, Najibeh, and their five children, the day Nadim earned his baccalaureate degree in 1952 (*from left*: Najibeh, Alfred Nicola, Emily, Nadim, Lodi, Nicolas, and Nada). The picture is annotated in Arabic by Emily with their names (she wrote mother and father for Najibeh and Alfred) and was sent to her aunt Zahia in Louisiana, where I picked it up.

42. Nadim earns his Master of Business Administration in 1956 from the American University of Beirut (formerly the Syrian Protestant College).

43. Nadim stands at the "Sisters of the Apostles" convent in Salima, Mount Lebanon, with the first batch of students at the newly established school, 1957.

44. The humble beginnings of the leather factory of Al-Kafaàt in 1964.

45. The poufs and bags sold well in international markets and turned Al-Kafaàt into an iconic social enterprise that provided work for people with disabilities, 1964.

46. Nadim with one of the workers, whom he regarded as "potentials, not handicaps," 1964.

47. Building the new Al-Kafaàt where the factory was relocated, along with a mainstreamed school, a therapy center, and a workshop for the production of orthotics and prosthetics, 1969.

48. The institute with the school as it looked in 1974, renamed the Lily Shwayri Center.

49. The leather factory in its new location as it looked on the eve of Lebanon's war of 1975, a successful enterprise employing 140 workers with disabilities.

50. Nadim, Najibeh, Nadim's three sisters, and Lily, at the fair organized by Al-Kafaàt in 1970 to celebrate the opening of the workshop for orthotics and prosthetics. Al-Kafaàt would later host training sessions for technicians from across the Arab world in 1972 and 1978.

51. Prime Minister Saeb Salam touring the institute with Nadim in 1972, when he stood "speechless in front of the miracle of Al-Kafaàt."

52. The first board of trustees of Al-Kafaàt. *From left*: Samir Khairallah, Nadim, Lily, Grégoire Haddad (*seated*), Ramez Aouad, and Laure and Joseph Moghaizel.

53. Nadim and Lily at the institute in 1974.

54. In the summer of 1982, I wore the uniform of an orthotics technician to "learn the mission," as my father used to say.

55. Al-Kafaàt did not escape the violence of Lebanon's war of 1975–1989. It would ultimately receive nine direct hits and was severely damaged on three occasions. This picture was taken in 1981.

56. Nadim signing his book when the first part of *We All Are Handicapped* (*Nous sommes tous handicapés*) was published in 1982.

57. Nadim enjoyed a unique relationship built on mutual admiration with the thinker and poet Said Akl. Here, Akl bestows the Michel Berty prize on him for *We All Are Handicapped*.

58. Nadim with George and Mela Markou on their visit to Beirut in 1998.

59. My father always kept in his study this picture of me with his lifelong friend Bob Clothier, 1970.

60. Visiting Martyrs' Square in Beirut with a friend from the United Kingdom in 1992. Fifteen years of sustained pounding completely devastated the capital city.

61. War is not a deterrent to a social entrepreneur as stoic and resilient as Nadim. In 1987, while war was raging and the future uncertain, Nadim began to prepare the grounds for what would become AL KAFAAT UNIVERSITY (AKU).

62. AKU as it looked in 2014.

63. The board of trustees of AKU with Tully Cornick, executive director of the American Council on Education's Higher Education for Development, Fellow of AKU and insignia holder for 2014 (*fifth from right*).

64. Sally Crimmins Villela, assistant vice chancellor for Global Affairs of the State University of New York, speaks at the annual commencement ceremony of AKU. Also pictured are the president of AKU, Professor Fathi Oueida (*left*), and the president of the board of trustees, Professor Ramez Aouad (*right*).

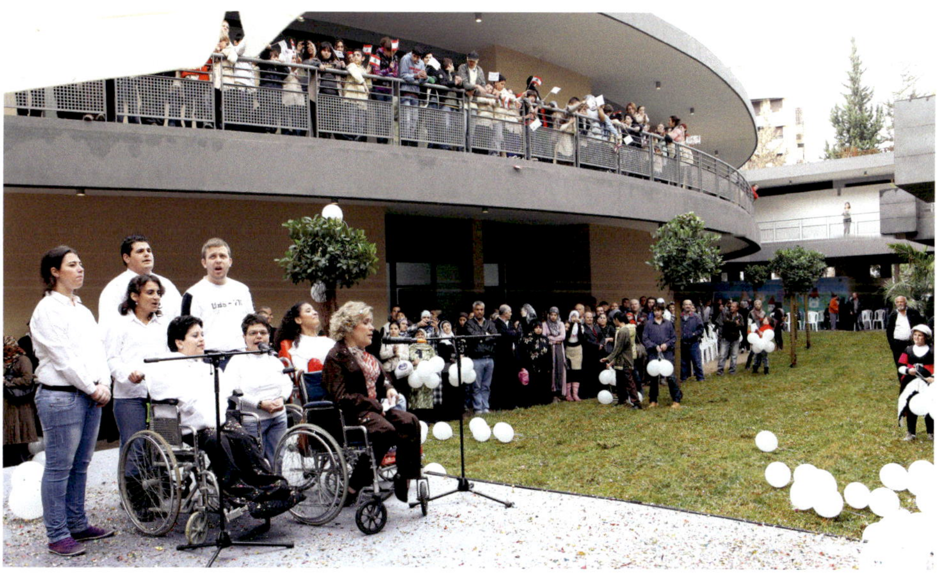

65. The inauguration of the Village center in 2012, which serves a large community of people with disabilities, after its war-afflicted buildings were renovated. This compound is the seventh of a series of institutions that Nadim built, serving a community of five thousand daily users in 2015.

66. Nadim in 2002, at his spiritual retreat in Cyprus.

67. Nadim and Lily with their children and grandchildren in 2012.

68. With my brother Ramzi (*center*) and my lifelong friend Daniel Turiel (*left*), partners in developing vocational training and employment programs at Al-Kafaàt. Daniel is the director of the Belgian ACTEC, a partner organization since 1994.

69. Chef Ramzi, the "King of the Lebanese Kitchen," as the *New York Times* called him in 2002, is the director of the Catering School of Al-Kafaàt. Here, with Nadim, on a photo shoot for *The Culinary History of Lebanon*, winner of the 2003 Gourmand Cointreau Award.

70. Roula in 2009 with my close friend Pierre David, the godparents of my youngest, Philip, at his christening. Pierre was my mentor in vocational training and brought his leading college in France, SEPR, to partner with Al-Kafaàt. Roula is today an associate professor of pediatrics and chief of the Developmental and Behavioral Pediatrics Division at the University of Massachusetts Medical School.

71. Myriam proved to be a remarkable ambassador for Al-Kafaàt. Here, at Englewood, New Jersey, she sits with Nadim at the table of His Eminence Metropolitan Philip (Saliba), whose Antiochian Orthodox Christian Archdiocese of North America has extended remarkable support to our care programs in Lebanon.

72. With Reina, my wife and friend, in 2012.

73. And our children, John, Helena, and Philip (*on the floor*), in 2014.

Appendices

Note: These brief historical essays are meant to provide context and depth to the central narratives of this book. They are not wholly inclusive of all the history that has been—or might yet be—written. Instead, they provide the reader with selected connections, from the personal and local to the regional and global.

1

Mount Lebanon in history

Like the mountain range it refers to, Mount Lebanon has been an indomitable presence throughout this book. Whether at the time of the caimaqamat or the mutasarifiya, or when the whole society revolved around the silk industry, Mount Lebanon was always in the background. I thought it would be valuable to introduce in an appendix the region where these political and economic structures took root, and I also felt compelled to convey a sense of the land where the Shi'a, Druze, and Maronite communities made their home. But more importantly, it is because Lebanon has been on the geopolitical exchequer of the region since the dawn of time that reading the past, I believe, would help the reader to understand much of the modern politics that still bring Lebanon in the fold of current Middle Eastern conflicts.

Since early times, Mount Lebanon—the western range of mountains that runs from the north to the south of Lebanon, parallel to the Mediterranean coast—has stood as a natural barrier, intersecting in the north with the Syrian Coastal Mountain Range and the Taurus Mountains in southern Turkey to form, with the Zagros Mountains in Iran, part of a constellation of peaks that closes in a crescent-shape and gives the enclosed lands a feeling of containment. For Gilgamesh, the king of Uruk on the lower Tigris and Euphrates, these were the boundaries of the known world back in the second millennium BCE, and these were the confines he stumbled into when he went seeking everlasting life, presumably on the foot of Anti-Lebanon, the eastern mountain range that forms the border between present-day Lebanon and Syria. This is where he came to encounter the aging Utnapishtim, who had built a giant ship to escape a cataclysmic flood and was subsequently granted eternal life. The epic is retold in the story of Noah, who built an ark according to God's instructions, the same floods that Utnapishtim had witnessed before him and that were not so uncommon in the lowlands traversed by the rivers of Mesopotamia. Noah's Ark is believed to have set sail on the Mountain of Ararat, north of the Taurus Mountains, in Armenia today, the "far end of the world."

When Abraham, the first Patriarch, came north from Ur and settled in Canaan, he took Sarah for a wife and walked to Egypt east of Anti-Lebanon, leaving his nephew in Jordan, by the Dead Sea. Later, with the unification of the kingdoms of Judea and Israel and the building of the First Temple to house the Ark of the Covenant, Solomon brought cedar trees from Mount Lebanon, caravans of them cut down and transported by his ally and father-in-law, King Hiram of Tyre. In the Song of Songs, Solomon sings about the beauty of a woman whose hair is "as black as the flocks of sheep from Lebanon," still a sight to enjoy today, driving across the hills of Mount Lebanon.

Although Mount Lebanon originally referred to the single mountains of Jbeil, Batroun, and Bcharreh in the north of modern-day Lebanon, the Europeans of the nineteenth century used "Mount Lebanon" to refer to the entire chain of mountains that stood as a natural divide between a coastal strip of harbor cities and a hinterland that had Damascus as its epicenter. It was a natural barrier throughout the troubled history of this part of the world, one that saw countless armies lay siege or march across to lay siege farther south in Palestine and Egypt. The majestic green mountain heights look impregnable when you contemplate them from the sea, as did numerous travelers in the nineteenth century who related their awe-inspired impressions in books and paintings. Impressive heights they may be, but more impressive are the depressions when these mountains that rise to nine thousand feet fall abruptly to the clear blue waters of the Mediterranean. Conquerors circumvented the steep falls, or tried to, but many, the most daring and arrogant, subjugated their armies to the impracticable terrain and left steles or commemorative inscriptions to signal their passage, as did Nebuchadnezzar when he crossed the Lycus River at the steep depression we call today Nahr al-Kalb, which marked the border in the times of the pharaohs between the lands of the Hittites in the north and those of the Egyptians in the south. Nebuchadnezzar was on his way to reprimand what was seen as a rebellion in Judea, which ended in the destruction of Jerusalem and a thirteen-year siege of Tyre. And the Assyrian conqueror was not the only one to have led an army across Mount Lebanon. Since the Egyptian pharaoh Ramses II, the mountains were the *passage obligé* for rival armies that camped on either side of the Lycus, standard-bearers of civilizations that mushroomed on the main confluents of the Middle East: the Nile in Egypt, and the Euphrates and Tigris in Mesopotamia. When you visit the Museum of Beirut, a gem for historians and archeologists alike, you see this very clearly. The influence of both civilizations, the one from the south and the other from the north and northeast, is clear from the various artifacts on display. But mostly, what is noticeable in there is the sequence of invasions, which were continuous across history, earning Mount Lebanon a provincial role, subdued in turns by Egypt and Mesopotamia.

The rise and fall of the tide over Mount Lebanon, from Egyptian rule to Mesopotamian, is also clear in the regional mythologies that indicate the commercial and cultural relations that once existed between the peoples. One of the earliest and most important Egyptian queen-goddesses, Isis, disguised herself as a nanny and entered in the employ of the queen of Jbeil (Byblos) to free her brother-cum-husband and primeval king, Osiris, who had been trapped in a tamarisk tree and placed as a pillar in the palace of the queen. This version of the story was probably developed during a period of intense relations between the mercantile harbor city of Byblos and Egypt and departs from the recorded myth of Isis. In the latter, she gathers the remains of Osiris scattered around the earth by his evil brother Seth (after weeping tears of sorrow in the Nile, which explains the yearly floods). Whichever story it is, it remains that on this side of the Mediterranean, Isis is believed to have wet-nursed the future king of Byblos while disguised as a servant in his mother's employ, a bonding that says a lot about the state of relations that existed between Egypt and Byblos at that stage. Still today, the Nabe'h al-Malak, the king's well, is marked on the tourist maps of old Byblos, the location where the tamarisk tree once took root. As for the Egyptian queen Isis, she was to be for a long, long time the patron goddess of Phoenician sailors in Byblos, the busy harbor at the foot of the Jbeil Mountain.

Then came from distant Persia the king of kings, Cambyses, and Mount Lebanon turned Persian. With him, a new civilization, the Achaemenid Empire, evicted the former rulers in the lands north and northeast from Mount Lebanon and settled in the elaborate remains of Assyrian, Babylonian, and Hittite cities and systems. Writing was known to the Mesopotamians, and a judicial system was even in place ever since Hammurabi laid his civic code in the second millennium BCE. Deprived of a written idiom for his administration, Cambyses adopted Aramaic, the lingua franca of the lands that he conquered and already spoken in Mount Lebanon, an advanced language that belongs to the Semitic family and whose script would give rise to the Arabic and Hebrew alphabets. The world under the Achaemenides wrote Aramaic, a language Christ himself would speak half a millennium later.

When Alexander showed up at the gates of Asia, the world of the *barbaros* (for the Greeks, anything outside of the Hellenic world was barbarian, no matter how refined and advanced) was already unified under the banner of the Persians. Alexander defeated the Persian king Darius's army a first time and, instead of pursuing his enemy into Asia, went south across Mount Lebanon, forcing all the Phoenician harbor cities into submission. Again, the island of Tyre resisted, as it had resisted Nebuchadnezzar when he showed up two centuries before, and did not open its gates to the mighty Persian conqueror. But Alexander was successful, and after having tamed the Persians and their allies down south, he went east on his long enterprise of conquering Asia and beyond, the lands across the Hindu Kush where Aristotle had ascertained that a world did exist, the writings of early historians notwithstanding. Those the Greeks had called "barbarians" were, in fact, quite civilized, as Alexander came to witness when he entered Babylon, and he endeavored, in his short life, to bring together the peoples of both worlds. He married Darius's daughter and took a second wife from Bactria (present-day Afghanistan), encouraging his men to do the same, which many did. Never before had the world been so homogenized and "borderless." In an attempt to Hellenize his new dominions, Alexander even encouraged the establishment of Greek settlements in Asia, a move that was sustained by his generals when Alexander passed away and they fought over its dismemberment. The swathes of land that are of interest to us in our story are those that fell in the laps of two of his close friends and generals after the long debacle called the Wars of the Diadochi: Ptolemy and Seleucus. The former took Egypt and had his seat in Alexandria, the marvel-city named after Alexander himself, while the latter earned Babylonia and thenceforth the entire Near East dominions of the conqueror. And again, as in previous millennia, Mount Lebanon stood as a natural divide between the two newly formed empires, with the high tide of the Ptolemaic and the low tide of the Seleucids switching it from one sphere of influence to the other.

The region was completely Hellenized when the Romans brought their sense of organization and their 250,000 miles of cobbled roads across the known world, and Mount Lebanon, again, was to play a prominent role. At a time when the Romans looked at Syria and Egypt as the granaries of Rome, Mount Lebanon enjoyed a central location between Phoenicia Maritima, coastal Phoenicia, and Phoenicia Secunda, that of the interior. It was the gatekeeper, in a sense, for the grains that were transited by land and by sea to feed the plebs in Rome, held in obedience by emperors with *panem et circenses*, bread and circuses. For bread, the grain stores were kept full in Rome and emperors gave it freely; for circuses, projects mushroomed across the empire, the most famous being the Colosseum, a gigantic venue for its time that hosted grand and bloodletting gladiator fights. Keeping the people happy and well fed was the key to power politics, and whoever controlled the harvests at the source was a step ahead. The builders of the Colosseum, Vespasian and his son Titus, were both generals in the provinces of Palestine before they became emperors. This is how powerful generals could become from playing politics where the grain was actually produced. Visit today the vestiges of the once-grandiose monuments and functions that the Romans spent decades to build in their provinces of Egypt, Syria, and Palestine: Tyre hosted Roman baths of a size that suggest an incredibly large population, large enough to justify the even larger temples of Baalbek, raised to honor Jupiter, Bacchus, and Venus. Monolith blocks of stone the weight of seven Boeing 747s each were quarried in Egypt and rolled across Mount Lebanon to sit as foundation stones for the temples in Baalbek, a show of force and grandeur that meant to show off the might of Rome to the populations of these provinces. Many other generals used this springboard to bounce back as emperors in Rome and, later, with the coming of the Severan dynasty and before the final decline of the empire, four others were themselves autochthones, of local origins.

With the advent of Christianity, the roads from Jerusalem to Rome were paved and a Roman toga meant the same whether on one side of the *mare nostrum* or the other, the large Mediterranean Sea shrinking to the size of a simple lake in the Roman vocabulary, a reflection of the Romans' ambition on a worldwide scale. Jesus came preaching in Mount Lebanon, accompanied by his mother, who waited for him in a cave, still there to visit today, a shrine called Our Lady of Awaiting (al-Mantara). They came to attend the wedding at Cana, where Jesus performed his first miracle. By turning water into wine at Cana, He sanctified Mount Lebanon as the place where Jesus, the son of man, gave proof of His divine Nature as Christ, two natures that became, there and then, as determined by the Second Council of Constantinople, "united with neither confusion nor division."

Because of the unified lands that were kept relatively peaceful under the Pax Romana, the teachings of Jesus of Nazareth could easily spread beyond the walls of Jerusalem and come to be known by the Corinthians and Philippians and Thebans and Romans, by Gentiles and Jews alike. Peter and Paul brought Christianity to Rome, and the Apostles took it to every corner of the inhabited world, treading routes that were paved by the Romans after having been cleared by Alexander and the Achaemenides before them. Then when Constantine, fighting under the banner of the cross, won over the horde of tribes who undermined the sovereignty of his dominions, Christianity became the religion of the empire. He moved his seat to Constantinople, the city that took his name, when Rome was in peril, and a new empire—the Byzantine—was born. It was Roman in structure and organization but Greek in the culture, in the writing, and in the liturgy it adopted. Temporal power was in the hands of the basileus, himself the head of a church that developed along the years into the Greek Orthodox Church, still called across Mount Lebanon today *Roum* Orthodox, to signal its Roman origins. Of the early emperors, Justinian was probably the most enterprising. He initiated many building projects, including one of the architectural marvels of the time, the great cathedral of Hagia Sophia, which for the next thousand years would remain the largest cathedral in the world. This is how a number of tribes came to master the art of stonemasonry, as I have shown in the appendix on the origins of the Moujaes family. Justinian needed iron to make the tools for cutting stone, indispensable for his building enterprises, as he did for making weapons and all sorts of equipment, and he had it within reach, in his own dominions, in Mount Lebanon. He sent to collect the ore and had a large mining operation in the vicinity of Shwayr, in the heights of the Metn Mountains, where my family traces its origins.

Falling from grace, the Ghassanids, the Arab tribes that were Christianized early on and sat on the marshes of the Byzantine Empire, forming one of its lines of defense, were forced into disintegration by the Byzantines themselves, just as a sweeping force was building momentum in Arabia under the banner of a new faith. Young and vigorous, Islam gained ground in no time, finding among the Arab tribes across the Middle East a good ear and practically no resistance from the aging and abated Byzantines. In record time, the marching armies under the first caliphs took city after city, till the entire region south of the Mediterranean, from present-day Turkey to the Maghreb, was conquered. The Byzantines were still there, but their empire had melted to the size of a city (Constantinople) and a few territories on either side, soon to be challenged by new invaders. In the meantime, Muawiya, the governor of Syria, in a move to contain the Byzantines, brought a tribe from Persia and installed it in Mount Lebanon, on the slopes of the Kesrwan Mountain (which took its name after the tribe, Kesra).

A new era was ushered in when Mount Lebanon became a sanctuary for runaways, a safe haven for dissenters, and a land of opportunity for many who understood early in history the important role it was destined to play on the regional exchequer. With the brutal changes taking place all around, many a people came to the mountains to lay low from strife they had at home. Different factions of Islam hence sought refuge in Mount Lebanon when their religious affinities or observances brought upon them the wrath of their coreligionists. The Druze were among them.

The Druze came into existence in the eleventh century under the Fatimids of Egypt, who observed Shi'a Islam. Followers of Ali, the Shi'a broke with Sunni Muslims in the seventh century after Ali was challenged by Muawiya, the governor of Syria and a contender to the caliphate. By acknowledging Ali, they became Alawi or Shi'atu Ali, which means partisans of Ali, shortened to Shi'a. They believed that the leadership of the Muslim community after Muhammad belonged to Ali and his successors, in contrast with Ahl al-Sunna, the Sunni, who claimed to be the keepers of the tradition of Muhammad and believed that the leaders should be the ones who were most qualified. The conflict between the two factions grew further when the son of Ali and his successor, Hussein, were ambushed and killed by the partisans of Muawiya. After that, the Shi'a laid low and ran from persecutions, giving a hand where they could to undermine the powerful empire Muawiya was successful at setting up in Damascus, which grew into a whole new civilization known to us today as the Umayyad. The Shi'a sided with the Sunni Abbasids, followers of Abbas, the uncle of the Prophet, which precipitated the fall of the Umayyads a century later, but they were again persecuted when the Abbasids came to power.

It took nearly 250 years before the Shi'a themselves succeeded in laying the foundations for their own empire. After a first attempt in Tunisia, the Fatimids came to power in Egypt, in Cairo, a city they founded and named Al-Qahira, the indomitable. The Fatimids were so called because they claimed to be descendants of Fatima, the daughter of the Prophet, who was also the wife of Ali, the fourth caliph and companion of the Prophet. Having Ali and Fatima to reckon with, the Fatimids had a dual claim to being the true descendants of the Prophet Muhammad. The Al-Azhar Mosque is still there to testify to their magnificence, though the mosque was turned into a Sunni seat when Saladin overturned the Fatimids in the twelfth century. Under the Fatimids, and for nearly three centuries, Mount Lebanon and much of the Syrian hinterland would see Shi'a communities settle and many of its original inhabitants adopt the new religion. The whole chain of mountains in Lebanon would remain under Shi'a rule until it fell under the sway of the Sunni Mamluk, who came from Egypt as well, brandishing their swords in 1305. The Shi'a then left their settlements and ran from the Sunni invaders, reorganizing their communities in the southern mountains (Jebel Amel), some of the highlands in the northern part (Akkar, Jbeil, and Kesrwan), in the Bekaa plateau, and beyond the Anti-Lebanon toward the Syrian interior.

As for the Druze, they were followers of the Fatimid caliph Al-Hakim, who, depending on whom you believe, was either a mad and despotic tyrant or a just and righteous ruler. After he disappeared one day (possibly assassinated by his elder sister, who became regent after his death), a group of his followers declared him occulted and praised him as the closing prophet, the last of a line of dignitaries whose return one day shall announce the end of times. Persecuted by Al-Hakim's elder sister, the Druze left Egypt, taking refuge in southern Lebanon and Syria. They proselytized for a certain time, expanding their community by bringing in new adherents to their doctrine, but they eventually closed the faith and stopped accepting new converts. The Druze boast a highly spiritual philosophy that rests on esoteric interpretations of the Koran and an Aristotelian view of human dimensions, both earthly and cosmological. Mind (or Intelligence), Soul (also called *Nafs*, which means the breath of life), and Wisdom (or *Kalima*, the Word), are the transient substances that form into a human body, which is defined by a complex set of universal parameters, and transmigrate into a different existence after the breath of life dies out. The spiritual leader of the Druze community is called after the first of these five dimensions, the Sheikh Akl, for in the Druze belief, intelligence is the essence of the Supreme Being. With no church or mosque, the Druze community is divided into the Uqqal (the sages, those who have received knowledge of their faith) and the Juhhal (the uninitiated, the unaware and unenlightened majority). From the onset, the Druze community was built on social divisions and strata, between the sages and the uninitiated, those who know and those who don't, masters and those who are governed. Their meetings in the *ḳhalwat*, the meeting halls, are community occasions where everything is debated—faith, social issues, and business alike.

Further north across the chain of mountains, and south of the borders with the Byzantine Empire, lived a small community of Christians, called Maronites after their patron saint, Maroun, who founded the community in the fifth century and whose creed was close to monothelitism. They believed that Christ had two natures, the earthly and the divine, yet that He only had one Will and It was divine. Though this creed was rejected by the third Council of Constantinople as early as the seventh century, the Byzantines later came to accommodate with the presence of the Maronites in their southern flank, who, though they considered them heretics, could nevertheless hamper any possible incursion from the Persian tribes further south, the advance guard of the Umayyad army of Damascus. But as with the Ghassanids early on, the Byzantines later rid themselves of the Maronites and sent them into exile to Mount Lebanon in the eleventh century.

Coming from Egypt in the eleventh century, the Druze preceded by a few years the armies sent by Pope Urban to regain Jerusalem from the hands of the so-called infidels. Led by Godfrey of Bouillon, the First Crusade marched across Mount Lebanon and took control of Jerusalem, remapping as it went the whole region into principalities and fiefdoms that suited the greed and ambitions of the barons. Conflict between Egypt's Saladin and Syria's Nureddin Zengi had brought the forces of Islam in the Near East to a stalemate, a turn of events that was favorable to the invading Franks. As the Crusades proceeded one after the other, hostility grew, not only from Muslim factions but also from the Christian Byzantines themselves, whose territories were reshuffled on more than one occasion. The Fourth Crusade, in 1204, undermined the forces of the Byzantine Empire to the extent that it never recovered, barely holding on to Constantinople, within the boundaries Emperor Theodosius had built seven centuries before. It managed, however, to hold together for another 250 years, taking advantage of the internecine fighting of the neighboring kingdoms.

During this tormented period, a new people migrated to Lebanon. Coming from Hauran, in the southwest of Damascus, the Shihab family escaped from getting bogged down in the war of attrition between Saladin and Zengi and fled to the opposite side of the Anti-Lebanon, settling in Wadi Taym, south of the Bekaa plateau, between the Mount Lebanon and Anti-Lebanon chains of mountains. Fighting ensued between the Shihab and a Frankish garrison that occupied the village of Hasbaya, and the Shihab won the day with a standing army of fifteen thousand fighting men. A family of Sunni princes from Mecca, having earned their titles from the early caliphs, who granted them lands in Hauran, the Shihab entered the stage of provincial politics in Mount Lebanon and would have a front-line role in the making of modern Lebanon, as we have seen in this book. They befriended the Druze, who preceded them to Mount Lebanon by a few years, in particular the Maan family, which had Fakhreddine in its lineage, the resilient figurehead, friend of the Medici of Florence, whose reign in the sixteenth century laid the grounds for the establishment of a social structure for Mount Lebanon.

By and large, the Druze and their new friends the Shihab stayed out of the wars of the Franks and the Arabs, as well as those between the Arabs themselves, and, by all means, eschewed the fighting of the Franks among each other and minded their own business. The Maronites, on the other hand, in their strongholds in the mountains further north, sent messages of sympathy to the Franks. The Maronite chronicles kept record of a Frankish king that was treated in Bcharreh, most likely the leprous King Baldwin. Later, the Maronite Church sent envoys to Rome to try to bridge the differences, hoping to gain the recognition of the papal authority, but the initiative was stonewalled by the Pope, who would have nothing to do with a church that appointed its own clergy without any acknowledged form of authority and, more importantly, one that had monothelite origins. Instead, he viewed the Byzantine Church as the true Church of the East, however conflicting this might have been with Roman Catholic credo (and politics). This difference led to the first schism, in 1054, between the Roman and Byzantine churches, partly because of distance and provincial politics but also because of language barriers and culture: the Roman Catholic Church adopted Latin, whereas the Orthodox Byzantine held on to its Greek language and heritage. Yet the schism was not a reason good enough to abnegate the existence of the Church of the East that was Roman at heart and obviously preceded the existence of the papal Church itself, and Rome maintained a normal level of relations with its counterpart despite the occasional clashes. This was to be the state of affairs until Rome felt let down by the Orthodox Church, now called the Melkite Church. The Byzantines asked Rome for support when the Ottomans were at the gates of Constantinople, alluding to a possible reunification between the two churches once the danger was out of sight, but the agreement reached at the ecumenical council of Florence in 1439 was not accepted by the rest of the Orthodox Church. This was reason enough for Rome to start taking an interest in the small Maronite community that lived in the heights of Mount Lebanon, a community of hard-working monks who excelled in terrace agriculture as much as they did in handling weapons. A Franciscan friar played the middleman and brought the head of the Maronite Church a miter, a pallium, and a signet ring from the Pope, a sign of endorsement. One thing leading to another, the Maronite Church was admitted into the realm of the Roman Catholic Church and a Maronite college was even founded in Rome, in the Vatican City itself. More significantly, the head of the Maronite Church was to become a Cardinal of the Catholic Church, a title bestowed on all the Patriarchs that have followed in the leadership of the Maronite Church till our present day.

In the middle of the thirteenth century, the threat from the Crusaders seemed less significant when Hulagu Khan, grandson of Genghis Khan, came knocking at the door with a Mongol army at his back. Sweeping over the seat of the caliph in Baghdad and then, with the help of Christian forces, taking Aleppo and Damascus, the Mongols marched south, only to be met with an equal force that came from Egypt: the Mamluks. Trained to be professional fighters and held in slavery by Saladin, mostly from Turkish origins, the Mamluks had rebelled against Saladin's successors and taken control of Egypt. The battle between the Mongols and the Mamluk forces was fought in Ain Jalut, in Galilee, and if the remaining Crusaders had sided with the (shamanist) Mongols instead of allowing the (Muslim) Mamluks to march north unimpeded, the outcome of the battle would have undoubtedly been favorable to the Mongols, and Islam would have taken a serious blow. But Hulagu was recalled home to gain his rightful throne after the unexpected passing of his brother, leaving twenty thousand men under the command of his favorite general, Kitbuqa, and the Mamluks, having better knowledge of the terrain, were able to lure the Mongol forces into an ambush. Egypt's high tide was thus over Mount Lebanon once more, and it was to overwhelm the region for another three centuries until the House of Othman decided differently.

With the vigor of newly founded ideologies, the Ottomans swept over the territories of the aging and corrupt empires of Byzantium, of the Abbasid, of the Mamluk, and of all their dependent kingdoms, and took hold of a large dominion that came to extend in its heyday from the Sinai to the walls of Vienna, across the whole Fertile Crescent, excepting the lands of the Persians. For the next four centuries, Mount Lebanon would live to the beat of the Sublime Porte in Constantinople, which fell in 1453 to the forces of Muhammad II, the Conqueror. The Moujaes family, whose saga we have followed throughout this book, moved to Mount Lebanon when Sultan Selim I came brandishing his sword across Syria. They had lived in Hauran and spread along what became the border of Syria and modern-day Jordan, many earning a living in stonemasonry, which they mastered along the years since the times of Justinian and even before. In the first half of the sixteenth century, they moved to Shwayr in successive migrations and turned into a large family that consisted of six main branches and no less than twenty offshoots.

2

The origins of the Moujaes family

A history

A tradition of stonemasons and a belief rooted deep in the Greek Orthodox faith are two realities that have sharpened my curiosity to delve in the history of the Moujaes family. To understand Alfred Nicola was to dig deep in his lineage, and the findings were telling. Does history repeat itself? We hear this said commonly, and we acquiesce quite spontaneously. What I found out is that mimicking does exist across the ages and a homogeneous school of thinking does transcend time no matter whether generations crossed over or even met, but history is what one makes of it. The following is my history of the Moujaes.

It all began in the Arabian Peninsula, a land of striking paradoxes, where heat and cold, dry and moist, are as marked as night and day. With the Red Sea to the west, the Indian Ocean to the south, and the Persian Gulf to the east, the Jazira, or the Peninsula as it is known to the Arabs, offers a plain and desolate desert. Yet, all around, from all sides, some form of vegetation exists, and in certain locations, the quality of life is good. In the north, the Syrian marshes of the Anti-Lebanon are fertile and hospitable. In the east, the river banks draw sediments that produce abundant vegetation. The north and northeast of the Peninsula form the Fertile Crescent, which arcs from the eastern tip of the Sinai through the mouths of the Tigris and Euphrates, across the lands of the Litani and the Jordan rivers. Then in the south, the mountains of Yemen draw the rainwater in profusion, sometimes in violent eruptions that cause the consternation of farmers. And there it was, in the south, the land of their origins. Many of the families that have entered the Moujaes clan have come from this Arabia Felix, as it was called by the early travelers, the "Happy Arabia." It was a land of wealth, where the kingdom of Sheba once existed, whose queen is said in the scriptures to have charmed King Solomon.

Down in Arabia Felix, there are big, thick trees that produce a resin that, when dried, has a bewitching smell. Frankincense, it is called, and the demand for it was big in Egypt, well before Christianity, for the rituals of the Pharaohs. It was later commonly used by the Byzantines, who established the new Rome in Constantinople in the fourth century and extended their kingdom across the whole of Bilad al-Sham, the "lands to the left," meaning the Fertile Crescent. In opposition, Yemen refers to the "lands to the right" (ancient cartography used the east, not the north, for orientation). From the early beginnings, merchants traveled the routes from the kingdoms of Yemen along the Red Sea to sell frankincense and myrrh, first to the Egyptians and then to the Christians when they came to inhabit the lands in the north. With economic trade came intercultural exchange, and thanks to these Arab travelers Christianity soon found its way south to the land of the Shebans and across the Red Sea to Abyssinia, our modern-day Ethiopia. Later, with the advent of Islam, the Prophet Muhammad sent his family and close friends to Christian lands in Abyssinia, to seek refuge from the House of Quraysh, his own tribe, which persecuted him. In view of the Prophet's monotheistic declarations, the Negus of Abyssinia looked at his prophecy as a variant of Christianity and extended his help. So Christianity went deep into the Peninsula in the early centuries of the Common Era, and a large number of convents were established. These were built by the Arabs themselves, who had been Christianized through the years. One of them, called Dayr Habib, or Convent Habib, indicates that Habib was a pre-Islamic name, one that we saw many times throughout this book when referring to the Shwayri family. In fact, not a single generation has passed, since as early as this book has ventured to dwell back, without one of the siblings of the Shwayri being named Habib. Another *dayr*, also located in the south of the Peninsula, is called Khanasser, a name that I suspect has the same etymology as the family Khneisser, who will befriend the Moujaes clan and follow its path to Shwayr.

To tame a rebellion in the land of Yemen, the Abyssinians ended up invading Arabia Felix on behalf of the Byzantines. During this period of incursion, many families and clans of Sheba and of the neighboring kingdoms left their homes. They went and took refuge further north, along the road to Najaf, requesting the hospitality of already established tribes. The code of honor in the desert meant that tribes always gave a safe haven to any family looking for asylum, no matter the reason for its plight or the foes it may have had. Tribes, and many Moujaes families among them, found sanctuary as far north as the marshes of Anti-Lebanon, the Hauran plateau and the northern regions of modern-day Jordan, well before the advent of the Byzantine Empire. Then, when Constantine the Great set his new capital in the East, Christian tribes living on the marshes of the empires were looked at with a favorable eye by the new lords of the land. The Byzantines had wealth and led a sedentary life with riches and abundant vegetation, which made them prone to raiding tribes. Against protection, the Byzantines gave the Arab tribes lands and titles. The settlers organized into a buffer state that kept the invaders away while maintaining an impeccable Arab hospitality that meant that the itinerant herders could disperse their livestock across the plains of Hauran during the summer seasons when the moss was dry elsewhere.

Early on, the Romans understood the ways of Arabia Felix and reveled in its riches. Not only did the Yemenites sell their self-produced frankincense and myrrh, they also traded products from across the Red Sea, such as ostrich feathers and ivory, and spices from across the Indian Ocean, selling these valued commodities up north. It was not long before they were outdone by the Romans. When the Romans walked the same routes and started their own trade, the economy of Arabia Felix dwindled. It kept regressing until the sixth century, when the great dam of Ma'arib broke. With the collapse of the dam, life in Arabia Felix became precarious, and many tribes migrated northward. Among them, there were families that mastered trade, agriculture, irrigation, and construction. For the purposes of this book, only two of these tribes are of interest to us. One went north to Hauran, the fertile plateau on the foot of Anti-Lebanon, and were called Ghassanids, after a well they settled next to, Ghassan. The other went northeast and settled on the marshes of the Sassanid Empire on the Tigris and were called Lakhmids, after their main tribe, the banu Lakhm. The former were Christian, though espousing a form of Christianity that was to be condemned later by the Council of Chalcedon and who believed that Christ had only one nature, not two, as was resolved by Byzantine orthodoxy (hence the name monophysites). The latter were pagan and would remain so until the advent of Islam in the seventh century, although some espoused the Nestorian creed, if only to stand in opposition to the Orthodox faith of the Byzantines (which others would ultimately come to embrace, building monasteries and many churches across central Iraq). A third tribe, less important in size and role, were the Salih, one that was eventually nurtured in the shadow of the Ghassanids though it would adhere to the Christian orthodoxy of the Byzantines.

If protection was needed against uninvited Arab looters, it also meant looking out for rival tribes that were, in turn, the guarantors for the safety of the competing empires in the region. At this moment in time and before the advent of Islam, there were two empires: the Byzantine and Sassanid. By the time of the establishment of the Byzantine Empire, the Sassanid Empire took hold of Persia on the ruins of the defunct Seleucid Empire. For defense, they left the Lakhmid tribe to organize as a buffer state for its security across its frontiers, though holding it in check from the onset by the force of weapons. And so Ghassanids and Lakhmids fought the wars of the Byzantines and the Sassanids and kept both empires safe from marauders.

Under the reign of the Byzantine emperor Justinian in the sixth century, the march for securing the frontiers of the empire was on. Engineers were summoned to produce designs for fortresses across the frontiers, and many were built. While the engineers (*mekhanopoios* and *mekhanikos*) were all Byzantines, the workers were recruited across Syria. The pay was substantially higher than what one might make elsewhere. If normal pay for a worker was one *kirateon* (which weighed two grams of silver) a day, stonemasons building the fortresses of Justinian earned four. Many tribes that would later build into the Moujaes family were among the countless Arabs who lent their hands to the construction works, mastering in the process the art of cutting stones. To involve the locals in the construction work, Justinian's generals usually commissioned Arab priests to oversee a project, themselves the figureheads of their respective communities. Compounded with their early knowledge in construction that they brought with them from Arabia Felix, the famous dam of Ma'arib being a fine example of their dexterity, builders from a number of families, and Moujaes among them, learned the art of stonemasonry from the Byzantines. This knowledge served them well throughout their existence, as we saw with Fares Bozeid Moujaes and his father in the first section of this book.

To quarry the stones and prepare them for construction, tools were needed, and tools needed iron. Justinian's empire extended all across modern-day Turkey and covered the whole of the Fertile Crescent, a large region rich in natural minerals, and iron ore was one of them. It was found abundantly in a few locations, two, in particular, in the vicinity of Shwayr, in the height of the Metn Mountains, at the modern-day villages of Mtein and Marjaba in Lebanon. There is no doubt that a number of craftsmen from the Moujaes clan took part in the expeditions to collect the iron ore from the mines in Shwayr. This is how they came to know the place that was later to become the village of their predilection. With iron, they made tools but also weapons, the sword being the ultimate possession of an Arab. One of the families of Hauran was named after the craft it mastered, Haddad, for blacksmith. Another, Haddadin, equally Ghassanid, followed a different path and ended up in Jordan today. Much later across the centuries, when the Moujaes came to settle in Shwayr, they brought with them, among other things, their Arabic zeal in manipulating swords. They were masters in the game of "sword and shield," a contest whereby two rivals improvise a fight on elaborate choreographies, performed to the beating of drums. Another art the Moujaes brought with them to Shwayr was that of poetry. With a sword at hand, a tent for a cover, a camel for travels, and the infinite desert to contemplate, the Arabs had only poetry for artistic expression. Pre-Islamic poetry is profound and is now part of the compulsory curriculum at secondary schools in Lebanon. The Moujaes mastered it, adding their Christian sensitivities to it, and are today as prolific in writing poetry as they were thirteen centuries before. Art was not all they brought with them to Shwayr. They also brought their rivalries with them, as in the clash that brought Yemenite clans against Qaysite clans, attested to have taken place in 1636 in the hills overlooking Shwayr. (The Qaysite clans originate from central Arabia, while the Yemenite clans come from the southwest of the Peninsula. Their different lifestyles and sociopolitical systems made them rivals from early on.)

For a number of reasons, not the least being to curb their growing power, the Byzantines decided to rid themselves of the Ghassanids. After a series of plots, the Ghassanids died out as a buffer state and the Byzantines were left to defend themselves. The emperor of the Byzantines in 634 CE, Heraclius, only realized his unforgivable mistake when the Muslim conquerors swept over his dominion in no time. Most of the families and clans remained there, on their properties on the marshes, only they now were the subservient subjects of the Umayyad Empire, which took Damascus for its capital. Some converted to Islam, but most remained loyal to Christianity.

The encounter would have certainly been softer between the Muslim conquerors and the Byzantines had the Ghassanids still been there on the marshes when the Muslims came invading. The tribes were both Arabs, with common origins. They spoke the same language and shared the codes of conduct of the nomads roaming in the desert. And Ghassanids were Christians, among the "people of the Book" and hence were not enemies of Islam. But they no longer had influence and were not any more the powerful confederation of tribes they once were, rulers over the Arab tribes and their kings polyarchs, as the Byzantine emperors once made them. The families were still there, but they no longer had the political organization of previous times. The other confederation, their foes of the past, the Lakhmid, had also undergone the same treatment. Their power dwindled till it finally vanished completely. The last princes of the Lakhmids espoused Christianity and lived in the court of the Byzantine emperors for a time. Many of the Lakhmid families, though pagans at the start, adopted Byzantine Orthodoxy when their political structure was undone (others espoused Islam, as did the Arslan tribe that would later settle in the Jurd in Lebanon and convert to the Druze faith). When the Muslim conquerors entered Syria, the defunct Ghassanid confederation had families still living across Hauran, while those of the Lakhmids lived along the mid-Euphrates and especially at Hira, their old capital city. The Byzantine Empire lost ground to the Muslims, who took hold of all of the Fertile Crescent, leaving the Byzantine Empire to shrink into the size and location of roughly modern-day Turkey.

And so, in 636 CE, the Umayyad dynasty came to govern much of the Fertile Crescent, taking Damascus as its stronghold. Early Islam was rather peaceful and tolerant of religious differences, and the first caliphs were even close to Christians, relying on them with respect to local matters. In that sense, administrations were kept very much the same as in the times of the Byzantines. One noticeable change that did prevail in Hauran came from the settlement of a new tribe to the lordship of a large patch of mountainous lands and fertile plateaus to the southwest of Damascus, home of the Goranitis (Golan) and the Auranitis (Hauran). The Shihab clan came from Mecca, adopted Islam, and fought with the previous conquerors. The leading figurehead of the clan, Harith Shihab, fought alongside Caliph Omar, and to reward him for his zeal at war, the caliph offered him lands in Hauran and Golan. The Shihabs came henceforth to govern part of the lands of the previous Ghassanid state, only now the new governors farmed taxes for the caliphate in Damascus and spoke fervently of Sunni Islam. I place the first encounter between the families that later came to constitute the Moujaes clan and the Shihabs to this early period of the seventh century. The rapport between the two clans was one that extended over the centuries, and was at its zenith when the Shihabs came to play an important role in the governance of Mount Lebanon under Amir Bashir. Having acquired their skills at building houses and fortresses as well as water conduits and aqueducts under the Byzantines, the Moujaes families lent their hands to the Shihabs and built much of their homes in Hauran.

The following five centuries were a period of relative tranquility in the lands governed by the Shihabs, despite the several changes that accompanied the rise of new empires and the waning of others. After the short-lived Umayyad, the Abbasid Empire came to power and would have obliterated its predecessor had not a prince of the Umayyad line escaped and started his own empire in Spain, one that had a particular taste for arts and luxury. The Abbasids took Baghdad for their capital city, and Damascus became a secondary city governed by a plenipotentiary prince appointed by the caliph. While Baghdad was gaining strength, the other regions of the new empire were turning into client states, all governed by ruthless strategists and warriors awaiting their chances-to-be. This would come at the turn of the millennium, when the Abbasid Empire was beset by internal dissension and bad leadership, as well as by a number of external contenders, among them the Mongols of Hulagu, the grandson of the great Genghis Khan, and the Turks, an Asian people who had invaded Anatolia, the deep land of the Byzantines. By then, the once great Byzantine Empire, the Rome of the East, was confined to the city of Constantinople and some neighboring lands. Although stories of Harun Rashid, the fifth Abbasid caliph, still tickle our imagination to this day, the Abbasid Empire in the second half of its five-century existence was but a shadow of its former self. The caliph still called himself the rightful standard-bearer of Islam, but his power was sapped by a multitude of growing new empires. There were the Latin kingdoms to watch out for, the Crusaders who came for Jerusalem and who established, on their way, kingdoms, duchies, and estates for their land-thirsty barons. There was the Fatimid Empire in Egypt, a stronghold for the Shi'a dissenters, followers of the fourth caliph, Ali, and who resented the orthodoxy of Sunni Islam. There was the Byzantine Empire, or what was left of it, and most of all, there was the Seljuk Empire, a Turko-Persian Empire that extended from the Hindu Kush in the east to the Mediterranean coast in the west. At its zenith, the Seljuk Empire would in fact engulf the Byzantine Empire, which had continued to contract.

The Seljukids sought no less than to unite the Arabs under their sway against the Franks. In the lands they occupied, they named *atabegs*, or governors, to rule in their stead, one of whom would have a particular role in the later events that interest us as we track the history of the Moujaes family. Nureddin Zengi ruled over Syria from 1146 to 1174 on behalf of the Seljukids, who confirmed him as ruler of Aleppo and endowed him with plenipotentiary rights. With Baghdad losing its grip on power, Zengi took matters into his own hands and carved a dominion that ran from Damascus to Mosul. He then sent one of his generals, a Kurd by the name of Sherkuh, to conquer Egypt from the Fatimids and expel the Franks, which he did with the help of his nephew, Salaheddine Ayyubi, better known in the West as Saladin. In time, Saladin would succeed at routing the Fatimid Empire altogether and sit his own empire in its stead, the Ayyubid, and become a serious competitor to his former patron, Zengi himself. War between the two was adamant.

War between Zengi and Saladin meant war between Syria and Egypt, and geographically, the Shihabs in Hauran stood in the middle. They came therefore to be solicited by both rivals to side with them, as their clan counted a large fighting group of disciplined warriors, all equipped with the swords made from the ore of Shwayr. Besides, they were Qurayshi and therefore belonged to the family of the Prophet Muhammad, a position that would lend religious legitimacy to whichever side they fought on. The Shihab chose not to fight either side, however, and decided to depart Hauran for good rather than stay and be compelled by the turn of events to wage war on Saladin or Zengi. They must have thought that by siding with the wrong adversary, the outcome might turn fatal to them, a mindset the Shihab would have on several more occasions in more modern times, as we have seen in this book. They simply packed what was theirs and left for the other side of the Anti-Lebanon, settling in Wadi Taym, between the Bekaa plateau and Galilee. They left with fifteen thousand people, a large caravan of families and subjects. Zengi and Saladin made overt attempts at bringing them back, but to no avail. However, on the western slopes of the Anti-Lebanon, the Crusaders had built their own strongholds and were not ready to surrender them. More fighting took place until the Franks ceded, leaving the way for the Shihabs to settle in what would become their homeland. What we know is that the Shihabs sent for the builders and stonemasons from Hauran to erect their new homes and castles, the same families who had built their homes in Hauran in the previous times, and among them were many Moujaes. The palace in Hasbaya, the capital city of Wadi Taym, is still there to see, built on the remains of the previous crusader fortress and well renovated by the Shihab descendants in more recent times.

With the start of the Fourth Crusade in 1202 and the sack of Constantinople two years later at the hands of the Latin Christians themselves, the remnants of the Arab tribes still living under Byzantine cover ran for their lives. The bulk had departed in previous centuries, every time the tormented epic of the Byzantine Empire was at a height, partly to seek refuge in Mount Lebanon[1] and partly to join the other tribes in Hauran. The Christianized Lakhmids, once the foes of the Ghassanids, were among them, as were the Salihids, the minor tribe we spoke of early in this appendix. One of the Salihid families was that of Zayd, whose followers were known as ben Zayd, or sons of Zayd. The evolution of namesakes that came along with the passing of time and when tribes settled down gave way to a new order: departing from a matriarchal order, names were given after the sons, and ben Zayd turned into bou Zayd, or Bozeid in today's English transliteration. This was the origin of the name of our stonemason in the first section, Fares Bozeid, my ancestor of the Moujaes clan.

And what with the Moujaes name? There is nothing on the radar; it is inexistent in any count from as far as the early Arab historians. I can only conjecture and for having delved with profusion into the ancient history of the Arab tribes, I sustain the hypothesis of Moujaes being a moniker that was attributed to the Melkite families in Hauran who decided to remain on the political sidelines and not take partisan sides in any conflict.[2] In ancient tribal Arabic, the name Moujaes would mean simply that, and I have a tendency to concur with this simplistic explanation. The Moujaes families were peaceful builders, lending their skills to the governing powers of the moment. In a way, their obsession with peace shows today in some practices at their village of Shwayr: it is the only place where all Christian denominations celebrate Easter on the same date, despite the differences between Roman Catholic and Orthodox liturgical calendars. More generally, the Greek Orthodox community has been neutral during Lebanon's wars ever since the country was endowed with a constitution in 1926. That says a lot about them wanting to remain on the sidelines, although many of them were praised for their righteous and responsible state counseling.

The Moujaes clan was formed of different families that came from a number of decomposed confederations, mainly the Ghassanid, the Lakhmid, and the Salihid. It was not spoken of as a clan at the time because it simply was not one when the constituting families lived in Hauran and across the Fertile Crescent. I believe it came to be later, when Islam took an ostensibly tighter expression with the coming to power of the house of Othman, a tribe that originated in Central Asia and

1. The Maronites, a Christian sect from northwestern Syria, acted as a buffer state for the Byzantines on their southern marshes in the times of the Umayyad and early Abbasid empires. The Byzantines later pushed them away into Mount Lebanon, where they had initial settlements as early as the seventh century and which became their final refuge in the eleventh century.

2. Melkite refers to the Christians who were followers of the Melek, the king, meaning the Byzantine basileus.

that blossomed into an empire of its own, overwhelming the entire region for four centuries: the Ottoman Empire. The fall of Constantinople in 1453 and the news of Muhammad the Conqueror riding on horseback into Hagia Sofia, the cathedral built by Justinian in the sixth century, must have been met with great horror by the Moujaes in Hauran. It took the Ottomans a very few years to sweep over the whole region, where they were met with negligible resistance. The old empires were battered and weakened by centuries of internecine fights. Sultan Selim I marched on Hauran in 1517. I place the time of the departure of the Moujaes families from Hauran any time between 1453 and 1517, perhaps in groups but not en masse, along a number of years. They left for Akkar in the northern mountains to join

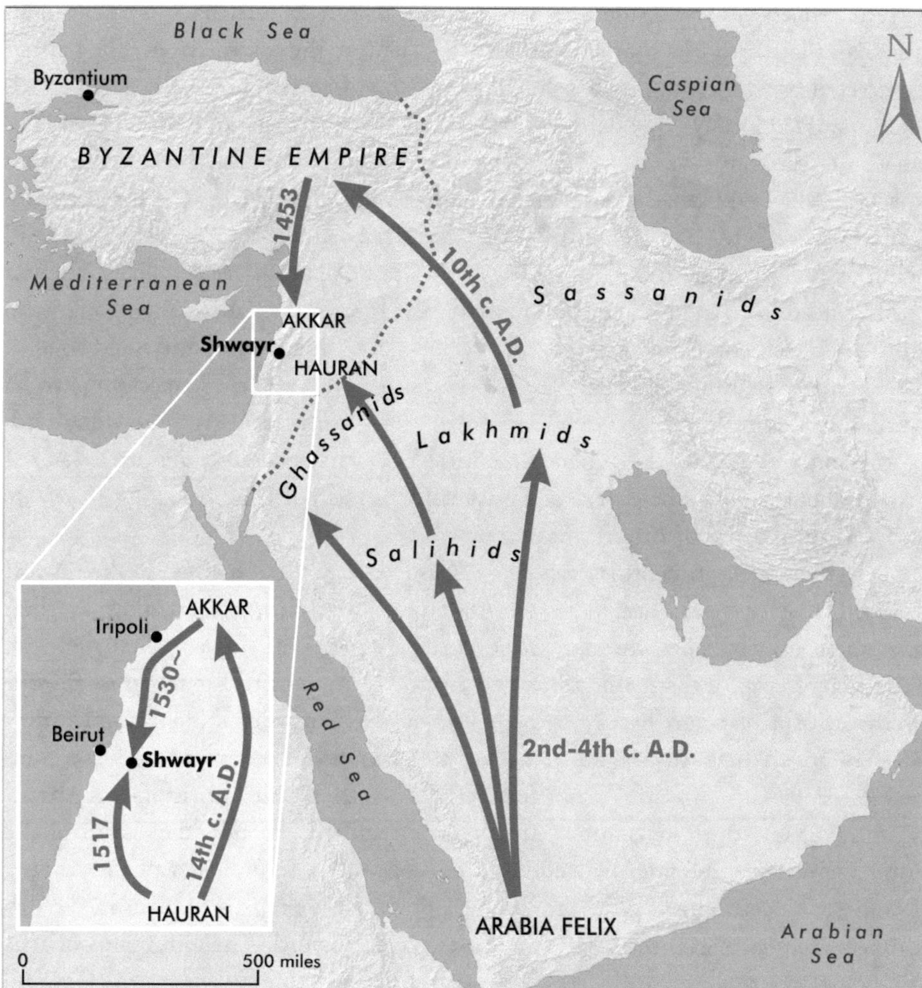

Map 10. Migration of tribes that formed the Moujaes families

others who left in previous periods and stayed in a village called Jubrayel for a time, then went to Shwayr, an ideal refuge where the Ottomans were probably not expected to turn up, in the heights of the Metn Mountains. They had traveled there countless times before to extract the steel ore from the mines to manufacture tools and weapons and may have also had a permanent settlement in the low villages, in Mtein or the surrounding villages.

Many explanations were given as to the etymology of the name Shwayr, some tracing it to an Aramaic root. I personally tend to stick to the simplistic account given from the depiction of a "small ravine," Shwayr being the diminutive form of *sheer*, which means "ravine" in Arabic. It was built on a precipice after all! Present only in contemporary literature from as late as the seventeenth century, I assume the name came to exist with this wave of settlers that left Hauran with the incursion of the Ottomans. On arrival, the new settlers built a church, one that rose next to an aging oak that spread its branches across what became the town center. The church was erected by the settling masons in 1532, within a few years of their arrival, with stones quarried locally. The date was transcribed in a half-coded, half-poetic ode to the Virgin Mary and was carved in stone in the nave of the church: "Piety is more expectant when addressed to the Virgin Mary" (*Al taḳwa arja' li Maryam al Batul*). In there, every letter had its equivalent in numbers: a for 1, b for 2, and so on, and each took a decimal position that corresponded to its place in the sentence. The use of this kind of a code to mark the foundation year says a lot about the people who built the church: a people of poetry and resilience, with a passion for creed so akin to the *asabiah* of the Arabs back in the Peninsula, the sense of belonging worth fighting and dying for. The ode is no longer there, unfortunately. The stone with the carving was broken up when the church was enlarged four centuries later. I learned about it from the elders of Shwayr, for it has been passed along the years with a faithful sense of oral tradition.

By the sixteenth century, when the Moujaes came to inhabit the heights of Shwayr, the Metn was allotted to the Abillamah family for tax farming. In their thirst for conquests, the Ottomans needed to rely on locals for land management. With a large empire that came to extend from the Balkans to Egypt, from Europe to Africa, control could hardly be achieved by the Turkish nationals, and a new model of governance was set. At the end of the day, the Ottomans needed to control the local clans and levy taxes from them to sustain their war efforts and to pay for the extravagant court in Istanbul. In this model of governance, the sultan of the Ottomans was the defender of Islam and the sole and absolute ruler of the empire. He ran a very centralized government and appointed his representatives in the different lands where his armies had vanquished by the sword. The Ottoman wali, the plenipotentiary representative, relied, in turn, on local families to control clans and levy taxes. The latter were chosen for their ascendancy over a certain number of other families, some gaining superiority by force. The tax-farming families earned their cuts in the process and ended up having a power base of their own, generally organizing into a landed family with feudal practices. The Ottomans referred to the head of such a family as *amir-iqtaa*, that is, a tax farmer appointed for a specific dominion, which was shortened to amir, a title that came to mean "prince." The fact of the matter was that an amir-iqtaa was bound by a contract, signed with the Ottoman wali, by which he was given the right to levy taxes on behalf of the Ottomans. The contract, called a muamala, was renewed every year.

In the late sixteenth century, the Ottomans appointed Fakhreddine, a notable figure from the Maan family, to govern Mount Lebanon. Fakhreddine was a Druze and, although he did not have the unanimous support of his coreligionists, he had the upper hand in the mountains. He managed to keep order and levy taxes for the Sublime Porte, the name given for the seat of the vizier, the head of the council appointed by the sultan and who, under certain rulers, turned out to be the strong figure of the empire. In turn, Fakhreddine gave some of his power to local families, who did much the same on smaller scale, managing land and selling the produce, remitting profits and taxes while taking a cut in the process. The Abillamah were part of this chain of governance, working first under the Maan and then under the Shihab when the Maan fell out with the Ottomans and were removed from power. But while the Maan were still in power, the Moujaes had dealings with them and with Fakhreddine in particular. The amir built Deir al-Qamar in the Shouf to be his stronghold and called on the stonemasons of Shwayr in the process. Fakhreddine was a builder in his own right, an enlightened despot who learned arts and architecture in the court of the Medici in Florence, where he took refuge for five years after his first falling-out with the Ottomans. On his return to Mount Lebanon, he took it upon himself to adorn Deir al-Qamar with shops and caravanserais, houses and public spaces, designed by the engineers who accompanied him to Tuscany and implemented by local builders and stonemasons, among them our Moujaes from Shwayr. The power of Fakhreddine was growing, and his vanity was not to the taste of the Ottomans, who brought the amir to Istanbul and had him beheaded. The Maan lost their privileges to the Shihab, the family we met early in this appendix and who had come to Hauran in the seventh century from Mecca, having fought valiantly with the third caliph, Omar. Leaving Hauran in the twelfth century to eschew a fight with Saladin and Zengi, the Shihab, once Muslim Sunni, had converted to Christianity by the time they came to play a role in the governance of Mount Lebanon. That was when the Ottomans drew them in to replace the Maan in the seventeenth century. Under Bashir Shihab, the Moujaes and other families from Shwayr put their knowledge of stonemasonry and building to use in the construction of Beiteddine, the famed palace of the amir.

Bibliography

Arabic sources

Abou-Nohra, Joseph. 2007.

الإكليروس *والملكية والسلطة؛ أبحاث في تاريخ لبنان الاجتماعي والاقتصادي*. بيروت: دار النهار،
أبو نهرا، جوزيف.

Fadlallah, Muhammad Hussein. 2001.

فضل الله، محمد حسين. *أمراء وقبائل*، خفايا وحقائق *لبنانية*. بيروت: منشورات رياض الريّس،

Ghannam, Riad. 1998.

اللبنانية في ظل حكم الأمير بشير الشهابي الثاني ونظام القائمقاميتين. بيروت: بيسان للنشر والتوزيع
والإعلام، غنّام، رياض. *المقاطعات*

Ghannam, Riad. 2000.

غنّام، رياض. *مقاطعات جبل لبنان في القرن التاسع عشر* . بيروت : بيسان للنشر وللتوزيع والإعلام،

Hallak, Hassan. 2008.

والقانونية لأوقاف المسلمين والمسيحيين في لبنان في العهد العثماني. بيروت : منشورات الحلبي
حلاّق، حسّان. *الأوضاع الشرعية*

Hallak, Hassan. 2009.

حلاّق، حسّان. *العلاقات الاقتصادية والاجتماعية*. بيروت: منشورات الحلبي الحقوقية،

Hamadeh, Saadoun. 2012.

حمادة ، سعدون . *الثورة الشيعيّة في لبنان ، (1985–1710)* . بيروت : دار النهار،

Moujaes, Adib. 2001.

مجاعص، أديب. *شوير القاهرة الـبتهزّ عامود الفلك*. الشوير : منشور خاص،

Moujaes, Adib. 2002.

مجاعص، أديب. *قصة فارس من لبنان*. ضهور الشوير : منشور خاص،

Pamphlet. 1997.

الشهابيين، جامعة الأمراء. *التراث الثمين في إمارة الشهابيين*. صادر: عن جامعة آل شهاب،

Pigoulevskaya, Nina. n.d.

العرب على حدود بيزنطية وإيران من القرن الرابع إلى القرن السادس الميلاد ينقله من الروسية صلاح
الدين عثمان هاشم. المجلس الوطني للثقافة والفنون الآداب. *بيغوليڤسكيا* ، نينا .

Rizhallah, Miled. 1923.

رزق الله ، ميلاد. *دليل الشوير ونواحيها*. بيروت: مجموعة المصايف اللبنانية،

Rustum, Assad. 1987.

رستم ، أسد. *لبنان في عهد المتصرّفية* . بيروت : منشورات المكتبة البوليسيّة،

Rustum, Assad. n.d.

رستم، أسد. *حروب إبراهيم باشا المصري في سوريا والأناضول* .بيروت : منشورات المكتبة البوليسيّة.

Rustum, Assad. n.d.

رستم، أسد. *تاريخ لبنان في عهد الأمراء الشهابيين* (3–1) ، بيروت : منشورات المكتبة البوليسيّة.

Rustum, Assad. n.d.

رستم، أسد. *لبنان في عهد الأمير فخر الدين المعني الثاني* . بيروت : منشورات المكتبة البوليسيّة .

Salameh, Antoine. n.d.

سلامة، أنطوان. *طانيوس شاهين ، من منارة الإقطاع إلى عجز الثورة*. بيروت : دار النهار للنشر.

Shwayri, Nadim. 1983.

معاقون»، معاني «الكفاءات» ومسيرتها في يوبيلها الفضّي(1982–1957). بيروت : منشورات الندوة
اللبنانية، شويري، نديم. «كلّنا

Shwayri, Nadim. 2000.

«كلّنا معاقون»، مسيرة «الكفاءات» في الحقبة 1982–2000 ، بيروت :منشورات الندوة اللبنانية،
شويري، نديم.

English and French sources

Abou-Hodeib, Toufoul. "Quarantine and Trade: The Case of Beirut, 1831–1840." *International Journal of Maritime History* 19 (2007): 223–244.

Akarli, Engin. *The Long Peace: Ottoman Lebanon, 1861–1920*. Berkeley: University of California Press, 1993.

Ammi, Kebir M. *Abd el-Kader*. Paris: Presses de la Renaissance, 2004.

Arboit, Gérald. *Aux sources de la politique arabe de la France: Le Second Empire au Machrek*. Paris: L'Harmattan, 2000.

Armagnac, Alfred, baron d'. *Nézib et Beyrout: souvenirs d'Orient de 1833 à 1841*. Beyrouth: Dar Lahad Khater, 1985. First published in 1844.

Armstrong, Karen. *A History of Jerusalem: One City, Three Faiths*. London: HarperCollins, 1997.

Arrigo, Joseph A., and Cara M. Batt. *Plantations: Forty-four of Louisiana's Most Beautiful Antebellum Plantation Houses*. San Francisco: Lexikos, 1983.

Barr, James. *A Line in the Sand: Britain, France and the Struggle That Shaped the Middle East*. London: Simon & Schuster, 2011.

Bayou Lafourche Folklife & Heritage Museum. "A Picture History of Lockport, 1835–1985." Picture compilation of exhibit displayed at the Holy Savior Elementary School, Lockport, Louisiana, on Founders' Day Celebration, August 23–25, 1985.

Betts, Robert Brenton. *The Druze*. New Haven: Yale University Press, 1988.

Bird, Kai. *The Good Spy: The Life and Death of Robert Ames*. New York: Broadway Books, 2014.

Boykin, John. *Cursed Is the Peacemaker: The American Diplomat versus the Israeli General. Beirut 1982*. Belmont: Applegate Press, 2002.

Braudel, Fernand. *Civilisation matérielle, économie et capitalisme (XVe–XVIIIe siècle)*. Paris: Armand Colin, 1967.

Buckingham, James Silk. *Travels among the Arab Tribes inhabiting the countries of East of Syria and Palestine including a journey from Nazareth to the mountains beyond the Dead Sea, and thence through the plains of the Hauran to Bozra, Damascus, Tripoly, Lebanon, Baalbeck, and by the Valley of the Orontes to Seleucia, Antioch, and Aleppo.* London: Longman, Hurst, Rees, Orme, Brown, and Green, Paternoster-Row, 1825.

Buheiry, Marwan R. *Beirut's Role in the Political Economy of the French Mandate, 1919–1939.* Oxford: Centre for Lebanese Studies, 1984.

Burrows, Mathew. " 'Mission civilisatrice': French Cultural Policy in the Middle East, 1860–1914." *The Historical Journal* 29, no. 1 (1986): 109–135.

Campanella, Richard, and Marina Campanella. *New Orleans Then and Now*. Gretna: Pelican, 1999.

Campanella, Richard. *Lincoln in New Orleans: The 1828–1831 Flatboat Voyages and Their Place in History*. Lafayette: University of Louisiana at Lafayette Press, 2010.

Candow, James E. *La déportation des Acadiens*. Grand-Pré: Société Promotion Grand-Pré, 2003.

Castellan, Georges. *Histoire des Balkans: XIVe–XXe siècle*. Paris: Fayard, 1991.

Chapot, Victor. *La frontière de l'Euphrate de Pompée à la conquête arabe*. Paris: A. Fontemoing, 1907.

Chevallier, Dominique. *La société du Mont-Liban à l'époque de la révolution industrielle en Europe*. Paris: Librarie Orientaliste P. Geuthner, 1971.

Chevallier, Dominique. *Villes et travail en Syrie: du XIXe au XXe siècle*. Paris: G. P. Maisonneuve et Larose, 1982.

Chiesa, Bruno, Valentina Colombo, Gabriel Crespi, Giovanni Garbini, Sergio Noja, and Michail B. Pietrovski. *L'Arabie avant l'Islam*. Aix-en-Provence: Edisud, 1994.

Chomsky, Noam, and Gilbert Achcar. *La poudrière du Moyen-Orient*. Paris: Fayard, 2007.

Choueiri, Raja. *Dhour-Choueir, ou, la paix des pins*. Beirut: F. Beryte, 1998.

Churchill, Charles Henry (Colonel). *The Druzes and the Maronites under the Turkish Rule, from 1840 to 1860*. New York: Arno Press, 1973, 1862.

Churchill, Charles Henry (Colonel). *Mount-Lebanon: A Ten Years' Residence, from 1842 to 1852*. London: Saunders and Oatley, 1853.

Cole, Catherine. *The Story of the Old French Market, New Orleans, 1855–1898*. New Orleans: The New Orleans Coffee Company, 1916.

Collinet, Paul. *Une "ville neuve" byzantine en 507: La fondation de Dara (Anastasiopolis) en Mésopotamie*. Paris: P. Geuthner, 1924.

Collins, Larry, and Dominique Lapierre. *Ô Jerusalem: L'épopée de la fondation d'Israël*. Paris: Poche, 2006.

Corm, George. *Le Liban contemporain, histoire et société*. Paris: La Découverte, 2003.

d'Arvieux, Laurent. *Mémoires*. Beyrouth: Dar Lahad Khater, 1982.

Davie, May. *Histoire démographique des Grecs-Orthodoxes de Beyrouth 1870–1939 (mémoire de Maitrise)*. Beyrouth: Université Saint Joseph, 1987.

Davie, Michael F. "Le cloisonnement confessionnel d'une ville: le modèle beyrouthin." *Mappemonde* 4 (1991): 8–11.

Davie, Michael F. "*Trois cartes inédites de Beyrouth: Eléments cartographiques pour une histoire urbaine de la ville*." *Annales de Géographie de l'Université Saint-Joseph* 5 (1985): 37–82.

Debbas, Fouad. *Beyrouth notre mémoire: Promenade guidée à travers une collection d'images de 1880 à 1930, 3ème édition*. Paris: Henri Berger, 1986.

Debbas, Fouad. *Des photographes à Beyrouth, 1840–1918*. Paris: Marval, 2001.

de Chateaubriand, François-René, Vicomte. *Itinéraire de Paris à Jérusalem*. Paris: Librairie de Firmin Didot, 1852.

de Laborde, Léon, marquis. *Voyage de l'Arabie pétrée*. Paris: Giard, 1830.

de Nerval, Gérard. *Voyage en Orient, 3e édition*. Paris: Charpentier, 1851.

de Perceval, A. P. Caussin. *Essai sur l'histoire des Arabes avant l'islamisme: Pendant l'époque de Mahomet, et jusqu'à la réduction de toutes les tribus sous la loi musulmane*. Paris: Firmin Didot Frères, 1847.

de Rochemonteix, Camille. *Le Liban et l'expédition française en Syrie (1860–1861): Documents inédits du Général Auguste-Alexandre Ducrot*. Paris: Picard, 1921.

d'Estailleur-Chanteraine, Philippe. *L'émir magnanime: Abd-El-Kader le croyant*. Paris: Fayard, 1959.

Ditto, Tanya Brady. *The Longest Street: A Story of Lafourche Parish and Grand Isle*. Baton Rouge: Moran, 1980.

Doucet, Jean P., and Stephen S. Michot, eds. *The Lafourche Country III: Annals and Onwardness*. Thibodeaux: Lafourche Heritage Society, 2010.

Dussaud, René. *Les Arabes en Syrie avant l'Islam*. Paris: E. Leroux, 1907.

El Halabi, Abbas. *Les Druzes, vivre avec l'avenir*. Beyrouth: Dar An-Nahar, 2005.

El Khazen, Ghassan. *La grande révolte arabe de 1936 en Palestine: Prémices et déclenchement*. Beyrouth: Dar An-Nahar, 2005.

Enkiri, Gabriel. *Aux origines du Liban contemporain: Le règne de Bechir II*. Beyrouth: Ministère d'information, 1973.

Fawaz, Leila Tarazi. *An Occasion for War: Civil Conflict in Lebanon and Damascus in 1860*. Berkeley: University of California Press, 1994.

Fell, Todd, and April Fell. *New Orleans: A City Named Desire, second edition*. New Orleans: Gris Gris, 2009.

Févret, Maurice. "La sericulture au Liban: Première partie—sa fortune passée." *Revue de géographie jointe au Bulletin de la société de géographie de Lyon et de la Région lyonnaise* 24, no. 3 (1949): 247–260.

Fisk, Robert. *Pity the Nation: The Abduction of Lebanon*. New York: Atheneum, Maxwell Macmillan International, 1990.

Forkner, Ben, ed. *Louisiana Stories*. Gretna: Pelican, 2004.

Friedman, Thomas. *From Beirut to Jerusalem*. New York: Farrar, Straus Giroux, 1989.

Fromkin, David. *A Peace to End All Peace: The Fall of the Ottoman Empire and the Creation of the Modern Middle East*. New York: H. Holt and Co., 2009.

Gemayel, Nasser. *Les échanges culturels entre les Maronites et l'Europe: Du Collège Maronite de Rome (1584) au Collège de 'Ayn-Warqa (1789)*. Beyrouth: Imprimerie Yousseff et Philippe Gemayel, 1984.

Gorton, T. J. *Renaissance Emir: A Druze Warlord at the Court of the Medici*. London: Quartet, 2013.

Grousset, René. *L'Empire du Levant: Histoire de la question d'Orient*. Paris: Payot, 1992. First published in 1949.

Guérin, Victor. *La terre sainte: Son histoire, ses souvenirs, ses sites, ses monuments*. Paris: E. Plon, 1882.

Guttman, Alain. *La guerre de Crimée, 1853–1856: La première guerre moderne*. Paris: Perrin, 2006.

Guys, Henri. *Beyrouth et le Liban*. Beyrouth: Dar Lahad Khater, 1985.

Habache, Georges. *Les révolutionnaires ne meurent jamais: Conversations avec Georges Malbrunot*. Paris: Fayard, 2008.

Hatton, Jean. *The Light Bearers: Carrying Healing and Hope to the Middle East Battleground*. London: Monarch/BibleLands, 2003.

Héneiné, Alice. *Lady Esther Stanhope et le Liban*. Beyrouth: Dar Lahad Khater, 1983.

Hitti, Philip. *History of the Arabs from the Earliest Times to the Present, tenth edition*. London: Macmillan, 1970.

Hokayem, Antoine. *La genèse de la constitution libanaise de 1926*. Antélias: Les Editions universitaires du Liban, 1996.

Hooglund, Eric J. *Crossing the Waters: Arabic-Speaking Immigrants to the United States before 1940*. Washington, DC: Smithsonian Institution Press, 1987.

Hourani, Albert. *A History of the Arab Peoples*. New York: Warner Books, 1992.

Joumblatt, Kamal, and Philippe Lapousterle. *Pour le Liban*. Paris: Stock, 1978.

Kassir, Samir. *Histoire de Beyrouth*. Paris: Fayard, 2003.

Kassir, Samir. *La guerre du Liban: De la dissension nationale au conflit régional, 1975–1982*. Beyrouth: CERMOC, 1994.

Khair, Antoine A. *Le Moutaçarrifat du Mont-Liban*. Beyrouth: Université libanaise, 1973.

Khater, Akram Fouad. *Inventing Home: Emigration, Gender, and the Middle Class in Lebanon, 1870–1920*. Berkeley: University of California Press, 2001.

Khouri, Robert. *Liban 1860: Chronique des événements*. Beyrouth: Self-published, 2003.

Khoury, Gérard. *Une tutelle coloniale: Le mandat français en Syrie et au Liban: Ecrits politiques de Robert de Caix*. Paris: Belin, 2006.

Labaki, Boutros. *Introduction à l'histoire économique du Liban: Soie et commerce extérieur en fin de période ottomane (1840–1914)*. Beyrouth: Université libanaise, 1984.

Labévière, Richard. *La tuerie d'Ehden, ou, La malédiction des Arabes chrétiens*. Paris: Fayard, 2009.

Lammens, Henri. *L'Arabie occidentale avant l'Hégire: Chrétiens et Juifs à la Mecque à la veille de l'Hégire*. Beyrouth: Imprimerie catholique, 1928.

Lammens, Henri. *La Syrie, Précis historique*. Beyrouth: Imprimerie catholique, 1921.

Laurent, Annie, and Antoine Basbous. *Guerres secrètes au Liban*. Paris: Gallimard, 1987.

Leary, Lewis Gaston. *Syria, the Land of Lebanon*. New York: McBride, Nast & Company, 1913.

Lewis, Bernard. *The Middle East and the West*. New York and London: Harper & Row, 1966.

Lockport Rotary Club. "A Sketch of the Louisiana Inter-Coastal Canal Route, from Morgan City to New Orleans via Houma and Lockport, 1910, a Reproduction." Lockport: Janlo Services, 1994.

Makarem, Sami Nasib. *The Druze Faith*. Delmar: Caravan Books, 1974.

Makdisi, Ussama Samir. *The Culture of Sectarianism: Community, History, and Violence in Nineteenth-Century Ottoman Lebanon*. Berkeley: University of California Press, 2000.

Meacham, Jon. *American Lion: Andrew Jackson in the White House*. New York: Random House, 2009.

Ménargues, Alain. *Les secrets de la guerre du Liban: Du coup d'État de Bachir Gémayel aux massacres des camps palestiniens*. Paris: A. Michel, 2004.

Mishāqa, Mikhāyil. *Murder, Mayhem, Pillage, and Plunder: The History of the Lebanon in the 18th and 19th Centuries*. Trans. Wheeler M. Thackston, Jr. Albany: State University of New York Press, 1988.

Moses, John G. *The Lebanese in America*. Utica: T. C. Peters Printing Company, 2001.

Mouawad, Ray Jabre, and Lévon Nordiguian. *Les Abillama, emirs du Metn: Histoire et palais XIIIe–XIXe siècles*. Beyrouth: Dar An-Nahar, 2013.

Nassar, Eugene. *My World, My Time: More Local Sketches*. Utica: Ethnic Heritage Studies Center, Utica College, 2012.

Nassar, Eugene. *Wind of the Land: Two Prose Poems*. Michigan: Association of Arab-American University Graduates, 1979.

Pappé, Ilan. *The Ethnic Cleansing of Palestine*. Oxford: Oneworld, 2006.

Peake, Frederick Gerard. *A History of Jordan and Its Tribes*. Coral Gables: University of Miami Press, 1958.

Peres, Shimon. *Un temps pour la guerre, un temps pour la paix*. Paris: R. Laffont, 2003.

Rabbath, Edmond. *La formation historique du Liban politique et constitutionnel*. Beyrouth: Université libanaise, 1973.

Raphaël, Pierre. *Les Maronites, leur histoire et leur rôle dans le retour des Eglises orientales*. Beyrouth: Dar Byblion, 2006. First published in 1934.

Rawlinson, George. *Phoenicia: History of a Civilization*. London: I. B. Tauris, 2005. First published in 1889.

Renan, Ernest. *Mission de Phénicie*. Paris: Imprimerie impériale, 1864.

Réveillé de Beauregard, Louis-Joseph-Pierre. *L'Emir Joussef Bey Karam, ou les Drames de Syrie, poème en six chants*. Marseille: Imprimerie de Gravière fils, 1875.

Richey, Emma Cecilia. *The New Orleans Book*. New Orleans: Searcy & Pfaff, 1919.

Rihbany, Abraham Mitrie. *A Far Journey*. Boston and New York: Houghton Mifflin Company, 1914.

Ristelhueber, René. *Traditions françaises au Liban*. Paris: F. Alcan, 1918.

Rose, Al. *Storyville, New Orleans: Being an Authentic, Illustrated Account of the Notorious Red-Light District*. Tuscaloosa: University of Alabama Press, 1979.

Salibi, Kamal. *A House of Many Mansions: The History of Lebanon Reconsidered*. Berkeley: University of California Press, 1988.

Saloom, Yvonne Nassar, and I. Bruce Turner. "Roots of the Cedar: The Lebanese Heritage in Louisiana." *Louisiana Library Association Bulletin* 54 (Summer 1994): 31–44.

Saxon, Lyle. *Lafitte the Pirate*. Gretna: Pelican, 1989.

Saxon, Lyle, Edward Dryer, and Robert Tallant. *Gumbo Ya-Ya: A Collection of Louisiana Folk Tales*. Gretna: Pelican, 1998.

Schulze, Kirsten E. *The Jews of Lebanon: Between Coexistence and Conflict, Second revised and expanded edition*. Brighton: Sussex Academic Press, 2009.

Schumacher, Gottlieb. *Across the Jordan: Being an Exploration and Survey of Part of Hauran and Jaulan*. London: A. P. Watt, 1889.

Seale, Patrick, and Maureen McConville. *Asad: The Struggle for the Middle East*. Berkeley: University of California Press, 1989.

Shahîd, Irfan. *Byzantium and the Arabs in the Fifth Century*. Washington, DC: Dumbarton Oaks Research Library and Collection, 1989.

Shlaim, Avi. *Israel and Palestine: Reappraisals, Revisions, Refutations*. London: Verso, 2009.

Shlaim, Avi. *Lion of Jordan: The Life of King Hussein in War and Peace*. London: Penguin, 2007.

Shwayri, Raif. *Nadim, un Liban généreux*. Paris: Les 2 Encres, 2008.

Spagnolo, John P. *France and Ottoman Lebanon, 1861–1914*. London: Ithaca Press, 1977.

Stanhope, Hester. *Memoirs of Lady Hester Stanhope: As Related by Herself in Conversations with Her Physician*. London: H. Colburn, 1845.

Thomas, Bertram. *Les Arabes (traduit de l'Anglais par Roland Huret)*. Paris: Payot, 1946.

Thompson, Elizabeth. *Colonial Citizens: Republican Rights, Paternal Privilege, and Gender in French Syria and Lebanon*. New York: Columbia University Press, 2000.

Touma, Toufic. *Paysans et institutions féodales chez les Druses et les Maronites du Liban du XVIIe siècle à 1914*. Beyrouth: Université libanaise, 1986.

Toynbee, Arnold, and Viscount James Bryce. *Armenian Atrocities: The Murder of a Nation*. London and New York: Hodder and Stoughton, 1915.

Traboulsi, Fawwaz. *A History of Modern Lebanon*. London: Pluto, 2007.

Tueni, Ghassan. *Une guerre pour les autres*. Paris: J. C. Lattès, 1985.

Unknown author. *Les massacres du Mont-Liban 1860: Souvenirs de Syrie par un témoin oculaire*. Beyrouth: Asmar, 2007. First published in 1868.

Unknown author. *New Orleans: A Descriptive View Book in Colors*. Denver: H. H. Tammen Co., 1913.

Urquhart, David. *The Lebanon (Mount Souria): A History and a Diary, Volume II*. London: T. C. Newby, 1860.

Vogüé, Eugène-Melchior, vicomte de. *Histoires orientales*. Paris: C. Lévy, 1880.

Vogüé, Eugène-Melchior, vicomte de. *Syrie, Palestine, Mont Athos; voyage aux pays du passé*. Paris: Hachette 2012. First published in 1876.

Waddington, W. H. *Inscriptions Grecques et Latines de la Syrie: recueilles et expliquées*. Paris: Firmin Didot, 1870.

Widmer, Mary Lou. *New Orleans, 1900 to 1920*. Gretna: Pelican, 2007.

Winslow, Charles. *Lebanon: War and Politics in a Fragmented Society*. New York: Routledge, 1996.

Yammine, Antoine. *Quatre ans de misère: Le Liban et la Syrie pendant la 1ère guerre mondiale*. Beyrouth: Byblion, 2005.

Films and documentaries

Belizaire the Cajun. Written and directed by Glen Pitre. New Orleans: Côte Blanche Productions, 2001. Special 25th anniversary ed. DVD, 100 min.

Ehden: Thirty years. The Massacre and the Pardon (in Arabic). Written, directed, and presented by George Yasmin. OTV, 2007. Two-part documentary, approximately 190 min.

Good for What Ails You: Healing Secrets of the Cajuns, Creoles, and Bayou Indians. Written, produced, and directed by Glen Pitre. Lockport: Côte Blanche Productions, 1998. DVD, 56 min.

Haunted Waters, Fragile Lands—Oh, What Tales to Tell! Written, produced, and directed by Glen Pitre. Thibodaux: Barataria-Terrebone National Estuary Program, 1994. DVD, 57 min.

La Fièvre Jaune/Yellow Fever. Written, produced, and directed by Glen Pitre. New Orleans: Côte Blanche Productions, 1978. DVD, 30 min.

Oklahoma! Directed by Fred Zinnemann. Beverly Hills: Twentieth-Century Fox Home Entertainment, 2006, 50th anniversary ed. DVD, 145 min.

Swamp People, Season One. A&E Television Networks, 2011. DVD, 410 min.

The War of Lebanon (Harb Lebnan): So That History Doesn't Repeat Itself. Written and directed by Omar Al Issawi. Al Jazeera Television, 2002. Fifteen-part documentary, 687 min.

Index

Page numbers in italics refer to maps. Subentries for major figures in the book are organized chronologically. All other subentries appear alphabetically.